Second Edition

SOCIAL SERVICES AND
THE ETHNIC COMMUNITY

Second Edition

SOCIAL SERVICES AND THE ETHNIC COMMUNITY

History and Analysis

Alfreda P. Iglehart
University of California, Las Angeles

Rosina M. Becerra
University of California, Las Angeles

WAVELAND

PRESS, INC.

Long Grove, Illinois

For information about this book, contact:
Waveland Press, Inc.
4180 IL Route 83, Suite 101
Long Grove, IL 60047-9580
(847) 634-0081
info@waveland.com
www.waveland.com

To all human services professionals who are committed to making ethnic-sensitive practice the norm rather than the exception.

Contents

Preface

Why is a book on social services and the ethnic community necessary?
With the growing literature on ethnic-sensitive practice, it may seem that
social workers and other social services providers have accepted the significance of race and ethnicity in the service delivery process. Models of practice
with specific groups and case studies found in the literature illuminate this
significance. In the midst of this growing body of literature, however, the
challenge of ethnic-sensitive practice continues to persist in a society that is
becoming increasingly diverse.

This book is for anyone who teaches and/or engages in social work and
social services delivery. This list includes social workers, human services
workers, caseworkers, case managers, practitioners, clinicians, other social
services-type designations, social-services trainers, social work educators,
anyone engaged in "social" work, and anyone who works with people. The
work settings may be schools, hospitals, public agencies, or private agencies.
Regardless of the job title or setting, those in the helping professions are part
of a complex sociocultural, historical, and political context that defines who
the workers are and what they do.

Social work as a profession continues to serve as an anchor for this book
because, as a profession, it is a dominant influence in shaping the services that
are to be delivered and to whom they are delivered. Many of the values and
norms of society are crystallized in this profession. A case might be made that
this book is not about social work at all but is rather an example of how services and professionals reflect the culture, values, and ideologies around them.

This book recognizes that no one worker or educator will be able to learn
all there is to know about every ethnic and racial minority group. The book
advances a fundamental knowledge base from which diversity practice with
any group can emerge. The past forms an essential building block for this
knowledge base, because today's dilemma is actually a snapshot in an album
that has been expanding for centuries. To effectively respond to the challenge
of ethnic-sensitive service delivery, those who provide social services and
those who educate social-services workers have to reach back to the past for
guidance and insight.

America's history is framed by the diversity of its citizens and its
responses to that diversity. This history aids in understanding some of the

patterns and trends that are visible today. Although parts of this past are inspiring and uplifting, other parts are painful and troubling. Some readers may feel that the past is dead and should not be resurrected. Others may feel that recounting the past will only dredge up negative feelings and anger. The purpose of this review is not to accuse, blame, or promote victimization. The past is reviewed as a crucial step toward the identification and implementation of effective ethnic-sensitive practice methods.

In the review of the past and evolution of social services in America, social work history is broadened to reveal facts and occurrences that may not be well known. Part of this history shows that the development of social work was closely linked to changing immigration trends. Some of the history reveals that ethnic minority communities were outside of the boundaries of the emergent profession. All communities, however, were identifying their needs and attempting to respond to those needs. Voluntary associations and the subsequent ethnic agencies capture this desire to respond. To some extent, the literature speaks for itself, and this book serves as a conduit for communicating its messages. The literature is provided for the reader's review and interpretation.

What is the goal of this book? Information and knowledge are forms of power, and this book should empower its readers, who will learn that the journey to ethnic-sensitive practice includes several pathways that involve the worker, the agency, the community, and the larger society. Perhaps some readers will conclude that truly effective ethnic-sensitive practice can only occur with a shift in the prevailing social structure. All should conclude that the discussions and proposed changes in technique cannot take place in a vacuum void of historical context.

Another goal of the book is the promotion of and support for open, honest, and frank dialogue about history, its significance, its impact on the present, and its role in forging links between diverse groups. Clearly, race and ethnicity remain sensitive and even controversial topics. Individuals, including social workers, may be hesitant to reveal their perceptions and feelings for fear they will be misinterpreted. A climate conducive to dialogue and cooperation has to be established so that social work professionals can trust and believe that there is no right or wrong side, only the side that leads to ethnic-sensitive practice. Everyone is on the same side, and all are in this together to seek solutions and breakthroughs.

Ethnic-sensitive practice should be a pathway to understanding and addressing community needs and problems. Each group in America appears to be looking in the mirror when serious efforts are undertaken to resolve community problems. Each group wants what is best for its members—people who look like them. Meaningful ethnic-sensitive practice takes place, however, when group members turn from their mirrors and look out their windows. From the window, other groups and the way they live their lives can be observed. While differences between groups exist, the commonality of community goals becomes the basis for collaboration, mutual aid, and problem resolution.

History and its effects are vital pieces to the puzzle of ethnic-sensitive practice. The dualism of mainstream social services and ethnic social services is a product of the evolution of systems and not just of individuals. If there is to be cross-fertilization between or even convergence of these dual systems, then those in both systems need to move beyond the familiarity and comfort of the image in the mirror to a greater appreciation of the diversity outside their window.

Acknowledgments

The authors are indebted to several individuals who generously shared their feedback about this book. They include Steve Clark, Joy Crumpton, Aurora Jackson, Karen Lee, Sean Lynch, and the late Jeanne Giovannoni. Various topics from the book were used as the basis of class discussions and student comments were insightful, honest, and stimulating. The authors gratefully acknowledge these students and thank them for their input.

Finally, this book is dedicated to all those who are sincerely striving to develop and provide ethnic-sensitive services.

CHAPTER 1

Introduction

The introduction to the first edition of this book began with the statement, "Social service delivery systems appear to be at another crossroads." One road signified the need to adapt and adjust service delivery systems and practices for an increasingly diverse population. The other road followed in the "one size fits all" direction. Clearly, in the years since the first edition was published, practitioners and delivery systems have struggled with the challenges of defining and practicing ethnic sensitive, multicultural, and/or culturally competent service delivery. Consequently, the road toward adaptability and adjustment has been identified as the target path. For social services in the United States, diversity has become equated with challenges rather than with opportunities. While the terms "diversity" and" multicultural" are frequently used to describe a changing populace, few would question the significance of race and ethnicity in discussions and debates on diversity. Because population shifts cannot easily be geographically contained, the ethnic minority presence in the United States is mushrooming from urban centers to Midwestern cities to Southern towns.

Recent Census Bureau projections further highlight the ethnic minority presence in the United States. When the first edition was published, the Census Bureau projected that, by the year 2050, minorities would make up 47 percent of the nation's population. While the percentage of this group was decreasing, it still was expected to command a majority of the population by the middle of the century. Increased immigration and higher birthrates for ethnic minority groups accounted for much of this demographic shift. In 2008, however, the Census Bureau issued a press release announcing that, by the year 2042, minorities would be the majority in the United States.[1] Population shifts are not static but, rather, are affected by numerous factors. As a result of more stringent, heightened national security in the post–9/11 era, and economic recessions, Asian and Latino immigration continues to increase but at a slower rate. As a result, Census Bureau population projections have been modified to show that non-Whites in America are not expected to comprise the majority of the population until 2050.[2] Because population increases are affected by rates of immigration, assumptions have to be made in order for projections to be calculated. For instance, if net immigration is held at a constant rate, the Latino population is expected to rise from its current 15 percent

1

to 28 percent by mid-century. The Asian population will grow from four percent to six percent, while African Americans will continue to hover around 13 percent. Non-Hispanic whites will decrease from 65 percent to approximately 49.9 percent. White population growth has been muted by relatively small fertility rates and because of aging of this group. These estimates may have to be adjusted again because ethnic identity may become more fluid and less static, categorizations used to label groups may change over time, and the number of individuals who self-identify as "mixed-raced" may increase over time.

Obviously, the expectation that racial/ethnic minorities will outnumber Whites in American society has received considerable attention. The implications for American society are virtually unknown and may be the source of some apprehension. Although it may not be so easily predicted or projected, it is eminently clear that a "tipping point" is in America's future. Issues of race and ethnicity are inexorably linked to American history, and many of these issues will resurface as America embarks on this new era.

To help meet the challenges of growing diversity, the National Association of Social Workers (NASW) has issued Standards for Cultural Competence in Social Work Practice.[3] These standards include the areas of ethics and values; self-awareness; cross-cultural skills; service delivery; empowerment and advocacy; diverse workforce; professional education; language diversity; and cross-cultural leadership. In addition, NASW's Code of Ethics[4] includes ethics governing discrimination and cultural competence:

- *Discrimination*: Social workers should not practice, condone, facilitate, or collaborate with any form of discrimination on the basis of race, ethnicity, national origin, color, sex, sexual orientation, age, marital status, political belief, religion, or mental or physical disability.

- *Cultural Competence:*

  1. Social workers should understand culture and its function in human behavior and society, recognizing the strengths that exist in all cultures.

  2. Social workers should have the knowledge base of their clients' cultures and be able to demonstrate competence in the provision of services that are sensitive to clients' cultures and to differences among people and cultural groups.

  3. Social workers should obtain education about and seek to understand the nature of social diversity and oppression with respect to race, ethnicity, national origin, color, sex, sexual orientation, age, marital status, political belief, religion, and mental or physical disability.

In addition, NASW asserts, "Discrimination and prejudice directed against any group are damaging to the social, emotional, and economic well-being of the affected group and of society as a whole.[5]

The Council on Social Work Education, the accreditation body that governs undergraduate and graduate social work educational programs, issues standards and guidelines for these programs. Among the Council's eight Educational Policy and Accreditation Standards is one on nondiscrimination and human diversity:[6]

The program makes specific and continuous efforts to provide a learning context in which respect for all persons and understanding of diversity (including age, class, color, disability, ethnicity, family structure, gender, marital status, national origin, race, religion, sex, and sexual orientation) are practiced. Social work education builds upon professional purposes and values; therefore, the program provides a learning context that is nondiscriminatory and reflects the profession's fundamental tenets. The program describes how its learning context and educational program (including faculty, staff, and student composition; selection of agencies and their clientele as field education settings; composition of program advisory or field committees; resource allocation; program leadership; speakers series, seminars, and special programs, research and other initiatives) and its curriculum model understanding of and respect for diversity.

Organizations associated with both social work and social service delivery have taken these steps to facilitate the development and implementation of a knowledge and practice base that supports culturally responsive interventions.

LEARNING FROM THE PAST

In order to understand the need for such ethics and standards, an examination of America's past should be undertaken. This examination reveals that Progressive Era thinkers and reformers of the nineteenth century were fearful that the massive influx of "new" immigrants—ethnic Whites from Southern and Eastern Europe—would seriously alter or even destroy the fiber and culture of native-born White society.[7] Widespread efforts to "Americanize" these new immigrants were launched with the intended effects of replacing immigrant language, traditions, and values with English and American values and culture.[8] The United States as the melting pot—an amalgam of people from diverse backgrounds with one language and one culture—was the image that guided popular thinking of the day and continued to do so for numerous years.

Deep, long-standing, and firmly entrenched values that defined what it means to be "American" have guided American social and political thought for centuries. Ethnic and racial differences are not value-neutral. In fact, it is difficult for citizens, including social service practitioners, to distinguish conceptions of differences from questions of inequality.[9] Furthermore, the history of racial and ethnic minority groups in the United States is filled with countless examples of prejudicial and discriminatory treatment. This is the foundation upon which racial/ethnic sensitivity must be built. Efforts to render this past invisible will only impede the movement toward cultural acceptance; therefore, knowledge of the past must be recognized, understood, and accepted as a means of elevating ethnic sensitive practice.

As immigrants of today—Asians and Hispanics, for example—seek solace on the shores of this country and as other citizens of color continued to seek equitable treatment, the melting-pot notion gave way to the concept of America as the "mosaic society." It may be argued that interracial relationships will pave the way for a blended society. In the intervening years from the new immigrants of the late 1880s and early 1900s to the new immigrants of the

1990s and 2000s, social service providers—and the rest of the nation—have come to realize that language, culture, tradition, and skin color cannot be easily erased or ignored. People continue to cling to what is important to their individual and group identity. In addition, color blindness was always more of a myth than a reality as particular ethnic groups were historically and continuously stigmatized by their color.

Demands and needs for social services will continue to come from groups that are more likely to suffer from poverty, discrimination, and their attendant consequences—groups that have a disproportionate number of ethnic minorities. Social service administrators and practitioners are urged to embrace the diversity surrounding these groups, and to implement culturally relevant and sensitive training for workers and programs for clients. As client populations change, the service delivery systems are expected to successfully adapt to these changes.

In the era of the mosaic and blended society, social service providers are charged with the task of responding to the needs of diverse groups in ways that recognize, respect, and tolerate group differences. In response to diverse client populations, the literature on clinical or treatment issues involved in ethnic-sensitive practice is proliferating.[10] These clinical issues often include the manner in which ethnicity affects the worker-client relationship, cultural beliefs that influence both the worker and the client, language and behavioral patterns that affect treatment effectiveness, cultural practices that do not support self-disclosure, and premature termination.

The role of the worker-client relationship in the delivery of ethnic-sensitive services is, indeed, vitally important. The client experiences the agency through the worker as the worker interprets the policies of the agency and implements its services. In addition, because of the relationship established between the client and the worker during the treatment process, acceptance of and respect for the client's ethnicity and culture foster the rapport and trust needed for effective intervention.

In response to the growing diversity of society, social work is stressing the need for social workers to increase their sensitivity to the cultures and values of minorities. Although treatment issues are crucial for effective individual, family, and small-group intervention, the worker-client relationship is but one aspect of service delivery to diverse populations. Furthermore, in some instances, the client's culture is treated as homogeneous and static while its social context and environment are overlooked.[11]

DIVERSITY AND SOCIAL CONTEXT

Lum describes *social context* as those crucial elements of the environment that help shape the individual.[12] In order for practitioners and administrators to acquire and implement the tools and techniques for working with minority populations and communities, the changing social context of both the ethnic minority community and the service providers must be considered. Intergroup communication and contact are influenced by the position of each group in society and by the historical and social context in which the communication and contact take place.[13]In an extensive review of literature on ethnic identity, Sanders presents the array of factors associated with ethnic identity formation.[14] These factors include situational, institutional, cultural, political, and geographical elements that serve to define and shape the ways groups see themselves and other groups. Jansson also argues that context is two-sided in that it offers both opportunities and constraints.[15]

Interaction is also a component of the social context in which social work operates. Historical constraints on interactions between groups frequently result in ignorance and stereotyping.[16] Distorted views of an ethnic minority group by those outside of that group may persist over time and become part of a prevailing, normative perception of a particular group. These stereotypic views may become so dominant and pervasive that a group member may encounter *stereotype threat*—the threat that s/he will be treated or judged in terms of that stereotype.[17] Stereotype threat is likely to occur when negative stereotypes about a group's abilities and potential are "in the air."[18] This means that individuals may "catch" or absorb stereotypes without any awareness of doing so.

Clients and their service providers are not just individuals but are also representatives of an array of networks that are bombarded daily with messages about who they are and how they should perceive others. These network and systems are bounded by ethnicity, culture, community, and a value-laden larger social environment. Client and social provider systems are shaped by the values and ideologies that define problems, help-seeking behaviors, and problem resolution. To ignore the other systems of which clients and providers are a part is to ignore a significant element of the world. Effective ethnic-sensitive service delivery also includes the utilization and incorporation of the client's community and community services in the service delivery process. In addition, the service provider's membership systems and worldview must be included. For numerous ethnic minority communities, community services are offered through the *ethnic minority agency*—that is, an agency with ethnic minority staff that provides services to members of that ethnic minority group. In the ethnic agency, the cross-group tension and conflict are not expected to be problems.

Still another aspect of service delivery involves recognition of the nuances of the service delivery system itself. Service delivery takes place in the context of an organization that is also shaped by the culture, values, and ideologies of the administrators and managers planning and implementing those services. These systems determine the "appropriate" problems to address and the "appropriate" ways to address them.

The preponderance of literature on technologies for individual-level interventions and the pronounced paucity of comparable literature on interventions at other levels have been held as proof that helping professions, particularly social work, have a preoccupation with changing people and not systems.[19] Epple considers both sides of the debate between micro and macro practice and notes that the tension between social justice and casework is rooted in the history of the profession.[20] The primacy of micro (or casework) literature over macro (social work) literature may suggest that the profession implicitly accepts existing social systems and explicitly omits critiques of social work and its nonclinical relations with minorities.[21] The clinical and casework interventions appear to render the client's social context as invisible.

Service delivery to ethnic minority communities illustrates the interface between service delivery systems and client systems. Consequently, the ethnic community is of central importance for the provision of multicultural social services. An examination of the ethnic community's responses to its own identified needs can provide a basis for understanding the ethnic community, its self-identified problems, and its problem interventions. The ethnic agency appears to capture an interface between a service delivery system and client system that blends service with community and ethnicity. The ethnic agency incorporates the social context of the ethnic minority experience in its processes and services.

In recognition of the historical context of the ethnic minority experience, this book provides a social and historical overview of (1) the experiences of racial and ethnic groups in nineteenth-century America; (2) social work's evolution and its implications for racial and ethnic minority groups; and (3) the emergence of ethnic services. This overview becomes the foundation for the delineation of macro approaches that supplement micro interventions to more effectively link mainstream social services with ethnic communities and ethnic agencies. The concluding section highlights recurring themes and dilemmas that continue to challenge service delivery.

HISTORICAL ANALYSIS

Mainstream social work and traditional social services have not historically shown themselves to be very flexible, adaptable, or malleable in service delivery structures and ideologies. The form and ideology governing social services have been evolving since the dawn of the twentieth century. Since then, there has been little deviation from the original underpinnings of service delivery that were derived from the social, political, and economic context of the day. Indeed, social work and social welfare, then and now, are products of the environments from which they emerge. Conservative underpinnings were in the forefront of the formative years of the social work profession when the country was coping with the arrival of diverse, new immigrant populations. These conservative underpinnings were reflected in charity organizations and settlement houses that were created by the White, Protestant, middle-class citizens who sought to assist immigrants in adjusting to American life.[22]

The history of social work with ethnic minority groups cannot be denied, although much of it appears to have been rewritten to shroud or omit the extent of racism and exclusion operative in the charity organizations and even in the settlement-house movement—the reform arm of social work's birth.[23] Although some early services aided ethnic minorities, the general disregard for the needs, concerns, and rights of ethnic minority groups is readily evident.[24] Actions on behalf of ethnic minorities were fragmented, sporadic, and sadly limited. Some ethnic minority groups were even seen as unsuitable for assimilation. For example, one settlement house director declared, "You can Americanize the man from southeastern and southern Europe, but you can't Americanize a Mexican."[25]

There often appears, however, to be a glorification and a vaunted view of the social-reform thrust of the early twentieth-century settlement work, and this period has been associated with a rise in the profession's commitment to social reform. Historical recollections, however, can often reflect more distortion and romanticism than realism. Although no deliberate deceit may have been intended, it has been fairly easy to equate the actions of the majority with those of a few reform-minded individuals. Today, service planners, administrators, and providers must recognize and confront the ambivalence with which mainstream social services have historically treated ethnic minorities. Acceptance of a group's history as *the group* experienced it is a vital step in reducing the gulf between mainstream social services and ethnic minority communities.

Years of distrust, apathy, neglect, and rebuff cannot, and should not, be minimized. The past must be confronted with all its undesirable baggage of differential treatment, benign neglect, and overt racism. Recognition of the past does not mean it should be condoned or condemned, however. It means that service delivery to today's diverse populations is predicated on history and responses to that history. Consequently, open doors and open arms will not automatically result in the masses of color flocking to partake of the services offered. Knowledge of history should be skillfully used to inform the development of effective service delivery strategies for today's diverse populations.

The embryonic years of social work are an appropriate starting point for the development of approaches that unite mainstream social services with ethnic minority communities. An examination of the past can be useful in identifying pitfalls and patterns that should be avoided as well as highlighting those actions and trends that should be replicated. This historical overview is not just a synopsis of past events; rather, it is an analysis and interpretation of social work history that examines racial ideology, social control, and social reform as they relate to ethnic minority communities. In addition, manifestations of the self-help ethos in these communities are also explored.

THEORETICAL PERSPECTIVES

The historical analysis and other analyses presented in subsequent chapters are derived from the systems and political-economy perspectives. Both are essential for interpreting the profession's responses to the needs of ethnic minority communities. In addition, these frameworks are used more generally to understand and frame the experiences of racial and ethnic communities during the early years of social work development.

Systems Perspective[26]

One of the unique advantages of the systems perspective is its applicability to numerous levels of social organization. It can be applied to families,[27] groups,[28] communities,[29] and professions.[30] The perspective can be used to discern the structure and behavior of these and other social entities. Bertalanffy, credited with originating the theory of general systems, wrote that "a system is defined as a complex of components in mutual interaction."[31] The systems perspective emphasizes the relationship between the system and its environment; interrelatedness of system components; the concepts of steady state, equilibrium or homeostasis; boundary maintenance; and system functions such as socialization, social control, communication, feedback, survival (adaptation and maintenance).

The environment is a significant aspect of the systems perspective. The importation of energy from the environment is necessary for system maintenance and survival. *Energy* here refers to those resources required for the system to act, affect change, and maintain itself. The system is bounded, but those boundaries are permeated by the dynamic exchange of energy between the system and the environment. Systems require *inputs* (people, raw materials, and/or other resources) from the environment, and these inputs are transformed by *throughputs* (technology or the series of processes/ activities applied to the inputs) into *outputs* (products) that are then released to the environment.

Systems can exist as tangible entities such as organizations, communities, states, or nations. A formal organization has discernible boundaries, can be distinguished for the environment, has varying components or subsystems, has a structure, socializes new members, has internal communication patterns, applies sanctions to member behaviors, and seeks to maintain itself. Systems perspective has been frequently used to analyze organizational processes and the organization-environment relationship. At the organizational level, systems characteristics appear more manageable for research and analysis. Organizational structure can be identified, formal communication channels can be investigated, and specific environmental factors can be explored.

The application of this perspective to communities and more complex levels of social organization has been more challenging because a community encompasses the individuals, families, other groups, organizations, and institutions within its boundaries. The United States, for example, exists as a complex social system with the same systems characteristics as a formal organization, and would include communities and all their components, states, regions, and all the social institutions that make up the nation. At these levels, the complexity of disentangling systems characteristics seems overwhelming. Rather than being a guide for research, the systems perspective emerges as a guide for understanding the numerous dynamics that affect a system's actions and responses. Thus, this perspective provides a conceptual framework for organizing and assessing complex systems.

In addition to geographical or spatial areas and organizations, systems can also reflect networks of individuals who are bounded by kinship. This type of system is referred to as *non-place communities*.[32] Kinship systems may be based on a blood, racial, or ethnic tie such as a family, an American Indian reservation, or a barrio. The African American community, the Hispanic community, or the Korean community may designate individuals who do not reside in the same geographical area but who are united by the domain of race or ethnicity. This blood, race, or ethnic non-place system is bonded by values, ideologies, interdependence among members, a strong belief in mutuality of goals and expectations, and a commonality of history, tradition, and culture. Members of these kinship systems also have similar perceptions and definitions of social status within the group.

Another type of non-place social system is one in which social network members share like-mindedness, as is the case with religious groups or professions. According to Anderson and Carter:

> An established profession claims for itself and is recognized by society as responsible for a symbolic territory or domain. Almost by definition, when a group carves out for itself a societal function or some part of the society's stock of ideas, it becomes established as a profession. . . . The major commonality among the professions is that they are formally legitimated by society to bring about change that is beneficial to the society and its components, as well as to maintain the society.[33]

Members of a profession often share similar ideologies, values, and beliefs that define the profession's "culture." Members of the same profession typically identify with each other and have a common loyalty to that profession. In addition, the functions of socialization and social control of members occur within the boundaries of the profession. Members are further bonded by the specialized knowledge and set of practices that generally distinguish one profession from another and distinguish the professional from the nonprofessional. As systems, non-place "communities of the mind" also strive to survive and maintain themselves and have all the other characteristics associated with systems.

A system can be both a part and a whole. That is, a system represents the parts that contribute to its wholeness while at the same time its wholeness represents a part or subsystem of some larger system to which it belongs. As a whole or complete system, the social entity strives to maintain its autonomy over the energy it receives, processes, and releases. Emphasis is on the internal dynamics of the system and its relationship with the environment. As a subsystem of a larger system, the social entity is perceived in terms of how it contributes to the larger system and responds to changes occurring in other subsystems. The larger environment also acts on a system and a system, in turn, acts on its environment.

Consequently, the systems perspective explicates systems functions, goals, adaptability, and boundary maintenance; the interdependence of subsystems; and energy exchanges (inputs and outputs) with the environment. The application of this approach to varying types and levels of social systems (from kinship systems to professions) adds to its significance for the topics covered in this analysis.

Political-Economy Perspective[34]

Because organizations are such an integral aspect of social work and service delivery, the political-economy perspective is also employed to further define and explain the dynamics occurring within organizational systems, between organizational systems, and between organizations and the larger environment.

According to Zald, "In its most generic sense, political economy is the study of the interplay of power, the goals of power-wielders, and productive exchange systems."[35] Power and economics guide an organization and community's development and maintenance. For organizations, in particular, the political economy affects goal direction, services, products, and definitions of effectiveness. For communities, the political economy determines their stability, cohesion, power status, and ability to achieve community goals. The political economy of an entity defines its system of power (*polity*), its system for acquiring and distributing resources (*economy*), and the interrelationship between the two. An entity's polity and economy refer to dynamics both inside and outside the entity. Thus, the community and organization are viewed as arenas in which various internal and external interest groups possess the resources needed by the organization and compete to optimize their values.[36] This framework has been applied to a number of different areas including the development of a settlement house,[37] responses to health care issues,[38] and group behavior.[39]

While the political economy perspective has relevance for understanding communities, it is particularly relevant for examining organizational behaviors. For the organization, internal polity defines its institutionalized patterns of decision making and its systematic processes for the exertion of influence in determining goals and defining ends to be met. This would encompass an array of structures, processes, and people within the organization. The power of individuals is derived from a hierarchical position or membership in the dominant elite faction that governs the organization formally or informally. This focus is on the manner in which goals and ends are determined and reified in the organization's political economy.

Organizations have constitutions or normative structures that direct their political economy.[40] Within the organizational constitution, several tasks are accomplished: incentives for participation are illuminated; discretion and decision-making responsibilities within the hierarchy are specified; those parties to whom the organization is accountable are identified; and goals, clients, and technologies are articulated. Power plays between special-interest groups inside and outside the organization shape, create, and re-create the organization's constitution. This constitution represents the embodiment of those values optimized by special-interest groups (dominant elite) of that organization.

Within the political-economy framework, the internal economy is specifically defined as the organization's processes for motivating, organizing, and guiding organizational participants to meet the organization's goals.[41] The distribution of resources reflects the organization's constitution and value commitments. The achievement of specific goals (the optimalization of values) involves the commitment of staff time, incentives for staff participation, allocation of fiscal resources, delineation of technologies, specification of tasks, and a hierarchy that supports goal attainment.

Special-interest groups outside the organization help make up the organization's external polity. Government agencies, legislative bodies, licensing/

accrediting bodies, sponsors/funders, other organizations that offer similar services, service beneficiaries, professional associations, and any other groups or individuals external to the organization with the power to influence the organization are examples of the external polity. These power brokers attempt to direct the organization in accordance with their own values that are derived from self-interests, moral imperatives, professional consider-ations, or some other mitigating belief system.[42] The Council on Social Work Education is part of the external polity of social work schools and programs because the council accredits such programs. In meeting accrediting stan-dards, programs often have to modify their curriculum and/or structure. Thus, through the power of accreditation, the council influences what goes on in social work programs, departments, and schools.

The external polity also has the power to legitimize the organization, and this legitimation acts as a magnet to attract clients, sponsors, and other resources on which the organization depends. Legitimation serves to reaffirm and sanction the organization's existence. In addition, legitimation reflects a correspondence between the external polity and the organization's constitu-tion. When this correspondence is challenged, external power brokers may force the organization to modify its constitution, internal power brokers may attempt to fight these challenges, or the external and internal power wielders reach a compromise.

The organization's external economy includes such environmental factors as the available supply of services, service demands, personnel costs, prevail-ing technologies, and clients. These factors constrain the organization's choices and constitution. In the systems perspective, these factors were referred to as inputs needed by the system in order to maintain itself and survive. Shifts in the external economy can also affect the organization's constitution by redi-recting the allocation of resources and shifting internal power relations.

The political-economy perspective thus highlights the internal and exter-nal political (power) and economic systems that determine and influence what an organization is and what it does. The organization's relationship with its environment is specified in greater detail, and particular factors of that environment are considered more significant than others. This perspec-tive clarifies power as it relates to organizations and operationalizes the uses of that power.

The systems perspective and the political-economy perspective form the framework for examining ethnic minority group history and the birth and development of social work as a profession.

DEFINITION OF TERMS

Ethnic group defines those who share a kinship system, a territory, belief systems, and biological characteristics. Thus, Mexican Americans, Cuban Americans, and Puerto Rican Americans may be members of the same race but belong to different ethnic groups. *Ethnicity* is more specific in that it rec-ognizes distinct cultural and racial groups, and it is used here to refer collec-tively to both ethnic and racial groups. *Ethnic minority* defines those ethnic groups that have a subordinated or disadvantaged status in U.S. society. In 1997, the Office of Management and Budget established racial and ethnic categories that are now widely recognized and accepted by social service agencies.[43] These groups are American Indian or Alaskan Native, Asian, Black or African American, Hispanic or Latino, Native Hawaiian or Other Pacific Islander, and White. *Ethnic agency* refers to the ethnic minority agency[44] (an agency with ethnic minority staff) that provides services to members of that ethnic minority group.

Ideology is defined as those beliefs that are held with great fervor, conviction, and tenacity and are accepted as fact or truth by some group.[45] It is mirrored in the prevailing political beliefs and is not typically alterable by science, logic, or rationality. Jansson lists and compares different political ideologies that range from conservative to radical in views of social problems and their causes.[46] The ideology of the group drives group action and defines social policy. These beliefs help the larger society in general and service providers in particular to define social problems and define solutions to these problems. Professions also have bodies of systematically related beliefs that guide practice.[47] Because many social workers have the ability to act autonomously, they are exercising their organizational discretion as they deliver services.[48] Social workers may embrace particular ideologies about specific racial and ethnic groups and through their discretion may incorporate these ideologies in their practice.

Social control is defined as those practices and policies designed to encourage, persuade, and/or coerce individuals to conform to values and behaviors defined by the larger society. This larger society is comprised of political elites, economic elites, and special-interest groups. Social control, as conceptualized here, is not closely related to neo-Marxian theory that sees the functions of social welfare institutions and personnel as promoting and perpetuating a capitalistic system. Neo-Marxian theory does not adequately reflect the range of issues that define the ethnic minority experience in this country. In the United States, there seems to be a dominant or national culture of which capitalism is but a part and this culture reflects the imprint of a dominant ethnic group in the institutions, values, and character of the country. This imprint determines what is truly "American" and who is truly "American," as well as identifying social problems, social-problem groups, and problem solutions.

The cultural imprint of U.S. society has historically made a distinction between racial minority groups and White ethnic groups. Although White ethnics have encountered deprivation and discrimination, they have not experienced the kind of exclusionary and dehumanizing treatment that deprived racial minorities of even the most basic rights and amenities for much of U.S. history.[49] The early years of what was to become social work practice dramatically emphasizes this point.

Social reform/social change is a concept whose definition often varies with the individuals using it. Conservative and liberal definitions abound that seem to represent opposite ends of a continuum. The concept can indicate major shifts and changes in the basic institutions of society or any change that is directed at levels other than the individual and groups of individuals. It is clear that when social reform is under discussion, the unit of analysis ceases to be the individual. The social reform nature of social work and social services will be examined as it relates to ethnic minorities, with particular attention to the ways social change was defined and the actions resulting from these definitions.

Ethnic minority self-help describes those actions and activities undertaken by collectives and/or other groups that result in the creation and organization of a service delivery entity (a service, a program, or an agency) that provides direct services to some identified ethnic minority group or community. These efforts may encompass political activism, but this activism is secondary to direct service provision for the amelioration or alleviation of particular social conditions. These efforts bring the service providers in direct, face-to-face contact with the service beneficiaries.

There seems to be a subtle irony in the use of the term *self-help*. The term connotes the ability of individuals to come together to develop their own solutions for the problem they identify; yet, the social and political environment surrounding the ethnic minority community poses constraints and conditions that often delimit community self-help goals and actions.

Welfare state refers to the institutionalization of policies and programs that support health, income maintenance, education, and welfare services. It reflects public (government) dominance in the policies, fiscal support, and implementation of a range of services that promote the general health and well-being of the citizens of the country. The private sector's influence is most noticeable in the implementation of social policy—through the operation of private institutions and programs.[50]

Mainstream, traditional, conventional social services are embodied in the practices of public and private, nonprofit, formal organizations established to address a particular problem or meet the needs of a particular group. Many of these formal organizations implement the policies and programs mandated by the public through legislation, whereas others are sponsored by special-interest groups. In this analysis, there are service sponsors (public and private), service providers (social workers and other human services personnel), and service recipients (typically referred to as *clients*). Mainstream social services also emphasize formal organizations that tend to be complex and hierarchical. Ideally, human services organizations would seek to provide services to all who need them within a community, but, in reality, many minority groups are unserved, underserved, or inappropriately served by the established human services system.[51] Unfortunately, this type of service delivery has evolved over the decades. *Mainstream social services represent the social practices of the welfare state.*[52]

Mainstream social work refers to the particular professional practice involved in the organization and administration of the complex machinery supporting the policies and programs of the welfare state. This practice is an outgrowth of the work of Charity Organization Societies and settlement houses of the Progressive Era (1895–1917). Clearly, professional social workers are but one piece of an intricate service delivery maze that includes numerous other human services personnel and professionals. The professional social work presence has, however, influenced the direction and tone of human services in this country. In fact, the development of the welfare state and the development of social work have been interdependent. The emergence of the roots of the welfare state in the New Deal of the Roosevelt administration contributed to a dramatic expansion of social work, as the number of social workers doubled during this period.[53] The welfare state depends on a massive social-practice labor force to carry out its policies. Social work is *the* social practice of the welfare state, and professional social work represents the professionalization of this practice.

DATA SOURCES

The analysis presented in this book is derived from a compilation and synthesis of existing empirical and theoretical literature and case studies. Historical records often provide indisputable documentation for the generalizations offered. Literature cited ranges from the historical *Charities and the Commons,* a turn-of-the-century journal, to more contemporary books and journals. Online databases and Internet sites have made resources more accessible and serve to enrich the information-gathering process. Although these sources are varied, they all provide insight into social services and the ethnic minority community.

To advance this consideration, literature outside of the social work and social services field are included in the knowledge base. Relevant literature in such areas as sociology, political science, and history offers perspectives on society, ethnic identity, and intergroup relations, serving to explain why challenges continue to persist in service delivery to racial and ethnic minority groups.

We reviewed literature that focuses on ethnic minority agencies—their history, forms, functions, and utilization—in order to formulate the dimensions and tenets underlying ethnic self-help. This literature included empirical discussions and a number of case descriptions and case studies. A systematic review of these cases led to the identification of some "universals" governing ethnic agency practice. Contained within these pages is a comprehensive compilation of literature on the ethnic agency. From this compilation are drawn the core features of practice that integrate community and ethnicity in the service delivery process. The ethnic agency thus becomes a model for ethnic-sensitive practice that utilizes the social context of the client system. Practice models derived from ethnic agency practice are generated for implementation in conventional social services.

Literature on the history of formalized service delivery, organizational behavior, organizational change, and interorganizational relations was also surveyed to generate a sound foundation for the explication of models for linking mainstream social services with the ethnic agency. There is no one "right" way to bridge the gulf between these two service delivery systems, and the models presented take into consideration the range of factors that influence the interorganizational relationship.

ORGANIZATION OF THE BOOK

Chapters 2 through 4 focus on the historical context of social work as it relates to the experiences of ethnic and racial minority groups during the profession's formative years. Because the history of ethnic and racial minorities in this country continues to influence social services and minority communities' reactions to these services, these chapters provide a detailed overview of the social conditions surrounding specific groups during the Progressive Era, including White ethnics. The White ethnics are discussed first in a separate chapter to provide a backdrop against which to compare and contrast their experiences with those of the ethnic and racial minorities.

Urbanization, industrialization, immigration, and migration created densely populated slums and a new kind of poverty. Writings that cover the history of social work often include descriptions of these social conditions, but the plight of ethnic and racial minorities are generally relegated to a brief discussion or to just a sentence or two. Those writings that do mention the social and discriminatory conditions of those groups often fail to discuss social work's specific responses to these conditions.

These chapters will present the unique histories of ethnic and racial minority groups to show that, although all groups suffered, all did not suffer equally. Furthermore, the histories of these groups are detailed so that students, practitioners, administrators, educators, policy makers, funding sources, and others interested in enhancing service delivery to diverse populations have a more in-depth knowledge of the histories of these groups. For those individuals who already possess this knowledge, these chapters serve as a stark reminder. These details are recounted for several reasons: to show that contemporary relations between social work and ethnic minorities are affected by the historical context of those relations; to emphasize that history can be dynamic with far-reaching consequences; to counter a tendency in social work to minimize its history with ethnic minority groups; and to stimulate thinking about how social work ought to relate to ethnic minority groups and communities.

Chapters 5 and 6 examine the way ethnicity and race affected the nascent profession's casework and reform responses. The role of race and ethnicity in the Charity Organization Societies and in the settlement-house movement is presented because of the significance of this history in the development of both contemporary micro and macro practice. These chapters also include discussions of professionalization and bureaucratization and how they affected the profession's reform impulse. Reform movements *within* the profession—the Rank-and-File Movement and the Human Services Movement—are also relevant for inclusion here.

In Chapter 7, social work's continued evolution as a profession is covered. Here, the debates and dilemmas surrounding professionalization are presented. Political economy theory will be applied to an examination of social work as a "middle course."

Chapter 8 covers the definitions and descriptions of ethnic services. As social work was evolving into a profession, the ethnic /minority communities were developing service delivery systems that, to a certain extent, paralleled the mainstream services. Each group developed its own approach to social service intervention and identified its own goals. Although some goals overlapped across communities, there were specific ways in which a particular group stamped the services with its unique culture and identity. The intersection of ethnicity and religion will also be discussed.

Chapter 9 focuses on the ethnic agency and offers an overview of its uniqueness. Chapter 10 covers the contemporary context of service delivery to ethnic communities. The historical analysis is used as a foundation for illuminating practice methods and approaches useful for service delivery to minority communities. The methods carry their own set of assumptions about agency values, leadership and resources.

In conclusion, Chapter 11 highlights the themes, dilemmas, and debates that continue to surround ethnic-sensitive service delivery. Particular issues seem to defy or resist resolution. Some of these issues are rooted in American history and some are rooted in the nature of American professions. Regardless, these issues need to be acknowledged and confronted if social work is to remain a viable profession in a multicultural country.

Historical analysis and organizational analysis are stepping stones to the development of (1) a sound knowledge base about the context of service delivery to ethnic minorities, and (2) effective methods of macro practice with these communities. Linking mainstream social services to ethnic communities and ethnic agencies can be effectively accomplished through an understanding of the history of ethnic communities and through an understanding of the traces of that history that are apparent today.

As this book shows, social work emerged from the needs of a changing society that was becoming more diverse. The arrival of immigrants from southern and eastern Europe began to challenge the prevailing assumptions about Americanism while the country was grappling with the meaning of citizenship for African Americans. At the same time, Asians and Mexicans were legally ineligible for citizenship as the American Indians languished on the reservations as non-citizens and non-persons. In this turbulent environment, forerunners of contemporary service providers addressed primarily the needs and issues surrounding the White ethnic immigrants. Historical analysis can uncover the factors that led to this focus.

As a result of the directions of these early workers, parallel service delivery systems emerged—one for mainstream social services and one for ethnic minority communities. These communities embraced a self-help ethos because not to do so meant, in many cases, limited or no relief from community problems. Formal and informal ethnic minority services were the forerunners of the ethnic agency and held significant meaning to the communities they served. At the same time, mainstream service providers often held patronizing and paternalistic attitudes toward these ethnic minority services. In general, ethnic agencies have been undervalued and unacknowledged by traditional social services and the social work profession.

Today, the future of social services and social work is again inexorably tied to ethnic groups, but now the ethnic groups are ethnic minorities of color.

The ability of service providers to respond efficiently and empathetically to the needs of these communities will shape the future of the human services. To remain viable and relevant, service providers—professional social workers and other human services personnel—must demonstrate their efficacy in meeting the challenges of this decade and the next.

Endnotes

[1] http://www.census.gov (accessed September 16, 2008).

[2] http://www.census.gov/population/www/projections/2009projections.html (accessed December 28, 2009); See particularly the Census Bureau report by Jennifer M. Ortman and Christine E. Guarneri, "United States Population Projections: 2000 to 2050."

[3] www.socialworkers.org?practice/standards/NASWCulturalStandardsIndicators2006.pdf (accessed March 2, 2009).

[4] http://www.socialworkers.org/diversity/newstandards.asp (accessed August, 3, 2009).

[5] http://www.socialworkers.org/diversity/defaulty.asp (accessed August 3, 2009).

[6] http://socialwork.iu.edu/media/EPAS.htm (accessed August 3, 2009).

[7] Roger Daniels, *The Politics of Prejudice* (Berkeley: University of California Press, 1962): 66; Florette Henri, *Black Migration: Movement North 1900–1920* (Garden City, NY: Doubleday, 1975), 146; Richard Hofstadter, *Social Darwinism in American Thought,* rev. ed. (Boston: Beacon Press, 1955), 170–200.

[8] Ruth Crocker, *Social Work and Social Order: The Settlement Movement in Two Industrial Cities* (Chicago: University of Chicago Press, 1992); Allen Davis, *Spearheads for Reform, The Social Settlements and the Progressive Movement: 1890–1914* (New Brunswick, NJ: Rutgers University Press, 1984); Howard Karger, "Minneapolis Settlement Houses in the 'Not So Roaring 20s': Americanization, Morality, and the Revolt Against Popular Culture," *Journal of Sociology and Social Welfare* 14 (June 1987): 89–110; Alvin Kogut, "The Settlements and Ethnicity: 1890–1914," *Social Work* 17 (May 1972): 22–31.

[9] Douglas Hartmann and Joseph Gerteis, "Dealing with Diversity: Mapping Multiculturalism in Sociological Terms," *Sociological Theory* 23 (June 2005): 235.

[10] See, for example, Paula Allan-Meares, "Cultural competence: An Ethnical Requirement," *Journal of Ethnic and Cultural Diversity in Social Work,* 16(3/4) (2007): 83–92; Larry Davis and Joe Gelsomino, "An Assessment of Practitioner Cross-Racial Treatment Experiences," *Social Work* 39 (January 1994): 116–123; W. M. Liu, D. B. Pope-Davis, and H. K. Coleman, *Handbook of Multicultural Competencies in Counseling and Psychology* (Thousand Oaks, CA: Sage, 2003); Flavio Marsiglia and Stephen Kulis, *Diversity, Oppression, and Change—Culturally Grounded Social Work* (Chicago: Lyceum Books: 2009); Jose Sisneros, Catherine Stakeman, Mildred Joyner, and Cathryne Schmitz, *Critical Multicultural Social Work* (Chicago: Lyceum Books, 2008); D.W. Sue and M. McGoldrick, *Multicultural Social Work Practice* (New York: Wiley, 2005).

[11] Marsiglia and Kulis, *Diversity, Oppression, and Change,* 178–215.

[12] D. Lum, "Culturally Competent Practice," in *Culturally Competent Practice,* 2nd ed., ed. D. Lum (Pacific Grove, CA: Thomson-Brooks/Cole, 2003).

[13] Jimy Sanders, "Ethnic Boundaries and Identity in Plural Societies," *Annual Review of Sociology* 28 (2002): 328.

[14] Sanders, "Ethnic Boundaries and Identity in Plural Societies," 386.

[15] Bruce Jansson, *The Reluctant Welfare State,* 6th ed. (Belmont, CA: Brooks/Cole, 2009).

[16] Sanders, "Ethnic Boundaries and Identity in Plural Societies," 386.

[17] Kay Deaux, Nida Bikmen, Alwyn Gilkes, Ana Ventuneac, Yvanne Joseph, Yasser Payne, and Claude Steele, "Becoming American: Stereotype Threat Effects in Afro-Caribbean Immigrant Groups," *Social Psychology Quarterly* 70 (December 2007): 386.

[18] Ibid.

[19] See, for example, Jillian (Mary Ann) Jimenez, *Social Policy and Social Change* (Thousand Oaks, CA: Sage, 2010): 219–258; Michael Reisch and Janice Andrews, *The Road Not Taken: A History of Radical Social Work in the United States* (New York: Brunner-Routledge, 2001).

[20] Dorothea Epple, "Inter and Intra Professional Social Work Differences: Social Work's Challenge," *Clinical Social Work Journal* 35 (December 2007): 267–276.

[21] Judith Trolander, *Professionalism and Social Change—From the Settlement House Movement to Neighborhood Centers 1866 to the Present* (New York: Columbia University Press, 1987). Author reviews the work of early historians who concluded that professionalism turned social work away from its reform roots.

[22] Herman Levin, "Conservatism of Social Work," *Social Service Review* 56 (December 1982): 613.

[23] Numerous historical overviews of social work's history either omit or briefly review the way early service providers viewed and responded to ethnic minority groups. Examples of this oversight can be found in June Axinn and Herman Levin, *Social Welfare: A History of American Response to Need,* 2nd ed. (New York: Harper and Row, 1982); Mary Ann Jimenez, "Historical Evolution and Future Challenges of the Human Services Professions," *Families in Societies* 72 (January 1990): 3–12; James Leiby, *A History of Social Welfare and Social Work in the United States* (New York: Columbia University Press, 1978).

[24] Examples of this racism and exclusion are contained in Davis, *Spearheads for Reform,* 94–96; W. E. B. DuBois, "Social Effects of Emancipation," *The Survey* (February 1, 1913): 572; Patricia Hogan and Sau-Fong Siu, "Minority Children and the Child Welfare System: An Historical Perspective," *Social Work* 33 (November 1988): 493–498; June Brown, "Primary Prevention: A Concept Whose Time Has Come for Improving the Cultural Relevance of Family and Children's Services in Ethnic-Minority Communities," in *Primary Prevention Approaches to Development of Mental Health Services for Ethnic Minorities,* ed. Samuel Miller, Gwenelle Styles, and Carl Scott (New York: Council on Social Work Education, 1982): 41; S. Wells Williams, "Chinese Immigration," *Journal of Social Science* 9 (December 1879): 110–111; Paul Wong, Steven Applewhite, and J. Michael Daley, "From Despotism to Pluralism: The Evolution of Voluntary Organizations in Chinese Communities," *Ethnic Groups* 8(4) (1990): 217.

[25] As quoted in Crocker, *Social Work and Social Order,* 182.

[26] Discussion in this section is drawn from Ralph Anderson and Ira Carter, *Human Behavior in the Social Environment—A Systems Approach,* 5th ed. (New York: Aldine De Gruyter, 1999); Ludwig von Bertalanffy, "General System Theory and Psychiatry," in *American Handbook of Psychiatry, Vol. I,* 2nd ed., ed. Silvano Arieti (New York: Basic Books, 1974); Daniel Katz and Robert Kahn, *The Social Psychology of Organizations,* 2nd ed. (New York: John Wiley and Sons, 1978), 23–33; David Nadler, "Managing Organizational Change: An Integrative Perspective," *The Journal of Applied Behavioral Science* 17(2) (1981): 192–194; F. Ellen Netting, Peter Kettner, and Steven McMurtry, *Social Work Macro Practice,* 4th ed. (New York: Pearson, 2008), 11–13; Christopher Petr, "The Worker-Client Relationship: A General Systems Perspective," *Social Casework* 69 (December 1988): 621–624; and Mary Zey-Ferrell, *Dimensions of Organizations: Environment, Context, Structure, Process, and Performance* (Santa Monica, CA: Goodyear, 1979), 40–42.

[27] Martha Cox and Blair Paley, "Understanding Families as Systems," *Current Directions in Psychological Science* 12 (October 2003): 193–195.

[28] Joanie Connors and Richard Caple, "A Review of Groups Systems Theory," *Journal for Specialists in Group Work* 30 (June 2005): 93–110.

[29] Amitai Etzioni, "Creating Good Communities and Good Societies," *Contemporary Sociology* 29 (January 2000): 188–195.

[30] Jan Wirth, "The Functions of Social Work," *Journal of Social Work* 9 (4): 405–419.

[31] Bertalanffy, "General System Theory," 1100.

[32] Ralph Anderson and Irl Carter provide a detailed discussion of nonplace communities such as kinship and professional communities in *Human Behavior in the Social Environment,* 73–76.

[33] Anderson and Carter, *Human Behavior in the Social Environment,* 92–93.

[34] The discussion presented here is drawn from J. Kenneth Benson, "Interorganizational Network as a Political Economy," *Administrative Science Quarterly* 20 (June 1975): 229–249; Yeheskel Hasenfeld, *Human Service Organizations* (Englewood Cliffs, NJ: Prentice Hall, 1983), 43–49; David Powell, "Managing Organizational Problems in Alternative Service Organizations," *Administration in Social Work* 10 (Fall 1986): 59–61; Gary Wamsley and Mayer Zald, *The Political Economy of Public Organizations* (Lexington, MA: Lexington Books, 1973); and Mayer Zald, "Political Economy: A Framework for Comparative Analysis," in *Power in Organizations,* ed. Mayer Zald (Nashville: Vanderbilt University Press, 1970), 221–261.

[35] Zald, "Political Economy," 223.

[36] Hasenfeld, *Human Service Organizations,* 44.

[37] See, for example, Robert Fisher and Michael Fabricant, "From Henry Street to Contracted Services: Financing the Settlement House," *Journal of Sociology and Social Welfare* 29 (September 2002): 3.

[38] See, for example, Merrill Singer, Ed., *The Political Economy of AIDS* (Amityville, NY: Baywood Publishing, 1998); and Judie Svihula, "Political Economy, Moral Economy and the Medicare Modernization Act of 2003," *Journal of Sociology and Social Welfare* 35 (March 2008): 157–173.

[39] See, for example, Patrice Hill Collins, "Gender, Black Feminism, and Black Political Economy," *Annals of the American Academy of Political and Social Science* 568 (March 2000): 41–53.

[40] Mayer Zald offers a detailed discussion of organizational constitutions in "Political Economy," 225–229.

[41] Powell, "Managing Organizational Problems," 59.

[42] Ibid.

[44] Office of Management and Budget, Federal Register Notice dated October 30, 1997. http://www.whitehouse.gov/omb/federeg_1997 standards/ (accessed October 24, 2009).

[44] For further discussions of ethnicity and race, see Beth Hess, Elizabeth Markson, and Peter Stein, "Racial and Ethnic Minorities: An Overview," in *Race, Class, and Gender in the United States*, 2nd ed., ed. Paula Rothenberg (New York: St. Martin's Press, 1992), 145–155; Benjamin Ringer and Elinor Lawless, *Race-Ethnicity and Society* (New York: Routledge, 1989).

[45] Lyman Sargent, *Contemporary Political Ideologies*, 7th ed. (Chicago: Dorsey Press, 1987), 2.

[46] Bruce Jansson, *The Reluctant Welfare State*, 6th ed. (Belmont, CA: Brooks/Cole, 2009).

[47] Burton Gummer, "On Helping and Helplessness: The Structure of Discretion in the American Welfare System," *Social Service Review* 53 (June 1979): 218.

[48] Michael Sosin, "Discretion in Human Service Organizations," ed. Yeheskel Hasenfeld, *Human Services as Complex Organizations*, 2nd ed. (Thousand Oaks, CA: Sage), 381.

[49] Ringer and Lawless, *Race-Ethnicity and Society*, 27.

[50] George Martin, Jr., *Social Policy in the Welfare State* (Englewood Cliffs, NJ: Prentice-Hall, 1990), 1.

[51] Wilbur Finch, Jr., "Alternative Service Organizations: The AIDS Community," in *AIDS—A Complete Guide to Psychological Intervention*, ed. Helen Land (Milwaukee: Family Service America, Inc., 1992), p. 79.

[52] See, for example, Bruce Jansson, *The Reluctant Welfare State*, 6th ed. (Belmont, CA: Brooks/Cole, 2009).

[53] George Martin, Jr., *Social Policy in the Welfare State*, 27.

The Progressive Era and White Ethnics
The Social Context of Early Practice

What does it mean to be White? It is clearly more than the color of a person's skin, as color differentiation is only a vague marker for ethnic identification in the United States.[1]

According to Tice and Perkins, the Progressive Era was an exciting time because this was a period when social work "blossomed as a profession, making a profound imprint on the society through its work in social welfare."[2] White ethnics represent the most significant population influencing the development of social work during this blossoming time. The historical emergence of social work was grounded in an era that adhered to distinct definitions of ethnicity, race, and "American." The country was forging a national identity steeped in values, ideologies, and norms that permeated the evolution of the profession. The historical and social context surrounding this evolution shaped the direction and destiny of the budding profession. An analysis of today's social work interventions with diverse communities must be grounded in the history of these diverse groups in the United States. Thus, the Progressive Era and the changing immigration patterns during this period become a significant starting point for this analysis.

Social work and human services publications do mention the Progressive Era, the social transition accompanying it, and, to some degree, the plight of ethnic minorities during this period. These topics often take up a few paragraphs or even a few pages that contain a broad, general, and sometimes simplistic overview without a serious analysis of the interplay between the social conditions affecting ethnic minorities and organized responses to them. The history of social work as it relates to particular groups should not be so easily dismissed, discounted, or denied. While much social work literature details the history of oppression and discrimination faced by minority groups during the Progressive Era,[3] little mention is made of how this discrimination and oppression influenced the profession's evolution.

General, brief historical summaries may erroneously convey a view that all groups suffered equally, horribly, and harmfully. Such a homogenized approach fails to distinguish the unique experiences of specific groups. These unique experiences were shaped by the way the larger society responded to each group—a larger society that included the nascent field of social work. For this reason, this chapter provides a more detailed description of the historical context in which social work emerged.

It is all too easy to believe that history has limited utility for contemporary practitioners and social delivery systems seeking proficiency in ethnic-sensitive practice. Some people may even think that only contemporary issues are relevant for this type of intervention—not the issues of the past. Yet, it is the specific history of each group that has contributed to the forms and functions of today's social work with that group. An understanding and appreciation of that history are paramount for explaining and addressing the tensions that have long existed between ethnic minority communities and mainstream social work.

Thus, an understanding of social work's contemporary relationship with ethnic minority communities does not begin with the present. Rather, the profession's response to the needs of these communities has been developing over time and the visible results today represent an accumulation of that history. The social work/ethnic minority community interface is predicated on the evolution of both the profession and the minority communities. Both sides had a specific agenda that led to the taking of divergent paths. It is the history of human services in general, and social work in particular, as it relates to ethnic minorities, that has shaped mainstream interventions in these communities. An understanding of social work's responses today is predicated on an understanding of responses during its formative years.

Modern social work has its roots in the Progressive Era (1895–1920), for it was during this period that increased immigration, massive migration, burgeoning industrialization, and unbridled urbanization dramatically changed the texture of U.S. society and created rampant social problems that begged for systematic, organized intervention. The acceptance of the idea that skilled professionals could assist individuals and families—and that the attendant rise of the human services can be linked to social and intellectual movements in the Progressive Era—set the stage for the emergence of social work, clinical psychology, and marriage and family therapy, among other human services.[4]

The actual years that define the Progressive Era appear to vary, depending on which source is consulted. For example, Cowan, Rose, and Rose described this period as 1900 to 1920,[5] whereas Jimenez used 1900 to 1917.[6] Davis targeted 1890 to 1914,[7] as did Kunitz.[8] More recently, Goldfield and his co-authors used the period from 1900–1917.[9] Because of migration rates, immigration patterns, changing laws, and shifting economic trends, clarity in defining the Progressive Era years is vital for assessing this period. Although the addition or subtraction of a few years may seem insignificant, these variations determine the specific events chronicled and their immediate and long-range effects. Some events included or omitted are minor in nature; others, such as World War I, are paramount. The actual definition of the Progressive Era has implications for the analysis undertaken.

Here, the years 1895 to 1920 define the Progressive Era and those historical occurrences falling within this period are emphasized. We use these
years because they capture the first signs of a change in the European immigration pattern, the peak of African American migration to the North, World
War I, and the period immediately following the war. World War I and its
aftermath were particularly relevant in defining the minority experience in
the United States. Discussing the historical antecedents and consequences of
the Progressive Era provides a more complete overview of the social context.

PROGRESS OF THE PROGRESSIVE ERA

The Progressive Era was so named because of the economic, social, and
political changes taking place during the time.[10] For example, this was the
period in which railroads linked areas that formerly had been separated by
weeks of travel. In 1865, the United States had about 37,000 miles of railroad
track, and by 1914, that figure had increased to 253,000.[11] Although the auto-
mobile was not a common family commodity, its presence was growing in
U.S. communities. Evolving transportation technologies meant that manufac-
tured goods and supplies could be carried to numerous parts of the country,
thereby increasing their distribution. Furthermore, industries and factories
developed with the utilization of cheap labor provided by migrants and immigrants. In 1914, there were 7 times as many industrial workers as there had
been in 1859, production had increased by about 12 times, and 69 percent of
the workforce held nonagricultural employment.[12]

The Progressive Era is noted for the reform efforts undertaken by progressives and reformers on behalf of workers, children, and widows. Furthermore,
this progressivism is generally associated with political liberalism directed
toward ameliorating the problems and injustices accompanying the transition
to an industrialized, urbanized society.[13] For example, in 1890, the National
American Women's Suffrage Association was established; in 1899, Illinois and
Colorado passed legislation that established juvenile courts; in 1904, the
National Committee on Child Labor was organized; in 1909, the White House
Conference on Care of Dependent Children was held; and from 1911 to 1920,
numerous states enacted mothers' pension legislation and workmen's compensation.[14] Indeed, the first systematic welfare programs were enacted at the
state level during this time, as reflected in the Illinois adoption of workmen's
compensation in 1911, which was viewed as a progressive innovation.[15]

The paradox of the Progressive Era is rather striking because it heralded
the dawning of a new American prosperity as well as a new American poverty. While thousands languished in the tenements of growing cities, thousands more were reaping the wealth of an industrializing country. At a time
when poverty was taking on a new and even more abject meaning, numerous
individuals were able to achieve success and wealth. During this era, the
number of millionaires increased significantly and industries were monopo-
lized by specific companies. The *World Almanac* named 4,000 millionaires in
1902, 47 percent of the nation's assets were held by 1 percent of the population during the early 1900s, Andrew Carnegie made $23 million in 1900, and

steel, oil, and agricultural machinery production were dominated by U.S. Steel, Standard Oil, and International Harvester.[16]

The Progressive Era also gave rise to organized efforts to assist the less fortunate. The origins of U.S. social work were primarily in the charity organization societies that emphasized control of pauperism by the regulation of charity through scientific principles (*Scientific Charity*) and by the assimilation of the poor and immigrants who suffered the harsh slum conditions. The settlement house movement—also a major part of social work history—provided for a focus on the environmental causes of poverty and on research into the factors leading to poverty. These two roots of contemporary human services are well known among professional service providers and have received extensive coverage in social work and human services texts and journals. What is often lacking in these discussions, however, is the plight of racial minorities and the manner in which the charity organization societies and settlement houses responded to these groups. [17]

The significance of the past has been emphasized by Ringer and Lawless:

> Thus the historical past of an ethnic group is not something that is relegated to its archives to be viewed as a curious but interesting relic. Instead it functions to organize sentiments, needs, aspirations of the present. Consequently to understand fully the meaning of the past for an ethnic group, it must be seen as filtered through the prism of the present. As such the past and present are inextricably interwoven in the life of the ethnic group, and the interaction between the two does much to define the group's vision of its future.[18]

A review of the general conditions of this period, the unique role of ethnicity in shaping immigrant experiences, and early social work history can provide insight into bridging the gap that separates social work from ethnic minority communities. These conditions and early responses to them become a legacy for modern multicultural social work practice. The historical context of ethnic and racial communities must be understood for contemporary social work to forge tools and techniques of multicultural practice.

The Social Conditions of the Progressive Era: Urbanization

The Progressive Era captures a snapshot of the urbanization of U.S. society along with significant population growth. In the decade preceding the advent of the Progressive Era—the 1880s—the U.S. population was 50.1 million, and 28.7 percent of this population resided in urban areas. At the beginning of the Progressive period, the population had grown to almost 63 million, and a little more than a third (35.1 percent) of the population was urban. By the end of this era (1920) the population had increased to over 105 million, and slightly more than half (51.2 percent) was found in urban areas.[19]

Much of the population increase occurred in specific major cities as migrants from rural areas and immigrants from other countries were drawn to them by the magnet of jobs and economic prosperity.[20] In 1860, there were 8 cities with populations over 100,000, and by 1900, that number had grown to 33.[21] Baltimore, Brooklyn, Boston, Chicago, New York, Philadelphia, and St.

Louis, for example, experienced unprecedented growth due to larger populations *and* changing city boundaries through annexation of adjacent areas that were already densely populated. For example, Chicago's population grew from 503,185 in 1880 to 1,099,850 in 1890—a rate of 118 percent; however, the city also grew in land mass from 35.66 square miles to 174.55 square miles—an almost 400 percent gain.[22] Thus, immigration, migration, and annexation contributed to the urbanization of U.S. society and the growth of urban centers.

Ideologies of the Progressive Era

In the period leading up to the Progressive Era, most social welfare efforts were generated by local and state jurisdictions. Some exceptions did exist, as was the case of a federally sponsored pension program for veterans of the Civil War.[23] For the most part, the general public did not assume the responsibility or obligation of caring for the needy. Poverty itself was not identified as a social problem that required widespread intervention. However, religious groups armed with teachings and social commitment filled this void with an ideology of caring for the downtrodden. *Social Gospel* emerged as an ideology that captured the ethos of the Pre-Progressive Era.[24] Extending charity and compassion to the poor was held as a primary mission for those seeking a Christ-like existence. This sentiment is reflected in the writings of Charles Loring Brace, a divinity school graduate who founded the Children's Aid Society in 1853.[25] He has been called the father of foster care because of his system of using trains (called orphan trains) to send New York street children to be placed with families in other, less urbanized parts of the country. In his book, *The Dangerous Classes in New York,* he wrote, "The central figure in the world's charity is Christ . . . Christ has indeed given a new value to the poorest and most despised human being."[26]

Numerous missionaries answered a calling to minister to the poor and the weakest of society. They visited asylums, almshouses, and often traveled to tribal reservations to educate Native American children. Although these ministers and missionaries may have come from privileged backgrounds, they were willing to make the sacrifices necessary to serve the poor. They placed their calling and their mission above the accumulation of personal wealth and status. Mission work became life's work for countless privileged, educated individuals (many of whom were women) who wanted to tend to the ills of society. The sacrifice and the work were expected to lead to spiritual rewards, contentment, and a sense of fulfillment.

A primary technology or method of intervention for the Social Gospel proponents was the establishment of home missions. Writing about the Social Gospel movement, Luker noted that in the antebellum South these missions were located in African American communities as a means of Christianizing the South.[27] Social Gospel followers launched a crusade to "uplift" the freedmen (former slaves) as a means of saving the nation. This view is captured in the words of a missionary who proclaimed that the goal was the creation of "a new Negro" and the "transformation of a vast population trained as slaves into a population with the character, habits, and virtues of free men."[28]

In the racially segregated communities of the South, the gospel of uplift actually translated into the gospel of self-help for the freedmen. Harsh social and political conditions meant that former slaves had few resources outside their own communities to support them. As the Social Gospel missionaries preached their messages in their home missions or in African American churches, the emphasis on self-help further confirmed to the freedmen that they would rise or fall through the works of their own hands. This message was also reaffirmed through the segregation and discrimination they encountered daily. (Chapter 3 offers a summary of the African American experience during the Progressive Era.)

While Social Gospel had rather limited appeal to the general populace, *Social Darwinism* seemed more consistent with public sentiment.[29] At a time when individuals were amassing wealth, this ideology could be used to rationalize the class distinctions that were evolving. Herbert Spencer authored the phrase "survival of the fittest" ten years before Charles Darwin's book, *Origin of the Species*, first appeared.[30] This ideology emanated from Charles Darwin's evolutionary explanation of species survival. By "survival of the fittest," Darwin meant, however, that species producing offspring that were better adapted for the immediate, local environment had a better chance of their characteristics and traits surviving over time.[31] In applying theories of evolution to human behavior, Social Darwinists believed they had a sound basis for explaining the ascendancy of Anglo-Saxons over other non-Anglo-Saxon groups. According to Claeys, Social Darwinism gave rise to a new definition of race that was tied more closely to skin color and to beliefs about racial supremacy that were linked with previous notions about "fitness."[32]

Social Darwinism further cemented beliefs that individual effort and ability accounted for success and prosperity in American society. A corollary of this belief was that poverty could be attributed to poor work, insufficient effort, and other factors over which the individual had control. Individual responsibility seemed to correlate well with American values of individualism, self-reliance, and the Protestant work ethnic.[33]

Social Darwinism also opened the door to scientific and pseudo-scientific investigations of biological differences between the races.[34] As a result, the perceived differences between so-called "higher" and "lower" races began taking on the aura of scientific fact. "Fittest" was equated with intelligence and whiteness. In this regard, Manifest Destiny (God's mission for Anglo-Saxons to conquer the new world) and the colonization of territories of color by dominant countries appeared to receive validation. Darwin and others concluded that the lower races could eventually be eliminated by the higher civilized races of the world. Thus, with Social Darwinism, Manifest Destiny was augmented by a racial destiny.[35]

ETHNICITY AND RACE IN THE PROGRESSIVE ERA

Ethnicity versus Race

Ethnicity and race represent distinct categories despite a common tendency to substitute one term for the other. According to Cox and Ephross, ethnic groups are bound by culture, identity, common past, attachment to a country, and a sense of "we-ness."[36] These authors also highlight the psychological (identity, perceptions of self and others, and solidarity) and social connotations (language, religion, community, and social roles) associated with ethnicity. Race, on the other hand, comes with social, psychological, *and* physical aspects. Distinctive physical characteristics appear impervious to the passage of time, while ethnicity seems to have a more fluid, malleable quality to it.

The White ethnics who immigrated to this country during the Progressive Era were deemed unfit because of their foreign ethnic heritage and culture. In addition, although they were not as dark as African Americans, they were still not as white as the native-born Whites. For some, these groups could be seen as occupying a type of "middle ground" in a racial hierarchy between Black and White.[37] Race, thus emerged as a central factor in determining the social status as well as social acceptance. The 1900 census, for example, recorded two categories for race—White persons and Colored persons.[38] Colored persons included those of Negro descent, Chinese, Japanese, and Indians. White persons were further classified as native born or foreign born.

In writing about the significance of distinguishing one's own group from those other groups that are different, Goldstein explains that the marginalization of the "other" promotes group identity, group solidarity, and group values.[39] The "other" can symbolize all the negative traits and characteristics from which the group wishes to separate itself. The "self" versus "other" or "us" versus "them" mentality can be depicted in the widely held belief that race was primarily a two-category designation consisting of Whites and Blacks or Whites and Coloreds. For this reason, the White ethnics posed a dilemma for native-born Americans since they were not quite fully the "other." These new immigrants had more in common with the native-born citizens and did not fall at the bottom of the racial order as did the "Coloreds" of the day. The perplexing status of the new foreigners resulted in myriad responses.

It should be noted, however that the definition of "other" has a fluid aspect to it that may change over time, as noted by Berbrier.[40] When the country was primarily English, the Northern and Western Europeans were the questionable foreigners; however, after these groups became dominant, then the Southern and Eastern Europeans became the unpopular masses. This suggests that the concept of "other" is dynamic rather than stable. This seems to be true in situations with ethnic groups as the "other." Historically, "black" or "colored" groups have remained entrenched as the "other."

White Ethnics

The history of White ethnics in the Progressive Era is a history of immigration patterns during this period. European immigration was largely unregulated prior to World War I (1914–1918), but this changed after the war.[41] Between 1880 and World War I, strong anti-foreign agitation erupted. This anti-foreign sentiment was tied to the dramatic change in immigration patterns of the Progressive Era—from the immigration of the desirable, sturdy stock of "old" European immigrants from northwestern Europe to the immigration of the less desirable peasants and "pales" from eastern and southern Europe (the "new" immigrants).[42]

Numerous immigrant groups (Germans, Scotch-Irish, Swedes, Dutch, French, Spanish, Portuguese, Jews) contributed to the emergence of an American identity during the colonial period, although the Anglo-Saxon element was predominant in determining U.S. political, legal, and social development.[43] Many of these groups with cultures that did not vary greatly from the developing U.S. culture had been assimilated as they already espoused or adopted English and Protestantism. Catholic and Jewish populations were relatively small and nonthreatening to mainstream America. Social Darwinism and racist imperialism reflected an adherence to Anglo-Saxon supremacy in the literature and science of the late 1800s.[44]

During the 1880s and earlier, the majority of European immigrants hailed from Great Britain, Ireland, Scandinavia, and other countries of the northwest. Census figures indicate that, in 1870, the overwhelming majority (96 percent) of the foreign born in the United States had come from these countries, and 61 percent of those immigrating to the United States in that year were from northwestern Europe.[45] These immigrants were considered desirable because their appearance, culture, and values were held as more compatible with U.S. culture. Thus, these immigrants were considered easy candidates for assimilation. German immigrants, although from central Europe, provide an example of such a group. In an article on African Americans in St. Louis published in 1903, Brandt noted that there was no German problem, "though the Germans form a large part of our population, because they are already in line with American ideals before they came over, and quickly become assimilated."[46]

In 1880, only 5.4 of the European immigrants coming to the United States were from eastern and southern Europe and, in 1890, that figure was 21 percent. By 1900, 49 percent of the European immigrants were from the "undesirable" countries. Immigration reached its peak in 1914 as 1,058,391 European immigrants traveled to the United States. Of this number, only 12 percent came from northwestern Europe, while more than half (58 percent) came from eastern and southern Europe.[47] In the minds of native-born White Americans, the threat was very real and very immediate.

White Ethnics and the Socio-Political Climate

Nativism was widespread in the country and was fanned by the visible presence of the new immigrants—Italians, Poles, Russian Jews, and Greeks. Native-born White Anglo-Saxon Americans believed themselves to be, through nativity and "stock," superior to others, while at the same time tolerating foreign-born people who were derivative of this stock.[48] Belief in the Anglo-Saxon legacy shaped political thought in the 1880s and took form in *nativism—the* view that native-born Whites of old stock (Nordic and Aryan ancestry) were superior to all other groups. The term "nativist" was apparently the outgrowth of a rumor that General George Washington only wanted native-born Americans on guard duty during a critical period during the War of Independence.[49]

The political environment captured the sentiment of the day. Daniels provides a detailed review of nativisim in immigration history and policy in American history.[50] Beliefs in nativism were powerful enough to dictate the operations of the federal government's immigration bureau, whose staff had increased from 28 in 1891 to 1,200 by 1906, a growth of 4,200 percent over this fifteen year period. While other bureaus sought to represent the interests of the groups they served, the immigration bureau did the exact opposite. Its fundamental mission was to shield the country from the unwanted effects of immigration. The growth of the bureau took place under the administrations of President William McKinley and President Theodore Roosevelt. Terence Powderly, the commissioner of immigration from 1897 to 1902, was a staunch supporter of immigration restrictions and was known to believe that British, German, and Scandinavians were the best immigrants for America.

Many new immigrants were Catholic or Jewish, while supporters of nativism embraced Protestantism. Progressives and other citizens feared that these new immigrants would outnumber the old immigrants from the sturdy-stock countries and threaten U.S. culture. Many of these new immigrants also were of darker skin color and were thought to be stupid, dirty, loud, drunken, sexually uninhibited, violent, and dangerously radical by native-born Americans.[51] In 1903, Brandt also noted that the Russians, Hungarians, and Poles "require more assistance to be converted into desirable American citizens."[52] Nativism can be seen as not just an anti-immigration sentiment but as a racist one that did not discriminate against all foreigners but against those deemed inferior to White, Anglo-Saxon people.[53]

Each ethnic group was subjected to a particular stereotype that was etched in the minds of many native-born Americans. For example, Roman Catholic Irish immigrants carried a dual stigma—one for their ethnicity and another for their Roman Catholic religion. Newspaper cartoons often portrayed them as monkey-like figures with a bottle of booze in one hand and a shillelagh (a curved headed small club) in the other.[54] Italians, on the other hand, were stereotyped as lazy, ignorant, and unclean, with a penchant for violence.[55] Arab immigrants were said to be un-American, criminal, poor, and ignorant of the American political system.[56] The Serbs, a Slavic group that practiced Serbian Orthodoxy, were referred to by the pejorative "hunkies," and a combination of Bohemian and Hungarian—Bohunk.[57] Eventually, many White Americans applied this designation to all Slavic immigrants. All of these negative depictions served to cast immigrants as outsiders (the "other"), thereby further solidifying the definition of "American" in the minds of native-born citizens.

The language of immigration can also carry with it metaphors that further cement a negative impression in the minds of citizens. Daniels identifies what he calls the hydraulic metaphor in which immigration is described as a flood, wave, torrent, or stream.[58] This author used the census to reveal that, despite public alarm, between 1860 and 1920, the percentage of foreign-born in the population remained constant at about 14 percent. The percentage decreased in subsequent decades. However, in the mind of the public during and after the Progressive Era, the country was awash with immigrants. The mind-set was related to the overall number of white ethnics in comparison to the desirable immigrants. According to the 1900 census, 1.6 million foreign-born Irish were in the United States while those from England totaled 0.8 million.[59]

Variations in Ethnicity and Location

Immigrants came from varied geographic areas and settled in all parts of the country. For example, Arabs, primarily Syrian and Lebanese, were immigrating to the United States. From 1900 to 1920, approximately 170,000 settled in this country and their numbers peaked in 1930.[60] From 1899 to 1910, approximately 60,000 Arabs immigrated to the United States.[61] Since many of these early immigrants were Christians, their religious identification may have buffered them from some of the harsh treatment experienced by non-Christian immigrants. Immigrants in far lesser numbers arrived in America from such countries as Cuba, Greece, India, South America, and the West Indies.

Not all the immigrants settled in urban areas of the East. According to the 1900 census, on the West coast, California had more Irish (over 44,000) and Italian (22,000) immigrants than any of the other western states. These numbers are dwarfed by the almost one-half million Irish and close to 200,000 Italians in New York. By 1910, the number of Italians in California had grown to 65,174.[62] According to Lothrop, California's location attracted those capable of financing the trip and those willing to settle in a rather remote state.[63] This author further notes that the Irish of California did not endure the same hostility as those in the east. In California, the "Mexicans and Orientals" were the targets of white hostility.[64]

Although White ethnics may have immigrated to all parts of the country, their massive numbers in the east propelled them into the center of attention and concern. Their lives defined the white immigrant experience in America.

Americanization

The Americanization movement represented institutionalized efforts to accelerate the process of assimilation of the White ethnics into American society—a process of moving them from deviancy to conformity.[65] It was believed that through this process these groups could become acculturated into mainstream America society.[66] The Americanization movement was consistent with the idea that destiny could be predetermined and controlled. Social interventions could be undertaken to transform White ethnics into "real Americans." The movement was directed toward thousands of the new immigrants who were of slightly darker skin tone, were of peasant, country stock, espoused non-Christian and/or non-Protestant religions, and had cultural values and practices that were "foreign." Nevertheless, these so-called undesirables were worthy of Americanization efforts. Although many "real" Americans were dubious because the task seemed so insurmountable, other reformers and progressives believed the problem could be resolved with serious effort. Indeed, many assumed that, over the years, the children and grandchildren of the new immigrants would blend in with the rest of America. This meant that the problems of Americanization were problems of the newly arrived, first-generation immigrants.

President Theodore Roosevelt predicted that eventually *all* White immigrants, through Americanization, would become assimilated into U.S. society.[67] To Roosevelt, Americanization meant Anglo conformity in addition to assimilation. He firmly believed that immigrants should rid themselves of ethnic names, ethnic identities, ethnic customs, and ethnic loyalties in order to become fully Americanized.

Americanization became a popular doctrine of the Progressive Era and suggested that the problems of the newer immigrants were problems of a temporary nature. Public schools and businesses developed Americanization programs to hurry along assimilation.[68] In writing about immigrant education in the early 1900s, Seller noted,

> Most old stock Americans, including educators, saw the southern and eastern European immigrants as morally, culturally, and intellectually inferior species which, if left unAmericanized, would destroy the American city. . . . Appropriate education for immigrants . . . was thought to be social and vocational rather than academic.[69]

Eventually, Americanization was broadened to include nationalistic loyalty in addition to Anglo-Saxon conformity.

According to Graham and Koed, the many sponsors of the Americanization movement included immigrant leaders, major employers, women's clubs, churches, unions, and eventually governments with as many as 30 state governments participating.[70]

Discrimination

Many of the Catholic and Jewish immigrants sought to maintain their own religious practices and teachings by sending their children to religious-based schools, thereby resisting pressures to assimilate. These educational practices often clashed with progressive goals for a homogeneous society.[71] For example, the policy of the Catholics that supported separate Catholic schools and institutions further kindled nativist, antiforeign sentiment.[72] This separatist desire for Catholic and Jewish institutions was often interpreted as a rejection of U.S. values and further reinforced the view that these "new" immigrants were troublemakers.

Many of the immigrants faced harsh discrimination in employment and housing. From 1880 to 1915, about 2 million Jewish immigrants from Eastern Europe came to the United States and were met with restrictive residential covenants that barred them from specific neighborhoods and employers who refused to hire them.[73] Much of this discrimination persisted beyond the Progressive Era, as Jews were frequently prohibited from holding particular offices and from entering most major universities.[74]

"New" immigrants were drawn to the United States for economic reasons as they left rural living behind them. Unfortunately, their agrarian skills could not be utilized in the large cities and they were forced to take whatever jobs and wages available. In 1900, 67 percent of the immigrants entered the country as laborers or without occupations.[75] They were forced to endure harsh slum conditions until they could better their plight through skill acquisition and assimilation. All unpopular immigrants did not endure the same type of discrimination. For example, among textile mill workers during this period, Italian immigrants were at the bottom of the pay scale when compared to other white ethnic groups.

Native-born American workers were bitterly opposed to Slavic, Italian, and other immigrants from Eastern and Southern Europe, and vocal proponents for immigration control advocated for the separation of the desirables from the undesirables.[76] Tensions between native-born Americans and the "new" immigrants influenced the U.S. labor movement as issues of class and ethnicity became entangled.[77]

Immigrants were also seen as the bearers of germs, disease, and contagion.[78] This stigmatization resulted in rhetoric and policies that reinforced public opinion. Any germs, diseases, and contagion they may have had can be associated with the conditions in which they were forced to live.

Health and Mortality

The new city dwellers and the cities themselves were ill equipped for the consequences of rapid demographic shifts. On one hand, the former rural life of migrants and immigrants was poor preparation for urban living with its dense population, poverty, poor working conditions, unemployment, and environmental conditions that fostered sickness and disease. Immigrants were also hampered by their lack of knowledge of U.S. culture and language. On the other hand, city services—such as sewer, water, street maintenance, and schools—often could not meet the needs of a swelling population. Housing needs also exceeded the availability of affordable, adequate housing. These factors contributed to the emergence of slums and tenement housing areas.

Conditions facing the poor of the urban centers were devastating.[79] Housing construction could not accommodate the thousands of people flooding the cities. Existing homes that had housed a single family were frequently partitioned so that several families could live in one room. The previous, more affluent owners deserted those areas, which were destined to become slums. These families could afford more spacious housing in the country or in other, more desirable parts of the city. The housing crisis led to the hasty construction of unsafe housing. In addition, most apartments had no hot water, no baths, no indoor plumbing, no windows, no ventilation, no sewers, and no other sanitation facilities.

New York City provided one of the worst cases of overcrowding, as a little more than 42,000 tenements were homes for about 1.5 million people in 1900.[80] According to Ehrenreich, "The tenth ward on New York's Lower East Side, with a population density of more than 700 per acre, was one of the most densely populated places in the history of the earth."[81] Population density exacerbated the problems of fires and sewage disposal. Fires were a common occurrence because coal stoves were used for heat, and because the tenements were practically on top of each other, fires quickly spread. Cities were also grappling with ways of disposing of sewage generated by the massive population. Garbage pickup was often unreliable as piles and piles of trash covered city sidewalks.

Death and disease plagued the slums; infants were particularly susceptible. For example, in Massachusetts, the infant mortality rate was 163 per 1,000 live births from 1890 to 1894. In the same state, in 1895, the death rate for infants under 1 year of age was an incredible 216. Furthermore, cardiovascular-renal diseases, influenza and pneumonia, and tuberculosis were killing the urban population at alarming rates.[82] Tuberculosis was a particular health problem in the crowded, unsanitary slums. In the absence of proper sanitation and refrigeration, immigrants also battled food poisoning. Many of the immigrants feared hospitals because they associated them with death; as an alternative, folk medicine and midwives were frequently utilized. Some medications readily available on the streets and promoted as cure-alls often did more harm than good because of their toxic contents.

The general environment may have been more polluted and stressful than those left in the immigrants' countries of origin. The streets of the urban centers contained numerous seen and unseen hazards. For example, in New York, at the turn of the century, about 150,000 horses produced over 2 million pounds of horse manure, and about 60,000 gallons of horse urine fell on the streets while about 15,000 dead horses had to be removed annually.[83] The streets held other hazards in addition to unsanitary conditions. City crime rates were high as gangs roamed the streets, and public safety was further hampered by poor or minimal street lighting.

Working conditions posed still another threat to the immigrants. About 35,000 Americans were killed and 536,000 injured each year during the Progressive Era. Railroad and steel plant jobs were particularly hazardous.[84] It was often cheaper for employers to replace sick and injured workers than it was to improve the working conditions. Workers toiled long hours in unsafe conditions for wages that could not adequately support them. Factory safety standards and restrictions on work hours were either nonexistent or poorly enforced. Workers appeared to be at the mercy of their employers and were thankful for whatever employment they had. Unfortunately, in cases of injury or death, these employers were often absolved of any responsibility; thus, many families were left destitute. Rising insurance costs, dramatic increases in work-related injuries, and economic uncertainties eventually led many businessmen to support workmen's compensation programs.[85]

Factories themselves were fire hazards due to poorly constructed or nonexistent fire escapes, the presence of debris, blocked exits, and the absence of sprinklers. In 1911, a fire at New York's Triangle Waist Company killed 145 workers, most of whom were young female Italian and Jewish immigrants who were either burned to death, crushed, or impaled on a fence as they tried to escape.[86]

Children were especially vulnerable as they succumbed to delinquency and/or lived on the streets as homeless street urchins. Those fortunate enough to secure employment found that it could be more of a curse than a blessing. Because the use of child laborers was rampant at the turn of the century, the employment of children raised its own unique set of issues.[87] These young workers toiled incredibly long hours for pennies in the canneries, factories, mines, mills, tobacco fields, and meat-packing plants where the work was often dangerous and poorly supervised. Others labored on the streets as vendors, messengers, and shoeshine boys. Children were often recruited from states with restrictive labor laws to those states with no such laws, and they worked as long as 12 to 14 hours a day for as little as 25 cents. In 1900, the number of child laborers in the South dramatically rose by three times over the previous decade and, nationally, over 1.5 million children were gainfully employed.

Racial Violence

Violence was often used as a form of social control to harness the immigrants as a means of protecting the interests of white workers. Senechal de la Roche notes that collective violence is personal injury by a group and usually takes the major forms of lynching, rioting, vigilantism, and terrorism and can be termed "popular justice."[88] Violence against the foreign born was particularly acute during the recessions of 1910 to 1911, 1914 to 1915, and the post–World War I years. In the latter years of the Progressive Era—the post–World War I years—bitter competition for jobs arose as the United States adjusted to its postwar economy. During this time, nativism fueled mob attacks against the foreign born, many of whom were Italian. Much of American frustration surrounding the changing economy and job situation found form and expression in violence and discrimination against those deemed "undesirable." Because the attackers strongly believed that they had the right to protect their interests, this violence may also be seen as a moralistic response to the deviance of other, outside groups.[89]

The American Protective Association was formed in 1887, was essentially anti-Catholic, and extended membership to any foreign-born who agreed to denounce Catholicism. Other such associations were formed to protect U.S. society from encroachment by outsiders. Labor groups, including unions, engaged in violence against immigrants who appeared to be taking jobs away from "real" Americans. The Ku Klux Klan found new life in 1915 and was just about anti-everything and everyone except those who the Klan believed were all-American and all-pure. The Klan terrorized African Americans, Catholics, and Jews alike. Particular individuals—those perceived as troublemakers and/or group leaders—were often singled out for attacks that resulted in serious injuries or death.

Injustices of the Law Enforcement/Justice Systems

Numerous groups lobbied for anti-immigration legislation that would delimit immigration from the "undesirable" countries of Europe. In 1887, Congress passed a bill that would use a literacy test to restrict immigration—a test of the immigrant's ability to read and write English (or another language) before entering the United States. In addition, the head tax on immigrants was doubled and the discretion of immigration agents to admit or deport was increased. Such a bill was necessary, according to legislators and other supporters, to reduce undesirable immigration. Although the bill had numerous exemptions based on age, physical condition, and family status, it was vetoed by President Grover Cleveland. Some years and several presidents later, Congress was able to override a presidential veto in 1917 to enact the bill. World War I had rekindled the nativism flame, and renewed agitation propelled the bill into law.

Neither race nor ethnicity was singled out as the thrust of the bill, but it was no secret that the wave of immigrants from eastern and southern Europe provided the impetus for the legislation. This was a subtle way of extending favoritism to one group without explicitly having to ban another. Since the poor, undesirable peasants among the new immigrants were limited in their literacy skills, the bill would curtail the flow of undesirables into the country.

Attitudes and legislation of the Progressive Era formed the basis of post–Progressive Era bills. Since the act of 1917 did not restrict immigration to the degree expected by its supporters, even more restrictive measures were passed later. For example, although the 1917 act implemented a process of screening applicants, the Quota Act of 1921 was passed to limit the *number* of immigrants entering the United States. A foreign country's quota was set as 3 percent of the number of its immigrant population in the United States in 1910. The Quota Act of 1924 went even further by setting the quota at 2 percent and using 1890 as the base year. This act favored the immigration of people from northern Europe because other immigrants were not a significant part of the U.S. population in 1890. Mexican immigrants were excluded from these restrictions because they were needed for labor in the Southwest farming industries and were not perceived as a national threat.

Systems Theory and the White Ethnic Community

In the Progressive Era, to be ethnic was to be deviant and the mechanisms of social control were applied at the local and state levels to achieve conformity.[90] The larger social system acted on and exerted influence over the white ethnic enclaves and communities. Legislation, discriminatory practices, ethnic violence, and unresponsive law enforcement agencies formed the parameters of the social system surrounding these communities and shaped their worldview. Ethnic groups, at that time, may have been likely to see themselves as victims in a hostile world. This chapter has recounted the numerous ways that native-born Whites attempted to convey that being foreign was undesirable and carried with it a degree of stigma.

White ethnics became subgroups in a social system that used race as a major criterion for social acceptance. In addition to assimilating to the values and beliefs about hard work and success, these new members were also socialized into the norms and behaviors dictating racial interactions. These norms and behaviors were so pervasive that they were intrinsic and inescapable in American society.[91] Immigrants also faced a political economy that conveyed ambivalent messages. On one hand, the rapid urbanization created a need for a larger workforce, and they filled this need. On the other hand, the political environment was hostile toward them. These were the forces that shaped the early experiences of immigrants during the Progressive Era.

A major vehicle for eradicating foreignness was the Americanization movement that found implementation in schools and industry. The social system functioned to socialize immigrant students in the norms and behaviors of their new country by offering Americanization classes. The certificates awarded for completion of these classes became symbolic treasures that many students and workers sought to obtain. Mob violence, as a mechanism of social control, was also used for defining undesirable behavior. In addition, this violence served to distinguish the outsiders from the insiders since the insiders (native-born citizens) were perpetrating violence against the outsiders (foreign born). Some native-born citizens may have participated in mob behavior as a way of solidifying their power over the outsiders and reaffirming their membership in the dominant group.

As subsystems, White ethnic enclaves and communities struggled to survive the oppressive conditions that engulfed them. Community members wanted to be part of America and lay claim to the American dream. They worked tirelessly to permeate the boundaries of society and to become real Americans. Many embraced the Americanization process as an opportunity to achieve that goal. Some groups promoted their assimilation by distancing themselves from marginalized outgroups and aligning with native whites in seeing these outgroups as incapable of assimilation. For White ethnics, the boundaries between them and mainstream society were pliable and permeable. The loss of ethnicity, however, came with sacrifice and cost.

Ethnicity Lost and Reclaimed

The subsequent decades witnessed the eradication of ethnicity from the White ethnic label. Indeed, over the years, the history of White ethnics has been written to extol the virtues of ambition, commitment, determination, and the ability to rise above insurmountable odds to achieve a legitimate place in the United States. Stories are written by and about immigrants who came to America with nothing but the clothes on their backs and a burning desire to be an American.

In this era, the myth of the "melting pot" was born. The idea was propelled into national consciousness by Israel Zangwill's play, *The Melting Pot.* In this play, a character utters,

> There she lies, the great Melting Pot. . . . Celt and Latin, Slav and Teuton, Greek and Syrian, black and yellow. . . . Yes, East and West, and North and South, the palm and the pine, the pole and the equator, the crescent and the cross. . . . Here they shall all unite to build the Republic of Man and the Kingdom of God.[92]

The play opened in 1908 during the period of arrival of mass numbers of new immigrants, and the melting-pot ideology offered an optimistic outlook about the country's future. In addition, the playwright, an organizer of the International Jewish Territorial Organization, believed in America's ability to assimilate the disparate masses. The popularity of the melting-pot perspective persisted long after the Progressive Era.

The gradual replacement of the White ethnic label with the White label has been detailed in several sources. For example, Ignatiev traces the process by which the Irish became White.[93] Roediger recalls the history of immigrant groups as they moved from ethnicity to whiteness.[94] At the end of this process, one monolithic white American identity was born and previous ethnic identities such as Italian, Irish, Jewish, Polish, or German were relegated to the past.[95] The process may now be complete, since the classification of federal data on race and ethnicity define white as a person having origins in any of the original peoples of Europe, the Middle East, and North Africa.[96]

Other infrequently mentioned factors encouraged and supported the assimilation of White ethnics. To conform to the values and norms of American society, White ethnics had to distance themselves from African Americans and other groups of color. These White ethnics had to show that they were distinct from the other marginalized groups and, therefore, should not be perceived or treated like them. As one example, Strickland provides a detailed history of how Germans in South Carolina moved from a position of close alliance with African Americans to identification with White Southerners and adherence to segregationist policies.[97] In some cases the distinction between White ethnics and African Americans was formalized. For example, in the late eighteenth century, the South Carolina House of Representatives declared that Moroccan Arabs should be treated as Whites and not as Blacks from Africa.[98]

Violence was also a powerful tool of coercion in the formation of a white identity for the White ethnics. In ethnic newspapers, stories of White violence against African Americans reinforced for ethnic Whites the extreme marginalization of the Black population. Zecker recounts articles in an 1896 Slovak newspaper that reported on the burning at the stake of an Irishman and his black wife and the lynching of a White man, his Black wife, and his Mulatto children.[99] Violence of this nature communicated the need for White ethnics to distance themselves from a group even more unpopular than they were. Eventually, African Americans became the "other" in the eyes of White ethnics.

More recently, an interest in White studies has been emerging.[100] This interest is based on the recognition that Whites do not form a single homogenous group. The rediscovery of ethnicity is leading to debates on how to study whiteness and how to interpret its meaning in a society that continues to cling to a Black–White racial dichotomy. The elimination of ethnicity from group identity was necessary for assimilation to occur. Reclaiming ethnicity emphasizes again the fluidity of ethnicity. For Whites, there appears to be an element of choice in this reclamation. Kibria asserts that racial minorities do not have the choice of defining their ethnicity since powerful external constraints impose a designation on them.[101]

The history of the "undesirable" immigrants in the United States has been used to reinforce U.S. values—for example, the beliefs that:

- those able to excel without help—the independent, rugged individual- ists—represent the best of America;
- "making it" is of paramount importance;
- everything is possible;
- the desire for material gain is the basis of work motivation; and
- those who fail have no one to blame but themselves.[102]

With this perspective, the social, economic, and political conditions that sur- round people were reduced to mere obstacles that tested the true worth and mettle of an individual. The new immigrants added another chapter to Amer- ican history that perpetuated those beliefs so tenaciously held in America. Thus, two histories of America were written—one for White ethnics and another for ethnic minority groups.

Endnotes

[1] Jillian Jimenez, *Social Policy and Social Change—Toward the Creation of Social and Economic Justice* (Thousand Oaks, CA: Sage, 2010): 142–143.

[2] Carolyn Tice and Kathleen Perkins, *The Faces of Social Policy* (Pacific Grove, CA: Brooks/Cole): 99.

[3] See, for example, Bruce Jansson, *The Reluctant Welfare State*, 6th ed. (Belmont, CA: Brooks/ Cole, 2009): 188–194; and Jimenez, *Social Policy and Social Change*, 142–173.

[4] Mary Ann Jimenez, "Historical Evolution and Future Challenges of the Human Services Profes- sions," *Families in Society: The Journal of Contemporary Human Services* 7(1) January): 3.

[5] Ruth Schwartz Cowan, Mark Rose, and Marsha Rose, "Clean Homes and Large Utility Bills 1990–1940," *Marriage and Family Review* 9 (Fall 1985): 53–66.

[6] Jimenez, "Historical Evolution and Future Challenges of the Human Services Professions," 3.

[7] Allen F. Davis, *Spearheads for Reform—The Social Settlements and the Progressive Movement 1890–1914* (New Brunswick, NJ: Rutgers University Press, 1984).

[8] Stephen Kunitz, "Professionalism and Social Control in the Progressive Era: The Case of the Flexner Report," *Social Problems* 22 (October 1974): 16–27.

[9] David Goldfield et al., *The American Journey: A History of the United States* (Upper Saddle River, NJ: Pearson Education, 2007).

[10] June Axinn and Herman Levin, *Social Welfare—A History of the American Response to Need*, 2nd ed. (New York: Harper and Row, 1982), 127.

[11] John Ehrenreich, *The Altruistic Imagination—A History of Social Work and Social Policy in the United States* (Ithaca, NY: Cornell University Press, 1985), 20.

[12] Ibid.

[13] Ronald Berger, "The Social Construction of Juvenile Delinquency," in *The Sociology of Juvenile Delinquency*, ed. Ronald Berger (Chicago: Nelson-Hall, Publishers, 1991), 4.

[14] Jansson, *The Reluctant Welfare State*, 111.

[15] Joseph Castrovinci, "Prelude to Welfare Capitalism: The Role of Business in the Enactment of Workmen's Compensation Legislation in Illinois, 1905–12," *Social Service Review* 50 (March 1976): 80–102.

[16] Ehrenreich, *The Altruistic Imagination*, 23; Philip Foner, *History of the Labor Movement in the United States, Vol. III: The Policies and Practices of the American Federation of Labor, 1900– 1909* (New York: International Publishers, 1964), 13–14.

[17] As noted in numerous publications, including David Wagner, "Collective Mobility and Fragmen- tation: A Model of Social Work History," *Journal of Sociology and Social Welfare* 13 (September 1986): 667; George Martin, Jr., *Social Policy in the Welfare State* (Englewood Cliffs, NJ: Pren- tice-Hall, 1990), 25–26; Louise Johnson, Charles Schwartz, and Donald Tate, *Social Welfare—A Response to Human Need*, 4th ed. (Boston: Allyn & Bacon, 1997); Rosemary Chapin, *Social Pol- icy for Effective Practice* (New York: McGraw-Hill, 2007), 45; Ralph Dolgoff and Donald Feld- stein, *Understanding Social Welfare*, 7th ed. (Boston: Pearson, 2007), 302–305; Jansson, *The Reluctant Welfare State*, 196–199.

[18] Benjamin Ringer and Elinor Lawless, *Race-Ethnicity and Society* (New York: Routledge, 1989): 6.

[19] U.S. Department of Commerce, Bureau of the Census, *Historical Statistics of the United States, Colonial Times to 1957* (Washington, DC: U.S. Government Printing Office, 1960): 9.

[20] Edmund James, "The Growth of Great Cities in Area and Population," *The Annals of the American Academy of Political and Social Science* 13 (January 1899): 1–30; Johnson and Schwartz, *Social Welfare*, 37; U.S. Department of Commerce, Bureau of the Census, *Historical Statistics*.

[21] Axinn and Levin, *Social Welfare*, 87.

[22] James, "The Growth of Great Cities," 18–19.

[23] Dolgoff and Feldstein, *Understanding Social Welfare*, 79–80.

[24] See Charles Hopkins, *The Rise of the Social Gospel in American Protestantism, 1865–1915* (New Haven, CT: Yale University Press, 1940); Robert Handy, ed., *The Social Gospel in America, 1870–1920* (New York: Oxford University Press, 1966); Ronald White, *The Social Gospel: Religion and Reform in Changing America* (Philadelphia: Temple University Press, 1976); Dolgoff and Feldstein, *Understanding Social Welfare*.

[25] Marilyn Holt, *The Orphan Trains* (Lincoln: University of Nebraska Press, 1992), provides a detailed review of Brace's work and of the orphan trains.

[26] Charles Loring Brace, *The Dangerous Classes of New York* (New York: Wynkoop & Hallenbeck, 1872) 13, 14 (part of the NASW Classic Series).

[27] Robert Luker, *The Social Gospel in Black and White* (Chapel Hill: University of North Carolina Press, 1991), 1–29.

[28] Ibid., 19.

[29] See Gregory Claeys, "The 'Survival of the Fittest' and the Origins of Social Darwinism," *Journal of the History of Ideas* 61 (April 2000): 223–240, for a detailed discussion and analysis of Social Darwinism.

[30] Peter Dickens, *Social Darwinism* (Philadelphia: Open University Press, 2000), 19.

[31] Claeys, "The 'Survival of the Fittest' and the Origins of Social Darwinism," 223f.

[32] Ibid., 238.

[33] See Jillian Jimenez, *Social Policy and Social Change* (Thousand Oaks, CA: Sage, 2010), 43–84 for a discussion of American values.

[34] Claeys, "The 'Survival of the Fittest' and the Origins of Social Darwinism," 238–240.

[35] Ibid., 239.

[36] Carole Cox and Paul Ephross, *Ethnicity and Social Work Practice* (New York: Oxford University Press, 1998), 6.

[37] Eric Goldstein, "The Unstable Other: Locating the Jew in Progressive-Era American Racial Discourse," *American Jewish History* 89 (December 2001): 384–385.

[38] United States Bureau of the Census. www2.census.gov/prod2/decennial/documents/33405927v1ch13.pdf (accessed August 12. 2009).

[39] Goldstein, "The Unstable Other," 383.

[40] Mitch Berbrier, "Assimilation and Pluralism as Cultural Tools," *Sociological Forum* 19 (March 2004): 32.

[41] Carl Wittke, "Immigration Policy Prior to World War I," *The Annals of the American Academy of Political and Social Science* 262 (March 1949): 5–14.

[42] Milton Gordon, *Assimilation in American Life* (New York: Oxford University Press, 1964), 87–88.

[44] Wittke, "Immigration Policy Prior to World War I," 5.

[44] Richard Hofstadter, *Social Darwinism in American Thought*, rev. ed. (Boston: Beacon Press, 1955), 170–200.

[45] U.S. Department of Commerce, Bureau of the Census, *Historical Statistics*, 56–57.

[46] Lillian Brandt, "The Negroes of St. Louis," *Publications of the American Statistical Association* 8 (March 1903): 205.

[47] U.S. Department of Commerce, Bureau of the Census, *Historical Statistics*, 56–57.

[48] Florette Henri, *Black Migration: Movement North, 1900–1920* (Garden City, NY: Anchor Press/Doubleday, 1975), 148.

[49] Roger Daniels, "Two Cheers for Immigration," *Debating American Immigration, 1882–Present*, ed. Roger Daniels and Otis Graham (New York: Rowan & Littleman Publishers, 2001), 13.

[50] Daniels, "Two Cheers for Immigration," 13–19.

[51] Henri, *Black Migration*, 146; Ehrenreich, *The Altruistic Imagination*, 22.

[52] Brandt, "The Negroes of St. Louis," 206.

[53] Henri, *Black Migration*, 147.

[54] See, for example, Marsha Woodbury, "Images of Irish Americans: Invisible, Inebriated, or Irascible," in *Images that Injure: Pictorial Stereotypes in the Media*, ed. Paul Lester and Susan Ross (Westport, CT: Praeger 2003).

[55] P. A. Sensi-Isolani, "Italians." In *A Nation of Peoples: A Sourcebook on America's Multicultural Heritage*, ed. E. R. Barkan (Westport, CT: Greenwood Publishing, 1999).

[56] Arab American National Museum, "Arab American History." (http://www.arabamericanmuseum.org/Arab+American+History.id.150.htm) Retrieved August 21, 2009.

[57] Peter Alter, "Mexicans and Serbs in Southeast Chicago: Racial Group Formation during the Twentieth Century," *Journal of the Illinois State Historical Society* 94 (Winter 2001/2002): 405; Karel Bicha, "Hunkies: Stereotyping the Slavic Immigrants, 1890–1920," *Journal of American Ethnic History* 2 (Fall 1982): 16–38.

[58] Daniels, "Two Cheers for Immigration," 7.

[59] United States Bureau of the Census. www2.census.gov/prod2/decennial/documents/33405927v1ch13.pdf (accessed August 12. 2009).

[60] Anan Ameri and Dawn Ramey, eds., *Arab American Encyclopedia* (Detroit: U X L, 2000).

[61] Nabeel Abraham, "Arab Americans—Overview," n.d. (http://www.everyculture.com/multi/A-Br/Arab-Americans.html) (Nabeel Abraham is Director of the Honors Program at Henry Ford Community College, Dearborn, MI). Retrieved June 18, 2009.

[62] Gloria Lothrop, "The Italians of Los Angeles," *The Californians* 5(3) (1987): 32.

[63] Ibid.

[64] Ibid.,34.

[65] Mitch Berbrier, "Assimilation and Pluralism as Cultural Tools," *Sociological Forum* 19 (March 2004): 32–33.

[66] James Barrett, "Americanization from the Bottom Up: Immigration and the Remaking of the Working Class in the United States, 1880–1930," *Journal of American History* 79(3) (1992): 996–1020.

[67] Roosevelt's views of Americanization are recounted in Thomas Dyer, *Theodore Roosevelt and the Idea of Race* (Baton Rouge: Louisiana State University Press, 1980), 123–142.

[68] Ehrenreich, *The Altruistic Imagination*, 31; Gerald Gems, "Ethnic Education: A Clash of Cultures in Progressive Chicago," *Explorations in Ethnic Studies* 14 (July 1991): 1–13.

[69] Maxine Seller, "The Education of the Immigrant Woman," *Journal of Urban History* 4 (May 1978): 308.

[70] Otis Graham and Elizabeth Koed, "Americanizing the Immigrant, Past and Future: History and Implications of a Social Movement," *The Public Historian* 15 (Autumn 1993): 28–29.

[71] Gerald Gems and Lucia Birnbaum, "Ethnic Education: A Clash of Cultures in Progressive Chicago," *Explorations in Ethnic Studies* 14 (July 1991): 1–13.

[72] Wittke, "Immigration Policy Prior to World War I," 10.

[73] Harold Bradley, *The United States from 1865 to 1890* (New York: Charles Scribner's Sons, 1973), 120; Henri, *Black Migration*, 148.

[74] Ehrenreich, *The Altruistic Imagination*, 46.

[75] U.S. Department of Commerce, Bureau of the Census, *Historical Statistics*, 60.

[76] Wittke, "Immigration Policy Prior to World War I," 10–11.

[77] Ehrenreich, *The Altruistic Imagination*, 21.

[78] See Howard Markel and Alexandra Stern, "The Foreignness of Germs: The Persistent Association of Immigrants and Disease in American Society," *The Milbank Quarterly* 80(4) (2002): 757–788.

[79] Descriptions presented here of slum conditions during the Progressive Era are drawn from Otto Bettmann, *The Good Old Days—They Were Terrible* (New York: Random House, 1974); Ehrenreich, *The Altruistic Imagination*, 20–22; Jansson, *The Reluctant Welfare State*, 112–115.

[80] Arthur Schlesinger, *The Rise of the City* (New York: Macmillan, 1951): 110–111.

[81] Ehrenreich, *The Altruistic Imagination*, 21.

[82] U.S. Department of Commerce, Bureau of the Census, *Historical Statistics*, 26, 30.

[83] Bettmann, *The Good Old Days*, 3; Ehrenreich, *The Altruistic Imagination*, 21.

[84] Bettmann, *The Good Old Days*, 70; Jansson, *The Reluctant Welfare State*, 114.

[85] Castrovinci, "Prelude to Welfare Capitalism," 80–102.

[86] Foner, *History of the Labor Movement in the United States*, 21.

[87] This discussion is based on the descriptions provided by Bettmann, *The Good Old Days*, 77–79.

[88] Roberta Senechal de la Roche, "Collective Violence as Social Control," *Sociological Forum* 11 (March 1996): 97–98.

[89] Senechal de la Roche, "Collective Violence as Social Control," 98.

[90] Berbrier, "Assimilationism and Pluralism as Cultural Tools," 33.

[91] Kay Deaux, Nida Bikman, Alwyn Gilkes, Ana Ventuneac, Yvanne Joseph, Yasser Payne, and Claude Steele, "Becoming American: Stereotype Threat Effects in Afro-Caribbean Immigrant Groups," *Social Psychology Quarterly* 70 (December 2007): 386.

[92] Clyde Kiser, "Culturalism Pluralism," *The Annals of the American Academy of Political and Social Science* 262 (March 1949): 128.

[93] Noel Ignatiev, *How the Irish Became White* (New York: Routledge, 1995).

[94] David Roediger, *Working toward Whiteness: How America's Immigrants Became White* (New York: Basic Books, 2005).

[95] Ronald Baylor, "Another Look at 'Whiteness': The Persistence of Ethnicity in American Life," *Journal of American Ethnic History* 29 (Fall 2009): 13.

[96] Office of Management and Budget, Federal Register Notice dated October 30, 1997. http://www.whitehouse.gov/omb/federeg_1997 standards/ (accessed October 24, 2009).

[97] Jeffery Strickland, "How the Germans Became White Southerners: German Immigrants and African Americans in Charleston, South Carolina, 1860–1880," *Journal of American Ethnic History* 28 (Fall 2008): 52–69.

[98] Arab American Museum, "Arab American History," http://www.arabamericanmuseum.org/Arab+America+History.id.150.htm (accessed June 9, 2009).

[99] Robert Zecker, "'Let Each Reader Judge': Lynching, Race, and Immigrant Newspapers," *Journal of American Ethnic History* 29 (Fall 2009): 31–68.

[100] See for example, Peter Kolchin, "Whiteness Studies: The New History of Race in America," *The Journal of American History* 89 (June 2002): 154–173; and Amanda Lewis, "'What Group?' Studying Whites and Whiteness in the era of 'Color-Blindness,'" *Sociological Theory* 22 (December 2004): 623–646.

[101] Nazli Kibria, "Race, Ethnic Options, and the Ethnic Binds: Identity Negotiations of Second-Generation Chinese and Korean Immigrants," *Sociological Perspectives* 43: 77–95.

[102] A list of American values and myths from which these were taken is provided by Ralph Dolgoff and Donald Feldstein, *Understanding Social Welfare*, 7th ed. (New York: Longman, 2007), 4–6.

African Americans and American Indians in the Progressive Era
The Social Context of Early Practice

The previous chapter detailed the experiences on White ethnics as they sought a new life in America. They encountered social, political, and economic barriers to their progress. If the White ethnics faced seemingly overwhelming odds, then those populations of color were facing odds even more daunting and potentially insurmountable. To fully understand the circumstances of non-White populations, it is important to detail the specific types of obstacles they faced and attacks they endured in order to provide a historical context for the development of the social work profession.

As noted in the previous chapter, non-Whites were perceived to be a separate class of people. The census reflected this belief, as did the social sciences of the day. In addition, Social Darwinism paved the way for the study of physiological and psychological studies to prove the innate inferiority of racial minorities. In 1916, one psychologist revealed that, according to test results, the low intelligence of Spanish-Indian, Mexican, and African American children was confirmed and concluded that "their dullness seems to be racial." When using Army test results, another psychologist plotted ethnic and racial groups along an intelligence continuum that placed Nordics at the highest end, Alpines and Mediterraneans in the middle, and African Americans at the lowest end.[1]

In 1900, non-Whites made up about 12 percent (9,312,599) of the U.S. population while Whites made up 88 percent (66,990,788), and that figure varied only slightly during the Progressive Era.[2] Of the non-Whites in the population, African Americans totaled 11 percent (8,840,789), whereas American Indians (266,760), Japanese (86,000), and Chinese (119,050) totaled slightly less than 1 percent. Mexicans were not counted separately in the statistics for this period. Thus, the 8.8 million African Americans in the United States at the turn of the century were the predominant racial minority.

43

Non-Whites did not fare as well as Whites during the Progressive Era. The infant mortality rates for non-Whites were almost twice that for Whites, and non-White mothers were almost twice as likely to die during childbirth as White mothers. Furthermore, a White person born in 1900 could expect to live an average of 48 years, whereas a non-White could expect 33 years of life. Tuberculosis and influenza claimed a higher percentage of non-Whites than Whites. For example, in 1914, 260 non-Whites per 100,000 and 169 Whites per 100,000 died from these causes.[3] These figures are indicative of the type of social conditions surrounding the non-White population.

Leading educators of the Progressive Era espoused views on the education of non-Whites that today would be called racist. For example, G. Stanley Hall, the educational reformer credited with bringing Freud and Jung to the United States, saw non-Whites as the *children* of the human race and advocated an educational approach that incorporated their culture and abilities. Decades ago, this position was considered one of reform; yet, it can be argued that it reinforced an inferior status for non-Whites.[4]

Although African Americans represented the dominant racial minority, it is important to look at them and other racial groups separately. This is necessary in order to underscore the uniqueness of each group's experience. The use of the category of "non-White" may lead to the erroneous assumption that all groups encountered the same type and degree of alienation and discrimination during the period that gave rise to social work. In addition, the uniqueness of each group's history has shaped its responses to the profession.

AFRICAN AMERICANS IN THE PROGRESSIVE ERA

While the Progressive Era is associated with major reform efforts described as "progressive," this era seems to have had limited progressiveness for African Americans. During this era, African Americans experienced harsh, widespread discrimination; dire health and mortality rates; unbridled racial violence; injustices of the law enforcement/justice system; and biased analyses and interpretations of their condition.

Northern Migration and Discrimination

Prior to the peak northern migration of southern African Americans, African Americans were virtually invisible to the people of the northern and western states. During the early years of the Progressive Era, it was more cost efficient to U.S. businesses for African Americans to remain in the South as cheap agrarian laborers. Those African Americans residing in the North were often less segregated than some of the "new" immigrant groups because their relatively small numbers in the population did not appear as a threat to other Americans.

Before the end of the Progressive Era, however, this situation changed drastically. The segregation of the South followed African Americans to the North. Even before the mass exodus of African Americans from the South, separation of the races was endemic in U.S. society. Indeed, in 1903, Brandt observed, "It is noticeable that there was a tendency to separation of the

White population from blacks as early as there was a free Negro population of any consideration."[5] When industrialization transformed farm work from labor dependency to machine dependency, when immigration restrictions curbed the flow of "new" immigrants, and when a major war drained the workforce, African Americans ventured North in record numbers. In the early 1900s, changes in African American migration patterns became apparent, and, by 1915, migration rates had risen significantly and peaked between 1916 and 1918. Figures for African American migration indicate that less than 100,000 migrated in the 1870s and 1880s; approximately 200,000 migrated between 1890 and 1910, and from 1910 to 1920, between 300,000 to 1 million made the journey.[6] As many as 700,000 African Americans are estimated to have migrated during a peak period from 1916 to 1917.

From 1910 to 1920, the total African American population of New York, Chicago, Philadelphia, and Detroit increased by about 750,000; and after World War I, New York, Chicago, Baltimore, and Washington each had an African American population over 100,000.[7] During this period, surveys of the reasons African Americans migrated found that poor wages, poor treatment by Whites, poor schools, problems with tenant farming, discrimination, and oppression were driving African Americans out of the South.[8] In 1917, DuBois noted that "the immediate cause was economic, and the movement began because of floods in middle Alabama and Mississippi and because the latest devastation of the boll weevil came in these districts."[9] DuBois also cited the cessation of European immigration and the violence against African Americans in the South as factors contributing to the migration.

Many African Americans assumed their own American nativity would foster acceptance by native-minded Whites. They found, however, that race took priority over nativity. Although they encountered prejudice similar to that experienced by the immigrant groups, this prejudice was intensified because of race. In documenting African American migration North, Goodwin observed, "Of all the major urban American immigrant communities of whatever ethnic or racial background, none faced the kind of systematic and restrictive measures upon its urban adaptation as did the American Black."[10]

African Americans appeared to represent a different class of people, and their growing presence in places where they had previously been rather invisible heightened racial problems. Even though they saw themselves as being as "American" as White Americans, they were confronted with a different reality. A group's self-identity is but one factor that defines its distinctiveness and status. The larger society also has its own set of definitions of the group and attempts to impose these definitions in its contact with that group.[11] To many Whites in the northern cities, African Americans were even more undesirable and "foreign" than were the "new" immigrants.

African Americans migrating North in search of economic security and freedom from oppression found the same conditions as experienced by the "new" immigrants—only more so. A 1905 issue of *Charities* described the housing problem facing African American migrants:

> Difficulty in obtaining a suitable place meets the Negro who comes to a large northern city. In many neighborhoods he cannot rent a house or

apartment no matter how well able he may be to pay the price for it, and in those places in which he is permitted to live his accommodations are frequently worse than the same money would buy *for any other race* [emphasis added].[12]

Sophonisba Breckenridge, an advocate of services for African Americans, provided a more detailed description in 1913 of the housing situation in Chicago:

> While half of the people in the Bohemian, Polish, and Lithuanian districts were paying less than $8.50 for their four room apartments; the steel mill employees less than $9.50, and the Jews in the Ghetto less than $10.50, the Negro, in the midst of extreme dilapidation and crowded into territory adjoining the segregated vice district, pays from $12 to $12.50.[13]

Breckenridge also observed that housing problems for African Americans were different from those of immigrants. While the *poor* Polish, Jewish, or Italian immigrant had to endure poor housing conditions, African Americans of *all* income levels suffered housing problems.

Many progressives in the North and the South saw education as the answer for African Americans. As with the newly arrived immigrants from southern and eastern Europe, manual training was at the heart of education proposed for African Americans. Although White philanthropists provided significant funding for education, many were only willing to support industrial education for African Americans.[14] In 1905, Gordon wrote,

> The strain of commercial competition, as well as the added stress of race prejudice has had a tendency to limit the opportunities of the Negro boy or girl in securing necessary work. . . . It would seem then, that manual training in a school for Negro children is even more essential and helpful than it is in a school for Whites.[15]

Gordon went on to extol the benefits of bench work, forging, woodcarving, and mechanical drawing for African American boys and the value of properly washing dishes, trimming lamps, making bread, and understanding the science of housekeeping for African American girls. Although White southerners in general opposed African American education, those who were somewhat sympathetic usually supported mechanical, industrial, and agricultural schools for this group.[16] Many Whites feared that too much of the wrong kind of education would make African Americans more difficult to control. African Americans themselves were more divided on the appropriate education for their people than were the Whites who actually controlled resources.

School attendance did not have the same meaning among African Americans as it did among Whites. In both the North and the South, since prejudice often prevented African Americans from working in the mills, factories, and other industries, they attended school instead.[17] Reformers who advocated compulsory education were ambivalent about the implications of such a bill for African Americans. Because school attendance was already high for many African Americans and compulsory education would put even more African Americans in the classroom, the potential threat of the "educated Negro" to White supremacy was widely debated.

As African Americans flooded the cities of the North, school segregation rose dramatically. Some schools were all African American, and those that purported to be integrated assigned African American students to the same classroom or sent them to branch schools. When African American and White schools existed in the same cities, African Americans had the most deteriorated buildings and the fewest supplies.

Other reform efforts were retarded by fear that the reform would also have to be extended to African Americans.[18] For example, the age of consent in Georgia was 10 years old and remained there until 1918 (when it was raised to age 14) because legislators did not want to extend legal protection to African American girls. Opponents of women's right to vote, particularly Southerners, feared that extending the vote to women would lead to African American women also voting. Thus, racism not only reduced the rights and privileges of African Americans but it also served to delimit the opportunities of Whites as well.

Pervasive racism against African Americans by persons outside this group affected the relations among members inside the group. For example, the "near-white" African Americans often saw themselves as different from the darker-skinned African Americans. Color became a status symbol that was associated with economic success. Because "whiteness" was more desirable than "darkness," African Americans adopted standards that favored the lighter-hued individuals of their race.[19] This may have carried over from slavery days, as mulattoes (as sons and daughters of slaveholders) and free African Americans had educational and economic advantages over the dark-skinned members of the race.[20] Furthermore, Whites may have extended preferential treatment to those African Americans who did not have the stereotypical "Negroid" features. The meaning of color in the African American community and the etiology of those meanings have been widely debated over the years.

Migration and Discrimination in Other Parts of the Country

While the vast numbers of African Americans were migrating to the northern cities, some did make their way to the Southwest and West. In 1900, for example, California had 11,045 African Americans in a total population of 1,485,053.[21] By 1910, African Americans numbered almost 22,000 of California's 2.3 million population.[22] Moore has provided a more detailed overview of African American migration to Colorado during the Progressive Era.[23] By 1900, about 8,516 African Americans were living in Colorado while the state had a population of about 440,000 native-born Whites and about 93,000 foreign-born Whites. Apparently, the animosity that many Whites felt regarding African Americans in the South and North was not apparent in the Southwest, as people there may have viewed them with amusement and curiosity. Acceptance of African Americans was facilitated by the presence of another group that was the designated "other" and treated with disdain. Whites in Colorado were fearful of Chinese competition for jobs and believed that African American migration "would help to keep out the Chinese, who were regarded as a threat to American labor."[24]

Moore's account of African Americans in Colorado in the early 1900s reveals the type of success this group found outside of the South and North. For example, the illiteracy rate was remarkably low for adult African Americans, which could be attributed in part to the state's urban and rural schools. African Americans were also able to take advantage of educational opportunities that may not have been available elsewhere. Furthermore, racial codes were not enforced, thereby permitting many African Americans to attain success. Moore also identifies several professional African Americans, including medical doctors, with thriving careers during the Progressive Era. A state like Colorado that was far removed from the hostile South and the discriminatory North suggests that the African American experience in America is as diverse as its people.

The impact of the gospel of self-help mentioned in the previous chapter was reflected in the rise of African American towns in various parts of the country. Numerous former slaves believed that the quest for freedom from oppression could be found in the creation of all-African American towns that would be self-governing and self-sufficient. One such example is the town of Allensworth that existed from 1908 to 1930 in California.[25] Like other leaders of all-African American communities, Colonel Allen Allensworth had a vision of an African American life free from the racial discrimination and the violent lynching he had witnessed. Colonel Allensworth believed that the African American race could rise by its own efforts if people were willing "to do for themselves" without having to rely on White philanthropy.[26]

The West, with its vast land seemingly in need of citizens, seemed to be the ideal location for the town Colonel Allensworth envisioned. He was able to maneuver around California's White-only Homestead Law by forming a corporation. Under the law, corporations were allowed to purchase land. The land was then resold to individuals who became the founding residents of Allensworth. According to Catlin, the 1910 census showed that Allensworth had 22 African American-owned farms on 12,890 acres with a total value of $260,270 and a population of 382 residents who occupied 72 buildings.[27] In addition, the town had 35 registered businesses that were owned by 23 separate people. Residents and area newspapers indicated that the town enjoyed harmonious relationships with the other towns in the area.

The town did have its shortcomings in that it had no public sewer system, no doctor, no financial institutions, and poor roadways. In addition to these factors, several others contributed to the decline of the town of Allensworth, including Colonel Allensworth's death; a dwindling water supply; the inability to start a vocational school that was to be patterned after Booker T. Washington's Tuskegee, Alabama, school; and the bypassing of the town by the Santa Fe Railroad. Today, the Allensworth site exists not as a town but as the Colonel Allensworth State Historic Park in Earlimart, California.

The description of this town is offered to broaden the historic focus on the lives of African Americans in the Progressive Era. Exclusive attention to the racial climate and living conditions of the South and the North fails to properly recognize the existence and experiences of those who migrated to other parts of the country.

Health and Mortality

Living conditions contributed to the health and mortality of African Americans. Migrating African Americans experienced a significant decline in general health in the northern environment, particularly the areas of infectious diseases and maternal and child illnesses.[28] These health and mortality patterns were present among African Americans in the North prior to the great migration period. In 1899, *The Charities Review* noted, "The negroes die twice as fast as the Whites; but the Whites have greater comforts and many advantages as regards skilled medical attention."[29] In 1897, *The Charities Review* attributed the high infant mortality rate among African Americans "to the fact that negro mothers are obliged, as a rule, to work out, thus leaving their homes and children, which is not only the cause of infant mortality, but also of neglected child life."[30]

While infectious diseases coupled with infant and maternal mortality decimated the African American population, a study at the close of the Progressive Era revealed that African American males were also more likely than Whites to be victims of homicide.[31] This fact underscores the violence that has historically seemed to stalk African Americans, and "black-on-black" homicides have been a part of the history of numerous African American communities. In addition to the personal and social upheaval that accompanied African American migration and urbanization, the concentration of alcohol and drugs in their communities has been correlated with violence.[32] The internalization of White attitudes that devalue African American life has also been posited as an explanatory factor.

Racial Violence

Violence against African Americans also escalated during the Progressive Era. In the decade prior to the Progressive Era, more Whites than African Americans were lynched, and during this era, the actual number of lynchings decreased as the percentage of African American victims rose. Mob action against this group increased, and lynchings as well as other acts of brutality became public spectacles. Of the 1,600 victims of mob action between 1890 and 1901, more than two-thirds were African Americans. A total of 3,000 known lynchings of African American men and women stained American history from 1885 to 1915.[33]

Although this violence generally plagued the southern states, other parts of the country also witnessed lynchings and race riots as the numbers of African Americans in the North increased dramatically. Wherever large pockets of African Americans settled, they faced the same conditions as the earlier "new" immigrants, *but their predicament was compounded by issues related solely to race.* According to Jansson:

> The situation was more favorable for African Americans in the North but only modestly so. . . . Neighborhoods occupied by African Americans were even more blighted than ones occupied by other immigrant groups, were more likely to be headquarters of organized crime and drug interests, and had virtually no health or other services. African Americans experienced

extraordinary discrimination in job markets; they were excluded from skilled trades and unions, were often used as scabs to break unions, and were subject to race riots and mob violence when they competed with whites for jobs.[34]

Racial hostility and hatred directed toward African Americans were more pervasive and lethal than that directed toward any of the "new" immigrant groups. Mob violence erupted in East St. Louis in 1917 and in about 25 other cities, including Chicago and Washington, as mobs of Whites burned African American ghettos and lynched, shot, and beat the inhabitants.[35] During the "Red Summer" of 1919, Chicago, Omaha, and other northern and southern cities were sites of brutal mob violence against African Americans that claimed numerous lives and left thousands homeless.[36]

The East St. Louis case is a vivid example of the magnitude and intensity of the racial mob violence that was inflicted against African Americans. The National Association for the Advancement of Colored People (NAACP) sent special investigators to collect data on the incident, and the results were published in the September 1917 issue of *The Crisis.*[37] According to this report, "On that day [July 2, 1917] a mob of White men, women, and children . . . drove 6,000 Negroes out of their homes; and deliberately murdered [sic], by shooting, burning and hanging between one and two hundred human beings who were black." Tension between Whites and African Americans had been unusually high for the past year in that city because African Americans from the South were used as strikebreakers when 4,500 White men in the packing plants decided to strike.

In a letter to delegates to the Central Trades and Labor Union, the East St. Louis union secretary wrote, "The immigration of the Southern Negro into our city for the past eight months has reached the point where drastic action must be taken if we intend to work and live peaceably in this community. Since the influx of undesirable Negroes has started, no less than ten thousand have come into this locality. These men are being used to the detriment of our white citizens."[38] The NAACP report, in response to this letter, noted, "It is not that foreigners—Czechs, Slovaks, Lithuanians—or whatever ethnic division is least indigenous to East St. Louis—it is not that *they* are ousting Americans of any color or hue, but the 'Southern Negro,' *the most American product there is* is being used to the detriment of our white citizens" [emphasis added]. [39] African Americans were faced with the stark realization that nativity did not override color and that they were considered the outsiders.

Injustices of the Law Enforcement/Justice Systems

Courts were not particularly sympathetic to African American rights and status as citizens. It was during this period in 1896 that the Supreme Court handed down its *Plessy* v. *Ferguson* decision that made "separate but equal" treatment of African Americans the law of the land.[40] The Court had already upheld segregation in an 1890 decision that let stand a Mississippi statute that called for separate railroad cars for Whites and African Americans. *Plessy* v. *Ferguson* dictated that the separate accommodations had to be of equal quality. This 1896 decision paved the way for widespread, court-sanctioned discrimination against African Americans.

In this historic decision, the Court declared that "legislation is powerless to eradicate racial instincts or to abolish distinctions based upon physical differences."[41] This ruling seemed to reaffirm the separation of the races as an innate or natural tendency that should not be challenged by law. Prejudicial attitudes thus became reified through laws that promulgated the inferior status of African Americans. Few people expected the "separate but equal" decision to be vigorously enforced. In fact, during the Progressive Era, other discriminatory laws were passed that limited African Americans' access to public education, housing, and jobs. These laws were often referred to as Jim Crow laws, derived from a nineteenth-century song-and-dance act that stereotyped African Americans in an offensive way. Because most of the African Americans (almost 90 percent) still lived in the southern states during most of the Progressive Era, Jim Crow laws and other discriminatory treatment occurred primarily in these southern states. The Jim Crow era is dated from 1890 to the 1960s although there are ongoing debates about its chronology, geography, and nature.[42]

African Americans' belief in the power of the federal government to protect them from discrimination was further shaken by the actions of the nation's president. Many African Americans felt abandoned by President Theodore Roosevelt when he unfairly discharged "without honor" 167 African American soldiers stationed near Brownsville, Texas, in 1906. An incident had taken place in which a White person was killed, and the soldiers refused to name those responsible. A military investigation yielded questionable evidence against the troops that may have been planted by Brownsville people as a way of having the troops removed.[43] Other White communities resented the presence of African American troops, and conflict between troops and community often arose during this period. For example, in 1917, as a result of racial conflict between police and African American soldiers in Waco, Texas, six African Americans were dishonorably discharged and sent to prison.[44] The Brownsville incident stands out because of the number of African Americans involved and because Roosevelt acted without the benefit of evidence.

African American support for Roosevelt practically vanished after he refused to seat African American delegates from the South at the 1912 political convention. Roosevelt may have been attempting to regain southern White support that was lost after he invited Booker T. Washington, the noted African American founder of Tuskegee Institute, to lunch at the White House. In the aftermath of White protest, Roosevelt later viewed the lunch as a mistake. These incidents led many African Americans to feel betrayed by a man who had once been regarded as an ally. These incidents were also indications of Roosevelt's belief that African Americans were inferior to Whites and needed aid to facilitate their assimilation into U.S. society.[45]

Actions by the federal government did little to raise African Americans' hopes for justice, fairness, and equal rights. The laws were against them and, as demonstrated in his arbitrary discharge of the Brownsville troops, so was the president of the United States. The evidence was overwhelming, mounting, and incontrovertible proof that "blacks were deserted by the federal government and must look after themselves."[46]

Massachusetts stands out as a unique case in the legal basis of equality for African Americans.[47] This state advanced race-neutral legislation including its desegregation act of 1855, an act that banned racial discrimination. Furthermore, this act gave African Americans hope that, through integrated schools, they could better their chances for success. The law also gave Whites basis to believe that, in the words of a White Bostonian, African Americans "need not look for any miracles to change their condition; to become elevated, they must cultivate and practice the same traits which are elevating others around them."[48] Historical reviews of the Massachusetts public schools confirm, however, that immigrant children commanded primary attention and were the focal point for Americanization efforts, as school authorities rendered African American pupils invisible. Many elite African Americans subscribed to a color-blind ideology that proclaimed, according to one, "A colored man must stand or fall on his merit." [49] For these elites, desegregation laws validated their belief in America as a meritocracy. In addition, for them and countless others, the American dream of achievement and success was becoming the African American dream as well. The law, however, was ineffective in erasing a color caste system that operated against African Americans. The law was powerless in eradicating the racial prejudice and discrimination that permeated society.

Because organized law-enforcement agencies were often perceived as agents for the social control of African Americans, these agencies also afforded little protection or security for countless members of this group. In almost every case of major racial conflict, the police refused to enforce the law and even led the mobs in attacking African Americans.[50] Consequently, poor or no law enforcement contributed much to the violence against African Americans.[51] A precarious relationship has historically existed between law-enforcement agencies and African American communities. Because no arrests were made in 99 percent of the lynching cases occurring between 1882 and 1903, it appeared that law-enforcement authorities virtually refused to intervene in "lynch law."[52] This lack of action did nothing to change African American attitudes about the police. The tensions between African Americans and law-enforcement agents are further captured in the 1921 study of homicides.[53] In this study, the majority of interracial homicides in the cities surveyed involved African American males who were shot by *police* for "resisting arrest."

In looking at arrests in St. Louis from 1876 to 1901, Brandt noted that a large part of the police force was Irish, and this resulted in tolerance toward the offenses of foreign-born individuals as well as "an abnormal vigilance over the Negroes."[54] In addition, the penal system has often been described as a replacement for the slavery system as a means of continued control of African Americans. For example, the state of New York legislated both the emancipation of slaves and the creation of the first state prison on the same day.[55]

Numerous African American communities in both the North and the South were crime-ridden, drug-infested areas. African Americans were forced to live in districts that included these vices—vices that appear to have been tolerated by the police.[56] For example, New York's major African American ghetto was home to saloons, gambling joints, prostitutes, pimps, and drug pushers. Also, African American areas of Savannah, Georgia, were great sources of "crime and immorality."[57] In the North and the South, African American crime rates exceeded that of Whites as African American men, women, and children filled the jails and penitentiaries. In 1910, 11 times as many African Americans were incarcerated for grave homicide, 8 times as many for lesser homicide, 6 times as many for assault, and 3 to 4 times as many for prostitution, robbery, liquor law violations, burglary, rape, and larceny.[58] The debate raged then, as it does today, as to whether these excessive crime rates are the result of differential police activity or differential criminal involvement on the part of African Americans. Regardless of the cause, penal institutions increasingly were becoming institutions of color.

"Wayward" children and "fallen" women were particularly prevalent among the incarcerated population. Surrounded by crime, poverty, and minimal prospects, countless African American children resorted to crime as a means of survival. In Georgia, for instance, children as young as 6 years of age were arrested and likely to be sentenced to the stockade or chain gang because of the absence of reformatories for African Americans.[59] Countless young African American women who migrated to the North eventually relied on prostitution, as well as other illegal activities, as a way of earning money. In the absence of reformatories for African American women, a significantly higher percentage was more likely to serve jail time than their White counterparts. Indianapolis, in the early 1900s, reflected this situation as White institutions refused to care for "fallen Negro girls."[60]

Systems Theory and the African American Community

The larger social system of the Progressive Era shouted its message to African Americans emphatically, legally, violently, and unrelentingly: You are not, and never will be, part of mainstream America. The history of slavery in the United States undoubtedly etched this deep-seated feeling in the minds of countless native Whites, and eventually, in the minds of the more recent immigrants. Society functioned, at that time, to reinforce this group's marginalized status.

The technology of discrimination and racism functioned to erect seemingly impenetrable barriers to the American dream for thousands of African Americans. Even when laws existed to ban discrimination against this group, attitudes and behaviors of the larger society were powerful enough to override them. For this group, negativity was so strong and pervasive that it was inherent. White ethnic immigrants, as distinct subgroups, were not immune to this "contagion" of the stereotypes and hostility surrounding African Americans.

The larger society, however, continued to rely on the labor of African Americans as an input to its growth and prosperity. This means that, historically, there has been a love–hate relationship between society and the African American. The value of this group has been in its labor contributions and not in the group itself. For this group, the boundaries between it and the larger society have been, at times, impenetrable.

Interpreting the African American Experience

The literature on African Americans during the Progressive Era contains valuable information about the lives and living conditions of African Americans, but it often reflects prevailing public attitudes about race in attempting to interpret the African American experience. Brandt, in a study published in 1903 on "The Negroes of St. Louis," noted that African Americans were not generally found in parts of the city that had large foreign populations. Housing segregation was attributed to landlords not wanting African American tenants because such tenants meant a depreciation of property value. Furthermore, African Americans were found to be absent from all trades in St. Louis because of exclusionary attitudes of labor unions.

In explaining the high incidence of infectious diseases among African Americans, Brandt reported:

> Negroes go insufficiently clothed in cold weather, are careless about wet clothing, are unwilling to call for medical attendance until the last moment, are ignorant of the laws of hygiene and sanitation, and live in surroundings that favor the spread of bacteriological diseases. . . . These figures [for patients treated for smallpox], like those for consumption and pneumonia, point to constitutions weakened by bad sanitary conditions, poor food, and general carelessness.[61]

When reporting on the pauperism among African Americans in St. Louis, Brandt wrote:

> The line between poverty and pauperism is farther down among the Negroes than among the whites, because of their lower standard of living. . . . Fruit and vegetables, especially, are obtainable in season for almost nothing, and a "nickel's worth" of bananas or watermelon will content a Negro for a day. For this reason, although poverty is palpably as great and widespread among the Negroes here, it probably does *not mean so much suffering as one would at first view suppose* [emphasis added].[62]

Warner's 1894 poverty study offers another example of the permeation of social science research by prevailing racial attitudes.[63] He studied the causes of poverty in American cities and categorized 7,225 individual cases by ethnicity and nationality. The causes of poverty were grouped as indicating (1) misconduct (drink, immorality, shiftlessness and inefficiency, crime and dishonesty, and roving disposition); (2) misfortune (e.g., lack of normal support as in the cases of an absent breadwinner, matters of employment as no work or insufficient work); and (3) matters of personal capacity as in cases of sickness or death of a family member, physical defects, insanity, and old age. When reviewing findings, Warner observed:

> Those who know the Colored people only casually, or by hearsay, may be surprised to find the misconduct causes running so low among them while sickness as a cause is of greater importance than in any other nationality. But to one who has worked in Baltimore or Washington it seems a natural result, and, indeed, a confirmation of the statistics. The

Colored people are weak physically, become sick easily, and often die almost without visible resistance to disease.[64]African Americans had the lowest percentage in the "Lack of work" category and the highest in the "Insufficient employment." Warner interpreted those two percentages as an indication of this group's "hand-to-mouth way of working at odd jobs rather than taking steady work."[65]

As these and other researchers offered subjective analysis of the social conditions of African Americans under the guise of objectivity, other writers sought to interpret the historical experiences of African Americans. Noted among these writers is Ulrich Phillips, a White scholar who helped to develop the history of slavery as a field of study.[66] Phillips held a rather sympathetic view of slavery and believed it to be a benevolent institution.

Even though racism and discrimination traveled with African Americans to the North, historical writing often overlooks the treatment this group received in that part of the country. The South continues to stand out as the seat of anti-African American sentiment while the North is left relatively unscathed. The experiences of African Americans reveal that no place in the United States provided a haven from White hostility, racism, and discrimination.

The Progressive Era witnessed the continuation of discriminatory treatment of African Americans and ushered in a wave of unrelenting segregation, discrimination, and violence in the wake of record migration and urbanization.

AMERICAN INDIANS IN THE PROGRESSIVE ERA

Since the economic development of the United States could not have progressed without the displacement and neutralization of the Native population, the policies of extermination, isolation, and assimilation that have competed for ascendancy all required the definition of Natives as savage, inferior, and less than human, and their cultures as inferior and deservedly doomed to extinction.[67] The history of the oppression of American Indian tribes in the New World has been extensively documented and only those aspects relevant for understanding historical and contemporary dynamics between mainstream social work and American Indian populations will be recounted.[68]

During the Progressive Era, reform aimed at the American Indian tribes was, in fact, a continuation of efforts started decades earlier. Many groups, organizations, and individuals dedicated their time to American Indian reform and set about to resolve the "Indian problem." This "problem" seemed to emerge when the tribes were dispossessed of their lands and America was struggling to determine what to do with the remaining American Indian population.

The American Indians represented a unique conundrum. They were of significance because of the lands they held. As a group, unlike other populations of color, they were not needed for their cheap labor and they sought to maintain their separateness rather than strive for assimilation and integration into the U.S. society. The American Indians had rebelled against White encroachment of their lands, fought fiercely for their lands and their way of life, and blatantly rejected White domination. The eventual subordination of these tribes resulted in rampant hostility and antagonism on both sides. With provisions in place for separating the tribes from their land, reformers could concentrate on "reforming" the American Indian.

Discrimination

According to Ahern, "The subordination of racial minorities by reform movements claiming principles antithetical to racism constitutes an important theme in the history of racism in the United States."[69] Reform efforts on behalf of American Indians at the turn of the century and earlier were predicated on assumptions, opinions, and beliefs that can now only be called racist. These reformers were typically White Protestants from middle- and upper-class society. Many were professionals or business people who believed they were acting in the best interest of the American Indians to make them a part of America.

These "Friends of the Indian," as they were called, saw education as the proper vehicle through which American Indians could cast their lot with other Americans. Adequately prepared, American Indians could then succeed or fail by their own hand or by their own mettle. In 1819, Congress began allocating modest sums of money (about $10,000 annually) for the employment of "capable persons of good moral character, to instruct them [American Indians] in the mode of agriculture suited to their situation; and for teaching their children in reading, writing, and arithmetic."[70] The funds were distributed to various societies that already operated or were willing to develop schools on the reservation. Missionary societies were active in this area and used their own resources to help support the schools.

Without educational intervention, reformers saw the tribes as doomed to existence as paupers, dependent on public dole. Through education, children would move away from tribal communal values and learn the meaning of individualism. Indeed, according to Senator Henry Dawes, a leading political figure at the turn of the century, the "defect of the [tribal] system was apparent. . . . There is no selfishness, which is at the bottom of civilization."[71]

In the minds of the reformers, the day schools of the reservations were viewed as inadequate for raising American Indians to the standards of a Christian civilization. First, reading and writing alone were not enough to accomplish the goals desired by the reformers. Manual labor instruction was another element that became identified as the cornerstone of American Indian education. Manual training would lead the tribes up the path to self-sufficiency and reduce dependency on government dole. In this regard, the requisite education would not only foster Americanism but also capitalism.

Second, and equally advocated, a move to locate the schools away from the reservations ensued. Many reformers believed that off-reservation boarding schools, in comparison to the day schools and the reservation boarding schools, provided the best setting for American Indian education. The push for separate, off-reservation schools was based, in part, on earlier attempts at American Indian reform. The reservations themselves had already been the target of reform efforts as reformers and missionaries tried to impose "civilizing" programs on them. A significant part of reforming focused on replacing American Indian spiritual practices with Christianity. However, missionaries often moved beyond religious instruction and urged tribes to abandon their old ways for a life of farming—a life that meant permanent residence in one place rather than following the herds they hunted. Many missionaries and reformers were so committed to particular beliefs that they failed to learn about the customs and beliefs they were trying to eradicate.

Programs to Americanize the American Indians were often useless to a people who suffered extreme poverty as they struggled with the demise of their old and independent way of life. This was particularly true for some of the plains tribes, since the conversion from a hunting culture to agriculture was destined to take years. In the meantime, these tribes were dependent on government support for the necessities of life. In many instances, food and materials supplied were insufficient, inadequate, and often inappropriate. It is conceivable that the transitional process was taking much longer than government officials and reformers anticipated, and tribal needs may have surpassed specified allocations. Indeed, Prucha argued, "In such an unlooked-for circumstance, it was perhaps understandable that the rations supplied were insufficient and often poor in quality."[72] Hagan, however, attributed some of the problem to "blundering or outright fraud by White Christians" who profited from government contracts by supplying reservations with shoddy goods or no goods at all.[73] The impoverished conditions of the reservations did little to encourage the tribes to enthusiastically embrace Christianity or the American way. Many tribal members were blatantly hostile to the reformers and missionaries, while others were merely passively resistant. Lack of progress in Americanizing the reservations led reform and missionary groups to reject the reservations as the focus of their attention. As noted by Prucha, "The realization that the Indians were not changing as the reformers had so confidently believed they would lead [sic] to an outright condemnation of the reservations as an unmitigated evil to be destroyed."[74] The reservations thus became the poisoned environment from which children needed to be rescued. In 1885, outspoken reformer Lyman Abbott told a reform-minded audience, "I declare my conviction then that the reservation system is hopelessly wrong; that it cannot be amended or modified; that it can only be uprooted."[75] These words captured the beliefs of numerous other reformers.

Surprisingly, the poor conditions of the reservations were held by some as necessary in order for American Indians to change their ways of life. Some argued that submission and destitution rendered the tribes more docile and obedient. Along the same line, others believed that the tribes needed to "hit bottom" before they would rise to a new and better life. However, even in the midst of the abject poverty on the reservations, American Indians continued to shun the guidance of missionaries and reformers.

Reformers and missionaries thus turned their zeal, attention, and force on the next generation of American Indians—the children. The tribal adults were already "lost" and could not be uprooted from "the blanket"—a reference to American Indian ways. The resolution to the "Indian problem" was seen in helping tribal children to "shed the blanket" so they could become part of the

American melting pot. Reformers believed that children literally had to be taken away from their families and their reservations in order to become "real" Americans. To facilitate American Indian assimilation, the reformers would "kill the Indian and save the man."[76] Separate, off-reservation schools for American Indians were proposed after American Indian education had been tried at a school originally developed for another ethnic minority group. In 1878, American Indian students were enrolled at Hampton Normal and Agricultural Institute, a manual training school for African Americans in Virginia. The school's administrator, General Samuel Chapman Armstrong, had been successful in securing the support of the American Missionary Association for the creation of the school in 1868. According to the memoirs of a Hampton teacher, a young White woman of "genteel New England upbringing," the American Indians formed a school within a school as the classes and dormitories "were entirely separate for the two dark races."[77]

Captain Richard Pratt, another military man and a vociferous advocate of American Indian industrial education, had been instrumental in gaining the students access to Hampton. Pratt, however, grew displeased with the arrangement because of conditions at Hampton and because he feared that prejudices against the "colored" would be directed toward the American Indian as well.[78] Pratt obtained support for opening a separate school for American Indians and in 1879 opened the Carlisle Indian Industrial School in Carlisle, Pennsylvania—probably the most famous of the boarding schools. From its opening enrollment of 82, Carlisle's enrollment eventually grew over the years to about 1,000 students. This school continued operating for 39 years until its closure in 1918.

While other boarding schools typically relied on private donations or churches for survival, Congress appropriated $67,500 to Carlisle in 1882 and the continued operation of the school became a certainty. With this and similar other appropriations, American Indian boarding schools symbolized a new direction in national policy. In addition, the boarding school became the most prominent and popular way of Americanizing the American Indian child and won substantial support from politicians, benefactors, missionaries, and other reformers.

The off-reservation boarding schools grew in importance to the reformers because such schools operationalized their belief that all vestiges of tribal life had to be stripped away before the new American could emerge. This meant that the children had to be separated from the reservation environment, tribal ways, and anything else having to do with their old life. The boarding schools became the most dramatic, powerful way for American Indian children to be "rescued" from the debilitating influences of the reservation. Children as young as age 6 were often enrolled at the schools that held hundreds, even thousands, of students in an institutional setting.

The boarding school period of American Indian history had long-term, far-reaching consequences for the youths who attended them and for their families. Appearance was critical and children were immediately groomed and dressed in the manner of White American children. Even though hair had much symbolic value in their culture, boys received haircuts upon their arrival. Visually, with the exception of color, the children were transformed into "Americans" and this transformation symbolized the psychological transformation that was to follow. Each child was given an English name and was instructed to answer only to that name.

Although variations existed across the schools, some commonalities were evident. All schools emphasized industrial training, English, and Christianity. Boys were taught to operate and repair machinery and girls learned food preparation among other skills. Runaways were common and, when apprehended, were often harshly punished. Large numbers of students died at the schools, and cemeteries adjacent to the schools were filled with hundreds and hundreds of markers. Student attendance ceased to be voluntary, as parents who refused to give up their children would not receive supplies or would suffer incarceration. Some children were even kidnapped for the boarding schools.

While education was to be the great equalizer in U.S. society, opportunities were extremely limited and the boarding-school experience did little to change public attitudes about the American Indian. Boarding-school attendees continued to be outsiders to U.S. society, and many also became outsiders among their own people. Hundreds returned to the reservation only to find that they could no longer communicate with their families because English had replaced the tribal language. Furthermore, the skills they had been taught were often useless on the reservation.

The success of the off-reservation boarding schools has been long debated. Some graduates were able to secure mainstream jobs and "shed the blanket." Several became writers and eloquently described their thoughts about and reactions to the boarding education. Others saw the schools as a way of escaping the impoverished conditions of the reservation. At the schools, children were regularly fed, adequately clothed, and life had a secure, predictable quality to it. Orphans could view the school as home and a place to belong. In general, however, this part of American Indian history is not warmly or tenderly remembered by those who were the most affected by it.

While denouncing any differences between Whites and American Indians, the reformers, nevertheless, advocated educational policies that were both dramatic and devastating for the American Indian people. *Separate* American Indian schools were a major component of the educational saturation plan—schools that emphasized *industrial* training—yet, reformers saw nothing racist or discriminatory in their proposals.

Reform efforts were instrumental in obtaining federal support of American Indian education. In 1870, the first federal appropriations were made, and by 1899, over $2.5 million was being spent annually on 148 boarding schools and 225 day schools that educated almost 20,000 children.[79] By 1913, 78 percent of all American Indian children were in school: 5,109 in mission schools, 26,028 in public schools, and 27,584 in the government's 216 day schools, 74 reservation boarding schools, and 37 off-reservation boarding schools.[80] The number of actual boarding schools decreased between 1870 and 1913, but the schools of 1913 boarded greater numbers of students than those of previous years.

Health and Mortality

Health and mortality are particularly important in this discussion of American Indians because during the turn of the century, these people had their *lowest* population census than at any other point—about 250,000. This population drop can be attributed to three primary reasons: epidemic disease, warfare, and genocide.[81] As with other groups, tuberculosis was a serious problem, and morbidity and mortality rates among American Indians far exceeded those among Whites *and* African Americans.[82] American Indians did not have immune systems that could protect them from the diseases of smallpox, cholera, typhus, diphtheria, and influenza that plagued Europe. Smallpox was particularly deadly and could wipe out entire villages in a matter of days. The number of deaths resulting from battles with the colonists and other tribes were significant but probably were less than those caused by disease. According to Snipp, assessing the number of deaths due to premeditated extermination is difficult as definitions of genocide vary.[83] Attempts to exterminate a race of people may extend from actual attacks to the forcible removal of people from their lands to the elimination of their culture. In this regard, the mortality rate for genocide may never be known.

Injustices of the Law Enforcement/Justice Systems

The courts played a pivotal role in further reducing the amount of land held by American Indian tribes. The Dawes Severalty Act of 1887 finally legalized what had been happening on a smaller scale. Prior to this act, numerous American Indians had either sold their land or had been defrauded of it. The Dawes Act stipulated that the president of the United States could allocate reservation land to American Indians with the title kept in trust for 25 years by the United States. Under the act, tribal land was divided into shares ranging from 40 to 160 acres. Family heads received the largest allotment and individuals received smaller parcels. After the allotments were made, any remaining "surplus" lands would be sold.

Under the Dawes Act, American Indians would become voting citizens if they lived away from their tribe and became farmers; however, since this stipulation went against tribal values, many American Indians would not concur and, consequently, lost their land.[84] Between 1887 and 1934, American Indians were separated from an estimated 86,000,000 of a total of 138,000,000 acres, and most of the remaining land was desert or semi-desert and considered worthless by the White population.[85]

The Dawes Act sought the redistribution of American Indian lands and also sought to remove the tribe as the core of American Indian power. Disbanding tribes and reservations would undermine the solidarity and cohesiveness of American Indians as a group and disperse tribal members throughout the territories. The separatism that promoted group identity and solidarity would be destroyed. This represents one example, albeit a legal one, of an attempt to force American Indians to assimilate into the American population.

Effects of the Dawes Act are visible today. In order for American Indians to be eligible for an allotment of land, they had to be accepted as eligible for tribal membership in one of the "Five Civilized Tribes": Cherokees, Creeks, Choctaws, Chickasaws, and Seminoles.[86] The resulting Dawes Rolls were formally known as the "Final Rolls of the Citizens and Freedmen of the Five Civilized Tribes in Indian Territory." The rolls have over 100,000 names recorded from 1898 to 1914, and the tribes currently use the Dawes Rolls as a way of determining tribal membership. To establish membership, individuals have to prove that they are a descendent of an individual whose name appears on the rolls. "Freedmen" are included in the names of the rolls because African Americans resided on the tribal lands and were thus counted as members of the tribe. In compiling the rolls, government workers listed those who "looked" Cherokee or Cherokee mixed with White as Cherokee and those who "looked" African American or Cherokee mixed with African American were listed as "Freedman."[87]

In 1975, The Cherokee people sought to revive their tribe and wrote a new constitution that limited tribal membership to those who could trace their lineage to one lineal ancestor named on the 1906 Dawes census. Those who were in the non-Indian category of freedman were deemed ineligible for tribal membership.[88] About 2,800 freedmen lost their tribal membership and have waged court battles to regain them. The rolls that were used to separate tribes from their lands have now become instruments for establishing tribal membership. These legal battles have become a wedge between two groups that had previously shared communal relationships. Thus, the power of legislation to influence and direct the lives of people for centuries cannot be denied.

In general, contracts and legal processes afforded little or no fairness for American Indians as treaties were routinely broken and congressional acts favored White Americans. Justice to Whites often meant injustices to the tribes. Violence against tribal groups was sanctioned and unpunished, while similar acts by American Indians resulted in vigilante justice or indiscriminate punishment of American Indians—"guilty" or "not. Consequently, American Indians had little protection under the law and no trust in the American legal system.

Systems Theory and the American Indian

The White ethnic community, as a subsystem, was able to penetrate the boundaries of the larger society to eventually become part of the mainstream. The African American community has been able to accomplish this on only a limited basis. The American Indian community, on the other hand, remained outside of society, particularly during the Progressive Era. Its unique history suggests that mainstream America did not want to include it and the community itself may not have wanted to be included. In the eyes of countless Americans, the American Indian did not have a place in the New World and was really a relic of the past. Through legislation and other acts, the country attempted to relegate the tribes to remote and barren lands. If they were really subgroups of the larger society, then their link to society was almost imperceptible. The ideologies of the time pushed thousands of indigenous people into a remote corner of American consciousness. American Indians did not stand a chance against the doctrines of Social Darwinism and Manifest Destiny. (The latter ideology is discussed in the following section.).

The reservations were greatly affected by the policies, programs, and practices of the larger environment. The boarding-school phenomenon removed children from their homes and plunged them into a totally foreign situation. The larger environment also controlled the amount and type of resources that were sent to the reservations. Most of the reservations were poor because the means for self-sufficiency had been stripped away and replaced with meager supplies. The larger society literally controlled the destiny of the reservations.

The internal dynamics of the tribes also dictated a tie to the larger society that was tenuous. The sovereign nations advocated for self-governance and control of their own destinies. If this had been granted, thousands of acres of rich and valuable land would have remained in their possession. As a subgroup, they were virtually powerless against attack and conquest. The desire to remain sovereign nations could not be realized in an era that equated race with deviance.

Interpreting the American Indian Experience

Hagan referred to the coercive assimilation of American Indians as "acculturation under duress."[89] In order for the educational programs to be proposed and implemented, reformers and educators had to believe firmly that the "American way" was the best way for all people of the United States. These "reforms" were grounded in a philosophy that held American Indian culture and people to be barbarian, savage, and in need of civilizing. The conversion to Christianity was a significant aspect of the Americanizing process.

With education, particularly off-reservation boarding schools, the American Indian was meant to acquire those tools necessary for American life. Education as a pathway to assimilation has been a cornerstone of the American belief system. With the proper skills, all people could become equal in the race for success. Thus, the reformers believed themselves to be doing the tribes a favor by aggressively advocating for their education. Because the tribes were often closed to this way of thinking, reformers, missionaries, and government officials took on the role of acting in the "best interest" of this group.

As White Americans interpreted and wrote history to conform to their rationalizations, numerous aspects of the American Indian experience were denied, ignored, or distorted. Only through prolonged interaction with Whites did the seemingly homogeneous group designation of "Indians" emerge.[90] Before these White American Indian interactions, American Indians were a diverse people, composed of many different Nations that had different languages and customs. Whites imposed a categorization that implied that all American Indians were similar, and from this similarity gross overgeneralizations could be made.[91]

The early history of White domination of American Indians was not grounded as much in nativism or Social Darwinism as was the subsequent domination of other groups. Rather, the colonists tenaciously believed they had a God-given right to take the land and its resources. This idea of *Manifest Destiny*, a term coined in 1845, crystallized the belief that God wanted the continent developed as a utopian example for the world of the successful fusion of democracy, capitalism, and Christianity.[92] Colonists also believed they were encountering an inferior, uncivilized "Red Race" that had to be subordinated through whatever means were necessary—a race that would ultimately benefit from White presence and White influence.

Reformers defined American Indians as childlike, ignorant people who did not know what was best for them. They could thus justify their proposals for "raising" the tribes while at the same time denying the role White America played in creating the American Indian's disadvantaged status. Furthermore, implicit in the reform ideology that, through education, the American Indian would either "sink or swim" was an underlying belief that the individual would then be responsible for his or her own failure.[93] The manner in which these reformers interpreted American Indian history and experiences, therefore, supported the coercive assimilation policies that were implemented.

This history underscores the tenacity with which reformers injected themselves and their beliefs into American Indian life. In operating in the "best interest" of and by "knowing what was best for" the American Indian tribes, reformers attacked tribal customs, values, and child-raising techniques. The removal of children from allegedly dysfunctional families and tribal environments was the most extreme case of racism, and it heightened the antagonism between White America and American Indians. Education alone was insufficient in lowering the barriers that existed between the two groups, and the boarding schools often led to greater alienation rather than assimilation. Although children were greatly revered as the next generation in American Indian culture, they also became a population that required protection from the good intentions of outsiders.

Endnotes

[1] Both examples are derived from Florette Henri, *Black Migration: Movement North, 1900–1920* (Garden City, NY: Anchor Press/Doubleday, 1975), 326, 328.

[2] U.S. Department of Commerce, Bureau of the Census, (http://www2.census.gov/prod2/decennial/documents/33405927v1ch13.pdf) Retrieved August 9, 2009.

[3] Monroe Lerner and Odin Anderson, *Health Progress in the United States 1900–1960* (Chicago: The University of Chicago Press, 1963): 114–120.

[4] David Muschinske, "The Nonwhite as Child: G. Stanley Hall on the Education of Nonwhite Peoples," *Journal of the History of the Behavioral Sciences* 13 (October 1977): 328–336.

[5] Lilian Brandt, "The Negroes of St. Louis," *Publications of the American Statistical Association* 8 (March 1903): 220.

[6] Henri, *Black Migration,* 51; E. M. Goodwin, *Black Migration in America from 1915 to 1960,* 9–10.

[7] David McBride, *From TB to AIDS—Epidemics among Urban Blacks since 1900* (Albany: State University of New York Press, 1991), 35.

[8] Goodwin, *Black Migration in America from 1915 to 1960* (Lewiston, NY: Edwin Mellen Press, 1990): 11, 13–14; Henri, *Black Migration,* 53–54.

[9] W. E. B. DuBois, "The Migration of Negroes," *The Crisis* 13–14 (June 1917): 63.

[10] Goodwin, *Black Migration in America,* 15.

[11] Benjamin Ringer and Elinor Lawless, *Race-Ethnicity and Society* (New York: Routledge, 1989), 20.

[12] The Housing Problem and the Negro," *Charities* 15 (October 7, 1905): 2.

[13] Sophonisba Breckinridge, "The Color Line in the Housing Problem," *The Survey* (February 1913): 575.

[14] William Pollard, *A Study of Black Self Help* (San Francisco: R & E Research Associates, 1978): 93–99.

[15] David Gordon, "Manual Training for Negro Children," *Charities* 15 (October 7, 1905): 84.

[16] Henri, *Black Migration*, 38.

[17] John Dittmer, *Black Georgia in the Progressive Era, 1900–1920* (Urbana: University of Illinois Press, 1977), 118–119; Henri, *Black Migration*, 242.

[18] Detailed discussions of both examples given are contained in Dittmer, *Black Georgia*, 116–120.

[19] E. Franklin Frazier, *Black Bourgeoisie* (Glencoe, IL: Free Press, 1957).

[20] Dittmer, *Black Georgia*, 61–62.

[21] Willi Coleman, "African American Women and Community Development in California, 1848–1900," in *Seeking El Dorado—African Americans in California*, ed. Lawrence de Graaf, Kevin Mulroy, and Quintard Taylor (Los Angeles: Autry Museum of Western Heritage, 2001), 103.

[22] Shirley Moore, "African Americans in California: A Brief Historiography," *California History* 75 (Fall 1996): 195.

[23] Jesse Moore, "Seeking a New Life: Blacks in Post–Civil War Colorado," *The Journal of Negro History* 78 (Summer 1993): 166–187.

[24] As quoted in Moore, "Seeking a New Life," 171.

[25] This description of Allensworth is drawn from Lonnie Bunch, III, "Allensworth: The Life, Death and Rebirth of an All-Black Community," *The Californians* 5 (November/December 1987): 26–33; and Robert Catlin, "Black Utopia: the Development of Allensworth, California, USA, 1908–1930," *Planning History* 23 (Number 3, 2001): 5–14.

[26] Bunche, "Allensworth," 28.

[27] Catlin, "Black Utopia," 10.

[28] McBride, *From TB to AIDS*, 35–36.

[29] "The Negro's Fitness," *The Charities Review* 9 (September 1899): 323.

[30] "The Negro," *The Charities Review* 6 (June 1897): 379.

[31] McBride, *From TB to AIDS*, 41–42.

[32] Henri, *Black Migration*, 40–41; McBride, *From TB to AIDS*, 43.

[33] Bradley, *The United States from 1865*, 146; Henri, *Black Migration*, 43–44; James McPherson, Laurence Holland, James Banner, Jr., Nancy Weiss, and Michael Bell, *Blacks in America: Bibliographical Essays* (Garden City, NY: Anchor/ Doubleday, 1971), 140–141.

[34] Bruce Jansson, *The Reluctant Welfare State*, 6th Edition (Belmont, CA: Brooks/Cole, 2009), 191.

[35] John Ehrenreich, *The Altruistic Imagination—A History of Social Work and Social Policy in the United States* (Ithaca, NY: Cornell University Press, 1985), 46.

[36] McBride, *From TB to AIDS*, 40.

[37] *The Crisis* 13–14 (September 1917): 219–238.

[38] As quoted in *The Crisis* 13–14 (September 1917): 221.

[39] *The Crisis* 13–14 (September 1917): 220.

[40] Discussion of this decision is summarized from Harold Bradley, *The United States from 1865*, 146; and Henri, *Black Migration*, 13–14.

[41] As quoted in Henri, *Black Migration*, 13–14.

[42] Raymond Givens, "Literature on Jim Crow," *Magazine of History* 18 (January 2004): 13–16.

[44] Events surrounding the discharge are detailed in Henri, *Black Migration*, 241–242.

[44] "Riots," *The Crisis* 13–14 (September 1917): 313.

[45] Thomas Dyer, *Theodore Roosevelt and the Idea of Race* (Baton Rouge: Louisiana State University Press, 1980), 89–122.

[46] Henri, *Black Migration*, 52.

[47] This discussion is drawn from Kazuteru Omori, "Race-Neutral Individualism and Resurgence of the Color Line: Massachusetts Civil Rights Legislation, 1855–1895," *Journal of American Ethnic History* 22 (Fall 2002): 32–58.

[48] As quoted in Kazuteru Omori, "Race-Neutral Individualism," 35.

[49] Ibid., 51.

[50] Henri, *Black Migration*, 261.

[51] John Dittmer, *Black Georgia in the Progressive Era, 1900–1920* (Urbana: University of Illinois Press, 1977), 137–138.

[52] Otto Bettmann, *The Good Old Days—They Were Terrible* (New York: Random House, 1974), 106.

[53] McBride, *From TB to AIDS*, 41–43.

[54] Brandt, "The Negroes of St. Louis," 252.

[55] Scott Christianson, "Our Black Prisons," *Crime and Delinquency* 27 (July 1981): 373.

[56] Sophonisba Breckinridge, "The Color Line in the Housing Problem," *The Survey* (February 1913): 575.

[57] Henri, *Black Migration*, 122; W. E. B. DuBois, *Some Notes of Negro Crime* (Atlanta, GA: Atlanta University Press, 1904).

[58] John Gillin, *Criminology and Penology* (New York: D. Appleton-Century, 1926), 60.

[59] Pollard, *A Study of Black Self Help*, 93.

[60] W. E. B. DuBois, *Efforts for Social Betterment among Negro Americans* (Atlanta, GA: The Atlanta University Press, 1909), 125.

[61] Brandt, "The Negroes of St. Louis," 229, 230.

[62] Ibid., 251.

[63] Amos Warner, "The Causes of Poverty Further Considered," *Publications of the American Statistical Association, New Series*, 4 (September): 49–68.

[64] Warner, "The Causes of Poverty," 60.

[65] Ibid.

[66] John Smith, "DuBois and Phillips—Symbolic Antagonists of the Progressive Era," *Centennial Review* 24 (Winter 1980): 88–102.

[67] Luis Kemnitzer, "Native Americans," in *Racial Discrimination against Neither White nor Black American Minorities*, ed. Kananur Chandras (San Francisco: R & E Research Associates, 1978), 9.

[68] This discussion is drawn from Wilbert Ahern, "Assimilationist Racism: The Case of the 'Friends of the Indian,'" *Journal of Ethnic Studies* 4 (Summer 1976): 23–32; Stephen Cornell, "Land, Labour and Group Formation: Blacks and Indians in the United States," *Ethnic and Racial Studies* 13 (July 1990): 368–388; Brian Dippie, *The Vanishing American-White Attitudes and U.S. Indian Policy* (Middletown, CT: Wesleyan University Press, 1982); Ralph Dolgoff and Donald Feldstein, *Understanding Social Welfare*, 7th ed. (New York: Pearson, 2007), 74–77; Henry Fritz, *The Movement for Indian Assimilation, 1860–1890* (Philadelphia: University of Pennsylvania Press, 1963); William Hagan, *American Indians*, rev. ed. (Chicago: The University of Chicago Press, 1979); Jansson, *The Reluctant Welfare State*, 131–134; Louise Johnson, Charles Schwartz, and Donald Tate, *Social Welfare—A response to Human Need*, 4th ed. (Boston: Allyn & Bacon, 1997); Francis Prucha, ed., *Americanizing the American: Writings by the 'Friends of the American Indian' 1880–1890* (Cambridge, MA: Harvard University Press, 1973); Francis Prucha, *American Indian Policy in Crisis: Christian Reformers and the Indians, 1865–1900* (Norman: University of Oklahoma Press, 1976); Francis Prucha, *The Churches and the Indian Schools, 1888–1912* (Lincoln: University of Nebraska Press, 1979); Russell Thornton, *American Indian Holocaust and Survival: A Population History Since 1492* (Norman: University of Oklahoma Press, 1987).

[69] Ahern, "Assimilationist Racism," 23.

[70] As quoted in Prucha, *American Indian Policy in Crisis*, 206.

[71] As quoted in Ahern, "Assimilationist Racism," 27.

[72] Prucha, *American Indian Policy in Crisis*, 223.

[73] Hagan, *American Indians*, 126–127.

[74] Prucha, *American Indian Policy in Crisis*, 224.

[75] As quoted in Prucha, *Americanizing the American Indians*, 35.

[76] The words of reformer Henry Pratt as quoted in Ahern, "Assimilationist Racism," 24.

[77] Kay Graber, ed., *Sister to the Sioux—The Memoirs of Elaine Goodale Eastman, 1885–91* (Lincoln: University of Nebraska Press, 1978), xi, 19.

[78] Prucha, *American Indian Policy in Crisis*, 273.

[79] Hagan, *Native Americans*, 135.

[80] Dippie, *The Vanishing American*, 186.

[81] C. Matthew Snipp, "Sociological Perspectives on American Indians," *Annual Review of Sociology* 18 (1992): 354–356.

[82] Thornton, *American Indian Holocaust and Survival*, 172.

[83] Snipp, "Sociological Perspectives on American Indians," 255.

[84] Dolgoff and Feldstein, *Understanding Social Welfare*, 75.

[85] Hagan, *American Indians*, 147.

[86] From http://www.archives.gov/genealogy/tutorial/dawes (accessed June 29, 2009).

[87] Jeninne Lee-St. John, "The Cherokee Nation's New Battle," *Time* in Partnership with CNN, Thursday, June 21, 2007. http://www.time.com/printout/0,8816,1635873,00.html (accessed December 5, 2009).

[88] Cherokee Nation, "History of Freedmen Descendents," http://freedmen.cherokee.org/Historyof FreedmenDescendents/tabid/724/Default.aspx (accessed December 5, 2009).

[89] Hagan, *American Indians*, 121.

[90] Cornell, "Land, Labour and Group Formation," 368–369.

[91] Johnson and Schwartz, *Social Welfare*, 96–97.

[92] Jansson, *The Reluctant Welfare State*, 131.

[93] Ahern, "Assimilationist Racism," 28.

Mexicans, Chinese, and Japanese at the Turn of the Century

The previous chapter presented a picture of the lives of African Americans and American Indians during the Progressive Era. Other racial and ethnic groups populated the country and encountered harsh treatment and conditions. These groups also contributed to the social context that gave rise to the social work profession. For this reason, a brief overview of their histories follows. These histories emphasize that, although they can be categorized together as racial and ethnic minorities, their experiences differed greatly from each other. Their histories are also relevant for gaining a fuller understanding of the social, political, and economic context from which social work emerged.

MEXICAN AMERICANS IN THE PROGRESSIVE ERA

> In a time when most Americans made no distinction between native-born Mexicans and newly arrived Mexican immigrants, Jim Crow attitudes and practices shackled the aspirations of both groups, regardless of nativity or citizenship.[1]

Historically, Mexicans as an ethnic population can be divided into two groups: Mexican Americans and Mexicans. The members of the first group are United States citizens, many of whom are descendents of the original Mexican occupants of the territories obtained by the United States. The latter group includes immigrants with varying amounts of time in this country. The histories of these two groups are intertwined.

At the beginning of the twentieth century, Mexican Americans in the United States were at a turning point in their history. In the middle to late 1880s, the vast amount of land they owned was coveted and eventually seized by White settlers through both legal and extra-legal means. As this seized land was mined, farmed, and developed, cheap labor was essential for production and profit. The indigenous people of Mexican descent in the Southwest and the immigrants from Mexico were significant to the nation

67

because they filled this labor need. The quest for land and the need for labor determined the nature of Progressive Era experiences and subsequent experiences of Mexican Americans and Mexican immigrants for years to come.

As issues regarding the illegal immigration of Mexicans and Central Americans continue to be debated, the pre-immigration history of Mexican Americans seems almost forgotten. The larger society may perceive anyone of Mexican heritage as being the first-, second-, or third-generation descent of a Mexican immigrant. Although this may be true for countless Mexican Americans, many others share a history in Texas and the Southwest that predates the establishment of White settlements. From the end of the Mexican War in 1848 to the beginning of unprecedented immigration from Mexico in 1910, the history of the Mexican people in the United States has been virtually unrecognized. This history, coupled with the treatment of Mexican immigrants, casts a shadow on mainstream social services to these groups today.

The history of Mexican Americans in the United States is tied closely to those events that occurred in Texas and the Southwest Territory.[2] White settlers moved into Texas in the early 1780s when it was still part of the state of Coahuila in the Republic of Mexico. Mexico welcomed these new settlers as long as they embraced Catholicism and pledged allegiance to Mexico. Once in Texas, however, the new settlers often forgot the oath and, in addition, continued to practice Protestantism. As a matter of fact, the settlers were able to circumvent numerous Mexican laws while challenging Mexico's power to enforce them. For example, Mexico's abolition of slavery in 1829 led many settlers to use lifelong indenture contracts signed by "former" slaves as a way of maintaining their slave population.

Hostility toward the Mexican government escalated and open rebellion ensued. The source of this hostility and antagonism can be traced to several issues. On one hand, the White settlers saw Mexican laws as interfering with their way of life, and their increasing numbers provided the strength they needed to openly rebel. On the other hand, it seems that the White settlers believed the Mexicans to be inferior in intelligence and refused to submit to a government that was also seen as inferior. At the time of the Texas War, the approximately 5,000 Mexicans inhabiting Texas did not join the White settlers in revolt against the Mexican government.

During the Texas Revolution, the battles in San Antonio (at mission Alamo), Goliad, and San Jacinto were fought. Although Mexico was victorious in the first two, the revolution ended with the defeat of the Mexican army in 1836 at San Jacinto. With this defeat, the Mexican Texas died a violent death and the Republic of Texas was born. According to Acuña: "More important was the hatred generated by the war. The Mexican was pictured as cruel, treacherous, tyrannical, and as an enemy who could not be trusted. These stereotypes lingered long after the war and can still be detected in Anglo attitudes toward the Chicano. The Texas War left a legacy of hate and determined the status of the Mexicans left behind as that of a *conquered* people" [emphasis added].[3]

The Mexican American War in the next decade recalled the hostilities between White Americans and Mexicans, and land again emerged as the

spark igniting conflict. During this period, belief in Manifest Destiny, Social Darwinism, and nativism spurred White settlers into the Southwest Territory with a fervor that could not be stopped. The territory, however, was already inhabited by 75,000 Mexicans, many of whom were *Mestizos*—descendants of the original Spanish conquistadors who created families with the American Indians of the area. In the aftermath of the Mexican American War and the signing of the Treaty of Guadalupe Hidalgo in 1848, thousands of Mexicans became Mexican Americans—citizens of the United States—as Mexico gave up the Southwest Territory in exchange for $15 million. This Southwest Territory was later to become the states of California, New Mexico, Utah, Nevada, and parts of Colorado, Arizona, and Wyoming.

People of Mexican ancestry residing in Texas and the Southwest suffered overt economic, political, and social subordination as White Americans began descending on the territory. This pattern was well established by the time revolution in Mexico drove thousands of Mexicans to the United States in the early 1900s. In 1900, those states with the largest number of individuals born in Mexico were Texas (71,002), Arizona (14,172), California (8,086), and New Mexico (6,010).[4] According to Ruiz, between 1910 and 1930, over one million Mexicans (approximately one-eighth to one-tenth of Mexico's population) came to the United States and eventually outnumbered Mexican Americans by two-to-one.[5] During this time, numerous White Americans ceased to make a distinction between native-born Mexican Americans and foreign-born Mexicans.

The Progressive Era embodied the historical hostility held by many Whites toward Mexican Americans, and this hostility was also directed toward Mexican immigrants. These sentiments, coupled with differential treatment, have followed Mexican Americans throughout their history in the United States.

Discrimination in the Southwest

Mexicans in Texas and the Southwest Territory embraced a culture rich in Spanish, Mexican, and American Indian customs, religions, and values. The Treaty of Guadalupe Hidalgo provided Mexicans

> the enjoyment of all the rights of citizens of the United States according to the principles of the Constitution; and in the meantime shall be maintained and protected in the enjoyment of their liberty and property, and secured in the free exercise of their religion without restriction.[6]

Unfortunately, this part of the treaty was not strictly enforced; as thousands of White settlers entered the territory, the rights of the indigenous inhabitants were trampled.

The Whites brought with them their own "American" values, customs, and laws. Implicit in this White presence was the belief that Whites were culturally superior to the Mexicans. Mexicans were not familiar with the "American" way of political and economic life, and no means were provided to educate them in these areas. In addition, many of the Mexicans spoke only Spanish, were poor, and worked for the *ricos* (the rich) who often owned vast acreage. The Mexican population was generally scattered throughout the territory in villages and small towns.

The treaty was not powerful enough to overcome the racial attitudes so firmly entrenched in the minds of the White settlers and reinforced by the Texas Revolution. These Texas and Southwest settlers eventually deprived Mexican Americans of political power even in towns with a predominant Mexican American presence. For example, in 1902, Texas adopted a poll tax that deterred Mexican Americans from voting.[7] In addition to losing political power, Mexican Americans were discriminated against in educational and economic opportunities. A master–slave caste system developed in which the Mexican Americans of Texas and the Southwest were relegated to the worst working and living conditions and became a cheap labor force for White farmers. As the territory grew in population, White establishments were known to post "No Mexicans Allowed," "No Mexicans Served," "Whites Only," and other similar signs indicating that Mexican or Mexican American clientele were not welcomed.

Thus, the Jim Crow laws associated with the South and the segregation of African Americans took on a similar meaning for the Mexican Americans and the Mexicans of the Southwest. Racist attitudes and discriminatory practices redefined Jim Crow from an African American–White phenomenon to a White–Mexican one. The commonality across both meanings is seated in the ideology of White supremacy. Even the Catholic nuns who aided the Spanish-speaking communities of Texas were not immune to the stereotypes and bigotry that were pervasive throughout the Southwest.[8]

This anti-Mexican hostility had a tremendous effect on the Mexican American population itself. This hostility was particularly fierce in the case of Mexican Americans who looked American Indian.[9] In Texas, *Tejanos* (Mexican American Texans) sought to distinguish themselves from Mexican immigrants, and eventually *Mexican* became a negative word to both Whites and *Tejanos*.[10] The Mexican American population was not a homogenous group but rather several groups as identified by their ancestry and physical appearance that ranged from the fairness of the Spanish to the darkness of the American Indian. These distinctions were captured in 1924 by McLean and Thomson, who wrote,

> The *Mexicans* are those who were born south of the Rio Grande in the Republic of Mexico, and who have emigrated to the United States, usually within the last five or ten years. They are not American citizens, and usually do not wish to become so. In many cases *their skin is slightly darker than that of the Spanish Americans* [emphasis added].[11]

This gradation was often associated with class, as the designation *Spanish American* symbolized Spanish blood, aristocracy, and wealth, whereas *Mexican* reflected American Indian and peasant stock. Because of the tremendous amount of anti-Mexican sentiment, people frequently sought to dissociate themselves from this group. Thus, racism and discrimination permeated the Hispanic population and influenced the self-identification of group members.

Even though the Spanish were already in the Southwest before the arrival of the White settlers, the descendants of these Spanish pioneers were not exempt from White condescension, *patronism*, and superiority. For example, McLean and Thomson wrote further in 1924, "It must always be kept in mind, however, that they [Spanish Americans] look on themselves as *real* Americans, and cordially resent any accusation of lack of patriotism" [emphasis added].[12] These authors provided descriptions of both the Mexican and Spanish American that reveal just as much about the writers as about the subjects. The Spanish and Mexican are presented as childlike, docile people without much capacity for leadership in the gold and silver mines in Colorado nor appreciation enough for the value of education to send their children to school.

The hostility toward Mexican Americans was so strong that, in 1904, when 40 orphans of White European background from New York were placed in the homes of Mexican Americans in the Arizona territory, the Whites in the area protested vehemently. The protestors claimed that the parents fed the children strange foods and were too poor to care properly for them. The racism of the attack was mirrored in the Whites' description of the parents as "half-breeds." Vigilantes forcefully took the children from the Mexican Americans and gave them to White families. The Arizona Supreme Court supported the action of the Whites and referred to the vigilante groups as "committees." The New York orphanage that originally placed the children was legally powerless in retrieving the children from the White families.[13]

The social conditions of Mexican Americans were exacerbated by the arrival of thousands of Mexican immigrants after 1900. Prior to 1910, Mexicans born in the United States made up 8 percent of the foreign born from the Americas and grew to about 25 percent in 1910.[14] From 1880 to 1910, the Mexican-born populations of Arizona, California, New Mexico, and Texas more than tripled. Jansson noted that many of these immigrants lived in remote areas and were subject to punitive labor policies of landowners who paid them little and brutally suppressed protest.[15]

At the turn of the century, Mexican immigrants and Mexican Americans made up 80 percent of the agricultural workforce, 90 percent of Western railroad workers, and 60 percent of mine workers.[16] In addition, others traveled to the northern urban centers for work or became migrant farm laborers in other parts of the country. In a 1912 article on the experiences of Mexican immigrants in the United States, Bryan noted that in 1908 and 1909, about 86 percent of the Mexican immigrants working as railroad laborers earned less than $1.25 a day, while the Greeks, Italians, and Japanese railroad workers were better paid, with some earning more than $1.50 a day.[17] In addition to poor wages, the Mexican immigrant also suffered poor living conditions that fostered diseases and criminal activities.

The Mexican immigrant was different from the Mexican American. Whereas the Mexican American was an American and saw America as his or her home, the immigrant had a much different view. According to Acuña:

> Like the European, the Mexican came to the United States because of his hunger; but unlike the European, he did not intend to stay, nor did his masters intend him to remain. He came as a temporary worker... and was constantly shuttled throughout the Southwest and Midwest... and would return to Mexico when the work was finished.[18]

This migratory pattern of the immigrant population and its supposedly temporary presence in the United States suggest that (1) assimilation was not the
intended goal for this group in the eyes of the larger society, (2) many immigrant communities were transitory, (3) the Mexican immigrant developed a
reputation for being a "floater," and (4) these immigrants were never intended
to be "real" Americans. Many of these generalizations, however, were
extended to Mexican Americans as well.

The federal government paid little attention to Mexican immigration
before 1924, and the various immigration commissions had little or nothing to
say about them.[19] The sentiment was that the Mexican immigrant was not a
factor in the employment of American workers. Business interests on the West
Coast emphasized the need for Mexican laborers, and immigration exemptions
were extended to allow them to enter the country. The labor unions did not
protest these exemptions because they, too, did not see these immigrants as
serious competitors for jobs.

Several additional factors influenced the encouragement of Mexican
immigration in the Western and Southwestern states.[20] One was the rejection
of the recruitment of African Americans from the South because they were
believed to be docile and lazy. Another was the description of the Mexican
immigrant temperament as docile, nonthreatening, and peaceful. Often, proponents of Mexican immigration believed that White workers were not suitable for the hard labor involved in farm work.

Regardless of what immigration advocates thought about the value of the
Mexican immigrant, one central belief reigned foremost in their minds: The
Mexican immigrant was not White. Furthermore, poor Whites were deemed
superior to the Mexicans because all White people occupied a status position
that placed them above Mexican immigrants. As Whites, they enjoyed privileges such as property and citizenship rights that were reified in the law. [21]

Americanization

Because supporters of Americanization saw many Mexicans, and even Mexican Americans, as unassimilated, some limited efforts were undertaken to boost
their assimilation through religious and state-organized Americanization
projects.[22] In the schools, for example, the curriculum typically included English
classes because the eradication of the Spanish language was viewed as a necessary step toward assimilation. It was not unusual for segregated schools to be
used as examples of Americanization at work. Legislation was passed in some
states that mandated the segregation of Spanish-speaking students. Decades
later, this history of segregation in California compelled families to file suit
against four school districts in 1945. In this case, the judge ruled that the "segregation of Mexican youngsters found no justification in the laws of California and
furthermore was a clear denial of the 'equal protection' clause of the Fourteenth
amendment."[23] This case, *Mendez v. Westminster,* is included here because it
predates the *Brown v. Board of Education* case that desegregated schools for
African Americans. The *Mendez v. Westminster* case captures the historic commitment Mexican Americans have had for the education of their children.

Racial Violence

Law enforcement agents provided no protection from the vigilantes who terrorized Mexicans in Texas and throughout the Southwest. For example, Mexican miners who were thrown out of the California gold mines were often attacked, shot, beaten, or even killed. These workers were seen as a threat to native-born White workers. Not only were they holding jobs that many thought belonged to Whites, but they were often willing to work for less money as well. In New Mexico and Arizona, violence against Mexicans was also widespread and frequent.

The situation in Sonora, California, provides an example of how racial violence, coupled with legislation, robbed Mexicans of land and livelihood. Mexicans from Sonora, Mexico, settled the area and were successful in mining productive claims. They fought off White attempts to drive them from the land and the lucrative claims. Mexican miners became the victims of raids and killings as the Whites' quest for the land knew no boundaries. In 1850, the state legislature imposed a tax on all foreign miners (aimed primarily at the Mexicans). Using guns to implement the regulation, Whites forced about 2,000 Mexicans to leave Sonora. The tax was so high that other miners, Whites included, were forced out of the mines. The tax was eventually repealed a year later, but by that time it was too late for the Mexicans.

In Texas, the Texas Rangers developed a reputation for shooting first and asking questions later in their dealings with Mexican Americans. A Mexican accused of a crime was often found guilty on the spot and punished immediately. In retaliation for a crime thought to be committed by a Mexican, Rangers shot or beat numerous Mexicans and assumed that the guilty party was somewhere among the bunch. To the Texas Ranger, a Mexican was a Mexican whether he or she lived north or south of the border.

Thus, the type of racial violence against African Americans in the South and later in the North was experienced by Mexicans in Texas and the Southwest, the overwhelming majority of whom were citizens of these areas. Many of the White settlers in Texas and the Southwest had migrated from southern states and merely redirected their racial animosity from African Americans to Mexicans. In some places, Mexicans were referred to as "yeller niggers."[24] According to Moquin, the number of Mexican American killings in the Southwest from 1850 to 1930 surpassed the number of African American lynchings for the same period.[25] Many of these victims were slaughtered for their land.

Carrigan and Webb present an analysis of Mexican lynching cases and make a comparison to African American cases.[26] Between 1880 and 1930, Mexicans were lynched at a rate of 27.4 per 100,000—a rate that surpassed that of African Americans in some of the southern states. Those states with the largest number of persons of Mexican descent also had the highest number of cases. For example, for the indicated period, 282 were lynched in Texas and 188 in California. The authors conclude that this history of lynching should be an integral part of any literature on lynching because it clearly shows that African Americans were not the only targets of extreme mob violence.

Injustices of the Law Enforcement/Justice Systems

Central to the history of Mexican Americans in the Southwest are the issues surrounding the land grants. The Treaty of Guadalupe Hidalgo opened the door to one of the "greatest land grabs in American history" since the dispossession of the American Indian tribes.[27] Pueblos, missions, and individuals possessed thousands of acres of "good" land in the Southwest through Spanish and Mexican land grants. The Mexicans who became Mexican Americans as a result of the Treaty of Guadalupe Hidalgo owned vast amounts of land that had been granted under a system originated by Spain.[28]

Although the treaty protected the rights of these Mexican landholders, White settlers used the U.S. court system to challenge land ownership. Congress passed the Land Act of 1851 that was to help clear up "confusion" about land titles. This act, however, paved the way for Whites whose claims were ruled on favorably. Rather than being a system of justice, the courts became a means of stripping Mexicans of their property rights. Here, the foundation for lack of faith and trust in the U.S. judicial system was formed.

Not surprisingly, Mexican immigrants were overrepresented in the jails and prisons of Texas and the Southwest during the early 1900s. As their percentage of the population increased, their incarceration rate also increased. The proportion of the incarcerated among the Mexicans was greater than among other foreign-born groups or among the native born.[29] In Arizona and California, the chief offenses were gambling and drinking. As with African Americans, these incarceration rates for Mexicans raise the issues of law enforcement as a means of social control, the differential enforcement of laws, and the differential use of imprisonment as punishment.

Mexicans in Other Parts of the Country

Mexican immigrants moved to other states during the Progressive Era. For example, Oppenheimer writes about the Mexican immigrants in Kansas during this period.[30] In 1900 there were only 71 Mexicans in Kansas, and ten years later that number had increased to 8,429 or a little less than one percent of the Kansas population. By 1920, the number rose to 13,770 or about one percent of the population. They hailed from every part of Mexico and worked in agriculture, meat packing, mining, and on the railroads. As a matter of fact, the Santa Fe Railroad and other similar companies actively sought Mexican workers. At the turn of the century, male laborers constituted the immigrant pool. As work became more permanent, the men were able to bring their families to the state and lay the foundation for communities.

These immigrants faced racism, discrimination, and segregation in Kansas. Some of this treatment had roots in the mid-nineteenth century when Mexicans traveled through the state and worked as wagoneers on the Santa Fe Trail. Since their job involved greasing the wagon wheels, they were labeled "greasers" by the Whites for whom they worked. This derogatory moniker greeted the Mexican immigrants decades later. The type of violence seen in the Southwest, however, was not replicated in Kansas.

The experiences of Mexicans in Louisiana and Mississippi were quite different from those of the Southwest and Kansas.[31] Those immigrants in the South traveled a different route from those of the Southwest, and their immigration was not fueled by the Mexican Revolution of 1910–1917. These immigrants traveled to the South from the Gulf Coast of Mexico. Their history is linked to Louisiana's historical relationship with Latin America. Louisiana and Mississippi had both been colonies of Spain, and New Orleans was known to be a safe haven for Latin American political exiles.

In the South, race was a black–white dichotomy and those who fell somewhere between the two often struggled to be legally defined as White. White status afforded protection from the Jim Crow laws that oppressed African Americans. Mexicans were able to utilize the Mexican government and Mexican nationalism to help forge a Mexican identity that aligned them with White immigrants. During the 1920s, Mexicans were living as Whites and the 1920 census counted 1,242 Mexican-born Whites in New Orleans. Mexicans learned that, if they distanced themselves from African Americans (the outgroup or "other") they increased their chances of being accepted as White. Since the South did not have the type of racial diversity that existed in the Southwest, the dichotomy of race as "black or white" may have made the White identity easier to achieve. In this regard, "white" meant anyone who was not "black."

Interpreting the Mexican American Experience

The history of Mexicans and Mexican Americans in the United States is often painted with broad strokes of heroism, romanticism, and expansionism. The Texas Revolution and the Mexican American War are depicted as righteous, just consequences of attempts to oppress the frontier spirit that knew no containment. To this day the battle cry "Remember the Alamo!" is synonymous with holding one's ground until the bitter end.[32] The rugged frontier seemed to beckon the rugged individual whose dreams were as vast as the land. Whites are perceived as having brought civilization, productivity, vision, and the American way to undeveloped territories. The Texas Rangers are depicted as the keepers of justice who valiantly defended the Texas borders and protected settlers from dangerous, savage intruders. The Texas Rangers Museum in Waco, Texas, today offers visitors an overview of the glorious and well-honored history and tradition of the Rangers.[33]

Acuña provides detailed descriptions of the romanticism that surrounds the Texas Rangers, the Texas revolt, and the Mexican American War.[34] He cites noted historians who dismiss the brutality that accompanied the conquest of Texas and the Southwest as justifiable and unavoidable. Acuña's message echoes loudly from the pages: Mexican Americans have a far different view of these events and their consequences. This history, as recounted by Mexican Americans, is one of oppression, racism, discrimination, and colonization.

At the same time, Mexicans in other states had somewhat varying experiences that underscore the heterogeneity of group history. Each part of the country had its own history and images of Mexicans. Texas (and the Southwest in general) proved to be the most brutal in its perceptions and actions. Other states seem to have acted less severely. Still other states embraced Mexican and Mexican Americas as equal partners in American citizenship.

Overall, the image of the Mexican American has greatly suffered. Over time, the distinctions between Spanish Americans, Mexican Americans, and Mexicans clouded and simply melted into one. Heritage and ancestry could not protect the Southwestern descendants of the first Spanish pioneers from being categorized as "alien" or "foreign" to U.S. society. As in the case of African Americans, nativity by birth and history could not shield numerous Mexican Americans from the differential treatment as "outsiders."

CHINESE IN THE PROGRESSIVE ERA

Chinese immigrants have experienced continuing exploitation in the workplace, from the early periods when they performed very dangerous work in building the nation's railways to the present time when newly arrived immigrants toil in urban sweatshops.[35]

By the time the Progressive Era began, the "Chinese problem" had already been resolved in the United States by the Chinese Exclusion Act of 1882 that prohibited Chinese laborers from entering the United States and prohibited Chinese from becoming naturalized citizens.[36] Between 1855 and 1877, it was estimated that 191,118 Chinese had entered the United States. In 1860, one-tenth of the Californian population was Chinese, and in 1870 the U.S. Chinese population was 63,199 according to census figures. The overwhelming majority of this 63,000 (99 percent) lived on the West Coast. Although immigrants of other countries were permitted unrestricted entry into the United States, Chinese were limited and, in some cases, those already in the country were driven out through a variety of means. Two years before the act, in 1880, Chinese constituted 105,465, or 2 percent of the 50,155,783 people in the United States. In 1882, the year the bill was enacted, 102,991 British and 250,630 German immigrants came to the United States in comparison to 39,579 Chinese. By the turn of the century, Chinese immigration was at a record low. Whites' perception of the Chinese in the United States had changed from being an invaluable labor supply to being the scourge of the earth.

The rise and fall of this group in America traces the ebb and flow of public attitudes shaped by a changing social, political, and economic climate. Although 2 percent of the population seems little cause for alarm, White workers viewed the Chinese as competitors who were willing to work any job for any wage. A country that had depended heavily on Chinese labor for the growth and maintenance of numerous industries in the past was now willing to denounce this group and deny any and all contributions it had made to the economic development of the country. Consequently, during the Progressive Era the status of Chinese individuals had been reduced to that of non-persons.

To grasp fully the status of Chinese individuals in the United States at the dawn of the twentieth century, it is necessary to trace a series of events that

climaxed in the Exclusion Act. In the mid-1880s, peasant uprisings, economic conditions, and political upheaval drove thousands of Chinese to flee China in search of new prosperity in other countries. The California Gold Rush acted to attract hundreds of Chinese, and the first arrivals were able to secure employment as cooks and servants. The Gold Rush period attracted some 35,000 Chinese, in comparison to the 2.5 million European immigrants entering during this same time. Many of the Chinese immigrants relied on resources, family assistance, or their own ingenuity to defray transportation expenses. With the later contract labor system, others entered into contractual agreements with U.S. companies that needed workers. These companies paid the travel cost incurred by workers and subtracted the amount from wages paid. Railroad companies used this system to meet the labor demands of the railroad construction. Some Chinese workers were recruited by large farming interests in the South with the expectation that these workers could fill some of the void left by the freed slaves. Many of the recruited Chinese eventually headed west when their contracts had been fulfilled.

When they came in modest numbers to the West before the 1850s, the Chinese were not perceived as any kind of threat. As a matter of fact, their style of dress, the pigtail, physical characteristics, and other indications of their cultural uniqueness made them a novelty in the Western towns. Many of the early arrivals worked in service areas such as restaurants and hotels that supported the growing population. Many were merchants and skilled craftsmen. When their numbers began to increase significantly in the 1850s, racism and discrimination became more blatant and more hostile. These were primarily Chinese peasants who were lured by the work in the mines. In the following decade, more Chinese immigrants were recruited for construction of the transcontinental railroad.

In the 1860s, Chinese workers were concentrated in the West in railroad and mining jobs. The railroad industry accounted for about 50 percent of the 30,000 Chinese workforce, and mining for a few thousand other workers. When the last spike was driven into the transcontinental railroad in 1869, about 25,000 railroad employers were out of work. By 1873, riches from the mines could no longer be extracted with an ax and a pan. More sophisticated mining procedures—those utilized by mining companies—were needed. The Chinese sought work wherever they could—in company mines, in factories, on farms, in domestic service. They often took jobs that were disdained by White workers and were working when thousands of Whites were not. The labor market thus became flooded and the depressions of the 1870s cast a negative, hostile shadow on the Chinese.

The Chinatowns that emerged as a result of these circumstances were made up of primarily men. For example, of the 100,686 Chinese in the United States in 1880, only 4,779 were women. Many of the early immigrants were hoping to save money and return to their homeland. In fact, about half of the men had left wives and families in China and anticipated returning home to them. Some men returned to China to find a bride with the hope of bringing her to America. Numerous immigrants planned to make the United States their new home and wanted to become Americans. About half of the immigrants

were "sojourners" and the other half were "settlers." For all, social activities were centered in the emergent Chinatowns, as Chinese merchants established shops and stores to provide culturally based goods and services. A Chinese merchant class eventually evolved that catered exclusively to the Chinese community. Like the original in San Francisco, small Chinatowns emerged in such cities as Chicago, Detroit, Minneapolis, New Orleans, and Augusta (Georgia).

During the Progressive Era, the Chinese population in the United States decreased from 107,488 in 1890 to 61,639 in 1920. The exclusion acts (discussed later in this section) contributed to this decline. The development of Chinatowns and the migration of Chinese to other parts of the country were attempts to escape racism, discrimination, and brutality of the West. This search drove many of the Chinese to seek safety in the Southwest, the Midwest, the East, and the South.[37]

Some members of San Antonio's Chinese population are descendants of the several hundred Chinese who were granted residence in the state by Congress because they assisted General Pershing in his 1916–1917 campaign against Pancho Villa. Hundreds of Chinese migrated to New York during the period of increased violence against them in the West. The Chinese population of Boston grew from 250 in 1890 to 1,000 in 1920. In some cases, the Chinese were brought in as cheap labor to work on specific projects and settled permanently in the area. In other cases, they migrated with the intent of establishing small businesses such as laundries, restaurants, and shops.

Discrimination

The Chinese experienced discrimination immediately upon their arrival in the United States. The racism against African Americans, American Indians, and Mexicans was extended to the Chinese on the West Coast. In addition to being non-White and non-Christian, they were considered an inferior race that was clannish, deceitful, and guilty of lowering the wage standard for White workers. They were referred to as "coolies," a term that meant transient laborers but took on an even greater derogatory, dehumanizing meaning when applied to Chinese laborers.

There was also a strong sense among Whites that the Chinese could not be assimilated into U.S. society and that their loyalty would always be to China. In the eyes of the American people, the Chinese were contract laborers who were only passing through the country to steal jobs and other resources from the more deserving White workers. The residential segregation that led to the development of Chinatowns only reinforced public attitudes that viewed the Chinese in a "we" versus "they" manner. Anti-Chinese attitudes were pervasive. In 1884, one writer noted:

> The Chinaman, unlike other immigrants, does not come to stay. He only seeks to accumulate as much during his foreign sojourn as will enable him to live at ease in his own country, to whose habits and traditions he closely clings. . . he can live more cheaply and compete advantageously in the labor market with the white workingmen who have families to maintain, and the usual duties of citizens to discharge . . . .[38]

Anti-Chinese sentiment grew so strong that societies were formed to address the "Chinese problem" and lobby for anti-Chinese legislation.

Racial Violence

Chinese were the victims of racially motivated violence from the beginning of their history in the United States.[39] The first documented violence against Chinese people occurred in 1849 in Tuolumne County (California) when 60 Chinese workers were chased out of their camps by White miners. Similar violence erupted in other California mining camps. In San Francisco, one of the largest riots was sparked in 1866 when the wage demands of White workers were rejected and cheaper Chinese workers hired. By the 1870s, such violence against the Chinese was the result of organized attacks, many of which were organized by anti-Chinese societies. With the economic crisis of the 1870s, violence against the Chinese escalated as they were blamed for the depressed plight of White workers. In one 1871 riot, 21 Chinese were slain, 15 by lynching. Raging racism fueled by a stagnant economy made the Chinese perfect scapegoats for White frustration.

Jew reviewed records of violence against the Chinese and reported that, from the 1850s to 1908, there were 153 such violent anti-Chinese incidents recorded with the following human costs: 143 Chinese murdered and 10,525 Chinese displaced.[40] A riot erupted in Milwaukee in 1889, although that city only had a population of 60 Chinese at the time. Up to 3,000 Whites took part in the rampage that lasted one day and one night and led to the destruction of the Chinese businesses. Overall, the decade of the 1880s has the distinction of being the period of the most extensive violence against the Chinese.

Chinese were attacked, injured, murdered, and/or driven from towns. Brutality against Chinese people took the form of shooting, lynching, burning, and stoning, and it became integrated into the history of the West. In 1879, Williams noted, "No country, no government, I undertake to say, has ever permitted the indignities to be cast upon any race of people, that the government and municipality of San Francisco and California have permitted upon this class."[41] The violence was not limited to California. It followed the Chinese wherever and whenever their numbers began increasing. The Denver riot of 1880, for example, destroyed every Chinese business and home in the city.

Health-Related Issues

In addition to the violence experienced by Chinese immigrants, Trauner maintains that they were also medical scapegoats in San Francisco from 1870 to 1905.[42] In 1870, San Francisco accounted for about a quarter of the state's Chinese population (the largest concentration in the state) but only totaled 5 percent of the city's population. In a matter of a decade, the Chinese lost their image of frugality and industriousness and became stereotyped as "a social, moral and political curse in the community."[43] In an example of foreignness being equated with germs and disease, outbreaks of malaria, smallpox, and leprosy in the late 1800s were erroneously linked to Chinatown, which suffered quarantines, fumigations, and the destruction of buildings in attempts

by the city to contain a targeted disease. While the city pounced on Chinatown to rid it of disease, little or no health-related services were made available to this community. While the advances of medicine led to the decline of
Chinese medical scapegoating, the city and county governments did not provide a medical clinic in Chinatown until the 1970s. This association between
disease and ethnicity was also extended to Japanese and Mexican laborers in
other cities such as Los Angeles during the Progressive Era.[44]

Injustices of the Law Enforcement/Justice Systems

Perpetrators of brutality were seldom brought to justice. Law-enforcement
agents many times witnessed racial attacks without interceding. Chinese
workers often retreated to the larger Chinatowns for protection. Although the
police provided little assistance in preventing the riots, they were instrumental in quelling some of them. This was little consolation for those who suffered
from these attacks. While law enforcement was lax in coming to the aid of the
Chinese, the law itself was being used as another weapon against this group.

The laws and policies against Chinese were so powerful during this
period that expressions such as "He doesn't stand a Chinaman's chance" were
quite popular. Such expressions mirror the lack of rights and privileges held by
the Chinese in America, particularly in California. The California Supreme
Court ruled that "the term Indian included the Chinese or Mongolian race,"[45]
thereby permitting the type of legal discrimination applied against American
Indians to be extended to the Chinese. Chinese individuals, therefore, were
barred from giving evidence against Whites in court. Writing of Chinese immigration in 1879, Williams asserted that this classification stigmatized the Chinese "by classing them with a race which has despised labor, has had no arts,
schools, or trade, and in the midst of the Californians themselves were content
to dig roots for a living."[46] This observation captures both the implications of
the ruling for Chinese individuals and the extent of prejudice against American
Indians. A judge of the United States District Court of California further ruled
that the Chinese could not become citizens because citizenship was extended
only to aliens who were free Whites or of African nativity or African descent.

In California, numerous state and local anti-Chinese legislation was
passed that taxed "foreigners," forced Chinese children to attend segregated
schools, targeted Chinese businesses for "special" licenses, restricted Chinese
fishing activities, denied Chinese admission to certain hospitals, and prohibited the hiring of Chinese workers for municipal jobs.[47] The anti-Chinese sentiment was so strong that a Democratic Party anti-Chinese rally in 1876 had
about 25,000 people in attendance.

It was the force of this sentiment that prompted Congress to pass the Chinese Exclusion Act of 1882. The act barred the entry of skilled and unskilled
Chinese laborers into the United States for 10 years, denied Chinese naturalization, and prohibited Chinese laborers' spouses from entering the country.
This act was not enough to satisfy its supporters, and other restrictions were
legislated. In 1884, the act was modified with more stringent restrictions, and
the Scott Act of 1888 banned the return to the United States of any Chinese

laborer. In essence, about 20,000 Chinese who had temporarily gone to China to see family and friends could never return to the United States. These people lost their businesses and whatever other possessions they had left behind in the United States.

Even though the law banned Chinese laborers, the Bureau of Immigration was so infused with prejudice that its informal policy held Chinese immigrants to be "deficient in a sense of the moral obligation of an oath," and immigration inspectors worked to exclude Chinese from admission to the country.[48]

During the Progressive Era, federal anti-Chinese acts continued to win support. In 1892, the Geary Act extended the Exclusion Act for another 10 years, and the Act of April 29, 1902, added yet another 10-year extension. Other acts restricted Chinese businesses, extended Chinese exclusion to the Philippines and the Hawaiian Islands, legislated funds for the use of a system to identify Chinese criminals seeking entry, and extended Chinese exclusion indefinitely. In 1913, one writer noted, "Every man in public life was under so binding a necessity to accept the popular belief in regard to the Chinese . . . that for one to seek the real truth of the matter was to end forthwith his political career."[49] Advocates for the Chinese people found themselves changing sides to avoid public attack. The Exclusion Act was not repealed until 1943.

According to Sung, "The Chinese were the only people specifically named in legislation to be excluded from the United States. It was an affront that still rankles in the hearts of many Chinese."[50] The racist nature of the exclusion acts and their legal perpetuation amplify the distinct history of this group in America—a history of how racism becomes converted into national policy.

Interpreting the Chinese Experience

The status of Chinese immigrants in the Progressive Era changed from sought-after laborers to a state of absolute rejection. Their contributions to the economic development of the West have often been rendered invisible. The type of racism and discrimination they endured required that their attackers deny or ignore all positive attributes, enabling them to categorize the Chinese in the vilest of terms. This shift in public attitude can be seen in an 1877 California State Senate report:

> We admit that the Chinese were, in the earlier history of the State, when white labor was not attainable, very useful in the development of our peculiar industries. . . . Now, to consider and weigh the benefits returned to us by the Chinese . . . they contribute nothing to the support of our institutions; *can never be relied upon as defenders of the State; they have no intention of becoming citizens;* . . . *and are a constant tax upon the public treasury* [emphasis added].[51]

These arguments subsequently were used against other immigrants of color, particularly undocumented Hispanics. In the case of the Chinese, the economic and political climates converged to identify a specific group of people as responsible for the ills befalling the West.

Opposition to the Chinese was strong enough to become a national policy agenda item. Once this happened, the history of the Chinese in the United

States was rewritten. This was strikingly apparent during the 1969 centennial celebration of the transcontinental railroad when then Secretary of Transportation John Volpe omitted from his speech any reference to the 12,000 Chinese who helped build the railroad. He credited "Americans" with tunneling through mountains and chiseling through granite to lay miles and miles of tracks. Since the Chinese railroad workers were not American citizens, Volpe's speech deliberately revised history to exclude the contributions of these "foreigners." Much of U.S. history has denied or minimized the significance of this group's involvement in America's development and the lasting effects of national exclusionary policies.

JAPANESE IN THE PROGRESSIVE ERA

Similar to the Chinese, the Japanese were at the outset welcome to our shores. . . . They took the place in large measure of the Chinese population that had begun to diminish year by year. However, the substitution of Japanese for Chinese was not a quantitative affair because Californians soon perceived that, unlike the docile, easy-going and subservient Chinese, the Japanese were ambitious, aggressive, and were backed by a proud, imperial government.[52]

Japanese presence in the United States became significant, especially in California, in the late 1880s as laborers immigrated from Japan and Hawaii.[53] Prior to this time, the census figures reported only 148 Japanese in the United States in 1880. Japanese immigration peaked between 1901 and 1908 when about 127,000 entered the country. In 1900, California had 42 percent of the country's 24,326 Japanese immigrants. By 1910, those numbers were 57 percent and 72,157, respectively. Some of this increase can be traced to the late 1880s when Japanese workers were recruited from the Hawaiian sugar plantations. The factors leading to the transmigration from Hawaii to California are not entirely clear. The Chinese Exclusion Act of 1882 created, no doubt, a need for another supply of cheap labor. This first generation of Japanese (Issei) was able to find work in agriculture (planting and picking crops), mining, and domestic service. In comparison to the Chinese, the Japanese, in some cases did work for lower wages. For example, in the 1890s, Japanese workers generally earned 50 cents a day while the going rate for Chinese workers had been twice that amount.

The Japanese seemed committed to upward mobility, and low-paying jobs were only a temporary means to economic improvement. Over time, Japanese workers were able to organize strikes that often resulted in wages comparable to those of other groups. In addition, working for someone else was also a stepping stone to land ownership, and numerous Japanese were gradually able to purchase land. Further, in their businesses, it was not uncommon for Japanese to employ other Japanese. Their strong desire for economic mobility meant that, in general, many Japanese were not satisfied to permanently occupy menial and low-paying positions.

Those Japanese immigrating to the United States were primarily male. For example, of the 23,326 entering in 1900, only 985 were female, and males continued to dramatically outnumber females during the Progressive Era. These laborers lived in segregated areas, often dubbed "Little Tokyo" or "Little Osaka," and maintained their culture and language. Japanese merchants were able make a successful living providing goods and services specifically to the Japanese community. A strong sense of community existed in the Japanese ghettos, and workers cooperatively joined together to save money. In describing the Issei pioneers, Mass stated,

> "Gaman," which connotes emotional self-restraint and the maintenance of strength and endurance in the face of hardships, was a primary value in the character of the Issei. A strong sense of family honor and esteem, requiring that one conduct oneself in a manner that will avoid ostracism, was also highly important.[54]

The success of the Japanese was documented in the growth of businesses and property ownership. The number of Japanese domestic servants decreased and the number of gardeners—a position of status among the Japanese—grew. In 1909, 1,380 Japanese-owned businesses were counted; land ownership grew from 2,422 acres in 1904 to 16,449 in 1909. By 1919, Japanese farmers owned over 74,000 acres, leased another 383,287 acres, and shared crops in still another 59,000 acres. In 1920, the Japanese farm income reached $67 million.

Economic success was powerless, however, in protecting the Japanese from discrimination as their ambition and industriousness were met with growing anti-Japanese sentiments among California Whites.

Discrimination

According to Kitano, the Japanese were in "the wrong country, the wrong state" at "the wrong time."[55] As they became economically competitive with Whites, much of the anti-Chinese sentiment was extended to include the Japanese. Fairchild summed up the similarity in public attitudes toward the two groups:

> With respect to the Chinese and the Japanese, typical American opinion has followed a similar pattern: first, a cordial welcome to these "quaint" and interesting foreigners who are willing to do unpleasant and menial work; then, as the numbers became sufficiently large to afford economic competition, violent and bitter opposition.[56]

Changes in public attitudes toward the Japanese coincided with the rise in Japanese worker strikes against White growers. Because there was not another readily available source of labor, growers felt cornered and thus yielded to the workers' demands for higher wages. This created an atmosphere of animosity in which employers held workers responsible for violating contracts.

By 1900, an anti-Japanese campaign was gaining momentum in California. This campaign may have been the perpetuation of anti-Asian attitudes that began earlier with the Chinese. In 1900, the mayor of San Francisco asserted:

> The Japanese are starting the same tide of immigration which we thought
> we had checked twenty years ago. . . . The Chinese and Japanese are not
> bona fide citizens. They are not the stuff of which American citizens can
> be made . . . they will not assimilate with us."[57]

Much of the initial anti-Japanese activity originated with the farm labor leaders and spread to the rest of the population. The newspapers stirred public outcry with warnings of a takeover by the Mongolian race. The San Francisco *Chronicle* was fierce in its attack of the Japanese with such headlines as "Crime and Poverty Go Hand and Hand with Asiatic Labor," "The Japanese Invasion, the Problem of the Hour," and "Japanese a Menace to American Women."[58] The Japanese, as the Chinese before them, were described by such epithets as "filthy beyond belief," "an inferior race," and "aliens whose presence is inimical to health and public morals."[59]

Japan maintained an active interest in those Japanese who immigrated to the states. This interest was magnified by its response to the 1906 San Francisco earthquake. The largest contribution from another country came from Japan and totaled $246,000. Japan also maintained a watchful eye on the social and economic conditions of its former residents. While San Francisco did, indeed, need the money for rebuilding efforts, many Whites interpreted Japan's act of generosity as further indication that the bond between Japan and the Japanese in California was impenetrable. As with the Chinese, beliefs in the loyalty of the Japanese to Japan intensified. In the minds of many, the Japanese could never be loyal to the United States. Beliefs in the disloyalty of Japanese to America have haunted the Japanese throughout their history in this country.

Labor meetings were organized in San Francisco and other California cities to promote Japanese exclusion. Labor leaders were also instrumental in establishing anti-Japanese leagues; the Asiatic Exclusion League, formed in 1905, was prominent among them. Active participants in this league included labor leaders who themselves were European immigrants. These individuals firmly believed, as did thousands of other European immigrants, that assimilation could be achieved with the European nationalities but not with non-Whites. In their eyes, assimilation of Japanese and other non-Whites went hand-in-hand with a reduced standard of living, a lower level of civilization, and a reduction of White superiority.

Boycotts were launched against Japanese businesses, and whites were admonished to support White-owned and operated enterprises. The public was warned about the risks involved in eating food picked and prepared by unclean Japanese hands. Labor leaders' and newspapers' unrelenting attacks on the Japanese heightened public fear of this group.

Japan's 1905 victory over Russia did little to ease White feelings about the Japanese. Prior to this demonstration of military force, the United States and Japan had cordial diplomatic relations. Japan's ascension to the status of a world power, however, altered public opinion about the country and led many to conclude that a Japanese invasion of the states was possible, if not imminent. With the rise of "Japan and the Mongolian race," political and military leaders advocated strong military preparation to ward off attacks on Anglo-Saxon power. Social Darwinism moved from encompassing individual species to including nations as well.

The fear of invasion by Japanese immigrants and the fear of military invasion by Japan were captured by the popular phrase "yellow peril." This phrase underscored both a racial and racist ideology. The defined "menace" was a specific non-White racial group. The defense of America from the menace of this "yellow peril" became a rallying point for those who advocated the continued domination of White civilization in the United States.

Organized anti-Japanese activities and fears of the yellow peril persisted in the United States long after the days of the Progressive Era, and they erupted in full force with the World War II internment of Japanese Americans. This is but one example of how the Progressive Era formed the foundation of sentiments and beliefs that persisted over the subsequent years. The World War II internment camps represented the manifestations of the racism that was expressed and acted upon during the previous decades.

Racial Violence

Kitano observed, "It is perhaps surprising that in spite of the continuous verbal and printed attacks on the Japanese, there were never any equivalents to the Chinese massacres, . . . or to the many Negro lynchings in the South."[60] Nevertheless, Japanese were assaulted and businesses were vandalized, especially during the labor-organized boycotts of their businesses. In these assaults, the Japanese victims typically did not sustain life-threatening injuries.

In cases of attacks on Japanese individuals, there were attempts by Whites to attribute the cause of the conflict to other than racial motives. For example, an attack on a Japanese businessman could be dismissed as simply having been caused by a labor dispute rather than by the victim's race. Furthermore, President Theodore Roosevelt authorized the use of troops, if necessary, to protect Japanese from mob attacks. This may have been done to protect the country's diplomatic relationship with Japan and not out of a belief in racial equality. Regardless of the motivation, this position may have tempered the use of violence against this group.

Injustices of the Law Enforcement/Justice Systems

Law-enforcement agents provided little or no protection to the Japanese or to their businesses. During the boycotts when assaults increased, the police failed to intervene and attackers routinely went unpunished. Complaints filed by Japanese individuals were also routinely dismissed. The law-enforcement arm of the criminal justice system simply refused to enforce the law against Whites who terrorized Japanese victims.

The most brutal battles fought by the Japanese were not fought in the street but "took place in the courts, and the most visible Japanese scars were from legal decisions."[61] The state of California was unrelenting in its quest for anti-Japanese ordinances. In 1906, the San Francisco Board of Education issued a resolution stipulating that all Japanese in public schools attend the

Oriental school in Chinatown. Although President Roosevelt was able to have the order rescinded, discriminatory educational practices against children of Asian descent became as much a part of the West Coast as the Pacific Ocean. The discriminatory laws against the Chinese also applied to the Japanese, who were also called "Mongolian." Thus, the Japanese could not become American citizens and could not vote.

California's 1913 Alien Land Act stipulated that Japanese could lease agricultural land for up to three years and prohibited additional land purchases. Land already owned or leased by Japanese individuals could not be passed along to their children. This controversial act was passed despite the protestations of then President Woodrow Wilson who was concerned with Japan's reaction to the act.

Organized lobbying for restrictions on Japanese immigration led to a "gentleman's agreement" between the United States and Japan in 1908. Unlike the Chinese exclusion acts that explicitly prohibited Chinese immigration, the gentleman's agreement was negotiated, voluntary, and reflective of the United States' respect for Japan's status as a world power. This agreement seemed to be a compromise that was acceptable to both nations. On one hand, the influx of Japanese immigrants could be curbed, and on the other hand, Japan itself would control the flow of Japanese to the states by restricting the number of passports given to laborers. The number of Japanese entering the United States was significantly reduced until 1914, when the number of wives entering the country caused the figures to increase sharply. American diplomats had not anticipated the number of wives coming to join Japanese men already in the United States. Many of the anti-Japanese leagues saw the unanticipated rise in Japanese immigration in spite of the agreement as another example of Japanese deception.

The Immigration Act of 1917 that instituted the literacy test also contained provisions for the curtailment of Asian immigration.[62] This act established the Asiatic Barred Zone that prohibited the entry of immigrants from southern and eastern Asia. The racially based immigration policies of the Progressive Era formed the basis of subsequent policies. The post-Progressive Era immigration bill of 1924 with its 2 percent quota based on 1890 census data also had restrictions directed specifically toward Japanese immigration. The bill placed *racial* restrictions on immigration by prohibiting the entry of persons who were ineligible for citizenship—a group that included Asians. In 1924, only White and "Negro" races continued to be able to gain naturalization. Even if Japan had been permitted a quota, that quota would have been so minuscule as to be nonexistent. According to census figures, there were 2,039 Japanese in the United States,[63] and this base would have given Japan an immigration quota that was 2 percent of this figure—which amounted to only 40. This bill, in effect, wiped out Japanese immigration. Since the "Chinese problem" had been taken care of with the exclusion acts and since the Japanese were barred because they could not be naturalized, the "Asian problem" had finally been resolved. Immigration policy, as related to the Japanese, was not changed until 1952.

Interpreting the Japanese Experience

The American dream became the dream of Japanese immigrants in the United States at the turn of the century and they struggled vigorously to achieve this dream. They came to succeed, and succeed they did. They rose from menial, low-paying jobs to positions of affluence in agriculture and business. They epitomized the "rags to riches" story that was heralded as the American way. Something happened, however, on their way to grasping that gold ring of success. They apparently were too good, too effective, and too productive in living the American dream. They seemed better at the success game than the "real Americans," who often felt more deserving of the economic benefits of this country.

Those traits that had endeared Japanese workers to American employers (willingness to work at any job for any wage, ambition, determination) became weapons of attack. When the Japanese became staunch economic competitors to "American" businesses, they were recast as deceitful, greedy, and unethical. Restrictions, legal and otherwise, had to be imposed to keep them in their place. A group with a commitment to upward mobility became feared as the "yellow peril" seemed destined to menace California and the world.

Over the years, this history of racism, discrimination, and legal restrictions against Japanese individuals at the turn of the century has faded in U.S. and social work history. Oppression seems less associated with Japanese Americans than with other people of color. In fact, the characteristics that helped the Issei achieve the American dream of economic success have been glorified and generalized, creating the stereotype of the "model minority." The myth of the model minority hides the history of oppression and has been used to counteract charges of racism. In an analysis of the model minority myth, Crystal asserted,

> Asian Americans' apparently successful efforts at assimilation . . . have earned them the dubious moniker of the "model minority." According to this "model minority" image, Asian Americans' cultural traits—diligence, frugality, and willingness to sacrifice—propel their upward mobility and win them public accolades.[64]

This rewriting of history and the emergence of this myth deny the differential treatment received by this group. Consequently, *oppression* and *discrimination* are words not typically used to describe the Japanese experience in America.

SOME CONCLUDING OBSERVATIONS

During the Progressive Era, ethnic and racial groups in the United suffered severe and extreme hardships. White ethnics, with their darker skin tones and "deviant" religions, were in danger of polluting the melting pot with undesirable traits. African Americans represented a separate class of people altogether. After separating the American Indians from their tribal lands, the "Friends of the Indian" were deeply invested in rescuing children from the harmful effects of the reservation. Mexicans indigenous to the Southwest were driven from their land and were relegated, along with Mexican immigrants, to servile positions in a caste-like system. The perception of Chinese as unwanted competitors with White workers and as unassimilable culminated in national policy that banned Chinese from entering the country. Ironically, their success in realizing the American dream caused the Japanese to be reviled as un-American, unassimilable, and unwanted.

Suffering is suffering—regardless of which group is being victimized. It is not a matter of whether one group suffered more or less than another group. The key point is that all groups suffered *differently*, and it is precisely this difference that should *not* be minimized, trivialized, or homogenized. Each group, then, has a history of contacts with White America, American institutions, and American policies. The United States, as a nation, responded differentially to each group, and each group in turn was influenced by the history and form of America's response.

Although there is no doubt that thousands of White ethnics confronted nativism, discrimination, violence, oppression, deplorable living conditions, and life-threatening work environments at the turn of the century, racial minorities and ethnic minorities seemed to have fared even worse. White ethnics still retained a White identity that made them worthy of Americanization efforts.

White Ethnics and People of Color

Although many old-stock Americans were hostile to the immigration of the "new" immigrants, national immigration policies did *not* explicitly target this group for immigration prohibitions. Immigration acts that affected these newer immigrants were based on *screening* procedures, not ethnic or racial membership. Through the literacy test, individuals rather than entire races of people were barred from entering the country. Chinese and Japanese immigrants were expressly singled out because of their race, and immigration acts specifically named Chinese immigrants and other immigrants as ineligible for citizenship—a group that included Asians. This was, in effect, a *racial* barrier to immigration.[65]

White ethnics were seen as "undesirable" immigrants because of their cultures, religions, and peasant background. In addition, they were also people with darker skin tones. With the turbulent rise of nativism and the drive to keep America pure and White, White ethnics failed to produce a national scare of the magnitude of the "yellow peril." There was no pervasive popular phrase or catchword that epitomized fear of White ethnics, as was the case with the "yellow peril." Although White ethnics significantly outnumbered other immigrant groups of color, vehement racial protest was directed at other groups such as the Chinese and Japanese. With the rise of Japan's military position, the fear of Japanese invasion biased White Americans against the country as well as its people in the United States. In his analysis of the anti-Japanese movement in the United States, Daniels indicated,

> Most of the charges against the Japanese—their nonassimilation, their low standard of living, their high birth rate, their vile habits—were also made

against European immigrants. But only against Orientals was it seriously charged that the peaceful immigrants were but a vanguard of an invading horde to come.[66]

White ethnics were shabbily treated and endured the worst of living conditions, yet they never experienced the loss of property that marks the American Indian and indigenous Mexican history in this country. Through the force of physical violence and the judicial system, both Indian and Mexican groups were dispossessed of vast acres of land. These lands were needed to feed the insatiable appetite of Manifest Destiny, White superiority, and what was perceived by Whites to be God's will. White Americans had a tremendous sense of entitlement, and nothing was permitted to hinder this great American quest.

White ethnics were not uniformly singled out for sustained and extreme treatment. Each city, each group, and each situation resulted in varying reactions from old-stock, "real" Americans. The treatment extended to the White ethnics was related to the economic climate, the type of work the groups sought, and the degree of perceived deviance of each group. This was not the case for African Americans who, *by law,* were mandated to receive separate treatment. Unlike White ethnics, African Americans were explicitly named and singled out in *national* policy for treatment that was at variance with the White population.

White ethnics and people of color were victims of racial attacks that claimed thousands of lives and even more injuries. However, the magnitude and intensity of the violence levied against southern and eastern Europeans never matched that levied against American Indians, African Americans, Mexicans, and Chinese. In some cases, entire communities of color were literally wiped out by angry mobs of White men, women, *and* children.[67] These attacks, some of which can only be described as *massacres,* often involved the participation of White ethnics.

Some of the discrimination against White ethnics, Mexicans, Chinese, and Japanese can be attributed to the values, cultures, and religions of these groups. Even though American Indians were not immigrants, they still had cultures and religions that were "foreign" to Americans supporting nativism. Differences heightened antagonisms between groups and were used to rationalize harsh treatment. As a result, a "we" versus "they" mentality emerged. Although White ethnics were outside mainstream America, in comparison to the racial/ethnic minority groups they were much closer to the native-stock "we" than were any of the other groups. In fact, many of the old-stock, native Americans favored any type of European immigration over immigration from China or Japan.

It is more difficult to argue that discrimination against African Americans was, in part, derived from cultural and religious differences or that their way of life was "foreign" to America. African Americans in the early 1900s were more "native" to the United States than many of the old-stock settlers who arrived in the country in the mid-1800s. African Americans were the products of U.S. society in that they were transformed from Africans to Americans through years of coercive servitude. In the post–Emancipation years, African

Americans were struggling to prove their Americanism and desired full integration into society. Nativity and cultural congruence, however, could not halt the discrimination and oppression heaped upon them. It seems that color alone was the paramount cause of their disfavored status.

At the beginning of the twentieth century, White ethnics and people of color were considered "social problems" in America. Each group was in need of some type of intervention capable of producing desirable outcomes. The Progressive Era and its reformers did not provide equitable responses to these social problems.

Systems Theory and the Mexican, Chinese, and Japanese Experience

The history of each subgroup in America is filled with countless efforts to achieve the American dream. This history reveals the impediments that barred access to this goal. In the history of Mexicans, Chinese, and Japanese in the United States, there is a common thread that ties them together. The larger social system questioned their willingness to become true Americans, their ability to assimilate, and their desire to cast aside their "foreignness." Their worth to the larger society was defined in terms of the labor they could provide. When recessions struck, these groups were expendable because White Americans were given priority for any available jobs.

The Chinese and Japanese created communities that supported cultural values and traditions. Others outside these communities interpreted this to mean that these foreigners did not want to become part of American society. White Americans regarded the cultural differences of these ethnic minorities as hindrances to the forging of an American identity. Few, if any, efforts were made to Americanize these two groups since, according to popular opinion, their loyalty was to their countries of origin. The immigration legislation and racial violence were both examples of the types of social control mechanisms that were employed to contain these groups.

Mexican American and Mexican communities also had to deal with questions of loyalty because of the proximity of Mexico to the United States. The Mexican Americans who predated the Whites in the West and Southwest were often overlooked. There was little effort, at times, to distinguish the Mexican American community from the Mexican immigrant community. The Mexican experience is a hybrid one. For the immigrant, labor was of supreme importance. For the original Mexican Americans, land was of supreme importance. In both cases, Whites exploited and manipulated these peoples to acquire both.

All ethnic and racial communities attempted to achieve a stability or homeostasis that routinized their daily lives. This stability could only be achieved through the acquisition of resources needed to support community life. For these communities, self-determination was often not an option, as the larger society imposed barriers that constrained their progress and development.

Ethnicity, Race, and the Reformers

The Progressive Era is associated with reform, enlightenment, and liberalism. The middle class was beginning to turn its attention to the pressing social issues of the day. There were, however, limits to the progressivism of the period. Although progressives liked to think of themselves as free from prejudice, they simultaneously insisted that separate races could not mix.[68] The *Plessy v. Ferguson* decision echoed this view and the voluntary, and sometimes forced, segregation of other racial groups reinforced this position. In fact, the Chinese and Japanese were often described as "clannish" because they seemed to prefer communities composed of members of their own race. The segregation of African Americans was also linked to prevailing attitudes about the inferiority of this group.

The progressives further believed that Anglo-Saxons were responsible for the country's expansion and industrial growth. The continuing development of the country in the Anglo-Saxon way was predicated on the Americanization of the new immigrants. The White ethnics could gain coveted membership in the elite group through assimilation into the country's melting pot. Assimilation meant undergoing the process of Americanization that replaced ethnic values and culture with American ones. For the White ethnics, learning English and acquiring useful skills were the way out of the deplorable slums. With upward mobility, the "new" immigrants could become true Americans, with children and grandchildren who would be indistinguishable from descendants of the White pioneers.[69]

Americanization was set as a goal for all White immigrants—adults and children. The adults were an integral component of the process and were deemed worthy of Americanization programs. This approach differed from the Americanization efforts undertaken by the "Friends of the Indian," who concentrated on the next generation—the children. The American Indian adults were viewed as a lost cause that only interfered with the children's assimilation. The two interventions represent a stark and racist contrast. All members of the immigrant population could be Americanized, yet only American Indian children were identified as the beneficiaries of this process.

Americanization, however, was not perceived as the goal for everyone. In fact, some groups were seen as unassimilable and incapable of becoming part of the mainstream. In 1949, Kiser asserted, "In view of common social attitudes, it is not expected that a similar assimilation of the colored groups will occur in the foreseeable future."[70] Indeed, no amount of Americanization would make African Americans, Chinese, Japanese, and other groups of color indistinguishable from the descendants of White settlers. Even when it was first introduced in the early 1900s, the melting-pot perspective failed to embrace people of color.

One explanation for the assumption that people of color were unassimilable lies in physical characteristics of these groups. Regardless of longevity in the United States, some groups will continue to look "foreign" and will continue to be linked with that group's country of origin. For example, in an 1992 undergraduate sociology class at a major Midwestern university, a Japanese American student offered emphatic support for the equalization of sex roles. A White student responded, "Would you feel that way if you were in your own country?" To which the Japanese American replied, "I *am* in my own country. I am a third-generation Japanese American." To this day, ethnic/racial minorities are often perceived as maintaining some type of allegiance to their countries of origin. This perception is applied to Mexican Americans, Chinese Americans, Japanese Americans, and other Americans of color. African Americans, however, are sometimes exempt from this stereotype.

These allegedly unassimilable groups were also considered inferior to White groups. Regardless of status, all Whites were seen as superior to all people of color. In the words of a progressive spokesman,

> Race . . . counts more than anything else in the world . . . an Italian of the commonest standing and qualities would be a more welcomed suitor [for the hand of an American's daughter] than the finest gentleman of Japan. . . . The instinct of self-preservation of our race demands that its future members shall be members of our race.[71]

Minority-group status thus defined a castelike system in which people of color, especially African Americans, occupied the lowest positions. This is clearly reflected in Brandt's 1903 observation: "There are certain processes in the preparation of tobacco where the heat required is so great that White laborers cannot be used; in these departments the [tobacco companies] employ about 350 Negroes."[72]

By looking at race and ethnicity as elements dictating a caste system, Whites' responses to people of color during the Progressive Era can be more fully analyzed. With the exception of American Indians, people of color served as an invaluable source of cheap labor for menial jobs detested by Whites. African Americans, Mexicans, Chinese, and Japanese all filled this need. As each group sought to rise above this lowly position, violent attacks, discrimination, and national policy served to contain their progress. African Americans were becoming too vocal and assertive in their drive for equality, and national policy acted as a ceiling for that drive. As Chinese and Japanese rose to the level of economic competition with Whites, various pieces of legislation halted their entry into the country and curbed their economic growth. Numerous Mexicans were robbed of their lands and forced to eke out a living in service to others. Vigilante terrorist groups made sure that the Mexicans stayed "in their place."

Thus, the Progressive Era reformers were greatly influenced by race and color in their determinations of the appropriate place for various groups in society. Progressives defined which groups could be assimilated and the Americanization process necessary for assimilation. They acted in "the best interest" of some groups (African Americans and Native Americans) and in blatant opposition to others (Chinese and Japanese). As an ideology, nativism attributed an inherently inferior status to people of color. They were perceived as *childlike* races and, as children, they needed the direction and supervision of the superior race. Woodrow Wilson reflected this perspective about African Americans when he said, "[African Americans are] a host of dusky children untimely put out of school [by emancipation]."[73]

The Progressive Era was thus one stage in the country's continued movement toward its Manifest Destiny. Reform was not enacted in the structures and institutions of society; rather, it was embodied in the attitudes of the middle class and wealthy who began to take notice of the disenfranchised masses around them. Progressives felt that some of these masses should not be left to rot in the urban slums—that efforts should be made to raise immigrants to the level of "true" Americans. To some extent, the Progressive Era was also a conservative period in that the activities of the progressives posed little threat to their economic or social positions.

Although the Progressive Era was a period of considerable change and reform in areas of social, legal, political and economic life, its history has been garnished with various myths.[74] Although middle-class progressives, reformers, and professionals were clothed in liberalism as they embraced the downtrodden, these groups also depended heavily on the financial and political support of big business, large corporations, and influential individuals. Orphanages, reformatories, welfare charities, children's aid societies, and numerous similar groups conducted their activities and maintained their organizations with large donations from businesses and powerful people. As a matter of fact, most reforms enjoyed the support of big business. Although the Progressive Era stands for reform and liberalism in U.S. history, the role of big business in this era is often minimized. Progressivism was in part a businessmen's movement, and big business played a central role in the Progressive coalition's support of welfare reforms.[75]

In addition to guiding many reform efforts, big business may have also served to constrain such efforts by sometimes defining inappropriate areas for intervention. Numerous reform activities and strategies were consequently discouraged and curtailed because they were not supported by big business. In order for business to be this influential, the reformers and the businessmen had to share similar ideologies and values. In this regard, the conservatism that comes with protecting vested interests and elite positions may have infiltrated Progressive Era movements, and reforms were to benefit those deemed deserving and appropriate. This progressivism and liberalism do not appear to have extended to non-White populations.

This is the era in which the roots of contemporary social work were planted. What were the positions of the charity organization societies, friendly visitors, and settlement-house workers on the issues of race and ethnicity? How did they respond to the controversial issues surrounding particular groups of color? These and related issues are addressed in the next chapter.

Endnotes

[1] Roberto Treviño, "Facing Jim Crow: Catholic Sisters and the 'Mexican Problem' in Texas," *The Western Historical Quarterly* 34 (Summer 2003): 140.

[2] This discussion is drawn from Rodolfo Acuña, *Occupied America—The Chicano's Struggle Toward Liberation* (San Francisco: Canfield, 1972); Rodolfo Acuña, *Occupied America: A History of Chicanos*, 7th ed. (Englewood Cliffs, NJ: Prentice-Hall, 2010); Frank Bean and Marta Tienda, *The Hispanic Population of the United States* (New York: Russell Sage, 1987); Arthur Campa, "Mexican Americans," in *Racial Discrimination Against Neither White nor Black American Minorities*, ed. Kananur Chandras (San Francisco: R & E Research Associates, 1978), 54–67; Bruce Jansson, *The Reluctant Welfare State—Engaging History to Advance Social Work Practice in Contemporary Society*, 6th ed. (Pacific Grove, CA: Brooks/Cole, 2009), 131–137; Matt Meier and Feliciano Rivera, *The Chicanos—A History of Mexican Americans* (New York: Hill and Wang,

1972); Wayne Moquin, ed., with Charles Van Doren, *A Documentary History of the Mexican Americans* (New York: Praeger, 1971); David Weber, ed., *Foreigners in their Native Land* (Albuquerque: University of New Mexico Press, 1973).

[3] Acuña, *Occupied America*, 19.

[4] U. S. Government, Bureau of the Census, http://ww2.census.gov/prod2/decennial/documents/33405927v1ch13.pdf (accessed August 9, 2009).

[5] Vicki Ruiz, "South by Southwest: Mexicans and Segregated Schooling, 1900–1950," *Magazine of History* 15 (Winter 2001): 23.

[6] As quoted in Acuña, *Occupied America*, 29.

[7] Weber, *Foreigners in their Native Land*, 147.

[8] A detailed description of this can be found in Robert Treviño, "Facing Jim Crow," 139–164.

[9] Meier and Rivera, *The Chicanos*, 82.

[10] Ibid., 88–89.

[11] Robert McLean and Charles Thomson, *Spanish and Mexican in Colorado* (New York: Board of National Missions of the Presbyterian Church in the U.S.A., 1924), viii–ix.

[12] McLean and Thomson, *Spanish and Mexican in Colorado*, 13.

[13] This incident is detailed in Weber, *Foreigners in their Native Land*, 191 and Marilyn Holt, *The Orphan Trains* (Lincoln: University of Nebraska Press, 1992), 136–137.

[14] Kingsley Davis and Clarence Senior, "Immigration from the Western Hemisphere," *Annals of the American Academy of Political and Social Science* 262 (March 1949): 76.

[15] Bruce Jansson, *The Reluctant Welfare State*, 6th ed. (Belmont, CA: Brooks/Cole, 2009), 192–194.

[16] Moquin, *A Documentary History of the Mexican Americans*, 253.

[17] Samuel Bryan, "Mexican Immigrants in the United States," *The Survey* 28 (September 12, 1912): 728.

[18] Acuña, *Occupied America*, 131.

[19] This discussion is drawn from Clare Sheridan, "National Identity and the Mexican Immigration Debates of the 1920s," *Journal of American Ethnic History* 21 (Spring 2002): 3–35.

[20] Sheridan, "National Identity and the Mexican Immigration Debates," 9–10.

[21] Ibid., 29.

[22] The discussion of education is based on Ruiz, "South by Southwest: Mexican Americans and Segregated Schooling, 1900–1950," 23–27.

[23] As quoted in Ruiz, "South by Southwest: Mexican Americans and Segregated Schooling, 1900–1950: 26.

[24] Bryan, "Mexican Immigrants in the United States," 728.

[25] Acuña, *Occupied America*, 131.

[26] William Carrigan and Clive Webb, "The Lynching of Persons of Mexican Origin or Descent in the United States, 1848 to1928," *Journal of Social History* 37 (Winter 2003): 411–438.

[27] Moquin, *A Documentary History of the Mexican Americans*, 190.

[28] A detailed history of the land grants can be found in Phillip Gonzales, "Struggle for Survival: The Hispanic land Grants of New Mexico, 1848–2001," *Agricultural History* 77 (Spring 2003): 293–324.

[29] Moquin, *A Documentary History of the Mexican Americans*, 259.

[30] Robert Oppenheimer, "Acculturation or Assimilation: Mexican Immigrants in Kansas, 1900 to World War II," *The Western Historical Quarterly* 16 (October 1985): 429–428.

[31] This discussion is from Julie Weise, "Mexican Nationalisms, Southern Racisms: Mexicans and Mexican Americans in the U. S. South, 1908–1939," *American Quarterly* 60 (September 2008): 749–777.

[32] Weber, *Foreigners in their Native Land*, 152.

[33] Moquin, *A Documentary History of the Mexican Americans*, 190–191.

[34] Acuña, *Occupied America*, 10–31.

[35] Rosemary Chapin, *Social Policy for Effective Practice* (New York: McGraw-Hill, 2007), 190.

[36] Discussion on this topic is drawn from Jack Chen, *The Chinese of America*; Chinn, "Chinese Americans," in *Racial Discrimination Against Neither White nor Black American Minorities*, ed. Kananur Chandras (San Francisco: R & E Research Associates, 1978), 19–33; Jansson, *The Reluctant Welfare State*, 134–135; Louise Johnson, Charles Schwartz, and Donald Tate, *Social Welfare—A Response to Human Need*, 4th ed. (Boston: Allyn & Bacon, 1997); Paula Rothenberg, ed., *Race, Class, and Gender in the United States*, 2nd ed. (New York: St. Martin's Press, 1992); Betty Sung, *The Story of the Chinese in America* (New York: Collier Books, 1971); U.S. Department of Commerce, Bureau of the Census, *Historical Statistics of the United States, Colonial*

Times to 1957 (Washington, DC: U.S. Government Printing Office, 1960), 9; Carl Wittke, "Immigration Policy Prior to World War I," *The Annals of the American Academy of Political and Social Science* 262 (March 1949): 5–14; S. Wells Williams, "Chinese Immigration," *Journal of Social Science* 9 (December 1879): 90–123; Paul Wong, Steven Applewhite, and Michael Daley, "From Despotism to Pluralism: The Evolution of Voluntary Organizations in Chinese American Communities," *Ethnic Groups* 8, no. 4 (1990): 215–233.

[37] The Chinese presence in other parts of the United States is detailed by Jack Chen, *The Chinese of America*, 248–269.

[38] Bryan Clinche, "The Chinese in America," *The American Catholic Quarterly Review* 9 (January to October 1884): 67.

[39] The history of violence against the Chinese is recounted by Chen, *The Chinese of America*, and Sung, *The Story of the Chinese in America*.

[40] Victor Jew, "'Chinese Demons': The Violent Articulation of Chinese Otherness and the Interracial Sexuality in the U.S. Midwest, 1885–1889," *Journal of Social History* 37 (Winter 2003): 390.

[41] Williams, "Chinese Immigration," 108.

[42] Joan Trauner, "The Chinese as Medical Scapegoats in San Francisco, 1870–1905," *California History* 57 (Spring 1978): 70–87.

[43] Municipal Reports of the San Francisco Board of Supervisors, 1876–1877. As quoted in Trauner, "The Chinese as Medical Scapegoats in San Francisco, 1870–1905," 71–72.

[44] Natalia Molina, *Fit to be Citizens: Public Health and Race in Los Angeles, 1879–1939* (Berkeley, University of California Press, 2006).

[45] As quoted in Williams, "Chinese Immigration," 110–111.

[46] Williams, "Chinese Immigration," 111.

[47] A list of anti-Chinese legislation is found in Chen, *The Chinese of America*, 137–139.

[48] As quoted in H. M. Lai, "Island of Immortals: Chinese Immigrants and the angel Island Immigration Station," *California History* 57 (Spring 1978): 89.

[49] As quoted in Sung, *The Story of the Chinese People*, 49.

[50] Sung, *The Story of the Chinese in America*, 57.

[51] As quoted in Chinn, "Chinese Americans," 29.

[52] Eliot Mears, "California's Attitude towards the Oriental," *Annals of the American Academy of Political and Social Science* 122 (November 1925): 210.

[53] This section is drawn from Kananur Chandras, ed., "Japanese Americans," in *Racial Discrimination Against Neither White nor Black American Minorities* (San Francisco: R & E Research Associates, 1978), 34–53; Roger Daniels, *The Politics of Prejudice—The Anti-Japanese Movement in California and the Struggle for Japanese Exclusion* (Berkeley: University of California Press, 1962); Richard Hofstadter, *Social Darwinism in American Thought*, rev. ed. (Boston: Beacon Press, 1955), 189–191; Jansson, *The Reluctant Welfare State*, 134–135; Johnson, Schwartz, and Tate, *Social Welfare*; Harry Kitano, *Japanese Americans* (Englewood Cliffs, NJ: Prentice-Hall, 1976); Tsutomu Obana, "The Changing Japanese Situation in California," *Pacific Affairs* 5 (November 1932): 954–966; and John Van Sant, *Pacific Pioneers: Japanese Journeys to America and Hawaii, 1850–80* (Urbana: University of Illinois Press, 2000).

[54] Amy Mass, "Asians as Individuals: The Japanese Community," *Social Casework* 57 (March 1976): 161.

[55] Kitano, *Japanese Americans*, 14.

[56] Henry Fairchild, "Public Opinion on Immigration," *The Annals of the American Academy of Political and Social Science* 262 (March 1949): 191–192.

[57] As quoted in Daniels, *The Politics of Prejudice*, 21.

[58] Ibid., 25.

[59] David Crystal, "Asian Americans and the Myth of the Model Minority," *Social Casework* 70 (September 1989): 406.

[60] Kitano, *Japanese Americans*, 26.

[61] Ibid.

[62] A detailed discussion of immigration policy can be found in Edward Hutchinson, "Immigration Policy since World War I," *Annals of the American Academy of Political and Social Science* 262 (March 1949): 15–21.

[63] U.S. Department of Commerce, Bureau of the Census, *Historical Statistics*, 9.

[64] Crystal, "Asian Americans and the Myth of the Model Minority," 405.

[65] Hutchinson, "Immigration Policy since World War I," 18.

[66] Daniels, *The Politics of Prejudice,*: 68.

[67] The 1917 East St. Louis, Illinois, riot that devastated the African American community, for example, included attacks by White boys and girls. Details of this youthful participation are contained in *The Crisis* 13–14 (September 1917): 219–238.

[68] Daniels, *The Politics of Prejudice*, 49.

[69] Clyde Kiser, "Cultural Pluralism," *The Annals of the American Academy of Political and Social Science* 262 (March 1949): 128.

[70] Ibid., 128.

[71] As quoted in Daniels, *The Politics of Prejudice*, 49.

[72] Lilian Brandt, "The Negroes of St. Louis," *Publications of the American Statistical Association* 8 (March 1903): 238.

[73] As quoted in Florette Henri, *Black Migration: Movement North, 1900–1920* (Garden City, NY: Anchor Press/Doubleday, 1975), 211.

[74] Anthony Platt, "The Child-Saving Movement and the Origins of the Juvenile Justice System," in *The Sociology of Juvenile Delinquency*, ed. Ronald Berger (Chicago: Nelson-Hall, 1991), 10. Platt also provided a detailed discussion on the role of big business in the Progressive Era.

[75] Ibid., 13.

CHAPTER 5

Ethnicity, Race, and the Emergence of Micro Practice

> The antecedents of social casework were the friendly visiting and scientific charity practiced by the Charity Organization Societies (COS). Friendly visiting was a peculiar synthesis of evangelical community service, positivism, Social Darwinism, and social control.[1]

As the social work profession grapples with the challenge of ethnic-sensitive service delivery, it is important to note that this challenge did not arise this year or even this decade. The challenge has been part of the history and evolution of the profession. As the previous chapters show, the Progressive Era, when the profession began to take shape, defined a period that was saturated with significantly diverse groups, both new and established. Immigrant groups from countries not previously considered as contributing to the American identity were dramatically increasing in numbers. The South was dealing with its own issues of adjusting to the recently freed African American slaves. The nation's equilibrium was being disrupted with the forces of industrialization, urbanization, and immigration.

Social work came of age in this period as new ways of responding to the social ills that accompanied this disequilibrium. Numerous social work books detail the history of the profession and include overviews of the micro and macro roots of the profession. More recent books have added sections on oppressed groups in America.[2] The inclusion of this content in the social work literature helps students and professionals grasp some understanding of the deeply rooted and firmly entrenched racial attitudes and behaviors that have plagued this country.

Often these discussions seem to place this history outside of, or loosely connected to, the roots of social work. A brief note might be provided about the manner in which prevailing ideologies may have influenced the early social workers. For example, Jansson states:

> If we place the emerging profession in the larger context of the Progressive Era, we can see that its leaders were captive to the intellectual currents and political assumptions of the period.[3]

In reality, all social workers (and everyone else) are products of the society and times in which they live. For this reason, it is imperative to delve into the budding profession's service delivery practices with ethnic and racial minorities. Because relief work was embarking on a new trajectory, the attitudes toward and practices impacting the Progressive Era's diverse populations warrant greater attention. Trends and patterns of that era may have implications for the twenty-first century. Thus, this review may help to offer insight into the contemporary challenges that confront the profession.

It is essential to begin with the initial roots of the profession. The review will then move forward with an analysis of significant milestones in the development of the profession that have had reverberating effects on the profession's relations with minority communities, in particular with African Americans. Central to this historical analysis is the integration of a theoretical framework that illuminates specific events and their consequences. The application of such a framework moves the overview from the purely descriptive to the blending of theory, history, interpretation, and assessment. The incorporation of a conceptual foundation suggests that associations and predictive inferences can be drawn and advanced.

THE BIRTH OF DIRECT PRACTICE

Most social work texts provide general descriptions of the origins of social work as a practice and as a profession. These descriptions include discussions of the charity organization societies (COS) and the settlement houses. The COS and settlement houses represent the two distinct arms of social work that are described in the table below. These descriptions encompass the various systems in which the intervention occurs. The direct/clinical practice arm uses the individual, family, and/or other small groups as the treatment unit. Indirect/macro practice, on the other hand, targets social systems (organizations, communities, institutions, and other social entities) for change or reform. The table below summarizes the differences between the COS and settlement houses.

Charity Organization Societies	Settlement Houses
direct/clinical, personal practice	indirect social practice
retail practice	wholesale practice
social casework	social reform
micro practice	macro practice

Social work historians agree that the COS and the settlement houses were not as involved as they could or should have been in the concerns and problems of ethnic minorities. However, the determinants of this lack of involvement seldom receive in-depth discussion. In addition, the reform history of social work is often held as the premier example of the profession's investment in the plight of the less fortunate and its commitment to changing or reforming hostile, oppressive environments. There seems to be general adherence to the view captured by Ehrenreich:

The proto-social workers—charity workers, settlement-house workers, reformers, a group made up disproportionately of those of the middle class and who experienced more intimate contact with the poor, the immigrant, and the black, in daily life as well as in time of crisis—were perhaps *less susceptible to nativism and racism than were many others of their class"* [emphasis added].[4]

It is possible that the history many social workers would like to believe did exist at the turn of the century. Ehrenreich's belief elevates the early workers above the racism and ethnic animosities that preyed on the rest of society. This position also casts these workers as individuals able to accept people as people despite the prejudice and discrimination surrounding them. As the previous chapters show, stereotypes and racism were widespread, and if Ehrenreich's perception is accurate, the ability of the mothers and fathers of the profession to rise about them is commendable.

Then, as now, every method of social work practice incorporates certain ideologies that serve to reflect either "dominant-subordinate" or "self-determining" social relationships among its participants.[5] These ideologies must be recognized and examined if progress is to take place. Social work should not be exempt from systematic scrutiny of its philosophies, practices, and popular beliefs.

Placing social work in the context of its political economy and viewing it as a subsystem of a larger social system can promote an understanding and appreciation of the dilemmas it faced during its emergence and evolution. An examination of the dynamics driving the early workers and organizations suggests that their goals and direction could have probably been predicted. In this regard, the question becomes: *Could the long-term outcomes of the evolution of social work have been any different?*

THE CHARITY ORGANIZATION SOCIETIES

The charity organization societies (COS) predated the settlement house movement in the United States, but both were inspired by similar activities in Great Britain. Prior to the importation of these interventions, almsgiving dominated U.S. responses to needy individuals and families. Accompanying the substantial increases in the number of those requiring assistance came widespread concern that pauperism was threatening the moral fiber of America. There was also growing fear that coffers once swollen with philanthropic contributions would be completely drained by the demands placed on them. Lack of coordination and the absence of any guiding principles resulted in what appeared to be indiscriminate relief giving.[6] In response to the rising demand for alms and their decreasing supply, the COS were established as a rational, scientific approach to serving needy populations. The COS consisted of local, nongovernmental agencies that were designed to *coordinate* relief efforts; however, some COS eventually began to *distribute* relief.[7] Through the COS, local charities could be organized under one umbrella so that the indigent would only be able to receive assistance from one charity.[8] Furthermore, the establishment of case registries meant that all relevant agencies, including law enforcement, could collaborate on cases.

The economic crisis of the 1870s brought with it unemployment, hordes of beggars and tramps, and huge relief bills.[9] The climate was ripe for the pursuit of alternatives to the fragmented, uncoordinated charity efforts that merely passed out money to those in need. A new approach was also supported by the prevailing belief that the existing responses actually perpetuated pauperism. The first COS in the world opened April 22, 1869, in London.[10] The first American COS was organized in 1877 in Buffalo, New York, by Stephen Humphreys Gurteen, an Episcopal clergyman, and it seemed to be the answer to combating pauperism. According to Watson's *The Charity Organization Movement in the United States,* by December of 1912 there were 154 COS in the country.[11] Fifteen were located in the Southwest and were established after 1905.

COS Inputs

From a systems perspective, the COS required numerous inputs for its development and maintenance as an organizational response to a social problem. One major input was the *ideologies* it adopted toward poverty and the poor. A number of ideologies served to propel the work of the COS. In *A Handbook of Charity Organization,* published in 1882, Gurteen detailed the philosophy and beliefs at the heart of the COS.[12] The COS captured the belief that people had a "natural tendency" to shirk duty and hard work for an easy and "unchurchly" life. Essentially this meant that, in the eyes of society, people were inappropriately seeking aid rather than supporting themselves. One of the dominant missions of the COS was to "investigate" the applications for assistance. Gurteen indicated, "No relief (except in the extreme cases of despair or imminent death) without previous and searching examination." In this manner, relief to the "accomplished cheat" could end while only "the deserving poor" would be helped. He cited the English rule of giving "no relief to able-bodied men, except in return for work done" and asserted, "This work-test is one of the most perfect touchstones for discriminating between the deserving and the undeserving that has ever been devised."

The ideology of *self-help* can also be found in the work of the COS. For Gurteen and other COS workers, charity had to be tempered with judgment in order to avoid fostering dependency among aid recipients. According to Gurteen, the COS mantra was, "Help the poor to help themselves." This was *not* to be accomplished by "small doles of money or by provisions supplied indiscriminately week by week." Rather, the COS sought to show the poor the way to independence, self-respect, and responsibility. In the minds of the organizers, COS could prohibit paupers from assuming that assistance was an entitlement and could inhibit the long-term dependency of individuals on public dole.

The ideology of *Scientific Charity* also bolstered the COS approach. According to Wagner:

> "Scientific Charity" originally favored the repression of pauperism by the regulation of charity by scientific principles as well as the socialization of

the vast numbers of poor and immigrants who were crowding the urban areas. The ideology of "Scientific Charity" reflected the harshness of Social Darwinism and the Poor Law tradition as well as the benevolence of Christian revival and the *noblesse oblige* of service which had a long tradition.[13]

Josephine Shaw Lowell, founder of the New York COS, wrote that the "task of dealing with the poor and degraded has become a science, and has its well defined principles, recognized and conformed to, more or less closely, by all who really give time and thought to the subject."[14] The science of the COS was based on the thorough investigation of all who applied for aid.[15] (The implementation of this ideology of Scientific Charity will be discussed in the technology section.)

Social Gospel (discussed in Chapter 2) was another central ideology that shaped the work of the COS. Many of those affiliated with the movement had ties to religious institutions and saw their COS work as an extension of their moral mission. In reviewing cases from social work's early years, Tice reveals how the workers thought of themselves as saviors of public morality whose mission it was to protect society from the damning effects of wayward clients.[16]

The moral underpinnings of the work suggest that workers were attempting to socialize clients in the ways and conduct that were expected of them. Women and men were expected to behave in particular ways, and the visitors and others affiliated with the COS may have felt that their duty was to help implement the values of the larger society.

In the midst of poverty, numerous individuals were able to rise above their humble beginnings to achieve enormous success and wealth. In this era the accomplishments of the *nouveau riche* were held as reflections of their efforts, perseverance, motivation, and capacity to overcome seemingly insurmountable obstacles. In contrast, the poor, in essence, were thought to be poor through their own fault and required a gentle nudge (or a firm push) in the right direction. It became the duty (Christian duty, for some) of those with abundance to reach down and help those in need. Indeed, views toward the poor were echoed in the writings of Robert Treat Paine, Jr., President of the Associated Charities of Boston:

> Among the pauperized classes of a great city, the chief obstacles are two, usually found together: lack of all skill, and lack of all hope. They can do nothing well enough to get work, and they are sunk in despair. They will make no effort to help themselves, or if you succeed in inducing them to try, there is so little they can do![17]

Inherent in these ideological inputs about poverty were perceptions of the larger society. For example, charity workers generally accepted the premise that America's abundance made it possible for all able-bodied persons to rid themselves of poverty through hard work.[18] In this light, poverty was a reflection of individual flaws that needed correction, rehabilitation, or socialization. Belief in the availability of work was so strong that after the 1890s depression, Mary Richmond asserted, "In ordinary times, there is still work somewhere for those who have the will and the skill to do it."[19] While the COS work addressed individual needs and focused on charity (benevolence), the investigative aspects emphasized its rigid standards (stinginess). COS organizers failed to see that poverty could not be stymied with this "benevolent stinginess" but was rooted in the structural societal transitions occurring at the economic and social levels.[20]

Individuals also served as inputs for the development and maintenance of the COS. In numerous cities, three groups were involved in the COS movement: charity workers, who were usually paid agents and administrators; boards of directors, who oversaw the operations of the COS; and volunteers who were referred to as "friendly visitors."[21] In 1880, the President of the Associated Charities of Boston wrote, "The paid agents must become, if only after long study and patient practice and many failures, experts in the art of helping struggling families permanently upward, as well as experts making a diagnosis of the causes of need."[22] By 1910, the paid agents and administrators would be calling themselves "social workers."[23] The paid staff and the friendly visitors were the immediate predecessors of professional social workers, and the friendly visitors, in particular, were the forerunners of caseworkers.[24]

The paid agents were seen as peripheral to the core activity—friendly visiting—and were apparently employed to do the jobs that were frowned on by the well-heeled friendly visitors (who were mostly middle- and upper-class women).[25] Administrative tasks were not deemed worthy of the time of the friendly visitors and, in essence, the paid agents were paid to be of service to the boards, COS committees, and the friendly visitors. Consequently, in the COS, each position carried its own responsibilities and a hierarchy was clearly in place. Agents often conducted investigations for well-to-do contributors and other interest groups; volunteer committees decided what approach to take with each case; and the friendly visitors used their personal influence to accomplish desired changes in the family.[26] Personal service and those who provided it ranked high in the hierarchy.

Boards were often composed of influential men from the business community and/or those of the upper class. Many board members donated money themselves or provided a liaison with other philanthropists and brought with them a desire to improve their tarnished image by demonstrating that wealth had social as well as personal significance.[27] Because the charity organization societies depended on this group for funding and legitimation, the goals and technology of the COS were often defined by these board members.

Another major input to the COS consisted of the thousands of *volunteers* needed to conduct the friendly visiting. While the interest of dominant elite males dictated the course of action of the COS, women were primarily responsible for realizing the mission of the sanctioning boards.[28] The ideology of the larger society was embraced by the friendly visitors as they conducted their daily visiting with the poor. Indeed, the friendly visitors were from the privileged segment of society—the segment that sought to control the tide of pauperism. Through this cadre of female friendly visitors, the COS was able to act on the motto coined by the Boston Associated Charities, "Not Alms But a Friend."

The individuals and ideologies were staunchly middle and upper class. The charity organization societies were a response to the fear that large num-

ently bad or unsalvageable but rather as wayward children, unable to know or act on what was best for them.[35] These attitudes reflect the paternalism that often dominated the personal service provided to the needy. The visitors envisioned themselves as being neighborly and trying to establish common bonds with a fellow neighbor. Although these may have been the images the visitors attempted to project, the visitors and "visitees" were definitely not equals and were separated by class and other boundaries. The likelihood of true friendships developing was minimized by these differences.

The use of personal service through friendly visiting was predicated on the assumption that the poor would be receptive to these visitors entering their homes. Indeed, the visitors were able to make hundreds, even thousands, of visits, and this could be used to attest to the value the poor placed in this service. It could also be argued that the visitors and visitees shared common goals and also had mutual interests. However, an alternative explanation for why the visitors were able to gain access to their cases can be found in the power–dependence relationship that existed between the two.[36] Because they had access to resources that were desired by the visitees, the friendly visitors were thus able to wield some influence over the families. Because they desperately needed those resources, needy families would be unlikely to refuse the visitors entry to their homes and even less likely to question or overtly resist their "guidance."

Although friendly visiting is championed as the mainstay of the COS and frequently cited as the core activity, it is not clear to what extent the COS actually utilized this personal-service approach to attacking poverty. In research on the history of the charity society movement, Lewis provided some data on this subject.[37] It is difficult to determine a pattern from the available data, but numbers for specific societies in 1892 were reported. For example, Boston had 683 visitors, Brooklyn had 532, and Baltimore reported 195. These were the only societies that appeared to have a pool to accommodate a significant portion of their caseloads. New York had only 218 friendly visitors and served about 7,500 cases a year. Data further revealed that 53 societies reported having over 3,500 friendly visitors, with 1,628 coming from the four societies just mentioned. Some 44 societies provided assistance to almost 75,000 cases. These figures, coupled with the fact that the visitors averaged a caseload of between one and four families, led Lewis to conclude that "the service of a friendly visitor was available to a small minority of the societies' beneficiaries."[38]

It appears that the exercise of discretion was also a significant aspect of the COS technology. The societies had to make some determination about the distribution of their friendly visitors since every case could not be assigned a visitor. This means that specific case factors, specific friendly-visitor factors, and/or specific organizational factors were instrumental in the decision-making process.

The charity organization societies had three other primary aspects in addition to relying on friendly visitations: (1) the careful study of every case, (2) the development and maintenance of central registration procedures, and (3) planning and coordination between charity agencies.[39] The thrust of the intervention was directed toward uncovering the circumstances surrounding an bers of poor people could become a dominant force in U.S. society and threaten the middle and upper classes. To a certain extent, the privileged classes banded together to create a mechanism for curbing the extinction of a society they cherished—a society with roots in small-town America and its small-town values. These groups were experiencing an America in a transition spurred by the urbanization, industrialization, and immigration detailed in the previous chapter. They were fearful that these changes would eventually lead to the demise of the America they loved and wanted to maintain. In a sense, the COS represented the middle and upper classes circling their wagon train against the onslaught of destructive forces. Although the COS promoted services to the lower classes, these organizations were a means of further solidifying the class boundaries that separated the haves from the have-nots. Through the COS, it was believed that the poor could learn the ways and values necessary to raise themselves from their unfortunate plight. According to Lubove, "Charity organization represented, in large measure, an instrument of urban social control for the conservative middle class."[29] This view has also been expressed by other writers.[30]

Technologies of the COS

In 1880, Robert Treat Paine, Jr., President of the Associated Charities of Boston, detailed the goals of the friendly visitor: to make sure that children did not grow up paupers, to aid in finding work for all who are able to work, to train in skill all who are deficient, to make sure that health and home are as well as may be, and to inspire new hope and self-respect.[31] When visiting the poor, the friendly visitor was expected to counsel family members and offer assistance in the context of friendship that was assumed to develop between the visitor and her charges. Ideally, through her presence, nurturance, concern, and example, the poor were to be moved to improve their lot. To some extent, assumptions about friendly visiting went beyond *noblesse oblige* because it captured the hope that interclass contact would benefit *all* classes and promote a sense of fellowship and community.[32]

While interclass contact had the potential of facilitating understanding between all parties, the role of the visitor in "showing" the poor the way to independence was the key element of friendly visiting. The Reverend D. O. Kellogg asserted in 1880 that pauperism was a "sign of moral weakness" and that the "victims of unsociable habits" needed "to see a world of pleasure and honor opened to them in the companionship of the refined and the pure-souled." He further noted, "Qualities of mind and heart are learned not only by imitation, but by contagion. . . . The educational power of association is of incalculable strength."[33] Also in 1880, Paine noted, "Volunteer visiting is the only hope of civilization against the gathering curse of pauperism in great cities."[34]

In the name of friendship, the friendly visitor would establish contact with a family. She sought to gain the family's trust as she exerted her personal influence over the family. The visitor often approached the poor as one would approach a child in need of molding—a gentle push in this direction, a more forceful nudge in another direction. The poor were not seen as inher-

Case-by-case investigations were a means of curtailing the willy-nilly almsgiving that had dominated charity work in previous years. This scientific approach to charity produced numerous detailed reports on the conditions of various groups in U.S. urban settings. For example, the Charity Organization Department of the Russell Sage Foundation, under the directorship of Mary Richmond, studied 985 widows known to nine COS in 1910.[43] This report captures both the emphasis on individual circumstances and the moralizing that so dogged COS efforts. Some 61 individual cases are presented to depict the most difficult cases. In noting the characteristics of these 61 widows as mothers, such categorizations as good, fair, immoral, intemperate, untidy with poor children, untruthful and extravagant, and having very low standards are used.

According to this study, for the 799 cases for which the cause of the husband's death was recorded, 29 percent of the deaths were due to tuberculosis, and other health-related causes accounted for approximately another 25 percent. This meant that over half the wives became widows because of illness or disease. In addition, 9 percent had lost their husbands through industrial accidents. Furthermore, over half of these industrial-death widows collected no compensatory damages for the losses caused by the accidents. As reported in the previous chapter, living conditions contributed to the incidence of illness among the poorer populations confined to the worst areas of the city. Chapter 2 pointed out that many workers toiled in unsafe jobs in hazardous settings. It is not surprising, then, that numerous families were thrust into destitution with the death of the breadwinner.

The COS did not tackle the larger structural problems surrounding the causes of widowhood. These organizations appeared to accept the environment as a given and to devote their efforts to helping families cope with and respond to their crises. The COS helped families secure medical assistance, provided dietary instruction, and offered the services of volunteer visitors. Volunteers acted in a variety of ways. For example, they taught children housework; monitored the schooling of the children; secured special medical help; taught cooking, sewing, and recordkeeping; found work for some women; and met many emergencies.

COS responses were, thus, predictable. The external and internal polities and economies blinded these organizations to the larger picture that placed individual ills in a social context. Because those involved in the COS movement were beneficiaries of the fruits of society and were convinced that success was a combination of hard work and moral living, they saw hardships as tests of human nature. The fact that thousands of individuals were being harshly tested may have reinforced the view that poorer classes were defective and in need of moral guidance.

The ideologies and individuals are not the only examples of the social control aspect of the COS. There was another means by which the COS sought to achieve their goals, and this vehicle is often overlooked in the historical COS literature. A concrete and vivid example is the organizations' reliance on the police for controlling immoral as well as illegal behavior. COS administrators often perceived poor communities with recreational activities consisting of penny arcades and small theaters to be a problem. Stage managers kept "a individual family's impoverished state and developing a unique response to that family's circumstances. The technology was, in fact, derived from the manner in which the societies' organizers and their supporters defined poverty and individual responsibility. The focus on the individual in problem definition gave rise to the focus on the individual in the search for problem resolution.

Investigations, or the careful study of every case (derived from the Scientific Charity ideology), became one of the dominant missions of the COS. In describing the methods of operation, McCulloch wrote in 1879 that, for the Indianapolis organization, the steps were as follows:

> The name and address of the applicant are entered upon the applicant book. Then [in] the record book are entered those facts which it thought necessary to know. These are: birth-place; previous residence; time in the city; landlord; physician; age; name of women before marriage; occupation; income; children—their names, ages, schools, earnings; rent and rent due; pawn tickets; help, if any, received from any other source; relations in the city or elsewhere able to assist.[40]

A personal visit was typically made to verify the information given by the applicant. This intake process was designed to ferret out the unworthy to guarantee that only the worthy would be extended relief. According to Abel, the COS emphasis on "science" was a response to the medical profession's advances in the diagnostic techniques used to treat disease.[41] These advances were giving medicine a significant claim to scientific authority. By also adopting scientific methods, the COS sought to gain social legitimacy.

The external polity and external economy of the COS dictated that the organizations pursue conservative approaches. These organizations emerged from political boundaries that favored the middle and upper classes and defined the "appropriate" change strategies to develop. Within the organizations, the polity and economy favored techniques that focused on individual-level interventions. Case-by-case investigations could reveal the underlying causes for a family's plight and form the basis of directed assistance. The organizational constitution was framed by (1) powerful volunteers who felt it was their duty to help the needy, (2) the power held by the providers of financial support to the organization, and (3) a reliance on investigation and friendly visiting.

Because the actual provision of monetary assistance was often secondary to scientific case investigations, the COS garnered a reputation for being miserly and stingy. An Irish poet, John Boyle O'Reilly, poked fun at the Boston organization by penning these sarcastic lines:

> The organized charity, scrimped and iced,
> In the name of a cautious, statistical Christ.[42]

This ditty also targets the role religion played in justifying the charity organization societies' approach to financial assistance. Clearly, with the COS, personal service rather than material help was seen as the major intervention strategy. The poor of the day may have not embraced this concept as enthusiastically as the COS organizers.

weather eye open for the social worker, with a policeman in tow, out to preserve the integrity of the American home."[44] As another example, the New
York COS hired a detective in 1886 to investigate beggars and then had 200
loiterers arrested and jailed.[45] One Chicago district COS agent, Eugene Lies,
advocated in 1905 for "close cooperation of police and charities"; the establishment of a "squad of state police" to apprehend and prosecute vagrants;
and the "establishment of a mendicancy police corps in Chicago."[46] Although
this position may have been extreme, its extremeness was not the reason for
its lack of implementation. The massive politics involved in such a plan and
the lack of interagency coordination can be blamed.

Numerous groups in society did not view police officers as helpful or supportive. In some cases, as noted in Chapter 2, the police themselves were
often involved in perpetrating acts of violence against specific groups. For the
COS, however, the police became a significant part of the "treatment" process.
Activities and individuals could be controlled with the swift action of a police
officer and the societies were not hesitant in applying the force of the law.

Some organizations had special departments that concentrated on elimi-
nating vagrancy. For example, the New York COS maintained such a special
department and reported on the 1885 activities of the special officer:

> Our special officer, in addition to daily inspection of some of their
> [vagrants and beggars] various resorts, has caused the arrest, warned,
> and investigated upwards of 700 beggars, of whom 63½% were able-
> bodied men and women capable of earning an honest living . . . 216 of
> these were arrested.[47]

In some ways, the COS exerted a heavy hand over those unfortunate enough to
seek out an existence on the urban streets. These enforcement activities seemed
to be aimed at the total removal of "immoral" people and "immoral" activities
from city landscape. For many individuals, the law-enforcement aspects of the
COS overshadowed the potential benefits of other COS interventions.

The COS and Immigrants

The COS devoted much effort in assisting immigrants in adapting to U.S.
society. After all, it was the rapid growth of cities and the concomitant social
ills (presented in Chapter 2) that triggered the search for more creative ways of
responding to these societal transitions. The economic cycles of growth, reces-
sion, and depression added to the already long list of problems facing both the
immigrant and native-born American populations. While the native-born
groups faced primarily economic hardships, the foreign-born population also
faced issues regarding adaptation to their new home. According to Johnson
and Schwartz, the COS did focus their concern on "this group of unadapted,
newly urbanized people" in their hopes of helping them "establish a life-style
congruent" with the "urban American societal system."[48] Ehrenreich went on
to assert that charity agencies and social workers imposed their "ideas of
proper living habits, family patterns, and behaviors" that defined "right living"
in their work with immigrants.[49] In addition, immigrants were not conspicuous

among the friendly visitors, paid agents, or directors, and this absence further attests to the middle-class Protestant American base of the COS.[50]

The COS thus became a vehicle for facilitating the Americanization of immigrant groups. Families were taught the art of housekeeping and the value of cleanliness. The social origins of the American emphasis on cleanliness can apparently be traced to the Progressive Era when immigrants were viewed as "dirty" and acculturation and assimilation required them to become "clean."[51] The COS became agents for transmitting the value of cleanliness. Many of the COS thus maintained the same position toward the new immigrants as did other Progressives (discussed in Chapter 2): They needed to be Americanized. With this goal in mind, numerous friendly visitors and paid agents set about the task of "encouraging" these newcomers to adopt American child-rearing practices, medical practices, diet, and clothing.[52]

However, the wave of "new" immigrants flooding the country at the turn of the century (as described in Chapter 2) posed unique challenges for the COS. Indeed, the COS rose to meet these challenges but carried with them the same nativism that marked other Progressives. As noted earlier, these antiforeign sentiments were directed against those immigrants with darker coloring and starkly "foreign" cultures, languages, and practices. The *Thirteenth Annual Report* of the Associated Charities of Boston, published in 1882, captured the frustrations experienced by COS workers and volunteers:

> Until the Italians became numerous, we had at least intelligent means of communication with most of the families we knew . . . [but the Italians] are truly foreign to us. We do not speak a common language; our standards have no meaning to them, and we may well doubt whether they have any applicability.[53]

In addition, in a review of the cases handled by the Minneapolis COS from 1900 to 1930, Stadum noted that culture and ethnicity were given slight attention and, in a third of the cases she studied, workers failed to indicate their nationality.[54] This slight attention may have been because the COS of this city did not include many of these "new" immigrants on their personal service caseloads. For example, the 1910 annual report of this organization stated that eastern Europeans did not understand America, nor did America understand them.[55]

These immigrants were not among those cases held in high regard by the friendly visitors. Although these families did receive services, it does not appear that they were offered with the same frequency and intensity as those offered to the more favored groups. This may be an area in which discretion was exercised to determine which cases would receive the attention of the friendly visitors.

The study of 985 widows known to COS in 1910 gives a glimpse into the caseloads of the COS.[56] In this report, 61 case summaries are presented with summary paragraphs that indicate the nationality of the widows. Of these 61, well over half were from the "desirable" immigrant countries of northern and central Europe. Only a quarter of the widows were from eastern and southern Europe. Approximately 16 percent were native-born Americans. Of those from the "undesirable" countries, 60 percent were Italian. Abel's review of records from the New York COS covering cases from the year 1916 showed that 30 percent of the cases were native-born Americans, the largest of all the groups receiving services.[57] These figures could mean that the friendly visitors and the paid agents were more comfortable working with those families who were more "American" and were further along on the assimilation continuum. It could also mean that those individuals with more "foreign" cultures were not socialized in the help-seeking process and did not have cultures that supported intervention by strangers. Whatever the reason, it does appear that personal and other services were available on a limited basis to the "new" immigrants.

Thus, the focus on the individual emerged in the COS work with the White ethnic groups. The key to the success of these groups, according to COS ideology, was adaptation, assimilation, and personal initiative. Many COS studied the extent of poverty within these various groups to ascertain those group characteristics that either encouraged or discouraged pauperism.[58] The charity organization societies, therefore, were committed to assisting the "new" immigrants in eradicating those traits deemed undesirable so that Americanization could be facilitated.

The COS and African Americans

> When one considers the size of the Negro problem in the South, and when one appreciates the fact that charity organization is a plant of slow growth, one is not surprised to learn that the problem of family rehabilitation among Negroes except in a few places such as Memphis has remained largely untouched.[59]

The COS were generally established in the urban areas of the North and East and began to extend their presence in other parts of the country. The above quote indicates that, even in the southern states with their large population of African Americans, the COS remained largely unresponsive to this group's needs. Watson further indicates,

> The feeling in Savannah and elsewhere in the South seemed to be to care for the needy white families first and gradually extend the work to the colored. This was sometimes justified by the low standards of living generally obtaining among the latter.[60]

While this was the case for COS in the South, it is important to study the relationship between the COS and African Americans in the areas where the COS existed in greater abundance.

Because the birth of the COS was in the northern and eastern states, the ethnic/racial minorities in those areas would appear to be the logical groups on which to focus. As noted in chapters 3 and 4, American Indians were confined to reservations, the Mexicans were concentrated in the Southwest, and the Chinese and Japanese were primarily located in the West. African Americans were the only group with a significant population in those areas with COS, and this group dominates the discussion here.

It has been generally asserted that African Americans were rarely the beneficiaries of COS services.[61] Because the COS engaged in several types of activities, an overview of their activities and services to and on behalf of African Americans is informative.

The Study of Social Conditions.   One major COS activity, as previously indicated, was thorough investigations of social problems. African Americans were the focus of some of these studies. The charity organization societies were instrumental in publishing reports and investigations in their journals on the *conditions* of African Americans. Although studies of other ethnic minority groups were also reported, these studies were relatively infrequent.[62] The COS provided significantly more coverage of *issues* pertaining to African Americans. For example, the June 1897 issue of *The Charities Review* reported on the second Atlanta University conference on problems of the urban African American that was held the month before. The September 1899 issue of *The Charities Review* contained an article on "The Negro's Fitness" that featured statistics on African Americans in educational pursuits. In addition, the October 7, 1905, special issue of *Charities,* according to its introduction, was "devoted from cover to cover to the social interests of the Negroes in the northern cities."[63] This issue offered reports on such topics as the West Indian Migration to New York, the housing problems faced by this group, and a census on the African American population of Baltimore.

Alvin Kogut, in an article entitled "The Negro and the Charity Organization Society in the Progressive Era," reviewed the discussions about "Negroes" in the journals of the COS and noted that interest in this group was probably at its highest from 1903 to 1906.[64] The review indicated that the COS did concern themselves to a certain extent with the issues surrounding the urban African American population. The COS reports have been particularly useful in documenting the extent of discrimination in housing and employment facing this group. Indeed, much of the information used in Chapter 2 to compare the plight of the "new" immigrants with that of the migrating African Americans came from early COS publications.

Kogut and others have also concluded that African Americans "probably benefited even less than other segments of the population from ongoing services of the COS and from COS support of such broader reform measures as housing code enforcement and labor legislation."[65] In writing of the African Americans of Philadelphia during the Progressive Era, DuBois likewise observed that, while African Americans receive "their just proportion" of the alms distributed, "protective, rescue and reformatory work is not applied to any great extent among them."[66] Consequently, the COS reports and investigations of the social conditions of Americans did not translate into hands-on services to African Americans.

Few African American Clients.   According to Kogut's content analysis, some COS believed that discrimination prevented them from obtaining employment for African Americans; thus, this minority group created unique problems for the COS. Rather than try to combat the discrimination impeding employment of African Americans, numerous charity organization societies concluded that their services were of little benefit to this group. This is further affirmed by the widow study conducted by the Russell Sage Foundation.[67] In the 61 case summaries, only 2 were "colored" widows. The lack of meaningful intervention between the COS and African Americans apparently fostered a particular reputation in this minority community. For example, one New York District COS experienced a substantial migration of African Americans but had few African Americans applying for relief.[68] Fueling the schism between the COS and African Americans was "the patronizing Lady Bountiful attitude of some of the social service groups" that irritated African Americans to the point that help from these social service groups was rejected.[69]

The COS seemed to have been unreceptive to the African American community. This attitude may have been conveyed in the projection of an unfriendly and cool atmosphere. Workers may have projected an air of disinterest and, perhaps, even disdain. Tice reviews the case of a worker who opened a case in 1905 for an African American woman. The worker noted in the record, "Because of the sentiment against colored people in that community, the visitor did not call again."[70] It is likely that the worker possessed some of the same attitudes that were prevalent in the community.

Ethnicity: A Credential or Means of Avoidance?   While the White friendly visitors may not have been visiting African American families, several organizations were still active in training African Americans to be friendly visitors.[71] For example, the availability of African American friendly visitors in the Baltimore area led to the establishment of separate boards in several districts. The Associated Charities of Washington had enough African American volunteers to hold a class to train them for friendly visiting. It should be noted that one COS was known to operate a separate "Negro auxiliary known as the Colored Federated Charities" that had "a board of Negro directors."[72] Hence, some COS agencies were helping African Americans learn to work with other African Americans.

In 1928, Jones noted:

> The first colored woman to be employed as a professional family case worker . . . was taken on as a case worker in the New York Charity Organization Society in 1902. . . . Thus it seems that [the COS secretary] was the first white social work executive to realize the value of using competent, trained Negro social workers *for work among their own people, whose problems they could understand and whose needs they could well interpret* [emphasis added].[73]

The assumption that a group member is better able to work with other like group members was fairly common in the Progressive Era and was not limited to COS. For example, African American settlement houses engaged the services of African American workers.[74] Mexican American nuns were used in the mission work with Mexican communities because "they understood the Mexican culture."[75] In the New York COS records studied by Abel, it was clear that indigent Jews were referred to the United Hebrew Charities.[76]

Race or group matching appears to have significant advantages in that the group member possesses knowledge of the group's history, culture, values. A major disadvantage, however, is that group matching allows nongroup members to avoid contact with the group in question. By hiring African American workers, White workers did not have to interact with a marginalized group and were able to maintain distance from the group, possibly serving to reinforce or even increase the marginal status of this group.

Factors Limiting COS Intervention with African Americans. In general, COS members were aware of the prejudice and discrimination that faced thousands of African Americans. Journals documented the extent of housing segregation and employment discrimination. The African American community's inability to escape the slums and the vices that the slums attracted was known to the COS. In the midst of this knowledge, the COS apparently had little to offer this impoverished group.

The lack of COS hands-on personal service work with African Americans can be attributed to several factors. According to Axinn and Levin:

> Such interest in the plight of blacks as might have developed from direct contact was stifled by the relatively few blacks in the caseloads of Charity Organization Societies. Again, the small number of blacks in the North was partially responsible. In Chicago in 1900, for example, blacks numbered 108,000 in a total of 1,698,000. They ranked tenth among the city's ethnic groups.[77]

As the numbers of African Americans increased with the tide of migration, COS practices may have been so firmly entrenched that expansion to include the "new" migrants was beyond COS capabilities. There were apparently other factors driving the COS responses that may have been masked by the small percentage of African Americans in the urban centers of the North. As the numbers increased, these other factors were able to rise to the surface.

The COS members were products of the society in which they lived; therefore, they were not immune to the *racial ideologies* that permeated society. As noted in Chapter 2, Progressives and reformers believed some ethnic groups could be "Americanized" and assimilated into mainstream U.S. society. These Progressives also perceived other groups as poor candidates for Americanization. The COS organizers had the same opinion. After studying the COS reports and periodicals, Kogut noted:

> Significantly missing from the discussion in the periodicals was talk of "assimilation," although assimilation played a prominent role in relation to immigrants and immigration. . . . The goal of assimilation was not, however, held out for the Negro. . . . This shift in goal . . . symbolized the profound difference in white America's perception of the white immigrant and the Negro migrant. . . . But perhaps the major reason for COS behavior in regard to Negroes lies in the *racism that permeated society* [emphasis added].[78]

Thus, most COS were not active in fighting for or even seriously advocating for the rights of African Americans.

The racial ideology of the COS is illuminated in specific articles of the COS periodicals. For example, the October 7, 1905, special issue of *Charities* endorsed the opinion of Booker T. Washington that "the masses of colored people are not yet fitted to survive and prosper in the great northern cities" and the position of anthropologist Franz Boas that the Negro "shows the traits of a healthy primitive people with a considerable degree of personal initiative, a talent for organization, an imaginative power, technical skill and thrift."[79] It is not surprising that Booker T. Washington was frequently cited in COS publications. No person better exemplified charity's goal of fostering individualism within an ethnic group than Washington.[80]

The COS aligned themselves with individuals, both African American and non-African American, who espoused their views about the status and inferiority of African Americans. These paternalistic, patronizing views were not thought to be racist by those who held them. These views were believed to be sympathetic and in the best interest of this racial group because they held an optimism that African Americans were in an early stage of group development and, with time, would make needed progress. It does appear, however, that, in the minds of the COS participants and other Progressives, no amount of progress would place this group on par with native-born Whites or White ethnics.

In this October 7, 1905, issue of *Charities,* an article on "West Indian Migration to New York" noted that among these migrants "it may be said that a very desirable class, including recently numbers of intelligent women, take to domestic work and are very much in favor with their employers."[81] Belief in the suitability of African Americans for domestic and manual work found among Progressives and reformers was also present among the COS members. The February 6, 1904, issue of *Co-operation,* the journal of the Chicago Bureau of Charities, echoed this view in an article on an industrial program for African Americans in Virginia: "In a single generation, these women [mothers of pupils in the program] had lost the practice of those domestic arts which made the cooks and seamstresses of the slavery period so celebrated."[82] The potential of this group for other kinds of pursuits was not recognized as COS defined the parameters of opportunities available to them.

Another explanation for the COS stance on African Americans lies in the fact that *the COS movement was not a reform movement.* Improvement in the status of people was the result of changing individuals, not of changing society. The host of ills facing African Americans could not have been effectively cured by friendly visiting. Indeed, the disenfranchisement of African Americans required some sweeping structural changes. The COS were not really invested in defining the problems of African Americans as structural problems and were not convinced the existing social system needed revamping. Consequently, the primary interest of the COS was not in African Americans, nor did they view their deprivation or segregation as factors requiring broad social reform.[83]

The COS and other reformers of the day supported and advocated individual responsibility while adding to it the concept of *ethnic group responsibility.*[84] Clearly, numerous problems confronted African Americans as they migrated to the North and fell victim to urbanization and industrialization. No one denied that color was a liability that exacerbated the social evils surrounding most immigrant and migrant groups. The COS were swamped with applications from those they felt they could help, and there was not much assistance available to the more difficult cases. It seems that whatever was to be done for African Americans, in the minds of the COS, had to be done by African Americans themselves.

An adherence to the doctrine of ethnic group responsibility as emphatically applied to African Americans is identifiable in the COS writings of the period. COS journals routinely reported on the efforts of African Americans to reform, improve, and assist themselves. The October 1897 issue of *The Charities Review* described and applauded the work of African Americans on behalf of their own people.[85] Named were a "colored philanthropist" in Chicago who established a home for the elderly and a man of youth, intelligence, and experience who was appointed as professor at Tuskegee Institute of Alabama. An industrial school in South Carolina "started by the colored people themselves" also received recognition.

The October 7, 1905, special issue of *Charities* contains several references to the efforts of African Americans to improve themselves and results of the Atlanta University study on Negro crime—a study that was directed by African Americans. Indeed, the section of the issue entitled "Opportunity and Responsibility" crystallizes the role of ethnic group responsibility: "In his [the African American's] deprivation of one or the other [opportunity and responsibility] lies the explanation of much of what we call the Negro's problem."[86] Examples are then provided to show how a lack of responsibility and accountability resulted in some of the social ills that befell African Americans.

The 1902–1903 annual report of the Indianapolis Benevolent Society observed that African Americans were becoming involved in philanthropic activities in their communities and stressed that "our citizens should give these movements all the encouragement and support possible."[87] The June 1897 issue of *The Charities Review* contained a report of the second Atlanta University conference on problems of African Americans in the cities, and this report conveys the COS doctrine of ethnic group responsibility. Although several resolutions were adopted at the conference, only one was actually quoted in the article—"that the negro must reform himself, and that he is not dependent upon charity or municipal regulations, but has the means in his own hands."[88] Because this resolution was synonymous with the sentiments of the COS, it was given prominence in *The Charities Review* article.

Concluding Observation. The COS did not entirely neglect or disregard the needs of African Americans. Investigations into the group's social conditions helped to expose the harsh realities surrounding the stigma of race in the United States. Almsgiving to this community and the provision of personal services to a limited few should not go unrecognized. The contributions of the COS to this racial minority group is, however, significantly less than those given to the White ethnic immigrants who also crowded the cities during this time. The charity organization societies were products of their environments and depended on the public for funding, support, and legitimation. Those individuals inside the COS implemented the beliefs and ideologies that were extant in the larger society. In order to survive and maintain themselves, these organizations had to continue to embrace the groups and ideologies that gave them life.

The lack of COS emphasis on the needs of ethnic minority groups has often been minimized due to the prominent place of the settlement house movement in the quest for social reform. It is often assumed that whatever deficits incurred in the COS movement were more than compensated for by the settlement houses. For this reason, the next chapter takes a closer look at the settlement house movement.

Endnotes

[1] Stanley Wenocur and Michael Reisch, *From Charity to Enterprise—The Development of American Social Work in an Market Economy* (Urbana: University of Illinois Press, 1989), 31.

[2] See, for example, Rosemary Chapin, *Social Policy for Effective Practice—A Strengths Approach* (New York: McGraw-Hill, 2007); Bruce Jansson, *The Reluctant Welfare State*, 6th ed. (Belmont, CA: Brooks/Cole, 2009).

[3] Jansson, *The Reluctant Welfare State*, 199.

[4] John Ehrenreich, *The Altruistic Imagination* (Ithaca, NY: Cornell University Press, 1985), 41.

[5] Michael Reisch and Stanley Wenocur, "The Future of Community Organization in Social Work: Social Activism and the Politics of Profession Building," *Social Service Review* 60 (March 1986): 74.

[6] Gary Lowe and Nelson Reid, "The Professionalization of Poverty," in *The Professionalization of Poverty*, eds. Gary Lowe and Nelson Reid (New York: Aldine de Gruyter, 1999), 11.

[7] Jansson, *The Reluctant Welfare State*, 197.

[8] Carolyn Tice and Kathleen Perkins, *The Faces of Social Policy* (Pacific Grove, CA: Brooks/Cole, 2002), 104.

[9] Ralph Dolgoff and Donald Feldstein, *Understanding Social Welfare*, 7th ed. (New York: Pearson, 2007, 1984), 261; Roy Lubove, *The Professional Altruist* (New York: Atheneum, 1969), 2.

[10] Watson, Frank, *The Charity Organization Movement in the United States* (New York: MacMillan Co., 1922), 53. http://books.google.com (accessed June 17, 2009).

[11] Watson, *The Charity Organization Movement*, 360.

[12] Stephen H. V. Gurteen, *A Handbook of Charity Organization* (Buffalo: The Author, 1882), 27–35.

[13] David Wagner, "Collective Mobility and Fragmentation: A Model of Social Work History," *Journal of Sociology and Social Welfare* 13 (September 1986): 667.

[14] As quoted in Emily Abel, "Medicine and Morality: The Health Care program of the New York Charity Organization Society," *Social Service Review* 71 (December 1997): 638.

[15] Abel, "Medicine and Morality: The Health Care program of the New York Charity Organization Society," 638.

[16] Karen Tice, *Tales of Wayward Girls and Immoral Women—Case Records and the Professionalization of Social Work* (Urbana: University of Illinois Press, 1998), 14–15.

[17] Robert Treat Paine, Jr., "The Work of Volunteer Visitors of the Associated Charities among the Poor," *Journal of Social Science* 12 (December 1880): 112.

[18] James Lane, "Jacob A. Riis and Scientific Philanthropy during the Progressive Era," *Social Service Review* 47 (March 1973): 39.

[19] As quoted in Verl Lewis, "The Development of the Charity Organization Movement in the United States 1875–1900: Its Principles and Methods" (D.S.W. diss., Western Reserve University, 1954): 185–186.

[20] Lubove, *The Professional Altruist*, 9.

[21] Kenneth Kusmer, "The Functions of Organized Charity in the Progressive Era: Chicago as a Case Study," *Journal of American History* 60 (December 1973): 659–660.

[22] Robert Paine, Jr., "The Work of Volunteer Visitors of the Associated Charities among the Poor," *Journal of Social Science* 12 (December 1880): 105.

[23] Kusmer, "The Functions of Organized Charity," p. 660.

[24] Dolgoff and Feldstein, *Understanding Social Welfare*, 261; Louise Johnson and Charles Schwartz, *Social Welfare: A Response to Human Need*, 2nd ed. (Boston: Allyn & Bacon, 1991), 8, 16. These roots of social work have also been noted in numerous other sources.

25 Wagner, "Collective Mobility and Fragmentation," 667.
26 Ralph Pumphrey and Muriel Pumphrey, "The Charity Organization Society," in *The Heritage of American Social Work*, ed. Ralph Pumphrey and Muriel Pumphrey (New York: Columbia University Press, 1961), 169.
27 Kusmer, "The Functions of Organized Charity," 672, 674.
28 Beverly Stadum, "A Critique of Family Case Workers 1900–1930: Women Working with Women," *Journal of Sociology and Social Welfare* 16 (September 1990): 74. See also C. A. Chambers, "Women in the Creation of the Profession of Social Work," *Social Service Review* 60 (March 1986): 1–33.
29 Lubove, *The Professional Altruist*, 5.
30 See for example, Ehrenreich, *The Altruistic Imagination*; M. E. Gettleman, "Charity and Social Classes in the United States," I, II, *American Journal of Economics and Sociology* 22 (April, July 1963): 313–329; 417–426; J. Leiby, "Charity Organization Reconsidered," *Social Service Review* 58 (December 1984): 523–538.
31 Paine, Jr., "The Work of Volunteer Visitors," 114.
32 Kusmer, "The Functions of Organized Charity," 662.
33 D. O. Kellogg, "The Principle and Advantage of Association in Charities," *Journal of Social Science* 12 (December 1880): 89.
34 Paine, Jr., "The Work of Volunteer Visitors," 113.
35 Lubove, *The Professional Altruist*, 14.
36 For a discussion of the power-dependence perspective, see Yeheskel Hasenfeld, "Power in Social Work Practice," *Social Service Review* 61 (September 1987): 472–475.
37 Lewis, "The Development of the Charity Organization Movement," 190–191.
38 Ibid.
39 Dolgoff and Feldstein, *Understanding Social Welfare*, 261; Ray Johns and David DeMarche, *Community Organization and Agency Responsibility* (New York: Association Press, 1951), 39.
40 Oscar McCulloch, "General and Special Methods of Operations in the Association of Charities," *Journal of Social Science* 9 (December 1879): 97.
41 Abel, "Medicine and Morality: The Health Care program of the New York Charity Organization Society," 638.
42 Quoted in numerous sources, including James Leiby, *A History of Social Welfare and Social Work in the United States* (New York: Columbia University Press, 1978), 116.
44 Mary Richmond and Fred Hall, *A Study of Nine Hundred and Eighty-five Widows* (New York: Russell Sage Foundation, 1913).
44 Albert McLean, as quoted in Kusmer, "The Functions of Organized Charity," 663.
45 Lane, "Jacob A. Riis and Scientific Philanthropy," 35.
46 As quoted in Kusmer, "The Functions of Organized Charities," 669.
47 As quoted in Lewis, "The Development of the Charity Organization Movement," 170.
48 Johnson and Schwartz, *Social Welfare*, 38.
49 Ehrenreich, *The Altruistic Imagination*, 31.
50 Lubove, *The Professional Altruist*, 16.
51 Ruth Cowan, Mark Rose, and Marsha Rose, "Clean Homes and Large Utility Bills 1900–1940," *Marriage and Family Review* 9 (Fall 1985): 53–66.
52 As noted in Jansson, *The Reluctant Welfare State*, 113.
53 As quoted in Lubove, *The Professional Altruist*, 17.
54 Stadum, "A Critique of Family Case Workers," 85.
55 As quoted in Stadum, "A Critique of Family Case Workers," 85.
56 Richmond and Hall, *A Study of Nine Hundred and Eighty-Five Widows*, 50–78.
57 Abel, "Medicine and Morality: The Health Care Program of the New York Charity Organization Society," 636.
58 Steven Diner, "Chicago Social Workers and Blacks in the Progressive Era," *Social Service Review* 44 (December 1970): 394.
59 Frank Watson, *The Charity Organization Movement*, 357.
60 Ibid., 352f.
61 This conclusion can be found, for example, in Andrew Billingsley and Jeanne Giovannoni, *Children of the Storm* (New York: Harcourt Brace Jovanovich, 1972), 38; Patricia Hogan and Sau-

Fong Siu, "Minority Children and the Child Welfare System: An Historical Perspective," *Social Work* 33 (November 1988): 494.

[62] An example is the report on "Mexican Immigrants in the United States," which was published in *The Survey* 28 (September 7, 1912): 726–730.

[63] "The Negro in the Cities of the North," *Charities* 15 (October 7, 1905): 1.

[64] Alvin Kogut, "The Negro and the Charity Organization in the Progressive Era," *Social Service Review* 44 (March 1970): 14–19.

[65] Kogut, "The Negro and the Charity Organization," 19–20.

[66] W. E. B. DuBois, *The Philadelphia Negro: A Social Study* (New York: Schocken Books, 1967), 357–358.

[67] Richmond and Hall, *A Study of Nine Hundred and Eighty-five Widows*, 50–78.

[68] Kogut, "The Negro and the Charity Organization Society," 13.

[69] Florette Henri, *Black Migration: Movement North 1900–1920* (Garden City, NY: Anchor Press/ Doubleday, 1975): 126.

[70] Tice, *Tales of Wayward Girls and Immoral Women*, 147.

[71] Kogut, "The Negro and the Charity Organization," 13–14.

[72] Watson, *The Charity Organization Movement in the United States*, 357f.

[73] Eugene Jones, "Social Work among Negroes," *The Annals of the American Academy of Political and Social Science* 240 (November 1928): 287.

[74] See, for example, Iris Carlton-Laney, "The Career of Birdye Henrietta Haynes, A Pioneer Settlement House Worker," *Social Service Review* 68 (June 1994): 254–273.

[75] Robert Treviño, "Facing Jim Crow: Catholic Sisters and the 'Mexican Problem' in Texas," *The Western Historical Quarterly* 34 (Summer 2003): 155.

[76] Abel, "Medicine and Morality: The Health Care Program of the New York Charity Organization Society," 636.

[77] June Axinn and Herman Levin, *Social Welfare-A History of the American Response to Need*, 2nd ed. (New York: Harper & Row, 1982), 151.

[78] Kogut, "The Negro and the Charity Organization Society," 20.

[79] "The Negro of the Cities of the North," 1.

[80] Steven Diner, "Chicago Social Workers and Blacks in the Progressive Era," *Social Service Review* 44 (December 1970): 394.

[81] "West Indian Migration to New York," *Charities* 15 (October 5, 1905): 2.

[82] As quoted in Diner, "Chicago Social Workers and Blacks in the Progressive Era," 395.

[83] Axinn and Levin, *Social Welfare*, 151.

[84] Andrew Billingsley and Jeanne Giovannoni, *Children of the Storm* (New York: Harcourt Brace Jovanovich, 1972), 23.

[85] "The Negro," *The Charities Review* 7 (October 1897): 718.

[86] "Opportunity and Responsibility," *Charities* 15 (October 7, 1905): 1.

[87] As quoted in Kogut, "The Negro and the Charity Organization Society," 13.

[88] "The Negro," *The Charities* 6 (June 1897): 379.

CHAPTER 6

Ethnicity, Race, and the Emergence of Macro Practice

This, then will be my definition of the settlement: that it is an attempt to express the meaning of life in terms of life itself, in forms of activity. . . . A settlement brings to its aid all possible methods to reveal and make common its conception of life.

—Jane Addams, 1899[1]

The settlement house movement, with its numerous and varied activities, sought to infuse poor communities with vitality and a drive to make living conditions better. This movement symbolizes the macro-practice roots of social work because of its focus on social reform. Macro practice encompasses community organization, policy practice, advocacy, and those other methods used for intervention at the organizational, community, and policy levels. Social workers embrace the history of the settlement houses as proof of the profession's ongoing commitment to social reform. While many in the profession can recount the significance of Jane Addams and Hull House, knowledge of other settlement houses is rather limited. In order to fully understand the range and depth of the settlement house movement, it is necessary to review the literature on Hull House and other settlement houses. Such an examination reveals that social reform was but one of the goals of the movement—the goal that continues to receive the majority of attention. Other perhaps less glamorous goals were achieved through the planned activities of the houses. The settlement houses that formed the core of the movement were as diverse as the populations they served. In addition, their technologies were just as diverse.

The dominance of Hull House in the profession's social reform history has resulted in generalizations about the overall mission of the settlement house movement. These generalizations offer little insight into the movement's interest in and contact with the racial and ethnic minorities that were streaming into the cities. The egregious treatment of these groups at the hands of the larger social systems in which they lived seemed to demand aggressive economic, political, and social interventions. For this reason, the reform-oriented nature of the budding profession was a potentially powerful resource for the ethnic and racial minorities in this country. Consequently, the historical role of social work's social reform in mitigating the conditions of these populations is well worth examining.

THE SETTLEMENT HOUSE MOVEMENT

Settlement houses, like charity organization societies (COS), were British imports.[2] In England, the houses created opportunities for university men to reside in the poorer sections of town to offer services and to plan strategies for addressing social problems. As developed in England, the settlement house "was simply a residence for university men in a city slum."[3] The first settlement house in the United States was the Neighborhood Guild, renamed University Settlement, established in New York in 1886. The goal of the first settlement house was to provide a place for the educated to settle among the poor immigrants to foster the kind of neighborliness that would develop good citizens.[4] Many of the first settlement houses in the United States were affiliated with educational institutions and religious groups. The idea spread as settlement houses proliferated in cities across the country. According to the 1911 *Handbook of Settlements*, there were 74 settlements in 1897, 103 in 1900, 204 in 1905, and 413 by the end of that decade.[5]

The University Settlement can be used to illustrate the goals and activities of a large settlement house located in a major urban city. It was located on the Lower East Side of New York City in a slum neighborhood.[6] As outlined in its constitution, this settlement wanted to

> bring men and women of education into closer relations with the laboring classes in this city, for their mutual benefit. The society shall establish and maintain in the tenement house districts places of residence for college men and others desirous of aiding in the work, with rooms where the people of the neighborhood may meet for social and educational purposes.[7]

The charter of Hull House, another well-known settlement established in 1889 by Jane Addams and Ellen Starr, described its mission: "To provide a center for the higher civic and social life; to institute and maintain educational and philanthropic enterprises, and to investigate and improve the conditions in the industrial districts of Chicago."[8]

According to the *Handbook of Settlements*, residents of the University Settlement conducted sociological investigations of the neighborhood, advocated for improved housing, worked for improved sanitation conditions, secured play areas and equipment for neighborhood children, served as school trustees, aided in the organization of unions, protested against corrupt politicians, opened their doors for a branch of a loan society to help ease economic hardship accompanying depressions, educated neighborhood residents about local politics, helped in the passage of a juvenile court law, and testified before state and national committees. The activities of Hull House and numerous other settlement houses were similar in nature to those of the University Settlement.

The settlement house movement is viewed as the reform history of social work because of the movement's efforts to improve the conditions of the slum neighborhoods. Strategies were crafted to promote legislation for improving the social climate of the neighborhoods in which they existed. Settlement house workers lived in the blighted areas and learned from personal experience the extent and consequences of poverty. These workers attempted to mobilize neighborhood residents to organize, advocate, and press for needed changes. Locally based actions often grew into social action, as settlement organizers recognized the power of the environment in the lives of individuals and fought to change that environment. The environment and its array of deleterious social conditions were the targets of change. In contrast to social casework, which started in the COS, the settlement house movement gave rise to social group work, community organization, and social action.[9]

While the settlement house movement addressed social reform issues, it still bore some resemblance to the charity organization societies.[10] Both organizations were devoted to teaching the poor the middle-class way of life and attached moral connotations to poverty. For both, the road to self-sufficiency was paved with hard work, commitment, and not yielding to the vices of life. In addition, Protestantism was a driving force in both the COS and the settlement houses. Furthermore, the settlement house worker was, to a certain degree, similar to the friendly visitor. The friendly visitor to the settlement house, however, worked from the inside out rather than from the outside in, and did not just visit but moved in for a rather sustained period of time.

Settlement house residents (or settlers) and charity organizers alike felt obligated to help those who were less fortunate and "to give something back" in exchange for the privileges they enjoyed. They wanted to use their education and class position to make a significant difference in the world in which they lived. Because the manner in which they made their contribution was so dramatic (changing their lives as well as place of residence), these organizers were also fulfilling a personal need to participate actively and meaningfully in the world around them—a world that included poverty, destitution, and countless examples of harsh human suffering.

Inputs for the Settlement House Movement

The settlement house movement relied on numerous inputs for its emergence and growth. Critical resources that were needed for the settlements to form, survive, and expand range from belief systems to funding, and they help define the crucial points in the environment on which the houses depended. Several of those inputs are discussed below.

Ideology.   The ideology of the settlement house movement reflected in varying degrees *noblesse oblige,* Social Gospel, socialism, social reform, and a belief in cooperation between social classes.[11] *Noblesse oblige* (or "a sense of duty of the privileged toward the unprivileged, of the 'haves' to the 'have nots,'" as it might have been called) was not, however, actually identified by Addams as a primary reason for settling in the houses.[12] She believed that the settlers were motivated by a desire to equalize the classes. The quest was to lift the poor *up* rather than to reach *down* to them. Some interpreted this equalization of the classes as a form of socialism, but this was a label imposed by others outside the movement. The belief in the cooperation between classes, however, found form in the nature of the activities pursued by the settlers of the houses.

Social Gospel emerges as a central ideology that shaped the settlement house movement. According to Boyer, when Addams founded Hull House in Chicago in 1889, she described her motives in Social Gospel terms.[13] The home missions of the Social Gospelers were similar to those of the settlement houses, and that similarity was not lost on the settlers. The settlers were often called upon to explain the difference between the two. Confusion between the missions and the settlements was one of the dangers facing the movement. Addams recognized this confusion and responded:

> The first is the danger that it [the settlement] shall approach too nearly the spirit of the mission which . . . will always exist, will always be needed, but which from its very nature can not be a settlement. Those who join it believe in some doctrines or methods which they wish to extend, it may be those of the church, of socialists, of teetotallers, of political party; but followers are enlisted and organized and a vast amount of machinery created for a given aim.[14]

To a certain extent, therefore, the settlement houses can be viewed as missions without the proselytizing.

Settlers believed in the capacity of people, regardless of their social status, for personal, economic, spiritual, and social growth. Settlement house residents extended their beliefs to encompass the duty of society to assist its citizens in maximizing their growth in these areas. Although the targeting of pauperism by the COS reduced the social problem to the individual level, the targeting of *poverty* by the settlement house organizers expanded the social problem to a more global, societal level. The settlement house philosophy also placed the "settlement" in the midst of the slums, to live among the poor, to share their lives and culture with the poor, to become a part of the neighborhood, and to experience life's hardships firsthand.[15]

Although it is difficult to summarize the settlement outlook (the word *settlement* was eventually used freely and loosely),[16] the writings of those closely affiliated with the movement provide some insight into the ideologies driving the movement. Addams saw the settlements as attempting "to add the social function to democracy." According to Graham Taylor of the Chicago Commons, "It [the settlement] seeks to unify and help all other organizations and people in the neighborhood that make righteousness and brotherhood. . . . [The settlement] aspires to be a center of the best social life and interests of the people." The second annual report of New York's East Side House reads, "All men of every class have something to give and something to get. Let the disposition to do good through others' agency be supplanted as far as possible by the desire to know and to do it first hand." Vida Scudder of the Philadelphia College Settlement echoed the significance of personal experience in the slum neighborhood by asserting that, through such an experience, "one has at least placed one's life at the point of greatest need in the modern world, between those alienated classes which cry out for a mediator."[17]

Addams summarized three major motives she felt drew settlers together: (1) a desire to push society from political democracy to social democracy by translating democracy into social terms, (2) a desire to "share the race life" of the masses and aid in racial progress, and (3) the desire to "express the spirit of Christ" by stimulating a Christian movement toward humanitarianism.[18] The settlement houses offered reformers an opportunity to practice their beliefs in a way that put them in direct contact with the impoverished classes. Unlike the friendly visitors who visited and then went home to their comfortable surroundings, the settlers changed their lives by moving into the slum neighborhoods, putting on their work gloves, and working alongside the poor. According to Wagner: "The settlements were the Peace Corps or Vista of a generation of young people (primarily women) in the 1890–1914 period who sought to escape home and join a vibrant, altruistic movement which also linked economic, political, social and philosophical concerns."[19]

The Value of Socialization and Americanization. The settlement house movement also achieved uniqueness by focusing attention on the socialization of the "normal, adequately functioning family."[20] With adequate resources and sufficient opportunity, the poor were envisioned as rising from the grips of destitution to take their rightful, respected place in society. The social ills confronting impoverished communities were attributed less to the moral weaknesses of the individual and more to the social and economic climate surrounding the individual. Thus, neighborhoods and communities were the target of intervention and the individual became the vehicle for affecting change at these levels. The settlers believed in the power of cooperation between settlement residents and community members in the quest to vitalize slum neighborhoods.

Even though the settlers wanted "oneness" with the slum residents, settlers were often aware of the schism that existed between them and those living around them. The settlers rarely actually suffered or experienced the poverty and destitution that afflicted families in the neighborhoods. Some settlers even believed that their presence in the neighborhoods was a sham and that the settlement was "nothing but a high flown 'ambassador' among these suffering swarms."[21] Although the mission of the movement was to reduce the social distance between the classes, some traces of that distance were difficult to erase. In addition, within the settlement house itself, settlers often maintained their own separate, insulated world, which further suggests that for many settlement houses integration into the communities was somewhat superficial.

Socialization for life often meant socialization for American life or Americanization of the immigrant communities. In fact, the Americanization movement was spearheaded by the settlement houses and spanned the period from the 1890s to the 1920s.[22] Settlers believed that immigrants needed to learn about U.S. culture and values in order to benefit from the riches offered in America. The settlement houses incorporated an adherence to the melting-pot view of society that was discussed in Chapter 2.

Examples of the significance of Americanization to the settlement house movement can be found throughout the 1911 *Handbook of Settlements*.[23] For example, a description of the neighborhood surrounding the Northwestern

University Settlement of Chicago noted, "All about us the problem of the Americanization of foreign peoples is being slowly worked out, and 'Americans in process' is the order of the day."[24] The goals of Friendship House, in Washington, DC, were "to promote temperance, thrift and self-control" and to "awaken an interest in civic improvement and establish the foundations of honest and progressive citizenship"[25] Zion House in New York was founded in 1893 to provide a place "where the elements of good citizenship can be inculcated and fostered."[26] In Erie, Pennsylvania, the Neighborhood House sought "to raise the standard of living and make better citizens of the foreigners in the neighborhood."[27]

The Settlers and their Motives. People who became settlers represented another settlement input. Settling in the slums of the city was a tremendous challenge for many of the settlement house residents. They faced the unsavory conditions of the slums that were detailed in Chapter 2. These educated, genteel men and women of comfortable means were willing to forego or temporarily put aside their lifestyle in order to touch a foreign, unseemly world teeming with every social ill imaginable. Many of the early settlers were daughters of ministers and by 1910, three-fourths of the 400 settlement houses had been founded by women.[28] The American settlement house movement drew on two sources for settlers—the clergy (as did the British movement) and the college woman (who was not part of the British movement)—and relied heavily on women, as college women made up 70 percent of the settlement residents.[29] Settlers, like the COS friendly visitors, were generally middle-class white women.

The charter of the College Settlements Association, organized in 1890, specifically addressed the role of women in the settlement house movement:

> The association would unite all college women . . . in the trend of a great modern movement; would touch them with a common ideal. Young students . . . should be quickened in their years of vague aspiration and purely speculative energy by possessing a share in a broad practical work.[30]

The settlements provided these women a chance for personal fulfillment, self-realization, and accomplishment beyond home, family, and the traditional role of teacher.[31] Many college-educated women felt stifled by prevailing norms that prohibited their participation in politics and gainful employment. Through the settlements, these women could satisfy their desire to do, be, or accomplish while at the same time helping the neighborhoods achieve their potential.[32]

Addams, the daughter of one of the richest men in northern Illinois,[33] wrote of the betrayal of educated women by a society that constrained the choices available to them. Addams saw settlement house work as the salvation for these women, including herself, because through "social mothering" and "civic housekeeping" the traditional role of nurturer was preserved.[34] The friendly visitors may have been responding to a similar need. Thus, women were creating a place for themselves outside of the home through their service in the COS and settlement houses.

While creating a place for themselves in administering to others, women were also defining for themselves a role steeped in service and practically void of substantial financial remuneration. Because many of the settlers either relied on the benevolence of others or had family funds, the volunteer nature of their work often came to be assumed. The reward for the work, consequently, lay not with financial compensation but with the meaning of the mission for the workers. For many, especially daughters of ministers, settlement work was an extension of the missionary movement as the settlers tried to uplift the poor.[35] The "calling" to a mission may still be viewed as a critical element of social work because of the continued prominence of the worker's motivation, moral incentive, and awareness of the greater good to be served.[36] Thus, the work itself becomes its own reward.

The External Economy and the External Polity.   The external economy and external polity formed another significant input to the settlement house movement. Settlement houses required legitimation and financial backing in order to be maintained and to expand. For many of the political progressives of the day, the settlement houses were "politically correct" in their focus and activities and therefore received support from philanthropists and corporate donors.

Levine and Levine provide a detailed discussion of the financing of the settlements.[37] Many settlers came with resources to sustain them, as did Addams. For settlers without this kind of financial support and for the paid staff (typically secretaries, domestics, janitors, and handymen), fund-raising became a necessity. When settlers entered the world of fund-raising, they were faced with several dilemmas. Fund-raising in the neighborhoods yielded limited results as the neighborhoods were poor. Wealthy patrons often made specific requests or recommendations about the actions and activities of the settlements. On occasion, funds were rejected because the donor's suggestion was not deemed appropriate to the settlement. Settlers were also fearful of accepting funds from local governments because they felt that freedom to make decisions and act independently would be compromised. Levine and Levine note:

> Settlement leaders felt their freedom to innovate and experiment would be seriously compromised if they worked within the framework of governmental agencies. . . . While the government might be benevolent, and in its benevolence promote important changes, there is probably a narrow limit to the changes government can tolerate at any point in time.[38]

As noted earlier, few reforms were enacted without the tacit approval, if not the guidance, of large corporate interests.[39] Within the dominant elite class of society, the Progressives were able to join forces with settlement house residents to push for reforms that were perceived as liberal. Many of the corporate leaders sought to polish their rather tarnished images by supporting worthy causes and groups. Numerous welfare reforms of the Progressive Era were the result of the businessmen's movement teaming with the settlement house movement.

This teamwork would suggest that major reforms during the Progressive Era provided some relief for the masses while at the same time offering something to the big business sector. The child labor, or child-saving, movement is an excellent example. Historical accounts of the fight for child labor legislation indicate that the abolition of child labor was, to some degree, a means of driving out marginal tenement operators and other marginal businesses. Such legislation was generously supported by those business interests that did not depend on cheap child labor. Children could be protected from exploitation, and big business could be stabilized, consolidated, and run more efficiently. At the same time, compulsory education was gaining more support, and child labor legislation fit neatly with such legislation. Furthermore, this child-saving movement was aligned with the traditional interest of women and was an appropriate area in which women could exercise social mothering.[40] In their quest for legislation to protect children, the settlement house leaders had the support of powerful, wealthy business leaders. This external economy and external polity were necessary for many of the reforms to be achieved.

The external polity and external economy also supported the settlement house Americanization efforts. Americanized workers were more productive and efficient workers. The settlement programs complemented the numerous programs provided by large companies. For example, the Ford Motor Company had mandatory English classes for the foreign born, and the first lesson commenced with a reading titled "I Am a Good American."[41]

On the other hand, these inputs acted as constraints to the reform activities of the settlement houses. Settlers had to be careful not to alienate wealthy supporters by taking up unpopular causes.[42] Settlement houses depended on large donations to operate their programs, and this dependency often defined the parameters of their reform targets.

The philosophy, the populace (service providers and service beneficiaries), external polity, and pecuniary base converged to form a service movement that has been heralded as the reform roots of modern social work.

Technologies of the Settlement House Movement

The settlement houses used a number of means to accomplish their goals: gathering and promulgating facts; local action; preparing legislation; mobilizing forces for the passage of legislation; securing employment for community members; teaching English, occupational skills, domestic skills, and hygiene; teaching the poor the middle-class values that contributed to success; and stressing the value of self-help.[43]

As did the COS participants, the settlers emphasized the importance of gathering facts and documenting the existence of problems. Jane Addams, Florence Kelley, and Julia Lathrop pioneered the social survey at Hull House and University of Chicago Settlement.[44] The Hull House Maps and Papers (1895) was the first systematic and detailed attempt to describe immigrant communities in an American city."[45] Harry Kraus, in The Settlement House Movement in New York City, 1886–1914, presented a detailed overview of the surveys and investigations that were completed by settlement house leaders.[46] The settlers saw the need to document social problems and compile data on housing, health, and employment. With this documentation, the settlers could then develop strategies for addressing and attacking the causes of social problems. More so than the COS, the settlers forged links with sociology and, therefore, colleges and universities. The basis for these linkages was reinforced by the college affiliation of the settlers and the settlement house appeal to college-educated women.

In terms of specific practices, the settlement houses offered space for union organizers to meet, provided a range of classes, organized clubs that facilitated community interaction, offered night classes, developed organizations that advocated for and protected the rights of immigrants, provided information and referred community residents to appropriate agencies for services, organized community residents to clean and improve their surroundings, invited community residents to house-sponsored recreational activities, and organized community residents to press local governments for such things as playgrounds, stricter enforcement of housing codes, and better city services. Settlers contributed to the push for child labor laws, women's labor laws, institutional care of the physically and mentally disabled, child welfare services, and juvenile courts.[47]

Not all settlement houses, however, engaged in all these listed activities. Some houses were concerned only with the provision of club activities, whereas others were actively involved in advocacy and legislation. The most notable and large houses—Hull House, Chicago Commons, University Settlement, for example—are frequently cited as the prototypical settlement houses; however, they probably fall at the reform end of a continuum that ranges from extremely conservative to extremely liberal (reform oriented). The number of settlement houses peaked at 500 in 1915,[48] and only a fraction of that number had ever participated in social reform work. The overwhelming majority had, however, developed clubs, classes, and recreation for their communities.

Children and young girls received a great deal of settlement house attention. Settlements generally provided day nurseries and kindergartens that freed mothers to work. Noel House (Washington, DC) settlers believed, as did most other settlers, that "the young people" were "in special danger."[49] With the exploitation of child workers and the seemingly inhumane treatment of juvenile offenders, passage of child labor laws and the creation of special services for youthful lawbreakers rose to the forefront of legislative activity. Settlers lobbied elected officials, sat on key boards and committees, ran for public office, and solicited the support of powerful individuals and groups. The perceived vulnerability of the young female worker facilitated launching efforts to protect this segment of their population. For example, the University of Chicago Settlement wanted "to secure a boarding house for immigrant girls in order to mitigate the evils attendant on the 'boarder' habit of immigrants."[50] Consequently, these vulnerable groups enjoyed the benefits of the "social mothering" provided by settlers seeking to find a niche for their skills.

As detailed earlier, the deplorable housing and sanitary conditions of the densely populated urban settings naturally led the settlers to focus on these areas. Creating a healthy, pleasant environment became the goals for numerous houses. Groups were organized to clean the streets themselves and/or to lobby for better services. Because children had no play areas except for the trash and manure-littered streets, playgrounds were also priorities. The settlement sometimes devoted some of its space to recreation activities for children. Cleaner streets and play areas were the products of the "civic housekeeping" of numerous settlement workers.

The settlement houses also evoked the strong arm of the law and law enforcement to assist in cleaning up neighborhoods. For example, the Settlement School in Frankfort, Kentucky, was able to have saloons closed, and the Irene Kaufman Settlement in Pittsburgh was instrumental in closing "obnoxious dance halls."[51] The work of the Thomas H. Swope Settlement in Kansas City, Missouri, vividly illuminates this side of the movement:

> After two years' agitation in regard to the motion picture show and muto-scope halls, valuable and necessary legislation was secured. [This settlement] cooperated with its neighbors in an effort to drive out prostitution and to exercise a certain moral supervision over the district.[52]

Just as the COS worked to improve the recreation activities of the communities, the settlement houses also attempted to rid neighborhoods of "undesirable" entertainment and recreation. To this end, the police assisted in driving out immoral elements by enforcing specific ordinances.

The primary settlement house technology used consistently across all houses was that of interaction with and between community residents. The contact the settlers had with each other and with their neighbors stimulated them to act on behalf of their neighborhoods. The energy flowing from these interactions inspired people to envision change in themselves and their surroundings and then work to achieve those changes. The core technology was the *process* of human dynamics derived from the interactions occurring in the houses. The importance of interaction was reflected in the goal of Hull House: "to make social intercourse express the growing sense of the economic unity of society."[53]

Settlement Houses and Immigrants

The settlement house movement is almost synonymous with immigration and Americanization as the houses emerged to meet the needs of the immigrants.[54] Since the settlement houses were residentially based, they experienced the transition of neighborhoods as the so-called new immigrants supplanted the old. The new immigrants were not shunned by the settlement houses; instead, they were embraced as groups that required more rigorous and extensive Americanization. The Chicago Commons noted the challenge that the new immigrants brought with them:

> In the place of every German, Scandinavian and Irish family removing, immigrant families still stranger to our American life and conditions arrive. Like the surf upon the sand, each new wave of immigration from southern Italy, Sicily, Poland, Armenia and Greece, breaks over us here, where twenty-four or more nationalities meet and try to live and work together.[55]

The University of Chicago Settlement also reported that the old Irish, Scotch, and English neighbors were supplanted by the Bohemian, Pole, Slovak, Lithuanian, Croatian, and Slovenian.[56] The same phenomenon was occurring throughout other parts of the United States as the settlement houses responded by opening their doors to their new neighbors. From Baltimore to Boston, Chicago to Cleveland, St. Paul to St. Louis, the new immigrants were changing the fabric of the neighborhoods as well as U.S. society.

While the doors were swinging open for the new immigrants, the welcome they received varied from enthusiastic to disdainful. Alvin Kogut examined the attitudes of key settlement house directors and concluded that these directors were guided by veiled racism or the spirit of egalitarianism.[57] Jane Addams of Hull House espoused cultural pluralism, recognized the special needs of the new immigrants, and valued their distinctive cultural heritage. Robert Woods of Boston's South End House, however, had a markedly different view of the new immigrants. He saw these immigrants as barriers to achieving national unity and advocated for immigration restrictions by joining the Immigration Restriction League. These examples highlight the diversity in opinions held by the settlement directors and their residents.

These attitudes toward immigrants are captured in the settlement house descriptions contained in the 1911 *Handbook of Settlements*. The La Grange House, one of the few settlements in the south (Augusta, Georgia), boasted of being in a neighborhood with a population "of pure American stock."[58] The Wrightsville House of Philadelphia was situated in an Hungarian neighborhood and the Hungarians were "almost over-thrifty, lacking the power to find the best of life, doing little else than earn, eat and sleep."[59] Furthermore, settlement house workers, in general, lacked wide variation in their position on legislation to restrict immigration. For example, according to Davis, "Most settlement workers also accepted the passage in February 1917 of the first immigration bill requiring a literacy test. There had always been disagreement over immigration restriction, but in 1917 not even the Immigrant Protective League launched an effective protest against the bill."[60]

The new immigrants were often seen as possessing values and customs that were not supportive of the American way of life. The answer for them, in the eyes of the settlers, was through the Americanization process. In fact, the push for Americanization was directed solely toward immigrants. They were seen as redeemable, and classes in English, sewing, cooking, housekeeping, mechanical drawing, and manual training were offered as the tools for success in America. Thus, the settlers agreed with many of the Progressives of the day: With proper training and guidance, the new immigrants could be transformed into true Americans. Numerous settlement leaders held attitudes similar to those of the larger society. These attitudes, as previously mentioned, included disdain for immigrant culture and religion, belief that foreigners were germ-ridden, and adherence to the stereotype of loose morality. Indeed, the early settlement house movement was encircled by the "benign form of paternalism" that prevailed during the Progressive Era.[61]

For the new immigrants, residence in a blighted neighborhood was but a stepping stone. With economic success, a family could relocate to better sections of town. In this regard, immigrant status could be held as a legitimate reason for living in a poor community. The native-born Americans did not have the excuse of immigrant status to protect them. For "real" Americans, continued existence in a community of destitution was often equated with personal failure or weakness. Attitudes toward the "real" Americans living in poverty areas are also found in the *Handbook of Settlements.* For example, the Union Bethel Settlement of Cincinnati described its neighborhood in these terms: "Much of our constituency is composed of the defective and dependent class. The people are largely Americans and Irish-Americans."[62] For the Southwark House in Philadelphia, the "Americans" in the neighborhood are described as "the dregs of a once prosperous community."[63] "The Nashville Wesley House was faced with many who were "of the unfortunate, shiftless, or immoral class."[64]

The settlement house movement, therefore, cannot be neatly summarized as reflective of a particular point of view or a particular vision. The views and visions were as diverse as the individuals moving into settlement work. In the telling of social work history, a few major settlement houses are singled out to exemplify settlement house work. The history that involved anti-immigration sentiment, belief in the individual as the cause of his or her own plight in life, the role of Americanization in settlement house work, and the social control aspects of this work is frequently minimized or ignored.

Settlement Houses and African Americans

In the Progressive Era, all racial and ethnic groups suffered but differed in the manner and extent of suffering. The social suffering of the minorities was exacerbated by their minority status. In the midst of this plight, it is relevant to determine the type of settlement house intervention that was taking place for the racial and ethnic minorities.

Because African Americans greatly outnumbered the other groups and moved into those cities in which the settlement houses flourished, the work of the settlement houses with this group is of particular interest. Generally, the settlement houses responded in one of five ways to the influx of African American migrants in those communities that had once been primarily composed of immigrants: They (1) provided services to the new migrants, (2) established African American branches, (3) refused to provide services to this group, (4) closed their doors rather than serve this new clientele, or (5) relocated to areas that did not include African Americans.

Examples of typical settlement house responses to African Americans are numerous: The board of the Eli Bates House in Chicago voted to close the house rather than admit African Americans; Kingsley House in Philadelphia excluded African Americans entirely; one New York settlement substantially increased its membership fee to discourage African Americans from joining; the director and board of Christamore Settlement in Indianapolis decided to move the settlement rather than integrate it; the Friendship House of Washington, DC, excluded African Americans; the Marcy Center of Chicago followed the Jewish families out of the neighborhood rather than provide services to the incoming African Americans; the Central Presbyterian Chapel and Settlement House in Kansas City (Missouri) accepted "all but Negroes" in its classes;

and the Neighborhood House of Ft. Worth noted that in its neighborhood the "people are Americans, foreigners, and many Negroes, the latter not touched by the work."[65]

The Integrated Settlement Example. Those settlements that welcomed African Americans were relatively few in number, and there were few settlement houses to serve any predominantly African American sections of town.[66] By the 1920s, when African American migration had already peaked, numerous cities were adjusting to the dramatic increase in their African American population and the settlement houses were experiencing the effects of these demographic shifts. The settlement house movement was a residentially based movement and, as such, could not ignore the changing complexion of the neighborhoods. The Abraham Lincoln Center of Chicago responded by offering integrated services that included African Americans and this response has been attributed to the center's "ultra-liberal" leaning.[67]

The Abraham Lincoln Center, founded in 1905, initially was situated in a neighborhood with people who were "largely American; many of them German, Irish and Jewish extraction."[68] The center controlled membership so that 50 percent African American membership could be maintained, provided interracial activities, and later sponsored a series of lectures by Melville Herskovitz, author of *The Myth of the Negro Past.*[69] Neighborhood House also approached a turning point in its history as African Americans replaced the immigrant population.[70] In 1925, the settlement staff decided to remain in its present location and begin providing services to these newest arrivals. By 1929 the settlement had hired its first African American social worker, but it was not until the 1940s, when its membership was two-thirds African American, that an African American joined the house's board of trustees.

To accommodate the growing number of African Americans in its neighborhood, the Greenwich House Settlement provided a room for African American residents to use for club meetings, classes, and a library.[71] While the provision of only one room may seem rather stingy, this was still far more than what many other houses provided.

Separation, Segregation, and Relocation. Some houses opened separate facilities for African Americans. For example, the Women's Federation of Elmira, New York, operated a small settlement "in the Negro quarter of Elmira"; the Henry Street Settlement in New York City established the Still Branch for Colored People; the College Settlement in Philadelphia opened the Starr Center to serve African Americans; Boston's South End House established the Robert Gould Shaw House for Africans; and the Wendell Phillips Settlement in Chicago was started with the help of Hull House residents.[72] According to Allen Davis in *Spearheads for Reform,* these separate houses for African Americans were based on specific beliefs of the settlers: "Many of the settlement house workers decided that special segregated facilities would best serve the interest of Negroes. This attitude was based partly on the idea that each neighborhood should have its own social center and partly on the fear that the presence of Negroes would drive others away."[73] In their 1922 book, *The Settlement Horizon,* Woods and Kennedy support separation by offering this perspective:

> A substantial number of settlements are situated in neighborhoods of
> white people which include a small number of Negroes. Where the ratio of
> black people to white is slight, the two races usually mix without friction.
> Large groups of colored people in a neighborhood predominately white
> may force a settlement, against its inclination, to choose between the two.
> In this case the soundest practice is to establish a separate branch, where
> special forms of work fitted to the needs of colored people are carried on.[74]

Judith Trolander provided a rather enlightening overview of the racial
segregation practiced at Chicago's Hull House.[75] By the 1930s, the second
largest African American community was situated in the Hull House neighborhood; yet, African Americans were not represented in the programs and services of the house. Even though the *Hull House Yearbook* listed a "black
mothers' club" organized in 1927 by Jane Addams, African American club
members were not invited to participate in house programs, were not on any
of the house's mailing lists, and did not receive any benefits from the program. Trolander described the practices of Hull House as de facto segregation.

Leaders of Pittsburgh's Kingsley House, founded in 1893, feared that their
neighborhood was "beset with persistent forms of degradation" and relocated
the settlement to an Italian neighborhood.[76] The population was increasingly
African American, so control of the original settlement building was given to a
group of churches that planned to operate an African American settlement.
Even though Kingsley House settlers fled the neighborhood, they did make provisions for their former building to be used for the new community residents.

A key to the settlers' response to African Americans can be found in the
attitudes of the settlers. Numerous settlers shared the attitudes of the larger
society toward African Americans. For example, Graham Taylor of Chicago
Commons saw African Americans as a problem—a "depraved" people who society was obligated to uplift and treat humanely.[77] Even Jane Addams seemed to
hold that African Americans were in the early stages of their development. At
the 13th Annual Conference for the Study of the Negro at Atlanta University in
1908, Addams remarked during her talk to an African American audience:

> The thing I feel most strongly as the difficulty among the Italians, among
> the Greeks and among the Russians (for these are the ones whom I con-
> stantly see), is the contrast they find between the life they have led at
> home and the life they are obliged to live in Chicago. . . . The advantages
> are that you are ready *to make your adaptation;* . . . the disadvantages
> are that *you lack some of the restraints of the traditions which the people
> I mentioned bring with them* [emphasis added].[78]

The voices of the settlement house movement did not convey a uniform attitude about African Americans. Some believed in racial integration while others endorsed racial segregation. Because the movement did not reach out to
embrace the African American communities, those voices that echoed racist,
separatist beliefs may have been the loudest.

The African American Settlement. The Eighth Ward Settlement House
of Philadelphia is a stark example of the way White settlers perceived and

approached an African American community. It was established in 1895 by private citizens for settlement work among African Americans. This population is thus described:

> In sharing its life with the colored people, our settlement has its unique problem, for it deals not with a race that is intellectually hungry, but with a race at the sensation stage of its evolution, and the treatment demanded is different. . . . The very material we have to deal with prevents us from being either attractive or successful. . . . And the peace we have not, we wish for others.[79]

The Eighth Ward Settlement House concentrated on cleaning and improving the streets. It provided sanitation work, kindergarten, public baths, a system for residents to save money, basket weaving, hammock making, a women's club, and a dancing class.

Most of the settlements providing services to African American communities focused on morality, temperance, religious instruction, neatness in domestic life, industrial uplift, singing classes, social meetings, drawing classes, instruction in thrift, and lectures.[80] One of the reports of Chicago's Frederick Douglass Center (founded by White settler Celia Parker Woolley) acknowledged, "Our treatment of the colored people in this country constitutes the greatest charge that can be made against our patriotism, our religion, our humanity"; however, the center's activities consisted primarily of "a women's club, sewing-class, children's singing-class, study-class, an orchestra, quartette and religious services Sunday afternoon."[81] Overall, White-controlled settlements that served African Americans, "instead of promoting racial reform, displayed a cautious reformism that bowed to racism and oppression."[82]

Those houses that served African American communities were generally not controlled by those communities. Most had White boards of trustees or white-dominated boards that directed the operations and guided the future of the house. For example, the Presbyterian Colored Missions of Louisville, Kentucky, was maintained by White Presbyterians and specialized in religious services and industrial classes, while the White Episcopalians supported settlement work in an African American section of New York and enrolled over 400 African American girls in cooking and sewing classes.[83] This point is significant because it mirrors the tendency of individuals outside the group to identify the group's problems and identify solutions to those problems.

Booker T. Washington received the support of many settlers because they agreed with his perspective that African Americans were not yet ready for equality and that the road to equality was paved with manual training. Such a position continued to place responsibility for overcoming discrimination at the feet of the discriminated. Indeed, African American settlement houses were not always designed to speak for the African American; rather, the separate houses often served to perpetuate racial segregation.[84]

Funding Issues.   Funding was often difficult to secure for programs that focused on African Americans. In writing of social settlement work among African Americans, Sarah Collins Fernandis observed in 1905:

The limitations of our activities may be easily measured by the fact that a year's expenditure, including three salaried workers, was six hundred dollars! That larger scope may be given to all our activities through generous financial assistance is our hope; that this line of work has its peculiar value as a corrective for delinquent conditions in districts where Negroes, ignorant and poor, form a segregated mass, is our firm belief.[85]

In 1908, Fernandis was continuing to seek funds for African American settlement work. She wrote, "Social settlement work for the colored people in needy centers should be helped in the struggle for financial foothold."[86] Trolander also noted that African American settlements, particularly branch houses, were poorly financed operations.[87] Established charitable organizations differentiated between White and African American clients, and little money was allocated for relief work with African Americans.[88] Although contributions were sufficient enough for the widespread settlement work with immigrants, the dearth of donations for work with the African American population reflected the attitudes of the external polity and external economy of the settlement houses. Even with the advent of the coordinated fund-raising activities of Community Chests, African American services still suffered from inadequate funding[89] and agencies were seldom rebuked for their discriminatory practices.

Ethnic Group Responsibility.   The doctrine of ethnic group responsibility may have been another factor influencing the practices of the White settlers. Perhaps the settlers felt the same as the friendly visitors: The responsibility for meeting the needs of African Americans rested with African Americans. It may have been expected that African Americans, when they reached that point in their evolution, would organize their own services for the benefit of their own people. This belief survived the Progressive Era and was reflective in the emerging social institutions of society. For example, John Murchison of the Department of Interior wrote in 1935, "It is difficult, however, to convince the Negro that he, himself, must accomplish his own deliverance and economic security."[90]

The establishment of the National Urban League seems indicative of this doctrine of ethnic group responsibility. It was organized in 1911, governed by a board composed primarily of conservative Whites and African Americans such as Booker T. Washington, operated primarily by African Americans, and had "Not Alms, but Opportunity" as its self-help slogan.[91] Settlement house worker Mary Simkhovitch was a member of its 39-person board.[92] Although the league was considered an African American organization, its goals and visions were set largely by Whites who acted in accordance with their views of what African Americans should be doing for themselves. Hence, the White-controlled external polity and external economy of these organizations dictated the technologies they used. These polities supported the doctrine of ethnic group responsibility.

Contributions of the Movement.   Although the movement did not distinguish itself as the champion of the African American, several individuals were able to distinguish themselves because of their work with and commitment to this group. Notable among these reformers are Jane Addams, Edith Abbott, Sophonisba Breckenridge, Lillian Wald, Mary White Ovington, Florence Kelley, Frances Kellor, and Celia Parker Woolley. Several of these individuals worked with African American community leaders to develop settlement houses for African Americans. For example, Lillian Wald was instrumental in the establishment of Stillman House in 1906, and Celia Parker Woolley established the Frederick Douglas Center in the African American section of Chicago. Mary White Ovington worked to improve housing in African American communities. Edith Abbott and Sophonisba Breckenridge advocated for services to African American children.[93]

One of the major contributions of settlement house reformers was the organization of the National Association for the Advancement of Colored People (NAACP). The organization was founded and funded by Whites, many of whom were associated with settlement houses and opposed racial discrimination. All of the original officers of the association were White, with the exception of W. E. B. DuBois.[94] Those who started the association feared that it would be perceived as too radical, so they enlisted the help of a journalist "to counteract the impression that the Association was made up of crackpots and radicals."[95] In its creation days, the NAACP may have been "radical," but the group envisioned carving a path to racial freedom through the established structures of society rather than by attacking or challenging the validity of these structures. Foster described the early days of the NAACP in this manner:

> In the beginning, the wealthy Northern white philanthropists who were interesting themselves in the Negro people, looked askance at the N.A.A.C.P. . . . Later on, however, the organization, by its increasingly conservative course, was able to win the support of these people.[96]

The NAACP organizers set the tone for an advocacy organization that sought reform by working within and through the existing legal and political system. These founders also espoused the trend of "outsiders" defining the problems and defining the appropriate solutions.

Settlement Movement and African Americans: Some Conclusions. African Americans represented a kind of anomaly to the settlement houses. Many were more "American" than the native-born population who may have had "foreign" stock in their family backgrounds. Consequently, African Americans did not need the "Americanization" treatment to which the immigrants were exposed. They already were Americans and were already grounded in U.S. values, beliefs, and culture. These Americans did not require proselytizing to direct their faith and souls to Protestantism, for they had already converted years before to American religion. Thus, it seems that the mission and technologies of the settlement houses would have to be modified for these groups to de-emphasize Americanization and emphasize social reform.

The external polity was strong enough to silence even the strongest reform voice. For example, when Roosevelt refused to seat an African American delegation from southern states during the 1912 presidential convention of the Progressive Party, Jane Addams debated leaving; however, she decided to remain.[97] Addams may have realized the futility of her protest but, by remaining at a convention of a supposedly reformist party that squelched the rights of African Americans to participate, she exemplified the fact that reform efforts did have their limits.

As far as African Americans were concerned, the settlement house movement cannot be generally characterized as a reform movement. The discriminatory practices that existed outside the settlement house found their way inside the settlement house. In addition, the creation of separate facilities to serve African American populations was a perpetuation of the prevailing belief that the races should be segregated. As with other services, segregation meant less—less service, less attention, less advocacy—for this group. The reform arm of the nascent social work profession was handcuffed by the pervasive racism that dominated the external polity and external economy, as well as by the racism that permeated the internal polity and internal economy of the settlement houses.

The verdict on the settlement house movement is that African Americans find the settlement houses guilty of overlooking the needs of African American communities. W. E. B. DuBois observed that social settlements excluded African Americans and "even where they are not actually discriminated against, they are not made to feel welcome."[98] Fannie Williams observed in 1905, "Only recently has it occurred to the social workers that those who speak a foreign tongue and belong to the 'submerged tenth' are not the only ones in need of guidance, protection and encouragement."[99] While this may have occurred to social workers, few were involved in extending that guidance, protection, or encouragement. In a 1936 analysis of settlement work with African Americans, Lindenberg and Zittel raised a critical question and then offered an answer:

> "What is the Settlement, the sponsor of the underprivileged and the champion of the immigrant, doing for the Negro who has settled on his doorstep?". . . . We find three factors which are altering . . . the composition of the settlement neighborhoods. . . . They are, namely, the decline of immigration, the shifting of the successful foreign born immigrant and his children out of the slum areas . . . and the influx of the Negro. . . . Let's face the issue! What are the settlements doing for the Negro in their neighborhoods? *In most instances absolutely nothing* [emphasis added].[100]

Consequently, the settlement house movement expended most of its energies on the White immigrant groups.[101]

Settlement Houses and Other Ethnic/Racial Minorities

If the settlement houses did little for African Americans, they did even less for other minority groups. The few settlements that developed in areas populated by other minorities provided segregated services or no services. The College Settlement in Los Angeles stands out as an exception because its participants included Mexicans. Settlement workers wanted to establish contact with the Mexicans newly arriving from Mexico, but the 1904–1905 report of the settlement asserted, "A race seeks its own."[102] This belief may have been the reason that house activities were often segregated by the ethnicity of the participants. Workers in this settlement house were active in lobbying for juvenile court services and served on numerous boards and commissions. The extent to which Mexicans were the beneficiaries of these activities is not clear because the neighborhood was changing from Mexican to Italian and Slovenian. As Mexicans left the Southwest and moved to other parts of the country, they continued to encounter racism and were generally excluded from participation in settlement houses.[103] In fact, the *Handbook of Settlements* makes little mention of the Mexicans as a service group.

As neighborhoods experienced changes in ethnic composition, exclusionary policies were, in some cases, reversed. The board of Neighborhood House, in Gary, Indiana, decided on November 17, 1925, to admit Mexicans to the agency.[104] In its work with Mexican families, this settlement house, like many others, appeared to focus on bringing religious teachings to this group, concentrating on saving souls rather than facilitating social reform. To reach this population, the house preached and delivered sermons in Spanish. There is little indication, however, that the economic and political issues facing Mexicans were addressed.

The Wesley House of Houston, Marston Hall of Thurber, Texas, and the Spanish Settlement of Brooklyn illuminate this emphasis.[105] Wesley House was located in a neighborhood that included native-born Americans, Germans, Armenians, Syrians, and Mexicans. Activities included night school for foreigners, kindergarten, nursing services, sewing school, and religious services in Spanish. Thurber, Texas, was a mining town with a population of 800 to 1,000—about three-fourths were foreign born and largely Italian and Mexican. Thurber provided religious services for foreigners, temperance society meetings, night school, kindergarten, housekeeping classes, and an array of clubs. The Spanish Settlement of Brooklyn taught English to Hispanic adults and featured classes in Christian Doctrine, sewing, singing, and dancing. However, advocacy and reform work on behalf of the Mexican population was not mentioned. To an extent, the limited settlement work with Mexicans was an extension and continuation of the missionary work with this group that predated the settlement house movement.

Other groups received practically no settlement house attention. For example, only one Chinese settlement is listed in the *Handbook of Settlements*.[106] True Sunshine Mission of San Francisco was established to provide work among the Chinese and was located in a Chinese quarter of San Francisco, across the street from the Chinese school. The mission maintained a playground, provided classes in English for adults, taught classes in sewing and kitchen gardening for children, had a dispensary, and conducted religious services. These activities focused on Americanization, not social reform; the anti-Chinese sentiment that dominated much of the West may have hampered any reform attempts. In addition, the settlers of True Sunshine Mission may not have recognized or accepted a need for any other types of activities.

Although not listed in the *Handbook of Settlements,* the Cameron House in San Francisco helped "Chinese women enslaved by the tongs in their brothels."[107] This work had begun in the 1870s with the Presbyterian Mission of Chinatown and was eventually led in 1895 by a Scotswoman named Donaldina Cameron. She was able to enlist the aid of the police in her efforts. This may be the only organized work on behalf of Chinese women during the Progressive Era.

Although located in the Chinatown and Bowery of New York, the China-town Rescue Settlement and Recreation Room was organized "for neighbor-hood work among erring" American, English, German, French, Hebrew, Italian, and Bohemian girls who "live with the Chinese and American men in Chinatown."[108] Substance abuse, disease, and prostitution associated with dance halls and saloons prompted settlers to intervene to rescue girls from this environment. Not surprisingly, the work of a settlement in Chinatown tar-geted the White ethnics in this community.

Settlement work never reached the Japanese communities. This may have been due to this group's economic success and the anti-Asian feeling that prevailed on the West Coast. It is doubtful that university or religious groups would commit their resources to assist a population that was per-ceived as taking property and business away from the "real Americans who deserved them."

American Indians were a special case; their confinement to reservations rendered the settlement house movement irrelevant. The reformers who advocated and implemented the boarding school model (discussed in Chapter 3) were drawn from the same pool as were the friendly visitors from charity organization societies and settlement house workers. In addition, many edu-cated middle-class women ventured to the reservation to teach and provide Americanization activities. These young women were called *missionaries* rather than social workers.

CONCLUSION

The reform of the settlement house movement excluded racial and ethnic minorities as the beneficiaries of that reform. The child labor reforms, the juvenile court reforms, and the creation of reformatories for children failed to incorporate minorities. According to June Brown:

> The literature of the era reveals a notable scarcity of the concern for the plight of Black children trapped in the neoslavery of sharecropping; for American Indian children subjected to many forms of . . . "acculturation under duress"; or for Hispanic and sometimes Asian children working in the fields of California and the Southwest.[109]

Consequently, from its very inception, social work was alienating ethnic minorities through practices that implied that the needs of these groups were not paramount.

Many of the issues confronting the ethnic minority groups were civil rights issues—issues that dealt with discriminatory policies and practices and racist perspectives. In general, social work, in its infancy and in its adulthood, has not been a civil rights movement. With a little stretch of the imagination, social work could be loosely perceived as a subtle civil rights movement for educated women who wanted to escape the confines of home and hearth. For these women, social work became a liberating force in their lives. Unfortunately, this liberation did not extend to other oppressed groups.

Endnotes

1 Jane Addams, "A Function of the Social Settlement," *Annals of the American Academy of Political and Social Science* 13 (May 1899): 36.

2 For a discussion of the English roots of the settlement house movement and the history of the movement in the United States, see James Leiby, *A History of Social Welfare* (New York: Columbia University Press, 1978), 127–135.

3 Leiby, *A History of Social Welfare*, 127.

4 June Axinn and Herman Levin, *Social Welfare—A History of the American Response to Need*, Second Edition (New York: Harper & Row, 1982), 112.

5 Robert Woods and Albert Kennedy, *Handbook of Settlements* (New York: Charities Publication Committee, Russell Sage Foundation, 1911), vi.

6 Alvin Kogut, "The Settlements and Ethnicity: 1890–1914," *Social Work* 17 (May 1972): 23; Leiby, *A History of Social Welfare and Social Work*, 128; Ralph Pumphrey and Muriel Pumphrey, "The Settlement Movement," in *The Heritage of American Social Work*, ed. Ralph Pumphrey and Muriel Pumphrey (New York: Columbia University Press, 1961): 193.

7 Woods and Kennedy, *Handbook of Settlements*, 228.

8 Ibid., 53.

9 Noted in social work literature such as Ralph Dolgoff and Donald Feldstein, *Understanding Social Welfare*, 7th ed. (Boston: Pearson, 2007), 303–305.

10 These similarities are discussed in greater detail in Dolgoff and Feldstein, *Understanding Social Welfare*, 299–305.

11 Axinn and Levin, *Social Welfare*, 111–113; Bruce Jansson, *The Reluctant Welfare State*, 6th ed. (Belmont, CA: Brooks/Cole, 2009), 178–179; Ray Johns and David DeMarche, *Community Organization and Agency Responsibility*, (New York: Association Press, 1951), 86; Kogut, "The Settlements and Ethnicity," 23; Leiby, *A History of Social Welfare*, 127–135; Pumphrey and Pumphrey, "The Settlement Movement," 192–193.

12 Addams, "A Function of the Social Settlement," 33.

13 Paul Boyer, "An Ohio Leader of the Social Gospel Movement—Reassessing Washington Gladden," *Oral History* 116 (2009), 89. Project MUSE, http://muse.jhu.edu/journals/ohio-history/v116/116.boyer.pdf (accessed January 12, 2010).

14 Addams, "A Function of the Social Settlement," 54.

15 Robert Reinders, "Toynbee Hall and the American Settlement Movement," *Social Service Review* 56 (March 1982): 39–54.

16 Kogut, "The Settlements and Ethnicity," 23.

17 The quotations in this paragraph are from Herman Hegner, "Scientific Value of the Social Settlements," *American Journal of Sociology* 3 (September 1897): 174–176.

18 Leiby, *A History of Social Welfare:* 129.

19 David Wagner, "Collective Mobility and Fragmentation: A Model of Social Work History," *Journal of Sociology and Social Welfare* 13 (September 1986): 671.

20 Axinn and Levin, *Social Welfare*, 113. Also mentioned in Pumphrey and Pumphrey, "The Settlement Movement," 192.

21 As detailed and quoted in Allen Davis, *Spearheads for Reforms—The Social Settlements and the Progressive Movement 1890–1914* (New Brunswick, NJ: Rutgers University Press, 1984), 87.

22 Howard Karger, "Minneapolis Settlement Houses in the 'Not So Roaring 20s': Americanization, Morality, and the Revolt against Popular Culture," *Journal of Sociology and Social Welfare* 14 (June 1987): 93.

23 Woods and Kennedy, *Handbook of Settlements*.

24 Ibid., 66.

25 Ibid., 31.

26 Ibid., 175.

[27] Ibid., 262.

[28] Dolgoff and Feldstein, *Understanding Social Welfare*, 303.

[29] Leiby, *A History of Social Welfare*, 127–129.

[30] Woods and Kennedy, *Handbook of Settlements*, 2.

[31] Clarke Chambers, "Women in the Creation of the Profession of Social Work," *Social Service Review* 60 (March 1986): 12; Harry Kraus, *The Settlement House Movement in New York City, 1886–1914* (New York: Arno Press, 1980), 37.

[32] Jansson, *The Reluctant Welfare State*, 185–186; Stanley Wenocur and Michael Reisch, *From Charity to Enterprise—The Development of American Social Work in a Market Economy* (Urbana: University of Chicago Press, 1989), 26–29.

[33] Anthony Platt, "The Child-Saving Movement and the Origins of the Juvenile Justice System," in *The Sociology of Juvenile Delinquency*, ed. Ronald Berger (Chicago: Nelson-Hall, 1991), 13.

[34] Chambers, "Women in the Creation of the Profession of Social Work," 12–13; J. Ehrenreich, *The Altruistic Imagination: A History of Social Work and Social Policy in the United States* (Ithaca, NY: Cornell University Press, 1985), 33–36.

[35] Dolgoff and Feldstein, *Understanding Social Welfare*, 263.

[36] James Gustafson, "Professions as 'Callings,'" *Social Service Review* 56 (December 1982): 510, 511.

[37] Murray Levine and Adeline Levine, *A Social History of the Helping Services* (New York: Appleton-Century-Crofts, 1970), 93–99.

[38] Levine and Levine, *A Social History of the Helping Services*, 94.

[39] Platt, "The Child Saving Movement," 13.

[40] These relationships and historical accounts are found in Platt, "The Child-Saving Movement," 11–15.

[41] Ehrenreich, *The Altruistic Imagination*, 31.

[42] As noted in Leiby, *A History of Social Welfare*, 132.

[44] Dolgoff and Feldstein, *Understanding Social Welfare*, 263–264.

[44] Wagner, "Collective Mobility and Fragmentation," 672.

[45] Davis, *Spearheads for Reform*, 85.

[46] Kraus, *The Settlement House Movement*.

[47] Louise Johnson, Charles Schwartz, and Donald Tate, *Social Welfare: A Response to Human Need*, 4th ed. (Boston: Allyn & Bacon, 1991).

[48] Kraus, *The Settlement House Movement*, 34.

[49] Woods and Kennedy, *Handbook of Settlements*, 33.

[50] Ibid., 71.

[51] Ibid., 87, 282.

[52] Ibid., 152.

[53] Ibid., 53.

[54] Dolgoff and Feldstein, *Understanding Social Welfare*, 263; Johnson, Schwartz, and Tate, *Social Welfare*; Kogut, "The Settlements and Ethnicity," 22; Kraus, *The Settlement House Movement*, 38; George Martin, *Social Policy in the Welfare State* (Englewood Cliffs, NJ: Prentice-Hall, 1990), 26–27; as reflected in the mission of the Women's Home Mission Society reported by Woods and Kennedy, *Handbook of Settlements*, 4.

[55] Woods and Kennedy, *Handbook of Settlements*, 40.

[56] Ibid., 69.

[57] Kogut, "The Settlements and Ethnicity," 22–31.

[58] Woods and Kennedy, *Handbook of Settlements*, 36.

[59] Ibid., 266.

[60] Davis, *Spearheads for Reform*, 227.

[61] Karger, "Minneapolis Settlement Houses," 91.

[62] Woods and Kennedy, *Handbook of Settlements*, 252.

[63] Ibid., 270.

[64] Ibid., 292.

[65] Ruth Crocker, *Social Work and Social Order: The Settlement Movement in Two Industrial Cities, 1889–1930* (Chicago: University of Illinois Press, 1992), 35; Judith Trolander, *Settlement Houses and the Great Depression* (Detroit: Wayne State University Press, 1975), 137–138; Woods and Kennedy, *Handbook of Settlements*, 32, 150, 295.

[66] Davis, *Spearheads for Reform*, 94; Trolander, *Settlement Houses*,136.

[67] Trolander, *Settlement Houses*, 137.

[68] Woods and Kennedy, *Handbook of Settlements*, 73.

[69] Trolander, *Settlement Houses*, 137–138.

[70] This history of neighborhood is reported in Crocker, *Social Work and Social Order*, 146.

[71] Steve Kramer, "Uplifting Our 'Downtrodden Sisterhood': Victoria Earle Matthews and New York's White Rose Mission, 1897–1907," *The Journal of African American History* 91 (Summer 2006): 258–259.

[72] Davis, *Spearheads for Reform*, 95; Woods and Kennedy, *Handbook of Settlements*, 177, 210; Trolander, *Settlement Houses*, 24.

[73] Davis, *Spearheads for Reform*, 94–95.

[74] Robert Woods and Albert Kennedy, *The Settlement Horizon* (New Brunswick: Transaction Publishers, 1990), 337. (Originally published in 1922 by the Russell Sage Foundation.)

[75] Trolander, *Settlement Houses*, 139–140.

[76] Woods and Kennedy, *The Settlement Horizon*, 51.

[77] Steven Diner, "Chicago Social Workers and Blacks in the Progressive Era," *Social Service Review* 44 (December 1970): 401.

[78] As quoted in W. E. B. DuBois, *The Negro Family*, Atlanta University Publications, No. 13 (Atlanta: Atlanta University Press, 1908), 152.

[79] Woods and Kennedy, *Handbook of Settlements*, 268.

[80] W. E. B. DuBois, *Efforts for Social Betterment among Negro Americans* (Atlanta, GA: Atlanta University Press, 1909), 121–126.

[81] As quoted in DuBois, *Efforts for Social Betterment*, 122.

[82] Crocker, *Social Work and Social Order*, 185.

[83] DuBois, *Efforts for Social Betterment*, 121.

[84] Trolander, *Settlement Houses*, 145.

[85] Sara Collins Fernandis, "A Social Settlement in South Washington," *Charities and the Commons* 15 (October 7, 1905): 66.

[86] Sara Collins Fernandis, "Social Settlement Work among Colored People," *Charities and the Commons* 21 (November 21, 1908): 302.

[87] Trolander, *Settlement Houses*, 145.

[88] Kraus, *The Settlement House Movement*, 217–218.

[89] M. A. Jimenez, "Historical Evolution and Future Challenges of the Human Services Professions," *Families in Society* 71 (January 1990): 7.

[90] John Murchison, "Some Major Aspects of the Economic Status of the Negro," *Social Forces* 14 (October 1935): 114.

[91] August Meier, *Negro Thought in America 1880–1915* (Ann Arbor: University of Michigan Press, 1966), 134.

[92] Trolander, *Settlement Houses*, 145.

[93] Sandra Sethno, "Public Responsibility for Dependent Black Children: The Advocacy of Edith Abbott and Sophonisba Breckenridge," *Social Service Review* 62 (September 1988): 485–503.

[94] Florette Henri, *Black Migration: Movement North, 1900–1920* (Garden City, NY: Doubleday, 1975). 202.

[95] Davis, *Spearheads for Reform*, 102.

[96] William Foster, *The Negro People in American History* (New York: International Publishers, 1954), 424.

[97] Axinn and Levin, *Social Welfare*, 152; Henri, *Black Migration*, 245; Jansson, *The Reluctant Welfare State*, 194.

[98] W. E. B. DuBois, "Social Effects of Emancipation," *The Survey* 29 (February 1, 1913): 572.

[99] As quoted in Edyth Ross, ed., *Black Heritage in Social Welfare 1860–1930* (Metuchen, NJ: The Scarecrow Press, 1978), 231.

[100] Sidney Lindenberg and Ruth Zittel, "The Settlement Scene Changes," *Social Forces* 14 (May 1935): 563, 564.

[101] Axinn and Levin, *Social Welfare*, 152.

[102] The Los Angeles Settlement Association, *The College Settlement* (Los Angeles: The Association, 1904–1905), 6.

[103] Crocker, *Social Work and Social Order*, 146.

[104] A discussion of the Neighborhood House and the Mexicans is provided by Crocker, *Social Work and Social Order*, 146–147.

[105] These settlements are described in Woods and Kennedy, *Handbook of Settlements*, 186, 296–297.

[106] Woods and Kennedy, *Handbook of Settlements*, 23–24.

[107] Jack Chen, *The Chinese of America* (San Francisco: Harper & Row, 1980): 184.

[108] Woods and Kennedy, *Handbook of Settlements*, 235.

[109] June Brown, "Primary Prevention: A Concept Whose Time Has Come for Improving the Cultural-Relevance of Family and Children's Services in Ethnic Minority Communities," in *Primary Prevention Approaches to Development of Mental Health Services* for *Ethnic Minorities*, ed. Samuel Miller, Gwenelle Styles, and Carl Scott (New York: Council on Social Work Education, 1982), 41.

CHAPTER 7

Ethnicity, Race, and the Evolution of Social Work

Caught up with internal and external struggles for control over markets, redefinition and expansion of its service commodity, and enhancement of its public image, mainstream social work largely ignored the racial and social class problems of minorities. Tackling them meant "rocking the boat," creating a dilemma for a group professing concern for the poor.[1]

The charity organization societies and the settlement house movement eventually converged into the profession of social work. Rather than providing a detailed history of this professional evolution, the goal of this chapter is to review and analyze critical aspects of this history that have had significant consequences for the profession's service delivery to minority individuals and communities. These aspects include professionalization, persistent ideologies, bureaucratization of the welfare state, and the rise and decline of movements within the profession. The chapter ends with a discussion of social work, social policy, and the public will.

SOCIAL WORK AND PROFESSIONALIZATION

There is little question that the prewar [World War I] acceptance of social reform as an integral aspect of social work gave way in the 1920s to a conception of social work as a constellation of skills and services designed to bring troubled individuals into functional harmony with society.[2]

For decades social work has selected as its main objective the enhancement of individual and social well-being within the contextual niche of the person in the environment.[3]

Social work began as a series of unpaid helping activities performed by a large population of educated, middle-class men and women at a time when American society was undergoing rapid change. The equilibrium of the social system was being disrupted by immigration, urbanization, and industrialization. The social conditions were extremely harsh and oppressive for White ethnics and people of color. The need for change served as the impetus for reorganizing charity work and agitating for legislative reform. The COS and settlement houses performed services that filled a void and helped create a more civil society.

As a new societal equilibrium emerged, social work leaders fought to transform social work into a legitimate professional with status, recognition, respect, and specialized expertise. This means that the paid social agent eventually replaced the volunteer friendly visitor as the dominant presence in the budding profession. Numerous factors shaped the direction of the new profession's development, and this development widened the schism between social work and ethnic/racial minority communities. Although the COS had been engaged in some limited reform activities, the move away from reform efforts for these societies is captured in Watson's 1922 observation:

> Social work, except possibly in the smallest communities, is no longer the undifferentiated field it once was. Although prevention is still the watchword of the day, housing reform and health campaigns need no longer claim the time and energy of family case workers, since others have now come forward to carry the burden of these important but specialized tasks. Leaders in family social work can turn with undivided attention to the basic work of their societies and to perfecting a technique for its accomplishment.[4]

Leaders in the field were alarmed by Abraham Flexner's pronouncement during his speech at the 1915 National Conference of Charities and Corrections that social work was not a profession because it lacked a specific skill as used with a specific function.[5] Social work leaders embarked on a mission to prove Flexner wrong, and to do so they would need to define their own particular niche of expertise. These individuals desired the professional designation enjoyed by other professions and the acceptance of the significance of the work they did. It may have seemed to some social workers that, in the absence of professional status, social work would be destined to remain an adjunct service rather than one that was indispensable and fully integrated into society.

No doubt, professional status also carried a special degree of significance to the educated women who wanted to elevate their "social mothering" and "civic housekeeping" to a higher plane. The seeking of professionalization also meant that women social workers needed to distinguish themselves from the other middle-class White women who worked under religious auspices in the missions.[6] Skills and expertise gained prominence over religious dedication and conviction. Paid work replaced volunteerism as social work gradually became a career choice for many educated women who, previously, had few outlets for their talents. Thus, the contributions to social work by numerous religious-affiliated women may have been overlooked in the writing of social work history.[7]

Professionalization became, in itself, a cause.[8] Volumes of time, energy, and other resources were invested in the establishment of social work as a full-fledged profession. Numerous social workers were invested in advocacy on their own behalf, since they were the major beneficiaries of the rewards of professionalization. Professional associations, training, and degreed educational programs became the goal as social workers attempted to define and redefine their work in terms compatible with the norms of professionalism. In essence, these pioneers believed that "the promise of American life" could be achieved if people placed their trust in the skills of those "exceptional" individuals who were expert in the control of social problems.[9] By pursuing professionalization, social work was following in the footsteps of other professions so that this goal was not deviant or atypical. As this mission was pursued, however, mainstream social work largely ignored the racial and social class problems of minorities.[10]

In this quest, personal services or social casework overshadowed the social reform activities associated with the settlement houses.[11] Personal or individual reform replaced social reform. Several major factors account for this ascendancy of social casework:

- Reform became unpopular as an activity,
- Social casework appeared more "scientific" and could easily lend itself to the development of a specific knowledge base,
- Social casework was less controversial than social reform,
- Restrictions on immigration seemed to reduce the significance of social reform activities,
- The power of the social work faction supported social casework, and
- Economic constraints led to reduced financial support for settlement house work and social reform.

The "cause" base of the profession that had been concerned with facilitating change was replaced by an emphasis on "functions" of social work and the expertise underlying those functions.[12]

The external polity of the budding profession frowned on radicalism, reform, and anything that remotely touched on militancy, particularly after World War I. The "Red Scare" of the 1920s caused many groups and individuals to cower in the face of witch hunts and mass intimidation. The climate was hostile toward agitation by or on behalf of any group, including racial and ethnic minorities. The public, including social workers, remained silent about the raids conducted by the Attorney General that led to the deportation of thousands of Russian immigrants who were alleged to be members of the Communist Party.[13] This hastened the decline of the settlement house movement and its attendant social reform. Jane Addams, yielding to the hostile polity by focusing on world brotherhood instead of Hull House activities, wrote of the effects of the raids: "Any proposed change was suspect, even those efforts that had been considered praiseworthy before the war . . . even social workers exhibited many symptoms of this panic and with a protective instinct *carefully avoided any phraseology of social reform"* [emphasis added].[14]

The decline of social reform was also linked to a reduction in unpopular immigration. Reform was generally seen as needed with White ethnic immigrant groups, not with the ethnic/racial minorities whose social situation had changed very little. The settlement house movement began to modify its emphasis and approaches. Social group work as reflected in recreation and educational activities surfaced as the primary technology, replacing social reform.[15] The settlement houses had to regain the financial support they had previously enjoyed, and to do this, they had to shed their reform image. For many settlers, *reform* became a word to avoid.

The noncontroversial nature of social casework became all the more important in this environment. In espousing social casework as the predominant method of social work, the profession shrouded itself with a cloak of conservatism. The primacy of individual responsibility was in step with prevailing political and social thought. It seems that, during this time, social work "success" was associated with a rejection of radicalism and militancy. This rejection can be seen as an indication that the profession was beginning to embrace more conservative methods of service delivery.

By narrowing their definition of social work to psychiatrically oriented casework, social workers minimized or completely eliminated public, social, and labor reform, as well as "less professional" techniques such as liaison and resource mobilization.[16] If the budding profession wanted public sanction and legitimacy from its external polity, the adoption of this narrow definition of social work seemed imperative. Consequently, the ideology of individual responsibility embraced during the Progressive Era was formalized in the teachings and practices of what was to become professional social work.

Grace Coyle, in 1935, offered a critique of social work when she wrote:

> As case work has "gone psychiatric" it has not only concentrated upon the individual, it has further centered upon his emotional life, giving decreasing attention to environmental factors, social and economic. It has even been claimed at times that the ills that beset the unemployed could be met by proper emotional adjustment.[17]

This concentration on the individual has resulted in what C. Wright Mills described as "an occupational incapacity to rise above series of 'cases.'"[18] For Mills, this trained incapacity was filled with political limitations. Because the social worker moves from case to case, he or she may be blind to a much larger picture or social context that may unify the cases. Awareness of such universal trends and commonalities may dictate an alternative professional response.

With professionalization came the "authority of expertise" predicated on the social worker's competence and the client's recognition and acceptance of that competence.[19] In addition to authority, paternalism has also been a part of casework practice. Paternalism involves acting in the best interest of clients even when their best interest is inconsistent with what the clients wish for themselves.[20] Thus, the social worker could act as a supportive father figure who could, when required, be authoritative.[21] Practices of the COS and settlement houses that identified for clients what they needed to do to become good Americans were institutionalized in the new profession.

To minorities, this social distance and paternalism seemed to be an extension of White superiority, since very few minorities were visible in the profession. Through the professionalization of social casework, social workers could legitimately define the problems of minority groups and the course of action necessary to combat those problems. This paternalistic attitude assumed that minority groups were underdeveloped and that assistance was needed to raise the values, aspirations, competence, and political sophistication of the groups.[22] This sentiment was very pervasive in post–World War I U.S. society, as it had been during the Progressive years. In social work, American society had found a profession that actually mirrored this belief.

Professionalization through casework practice placed the worker–client interaction and relationship at the core of social work practice. The expertise of the professional separated those who provided help from those who received help. The distance that existed during the Progressive Era between the friendly visitor and the service beneficiary was perpetuated by the distance between the expert and the client. This distance promotes practitioner objectivity and leads to assessments that may minimize client definitions of the problem. The power of the professional increases when problems are attributed to individuals, making diagnostic skills more crucial.[23] Furthermore, the power of the worker over the client became an integral part of professional social work practice.[24]

The Persistence of Ideology

Social casework stressed the social diagnosis of the individual, and Freudian approaches came to be accepted as a social diagnosis technology.[25] Social workers supported an ideology that carried a psychological orientation to social problems.[26] Social problems started and stopped with the individual as social work defined problems in individual functioning terms. How a problem is defined also defines the solution proposed. Environmental, institutional, and/or structural bases of social problems were virtually ignored and social workers strove to change, treat, socialize, or rehabilitate the individual. Herein lies the thrust of the conservatism of social work: Society is fine and would be better if the "broken" people could be "fixed." This meant that, at that time, social work virtually ignored the problems of large-scale institutional change.[27] This sentiment is further reflected in Watson's 1922 pronouncement, "Case work is spoken of in some quarters as 'the art of untangling and reconstructing the twisted personality' in such a manner that the individual can adjust himself to his environment."[28]

The ideology of social work may differ markedly from that of ethnic/racial minorities. These groups are more likely to attribute the cause of their social condition and situation to the unrelenting discrimination and racism they historically faced.[29] Over time, many minority individuals continued to believe that White racism was the major mental health problem that needed to be addressed.[30] Chapters 3, 4, and 5 clearly revealed that the passage of time did little to lessen the racism and discrimination that many groups of color faced. By adopting social casework as its dominant method, the profession of social work was ignoring the beliefs and unique histories of racial/ethnic groups in the United States—a history that is replete with institutional oppression. Social work was not just turning its back on social reform—it was turning its back on the thousands of individuals who had suffered extensively and primarily because of discriminatory treatment they received.

Social work did, however, apply its method to work with minorities. These groups were often seen as victims who were damaged by their history of oppression.[31] This led to what Henry Miller refers to as *clinicalism*—the presumption of damage and the use of psychological assistance to overcome this damage.[32] According to Miller, the history of minorities was, indeed, noted in this social work response. For African Americans, for example, this meant that slavery, exploitation, and victimization significantly damaged this group, and the results of this damage were visible in lifestyles that were viewed as maladaptive. This "clinicalism" was applied to other groups as well. American Indians have been perceived as vulnerable to psychological problems because of their forced acculturation to U.S. society.[33] Social work's role, therefore, was to "correct" this damage by working with individuals because, with social casework, only individuals are "sick," not entire ethnic groups.

Sociologically, social work was often considered one of the many ways in which society exerted control over its "deviant" members.[34] Ideologies and beliefs are examples of the kinds of social control that exist in U.S. society.[35] By denying the forces of discrimination in the institutions and structures of society, social work as a profession was validating those very institutions and structures. The endorsement of individual treatment communicated to minorities that the new profession of social work would be of little assistance in the struggle for racial equality because it perceived that efforts at social change were unnecessary. In addition, those in need of relief would have to look elsewhere as Watson, in 1922, wrote that "relief, though important, is nevertheless but incidental in good case work.[36] These subtle messages defined what the profession saw as the "appropriate" ways to combat social problems and attempted, either intentionally or inadvertently, to steer minorities away from social reform and social change. Social work seemed to capture America's ambivalence about the causes of social problems by trying simultaneously to enable and to control clients.[37]

Had more minorities been involved in the profession during its developmental stage, perhaps the outcome would have been different. As it was, African American and other minority social workers were extremely rare. Figures for 1928 show that there may have been as many as 1,500 African American social workers in the country, but only about 500 were believed to have had any form of special social work training.[38] African American social workers included 270 in private settings in 65 cities in 1932, another approximately 600 in other settings around the country, and the teaching staff at the African American schools of social work, Atlanta University and Howard University.[39] In fact, the National Urban League was one of the largest employers of African American social workers. These workers were needed for the numerous service sites the league operated. Training and other educational programs would not admit African Americans, and countless White agencies would not employ them. Jewish and Catholic social services were well-organized exceptions to the dominance of social work by White Protestants.[40] The need to increase the minority presence in social work has been a concern for years.[41]

Professionalization further removed mainstream social work from ethnic/minority communities. The external polity and external economy guided the path of the new profession. Legitimacy and public sanction could not be jeopardized by endorsing unpopular methods and groups. The development of any profession cannot be separated from the environment in which it forms. The internal polity of the embryonic profession charted a direction that was in consonance with the environment. The direction taken may have assured the profession of survival and public support. Any critical analysis of the profession's development must consider the internal and external forces that not only shaped but also dictated particular responses. The intent here is not to rationalize or blame, but to support the contention that service delivery to minority communities must take into account the history of the alienation between the profession and those ethnic minority communities it now seeks to serve.

The Bureaucratization of the Welfare State

The Great Depression of 1929 marked another turning point for social work. Massive unemployment overwhelmed local charities and state governments. Strategies to revive the business sector proved unsuccessful as the nation labored under the widespread discontent of the public. As an almost last-ditch effort, President Roosevelt signed into law the Social Security Act of 1935 that changed the role of the federal government in caring for its citizens. It was the passage of this act and the public funding of social programs that catapulted the United States into what became known as a *welfare state*. With this law, the federal government transported social services from the private to the public sector and became the predominant sponsor of social programs. These programs required thousands of social workers and the organizations that employed them. As a result of this and other relevant legislation, the number of social workers doubled during the 1930s to number about 30,000.[42] Years earlier, apprehension had been expressed about the "red tape of official machinery" when the Los Angeles became the first city in the nation to create a Municipal Charities Commission to oversee social work in that city.[43] The red tape of a city was surely dwarfed by the red tape associated with the federal government.

With the welfare state came social work's dependency on federal sponsorship that cemented a bond between social work and the "establishment." If government is deemed an impartial provider of funding, then the social work–government relationship could be neutral. If, however, government is a vehicle for the expression of particular values, particular special-interest groups, or particular ideologies, then social work could be jeopardizing its effectiveness as a profession. For many social workers, a welfare state potentially meant that social work could end up preserving the status quo and protecting the institutions that financed the profession.[44] Because previous social policies of the federal government had exerted an oppressive influence over ethnic/racial minorities (as discussed in previous chapters), social work's growing relationship with the government did little to raise the profession's status in their eyes.

Funding imperatives imposed by the federal government, as well as bureaucratization, are additional factors that have significantly influenced social work's response to ethnic minority communities. With the rise of the welfare state, the consumption of services was separated from the control of the services. As the federal government became a dominant sponsor of social services, consumption was separated from financing; this is one way that control is separated from consumption.[45] With this funding arrangement, agencies become accountable to the service sponsor and not to the service consumers. The voice of clients became heard indirectly through taxation and social policies. The separation of consumption from control reinforced the ideology of professional social work. Etzioni noted:

> The professionals are in a difficult place in this continuum. Their services, especially when organized in any administrative form, are separate from the fee charged and therefore from direct pressure by the client. Here the separation between consumption and control is supported by a strong ideology. . . namely, that *those who administer the service are in a better position to judge what is good for the consumer than he is for himself* [emphasis added].[46]

With the emergence of the welfare state, ethnic and racial minorities remained outside of the mainstream as consumers rather than power brokers. To a certain extent, the welfare state solidified their powerlessness, since these groups could not shape social policies—not even those policies that directly affected their lives.

Bureaucracy became the predominant organizational form for the complex, specialized programs that were created. According to Weber, the bureaucratic organization is characterized by its reliance on technical expertise, administrative hierarchy, specialization, formalized procedures, rationality, efficiency, and depersonalization.[47] The bureaucratic structure further distanced the client from the worker as services became administratively driven rather than client driven. The organizations also promoted a rigidity that often defied attempts at change and innovation; hence, they became less likely to adjust to changes in society. These organizations also became settings for socializing social workers into the values and norms governing bureaucratic practice.[48]

Ethnic minorities perceived these organizations as bastions of the status quo that seemed incapable of responding to their needs. They became entities to be manipulated, circumvented, or avoided. The impenetrable walls of bureaucratic rigidity, red tape, and coldness alienated numerous minorities as they experienced the welfare state organizations as unresponsive.

Even some of the very programs that gave rise to the welfare state under the Social Security Act of 1935 further alienated ethnic minorities.[49] African Americans were discriminated against in the programs of Roosevelt's New Deal as some work and housing programs practiced segregation, and other programs had requirements that could not be met by African Americans. In 1933, African Americans totaled 10 percent of the population yet represented 18 percent of relief recipients.[50] They filled relief rolls because many of them had been fired from jobs and replaced with Whites. Discrimination and racism found their way into the operations of the very social programs designed to combat the Great Depression. In 1935, John Murchison of the Department of the

Interior observed, "In the broad programs for economic security for the masses, moreover, the Negro in actuality still remains outside the total picture."[51]

When thousands of unemployed Hispanics applied for relief during the 1930s, they were often forced to return to Mexico. This happened to about 400,000 Hispanics from 1929 to 1934. Many, with $14.70 given them by the government, were indiscriminately railroaded to Mexico without regard for effects of deportation on families. Cornelius observed, "The door was slammed shut, and mass roundups and less obvious forms of coercion were employed to rid ourselves of the 'intolerable burden' of Mexican workers who did not leave of their own volition."[52] (The repatriation of Mexicans during the Great Depression will be discussed in greater detail later in this chapter.) In addition, during the Depression numerous Nisei (second-generation Japanese) could not find employment in engineering, manufacturing, or other areas in which they had received training. Racism toward this group contributed to the fact that almost no Nisei were employed by Whites.

For the Mexicans and Mexican Americans remaining in this country, discrimination was rampant during the Depression. They were often excluded from the New Deal programs. For example in Arizona, the Pima County Welfare Board had 1,000 Civilian Conservation Corps (CCC) slots to fill in 1933.[53] Only one-fifth of them were given to workers of Mexican descent, even though the county had a significantly higher population of this group. When local groups complained about the underrepresentation of Mexicans, county officials said that they felt it would be disruptive to raise the standard of living for Mexicans while letting the White standard decline. In addition, the CCC camps were segregated for both African Americans and Mexican Americans. Although the federal legislation did not mandate Mexican segregation, Whites pushed for it and, eventually, segregation became common practice in the CCC camps.

As with the COS and the settlement house movement, the welfare state was not initially designed to address the issues of ethnic minority communities. The intended recipients of the services, employment, and relief were White Americans. For the most part, the emergence of the welfare state and the bureaucratization of services that accompanied it deepened the wedge between social work and ethnic minority communities.

The Rise and Decline of Movements in the Profession

The rank-and-file movement (RFM) of the 1930s[54] and the human services movement (HSM) of the 1960s and 1970s[55] were dramatic attempts to realign the goals, practices, and administration of the profession. Both movements were sparked by social policies that attempted to alleviate social suffering—policies of Roosevelt's New Deal and Johnson's Great Society's War on Poverty, respectively. With both plans, new, untrained recruits from outside the profession staffed the new social programs and brought with them a different perspective of their employment, their mission, the social work profession, and social service delivery. At its peak in 1936, the RFM had about 15,000 members who were employed primarily in public relief agencies.[56]

The RFM social workers held talks on the worker–client relationship, sought to redefine the professional focus to emphasize client needs rather than professional status, took part in protest activities and radical movements, identified with the clients, and supported unionization. By the mid-1930s, however, the RFM workers had quieted their attack on social work and tried to develop their own method of casework that valued client-related goals. Much of the movement's push for social reform over casework and rethinking the worker–client role disappeared as "professional and movement interests converged around the narrower protective concerns of raising the standards of service through job classification, salary schedules, training, and personnel practices.[57] The resulting civil service bureaucracy served as a way of shielding public sector jobs.[58] Near the end of the 1930s, these responses to policies and practices made the RFM a part of mainstream social work. This would seem to represent a striking example of co-optation.

The agitation of the RFM did leave a mark on the profession, which expanded its scope to integrate some of the movement's issues. For example, because of the RFM, the profession accepted the following: public welfare as a field, even though it has never achieved a status base comparable to private agency work; groupwork and community organization as legitimate methods, even though they have continued to be overshadowed by direct practice; and a broader view of casework that fostered the "person-in-environment" perspective.

Spano offers an overview of the RFM goal of achieving social justice for minority groups, especially African Americans.[59] Rank-and-filers spoke out because of their conviction that racial injustice was actually symptomatic of the class divisions in society. The eradication of injustice and oppression would benefit everyone regardless of race or ethnicity. The meetings, writings, and speeches of the RFM were filled with support for African Americans. As the momentum of the movement ebbed, the benefits of this advocacy for minority groups remain unclear.

The turbulent 1960s with its civil rights movement, Chicano movement, protests, riots, and general social upheaval formed the backdrop for the human services movement. The War on Poverty was a compilation of job training, community action, and youth employment programs. The community action programs mandated "maximum feasible participation of the poor" that was interpreted in varying ways at the local level. Newly developed community programs recruited paraprofessionals, minority group members, poor people, and others not typically identified with social work.

A community organization movement also developed that was at odds with the traditional theme of profession building. This movement developed outside the profession and acknowledged the role of race and class in dividing U.S. society. Individuals who were not professional social workers, such as Saul Alinsky and Caesar Chavez, were instrumental in catapulting community organization to national prominence.

Client and community groups challenged the tenets of mainstream social work. National Welfare Rights Organization members, minority social workers, and other activists launched protests that disrupted professional conferences. These protests were used to force the profession to rethink poverty and racism. The HSM focused on social change, social reform, grassroots organizing, client rights, and community development. HSM workers wanted to be agents of social change, not agents of social control, and they wanted to start with the places where clients were the most oppressed (prisons and welfare offices, for example). As with the RFM, the profession's internal polity now included a vocal faction that wanted to change the course of the profession's development.

During this period, African American social workers grew increasingly dissatisfied with the National Association of Social Workers' (NASW) inactivity in fighting racism and advocating for African Americans. They formed the National Association of Black Social Workers in 1966 and split from NASW in 1969.[60] Because many of the Chicano social workers perceived NASW as not responding to their needs, they formed their own national social work organization, the Trabajadores de la Raza, also in 1969.[61] While the African American social workers challenged the profession's stance on matters of race, the Chicano social workers wanted more aggressive recruitment of Chicanos for the profession, as the Chicano presence in the profession was minuscule.

As with the RFM, the agitation of the HSM waned due, in part, to powerful organizational and professional norms that resisted change. Social work, for the most part, returned to business as usual. Although it was not self-sustaining, the HSM, nevertheless, left a legacy to social work: Undergraduate social work education was strengthened as the Council on Social Work Education established standards for accrediting undergraduate programs; the Bachelor of Social Work (B.S.W.) became an entry-level degree for professional practice; a human services profession emerged with its own educational program and schools; interest in community organization was renewed, even though that interest declined over time; the profession accepted the role of social advocate; and the practice of casework was critically revisited.

Wagner hypothesized more conservative changes to the profession as a result of the HSM:

> While Human Service and BSW workers will seek *increasing professionalization, including dissociation from lower status work and increased association with MSW workers,* the MSWs will seek increasing work differentiation in which non-MSWs perform most direct practice, while MSWs can become supervisors, consultants, and administrators [emphasis added].[62]

It seems likely that the dominant internal polity of the profession will continue to co-opt dissidents and fractious factions while not straying too far from its conservative leanings toward professionalization. As a matter of fact, many social workers with a bachelor's degree as their highest degree are providing case management services—services that have a history based in the charity organization societies.[63] According to Jansson, even the introduction of the environmental systems and ecological frameworks in the 1970s and 1980s were translated into tools for casework. He stated,

> As Mary Richmond advocated decades earlier, emphasizing the environment encourages social workers to gather information about clients' living

conditions. In this way, social workers need not try to change environmental conditions themselves, but can use conditions to aid clinical work.[64]

Two major movements within the profession were not powerful enough to deter the profession from its quest. As social work continues with and maintains its professionalization, it appears to be moving away from serving minority communities, poor communities, and other groups that need advocacy and empowerment.[65] Those it now serves include fee-paying or third-party payment clients as the number of social workers in private practice increases.[66] Historically, the profession devoted more of its political influence to support licensure and vendorship privileges for social work clinicians than for services to disenfranchised populations.[67]

SOCIAL WORK, SOCIAL POLICY, AND PUBLIC WILL

In 1957, Styz described the "middle course" that some social workers took on racial issues—a course that, at that time, saw social workers working within the segregation framework without necessarily agreeing with it.[68] Social work has had numerous demands placed on it by numerous constituencies. For its viability, it may have been prudent to respond to controversial issues in a manner that did not alienate factions. That middle course appears to support "soft determinism" as a way of specifying the causality of social problems.[69] On one hand, there is acknowledgment of factors beyond the individual's control; on the other hand, there is acknowledgment of individual responsibility. It is the hand of individual responsibility, however, that receives the manicure.

Societal Sanction

As a profession, social work has had to balance the demands and expectations of its numerous and powerful constituencies that include the dominant elite both outside and inside the profession. To a large extent, social work as a profession has continued to be vulnerable to and dependent on its external polity and external economy. This dependency has permitted these polities to exert potent influence over the profession's position on matters of race and ethnicity. This dependency has also steered the profession along the middle, and sometimes even conservative, course.

Social work, as a nascent profession, could not afford to alienate those factions that conferred the designation of "profession." Professions require societal sanction in order to be legitimate. In defining societal sanction, Meinert, Pardeck, and Kreuger write:

> There exists societal sanction and support for activities in a specific domain (niche) of human need. This sanction manifests itself by approval for, legitimation of, and the creation of official organizational structures to provide services within the domain of need. The practitioners and the services to be delivered are seen as trustworthy by recipients.[70]

The profession had to equivocate on the controversial issues of race because to do otherwise would endanger its status and legitimacy to the rest of society. It needed to be in step with the rest of society and with the social and political institutions of society. Social work has been guilty of complicity with those institutions that maintained and implemented discriminatory treatment of racial and ethnic minorities. When segregation was the modus operandi of the day, social work agencies segregated despite their policy statements on nondiscrimination.[71] Racial minority clients and staff were subjected to differential treatment and differential access to services and employment. To do otherwise would have endangered the profession's credibility in the eyes of its resource holders. Social reform was held in abeyance as the profession acquiesced to the ideologies and practices of mainstream society. The middle course emerged as a reasonable response to environmental constraints. Indeed, the history of the profession appears to be a history of responding to the external environment.[72]

It took a major social movement—the civil rights movement—to shake racial attitudes and challenge race-related practices. Social workers were not in the forefront of leadership in this movement. The profession hovered around the borders of the movement with ambivalence about its role in it. Once desegregation became the law of the land, however, the profession was free to embrace the new mandate without fear of reprisals, for it was only acting in accordance with changing policies and changing mores. Social work schools and agencies could then actively begin to recruit minority group members.[73]

This dependency of the profession has muted its reform impulses and has given the profession a "bandwagon" quality. It seems to move with the trends and practices of society, not against them. It can jump on the bandwagon once the parade has begun but it cannot afford to lead the procession. This type of response may continue to promote the profession's survival and legitimacy, but it does little to endear the profession to ethnic and racial minorities. Such a response appears to make social work compliant with prevailing dominant racial attitudes, whatever they may be. For these reasons, social work's image and reputation as an establishment-oriented profession may have some credibility. As a system seeking survival and growth, this establishment-oriented image may have been in the best interest of the profession. The middle course may be the profession's attempt to manage its environmental dependencies.

Bureaucratization has also curtailed the reform impulse of the profession through rigid structures and procedures that seem immune to change and innovation. These systems seek to preserve a status quo and to continue doing business as it has always been done. Because of this, an external impetus—the civil rights movement and the resultant policy changes—was required to penetrate bureaucratic barriers to produce change. With the bureaucratization of social work, the profession became organizationally committed to the middle and conservative course.

The leadership of the elite within the profession that knighted social casework as *the* method of social work also serves to mute the profession's reform impulse. The profession may act as an agent of social control for its members who venture outside the social work mainstream. Practitioners and scholars who challenge and critique the profession are often dubbed "radical," and their perspectives are referred to as "radical social work."[74] This so-called radical social work has challenged professional social work education, the role of social work in society, and the way the profession has related to disenfranchised groups. The very imposition of the "radical" label denotes that these perspectives are deviations from the mainstream of social work. This labeling may further serve to prevent these alternative views from being fully integrated into the profession. The profession's dominant elite appears to have supported and further forged the middle and conservative course of the profession.

The argument that social work is also an agent of social reform seems rather specious. While numerous social workers may truly believe in the profession's commitment to reform, the profession's liberalism may be associated with *individuals* within the profession rather than with the *profession* itself[75]—as was true with the settlement house movement. Those individuals who have been capable of achieving some type of social change or social reform may be held as examples of the profession's long-standing dedication to social work. The acts of a few reform-minded individuals are perhaps generalized to the profession as a whole. In fact, these activists may be individuals who also happen to be social workers and who were successful despite being social workers.

Social Work and Social Reform: Implementing the Public Will

During the Progressive Era, educated individuals with privilege, means, influence, and access banded together to propose and implement methods for alleviating the widespread social problems of the time. The social conditions were ripe for social reform, in the form of legislation, to address the social problems of the day. There were voids that needed to be filled and action that needed to be taken. Poor housing conditions, harsh working conditions, and the absence of child labor laws formed the foundation for action. Conditions had converged to create opportunities for change in a society that was ripe for change. All the necessary inputs for social reform were available for use. Reformers who had a commitment to improving the lives of others needed a fulfilling arena in which to devote their time and energy. To a certain extent, they were in search of a cause worthy of their attention.

As reformers began to achieve success in proposing legislation and improving social conditions, that void started to fill. Society moved in the direction of greater stability and the crisis was abating. For the larger society, the deed was done and a different political climate began to emerge. By this time, the reformers and COS alike had become invested in the work they were performing and moved to make it a permanent part of American society. One way of doing this was to establish social work as a profession.

The goal of survival gained dominance, and professionalization became the means through which survival could be achieved. A domain had to be identified and then, once identified, it had to be protected. For societal sanction and the resulting legitimacy, the domain had to be consonant with prevailing values and ideologies. Clearly, the domain of casework with the dependent and vulnerable of society was a socially acceptable choice. It has traces of several American values and ideology: individualism, independence, self-reliance, Social Darwinism, and the Protestant work ethic.[76] Casework seemed the ideal choice in a society that was beginning to feel that social reform was no longer needed. The dominance of casework began to surface during the latter part of the Progressive Era as legislative reforms were passed.

The ascendancy of casework can also be attributed to the fundamental differences between Mary Richmond and Jane Addams. [77] To advance this method, Mary Richmond's *Social Diagnosis* became the authority on the casework method.[78] At a time when medicine was making significant advancements, the diagnostic-oriented title was effective in portraying the developing social work profession as one with a solid knowledge base. Thus, the technology of casework was crystallizing while reformers like Jane Addams did not produce a comparable tome of its methods. Addams apparently had not defined methods for challenging institutional and structural barriers. In addition, she lost favor with her social work colleagues for not supporting professionalization and paid employment for social workers. Thus, it seems somewhat inevitable that casework would ultimately prevail.

Much of the actions of social work leaders during the professionalization process can be described as defining and protecting that domain. In addition, dependency on the environment for vital inputs such as validation and legitimation served to mute any reform tendencies that may have remained. The seeking of societal approval may have served to exert a degree of social control over the new profession. It could not afford to alienate the very source to which it looked for validation.

Because people of color had been marginalized, all the benefits of social reform may not have been extended to them. The populace believed at that time that these groups should have the power, motivation, and commitment to help themselves. There was no belief in, or recognition of, the need for any specific reform for them. It cannot be stressed enough that some groups remained on the periphery of society. In the absence of being White, they were denied many of the privileges extended to others.

Each profession serves a unique purpose for society because it fills some need that society has. While the uniqueness of professions like law and medicine are readily known, such was not the case with social work. With the advent of the welfare state, however, the profession's role became more easily identifiable. According to Popple and Leighninger, social work is the core technology in the social welfare institution, the institution in society that deals with the problem of dependency.[79] Social work represents the implementation arm of social policy. Van Meter and Van Horn define policy implementation as "the performance of the policy as it is actually delivered to clients." [80] Social policy reflects the will of the public; therefore, social work is responsible for implementing the public will. This is a critical supposition because it means that social reform can only be undertaken if it is desired by the public.

For the profession to engage in social reform efforts, as a profession, the mandate would have to come from the larger society. An alternative approach is for the agitation to erupt from the profession itself. This seems rather unlikely for a profession with significant resource dependency on the larger society. For this reason, social work is cast as an unlikely leader of a social movement. While abstention from reform activity may seem rational for survival, it does not endear the profession to marginalized minorities.

Examples of Implementing the Public Will

Because they relate specifically to racial and ethnic minorities, two key examples of professional social workers implementing the public will—Mexican repatriation during the Great Depression, and the internment of Japanese Americans during World War II—are discussed below.

Social Work and Mexican Repatriation.[81]   During the years of the Great Depression that began in 1929, thousands of Mexicans and Mexican Americans found themselves out of work like people all over the country. They applied for welfare relief to which they were entitled. Because of the burden this placed on welfare departments, countless local and state governments began repatriating Mexicans. Mexicans were transported, voluntarily and involuntarily, to Mexico. Because of the stereotypes people held, no distinction was made between the Mexican and the Mexican American, so thousands of native-born Mexican Americans were rounded up and sent to Mexico. An estimated 400,000 Mexicans were escorted out of the country by bus, train, or truck from 1929 to 1934. In 1931 alone, an estimated 50,000–75,000 Mexicans and Mexican Americans left the Southern California region. Between 1930 and 1932, approximately 18,520 Mexicans were escorted from Arizona. In 1928 Detroit had a Mexican population of 15,000, but during the Great Depression that number was cut by half. The process varied from state to state, but the overall intent was clear. Public attitudes were against Mexicans because they were thought to be a monetary drain during the financial crisis. The public perception was that Mexicans were not real Americans and retained their loyalty to Mexico (as was discussed in Chapter 3). According to one writer of that period:

> The repatriation program is regarded locally as a piece of consummate statescraft. The average per family cost of executing it is $71.14, including food and transportation. It cost Los Angeles County $77,249.29 to repatriate one shipment of 9,024. It would have cost $424,933.70 to provide this number with such charitable assistance as they would have been entitled to had they remained—a saving of $347,468.41.[82]

In Los Angeles the program was administered by the Los Angeles County Bureau of Welfare, a branch of the county department of charities. In Detroit, the Detroit Department of Public Welfare created a "Mexican Bureau." Any Mexican who applied for relief was sent to the Mexican Bureau where he or she was encouraged to consider repatriation. It has been estimated that about half of those repatriated were actually born in the United States. Many of those who were repatriated wanted to return to Mexico and welcomed the assistance to do so. For countless others, however, this was repatriation under duress. For some repatriated individuals, the return to the United States would take months or even years. Mexicans had become scapegoats for an economic crisis for which they were not responsible.[83]

Social workers represented the implementation or enforcement of a policy that was clearly the public will. Whether they agreed with it or not, their duty as social workers required them to follow through with this mission. Since enforcing this policy was part of their responsibility, Rich penned an article published in 1936 entitled, "Case Work in the Repatriation of Immigrants."[84] She reported that, for Chicago, Mexicans had the largest number of repatriations for 1931 (14,406) and 1932 (36, 992); however, she offers no explanation for these high figures. The author outlines the issues to be considered by the worker for *voluntary* repatriation cases but does not provide a similar discussion of the use of *involuntary* repatriation as a means of suppressing welfare expenditures. The author does mention the "removal clause" in immigration legislation that permitted the deportation of people who fell into distress, needed public assistance, and/or posed an employment threat to native workers. For these situations, the author merely indicates that social workers should be consulted by those who wish to utilize this clause. The reason for this lack of detailed discussion is not clear, but the role of the social worker in the removal process is minimized. What is clear is that voluntary *and* involuntary repatriation had, by that time, become a routine feature of the county social work position.

The political climate of the Great Depression had singled out the Mexican as the cause of White unemployment. Many social workers may have agreed with this sentiment. Regardless of their personal opinion, they carried out their duties efficiently. The consequences of this period in American history for Mexican and Mexican American families would linger for years. The impressions this left of social workers may have been irreversible.

Social Work and Japanese Internment.   Another example of social workers carrying out the public will can be found in the internment of Japanese Americans during World War II. Much has been written about this period in American history and the factors and forces that led to this internment. Park, however, provides details about social work's involvement in the actual internment process.[85] About 120,000 Japanese and Japanese Americans were relocated to camps, while no persons of German or Italian descent (countries at war with the United States) were subjected to this treatment. By this time, these White ethnics may have become so assimilated that their ethnic heritage was no longer apparent. The Japanese, however, were deemed potential enemy aliens and a threat to national security. The stereotypes that had dogged this group since the late nineteenth century were manifested in this treatment. Their loyalty to the United States was being questioned as it had been decades earlier. In fact, that questioning may never have ceased.

State and local social workers loaned by the California State Department of Social Welfare processed and interviewed these individuals. In addition, private agencies offered volunteer workers and other agencies provided consultation. The records are silent on how the social workers felt about their duties or if they protested the discriminatory actions in which they were engaged. It is likely that some may had misgivings about the situation but felt powerless to confront it. By this time, many may have had too much to lose (employment, careers) to challenge the role they played in the internment process. On the other hand, these social workers were members of the same society that harbored negative views about Asians, so involvement may have filled some of them with pride for aiding in the country's security.

Mexican repatriation and Japanese internment both represent actions of the profession that may have tarnished its image in the eyes of those most affected. The point here is that, in these cases, the role of the profession was to implement social policy, and that role still exists today. As was predicted years before, resource dependency affects reform tendencies. Furthermore, as has been previously emphasized, attitudes about race and ethnicity are so firmly embedded in American norms, behavior, and culture that they are virtually contagious. People "catch" them without any awareness that they have been "infected" with these attitudes.

The Professionalization of Reform

The evolution of social reform into macro practice may also reflect an adherence to a safe course of action. The authors of a text on macro practice define this practice as "professionally directed intervention to bring about planned change in organizations and communities" and involves the practitioner in the areas of organizations, communities, and policy.[86] It is a problem-solving method that defines and assesses needs in organizations and communities, leads to the development of strategies for intervention, and guides the selection of an appropriate tactic to bring about the planned change.

Macro practice, as currently defined, is a fairly benign practice concentration because it acknowledges the role of external systems in shaping organizations and communities while at the same time working *within* the existing systems to bring about change. By working within these systems, the macro practitioner accepts them as impartial, effective, valid, and responsive. Civil disobedience, protests, activism, and other blatant, direct challenges to these systems that once characterized social action, social reform, and social change are approached with great trepidation, as reflected in the following observations in a macro text:

> The goal of *social action* is both process and task oriented in that participants seek to shift power relationships and resources in order to effect institutional change. Beneficiaries of this type of intervention are often perceived to be victims of an oppressive power structure. . . . Although the language of social action is often espoused by social workers, it is important to realize that this approach to community practice is based in conflict, power dependency, and resource mobilization theories of power and politics. The confrontation required in this model is energy draining and time consuming, and sometimes the focus on task becomes so important that process is forgotten.[87]

Social reform or social change activities are not mentioned and, as can be detected, social action is not encouraged as a community change strategy.

The social action or social reform element of community organization has virtually disappeared from macro practice to be replaced by administrative practice, community development, and social planning.[88] As the reincarnation of social reform, macro practice may represent the transformation of social reform into elements that are compatible with mainstream social work. These limited perspectives on structural-level change seem also to tie social work to nonthreatening, nonconfrontational methods of intervention.

Ethnic and racial minorities are aware of the partiality, ineffectiveness, and nonresponsiveness of social systems. An acceptance of the status quo inadvertently supports the inequality these systems have perpetrated. It is difficult for many minority group members to place this awareness aside and see social and political systems as neutral, fair, and benign entities. Furthermore, social action or activism may not be the intent of these groups; rather, an awareness of the oppressive nature of these systems seems to be the crucial point. Methods of social work that recognize the injustices of institutions in society convey the profession's commitment to advancing civil rights. An absence of this recognition seems to minimize or disregard the historical experiences of ethnic minority groups. The faith that social work has in the integrity of society's institutions and structures may not be shared by many members of ethnic and racial groups. With mainstream definitions of macro practice and community organization, the gap between social work and these communities may grow even wider.

CONCLUSIONS

The legacy of the charity organization societies is visible throughout social work. The COS evolved into family services[89] and many of the preachings, practices, and personnel patterns are firmly imprinted on contemporary family casework. The influences of the COS on the development of social work as a profession are striking:

- continued adherence to individual responsibility,
- the dominant polity defining social problems and their solutions,
- an emphasis on cases rather than population aggregates,
- the social distance between helper and service recipient,
- adherence to the doctrine of ethnic group responsibility,
- reliance on women for the provision of social services, and
- continued ties to the "establishment" that raises questions about the social control functions of social services.

From the settlement house movement, social work inherited advocacy, social action, policy practices, community/locality development, and social/ community planning. Services to ethnic and racial minorities were not significantly integrated into this movement. Settlers focused on socializing the individual as a central goal—a focus that is typically minimized when the reform roots of social work are reviewed. Individual-level focus is generally associated with micro practice and not the reform arm of the profession. As with the

COS, the settlers also defined the needs of the communities in which they resided. In this case, however, they invited community residents to participate in achieving the goals and missions of the houses. In addition, individual responsibility also figured heavily in the beliefs of the settlers. The settlement houses did, however, stimulate the development of social policies and the provision of services. Intervention with social systems, although perhaps not to the extent or degree commonly believed, dramatically divided the settlement movement from the COS.

The reform arm of social work, however, has been continuously overshadowed by the personal or direct practice thrust of the profession. Protest movements within the profession have been unable to deter the profession from its middle course. As social reform is also professionalized and integrated into the profession as macro practice, social work's allegiance to mainstream society becomes even more entrenched.

Ethnic minorities feel that the profession and its evolution have had little to do with them and their history. They have often had to struggle to provide for the service needs of their communities. The next chapter provides evidence of the need for and capacity of ethnic minority communities to develop their own services.

Endnotes

[1] Stanley Wenocur and Michael Reisch, *From Charity to Enterprise—The Development of American Social Work in a Market Economy* (Chicago: University of Illinois Press, 1989), 259.

[2] Mina Carson, *The Settlement Folk* (Chicago: The University of Chicago Press, 1990), 166.

[3] Roland Meinert, John Pardeck, and Larry Kreuger, *Social Work—Seeking Relevance in the Twenty-First Century* (New York: The Haworth Press, 2000), 7.

[4] Frank Watson, *The Charity Organization Movement in the United States* (New York: MacMillan Company, 1922), 408. http://books.google.com (accessed August 22, 2009)

[5] Roy Lubove, *The Professional Altruist* (New York: Atheneum, 1969), 106.

[6] Regina Kinzel, *Fallen Women, Problem Girls: Unmarried Mothers and the Professionalization of Social Work* (New Haven: Yale University Press, 1993).

[7] See for example. M. Christine Anderson, "Catholic Nuns and the Invention of Social Work: The Sisters of the Santa Maria Institute of Cincinnati, Ohio, 1897–1920s," *Journal of Women's History* 12 (Spring 2000): 69–88.

[8] Wenocur and Reisch, *From Charity to Enterprise*, 259.

[9] Stephen Kunitz, "Professionalism and Social Control in the Progressive Era: The Case of the Flexner Report," *Social Problems* 22 (October 1974): 26.

[10] Wenocur and Reisch, *From Charity to Enterprise*, 259.

[11] Numerous sources provide detailed accounts of the ascendancy of casework over social reform. The discussion presented here is based on the following readings: Axinn and Levin, *Social Welfare*, 152–158; Herman Borenzweig, "Social Work and Psychoanalytic Theory: A Historical Analysis," *Social Work* 16 (January 1971): 7–16; Mina Carson, *The Settlement Folk*, particularly 166–167; Rosemary Chapin, *Social Policy for Effective Practice* (New York: McGraw-Hill, 2007); Ralph Dolgoff and Donald Feldstein, *Understanding Social Welfare*, 7th ed. (New York: Pearson, 2007); Bruce Jansson, *The Reluctant Welfare State*, 6th ed. (Belmont, CA: Brooks/Cole, 2009); Josefine Figueira-McDonough, *The Welfare State and Social Work* (Thousand Oaks, CA: Sage Publications, 2007); Jillian Jimenez, *Social Policy and Social Change* (Thousand Oaks, CA: Sage Publications, 2010); James Leiby, *A History of Social Welfare and Social Work in the United States* (New York: Columbia University Press, 1978), 181–190; Lubove, *The Professional Altruist*, 53–84; Gary Lowe and Nelson Reid, eds., *The Professionalization of Poverty* (New York: Aldine de Gruyter, 1999); Meinert, Pardeck, and Kreuger, *Social Work—Seeking Relevance in the Twenty-*

First Century; Philip Popple and Leslie Leighninger, *The Policy-Based Profession*, 4th ed. (New York: Pearson, 2008); Wenocur and Reisch, *From Charity to Enterprise*.

[12] The cause-versus-function discussion can be found in numerous writings, including Dolgoff and Feldstein, *Understanding Social Welfare*, 326–327; Lubove, *The Professional Altruist*, 157–158.

[13] A more detailed discussion can be found in Borenzweig, "Social Work and Psychoanalytic Theory," 11–12.

[14] As quoted in Borenzweig, "Social Work and Psychoanalytic Theory," 11.

[15] Axinn and Levin, *Social Welfare*, 157.

[16] Philip Popple, "The Social Work Profession: A Reconceptualization," *Social Service Review* 59 (December 1985): 564.

[17] Grace Coyle, "The Limitations of Social Work in Relation to Social Reorganization," *Social Forces* 14 (October 1935): 100.

[18] C. Wright Mills, "The Professional Ideology of Social Pathologists," *American Journal of Sociology* 49 (September 1943): 171.

[19] Sally Palmer, "Authority: An Essential Part of Practice," *Social Work* 28 (March /April 1983): 123.

[20] Marcia Abramson, "Autonomy vs. Paternalistic Beneficence: Practice Settings," *Social Casework* 70 (February 1989): 102; Frederic Reamer, "The Concept of Paternalism in Social Work," *Social Service Review* 57 (June 1983): 259.

[21] Elizabeth Irvine, "Transference and Reality in the Casework Relationship," *British Journal of Psychiatric Social Work* 3 (December 1956): 15–24.

[22] Miller, "Social Work in the Black Ghetto," 276.

[23] David Powell, "Managing Organizational Problems in Alternative Service Organizations," *Administration in Social Work* 10 (Fall 1986): 65.

[24] Yeheskel Hasenfeld, "Power in Social Work Practice," *Social Service Review* 61 (September 1987): 467–483; Yeheskel Hasenfeld, "Worker Client Relations," in Yeheskel Hasenfeld, ed., *Human Services as Complex Organizations* (Thousand Oaks, CA: Sage Publications, 2010), 405–425.

[25] Discussions of the place of Freudian approaches in social work history can be found in, for example, Borenzweig, "Social Work and Psychoanalytic Analysis," 12–16; Lubove, *The Professional Altruist*, 88–89; George Martin, *Social Policy in the Welfare State* (Englewood Cliffs, NJ: Prentice-Hall, 1990), 27.

[26] Burton Gummer, "On Helping and Helplessness: The Structure of Discretion in the American Welfare System," *Social Service Review* 53 (June 1979): 218–219.

[27] Harry Specht, "The Deprofessionalization of Social Work," *Social Work* 17 (March 1972): 3–15.

[28] Watson, *The Charity Organization Movement in the United States*, 415.

[29] Linda Gordon, "Black and White Visions of Welfare: Women's Welfare Activism, 1890–1945," *The Journal of American History* 78 (September 1991): 559–590; Jimenez, *Social Policy and Social Change*, 138–176; Maxwell Manning, Cornelius Llwellyn, and Joshua Okundaye, "Empowering African Americans through Social Work Practice: Integrating an Afrocentric Perspective, Ego Psychology, and Spirituality," *Families in Society* 85 (April–June 2004): 221–228.

[30] Charles Sanders, "Growth of the Association of Black Social Workers," *Social Casework* 51 (May 1970): 279.

[31] Miguel Montiel and Paul Wong, "A Theoretical Critique of the Minority Perspective," *Social Casework* 64 (February 1983): 112–113.

[32] Henry Miller, "Social Work in the Black Ghetto: The New Colonialism," in *Dynamics of Racism in Social Work*, ed. James A. Goodman (Washington, DC: National Association of Social Workers, 1973): 271–287.

[33] Teresa LaFromboise, "American Indian Mental Health Policy," *American Psychologist* 43 (May 1988): 388.

[34] Robert Taylor, "The Social Control Function in Casework," *Social Casework* 39 (January 1958): 17–21.

[35] Margaret Vine, *Sociological Theory*, 2nd ed. (New York: David McKay Company, 1969), 171.

[36] Watson, *The Charity Organization Movement in the United States*, 414.

[37] Robert Halpern, "Supportive Services for Families in Poverty: Dilemmas of Reform," *Social Service Review* 65 (September 1991): 343, 344.

[38] Eugene Jones, "Social Work among Negroes," *The Annals of the American Academy of Political and Social Science* 140 (November 1928): 287–293.

[39] Jacob Fisher, *The Response of Social Work to the Depression* (Boston: G. K. Hall & Co., 1980), 135, Leslie Leighninger, *Social Work Search for Identity* (New York: Greenwood Press, 1987), 10.

[40] Fisher, *The Response of Social Work*, 10.

[41] Ruth Berger, "Promoting Minority Access to the Profession," *Social Work* 34 (July 1989): 346.

[42] Martin, *Social Policy in the Welfare State*, 27.

[43] Watson, *The Charity Organization Movement in the United States*, 404.

[44] John Ehrenreich, *The Altruistic Imagination: A History of Social Work and Social Policy in the United States* (Ithaca, NY: Cornell University Press, 1985), 104–105.

[45] Amitai Etzioni, *Modern Organizations* (Englewood Cliffs, NJ: Prentice Hall, 1964), 94–96.

[46] Ibid., 97.

[47] Max Weber, "Bureaucracy," in *The Sociology of Organizations*, 2nd ed., ed. Oscar Grusky and George Miller (New York: The Free Press, 1981): 7–36; and as described in Lubove, *The Professional Altruist*, 161–162.

[48] David Bargal, "Social Values in Social Work: A Developmental Model," *Journal of Sociology and Social Welfare* 8 (1981): 53.

[49] This discussion is drawn from Jansson, *The Reluctant Welfare State*, 185–192.

[50] Wenocur and Reisch, *From Charity to Enterprise*, 256.

[51] John Murchison, "Some Major Aspects of the Economic Status of the Negro," *Social Forces* 14 (October 1935): 116.

[52] Wayne Cornelius, "Mexican Migration to the United States: Causes, Consequences, and U.S. Responses," in *Crisis in American Institutions*, 5th ed., ed. Jerome Skolnick and Elliott Currie (Boston: Little, Brown, 1982),159.

[53] This discussion is from Eric Meeks, "Protecting the 'White Citizen': Race, Labor, and Citizenship in the South-Central Arizona, 1929–1945," *Journal of the Southwest* 48 (Spring, 2006): 103.

[54] As discussed in Ehrenreich, *The Altruistic Imagination*, 102–138; Fisher, *The Response of Social Work*, 91–135; Leighninger, *Social Work*, 39–44; Popple, "The Social Work Profession," 564–565; Rick Spano, *The Rank and File Movement in Social Work* (Washington, DC: University Press of America, 1982); David Wagner, "Collective Mobility and Fragmentation: A Model of Social Work History," *Journal of Sociology and Social Welfare* 13 (September 1986): 657–700; Wenocur and Reisch, *From Charity to Enterprise*, 182–207.

[55] As discussed in Ehrenreich, *The Altruistic Imagination*, 187–264; Katherine Kendall, "A Sixty-Year Perspective of Social Work," *Social Casework* 63 (September 1982): 427–428; Neil Gilbert and Harry Specht, "The Incomplete Profession," *Social Work* 19 (November 1974): 667–668; George Lockhart and Joseph Vigilante, "Community Organization, Planning and the Social Work Curriculum," *Community Development Journal* (January 1974): 64–70; Reisch and Wenocur, "The Future of Community Organization," 82–85; Robert Ross, "The New Left and the Human Service Professions," *Journal of Sociology and Social Welfare* 4 (May 1977): 694–706; Stephen Sunderland, "Creating the New Profession-The Human Services," *Education and Urban Society* 7 (February 1975): 141–171; David Wagner, "Radical Movements in the Social Services," *Social Service Review* 63 (June 1989): 264–284.

[56] Wenocur and Reisch, *From Charity to Enterprise*, 182.

[57] Ibid., 184.

[58] Jimenez, *Social Policy and Social Change*, 246.

[59] Spano, *The Rank and File Movement*, 222–237.

[60] Johnson and Schwartz, *Social Welfare*, 106; Charles Sanders, "Growth of the Association of Black Social Workers," *Social Casework* 51 (May 1970): 277–284.

[61] Alejandro Garcia, "The Chicano and Social Work," *Social Casework* 52 (May 1971): 278.

[62] Wagner, "Collective Mobility and Fragmentation," 687.

[63] Diana DiNitto and C. Aaron McNeece, *Social Work Issues and Opportunities in a Challenging Profession* (Englewood Cliffs, NJ: Prentice Hall, 1990), 114; W. Joseph Heffernan, *Social Welfare Policy* (New York: Longman, 1979), 57.

[64] Bruce Jansson, *Social Policy—From Theory to Policy Practice*, 2nd ed. (Pacific Grove, CA: Brooks/Cole, 1994), 20.

[65] Jan Hagen, "Women, Work, and Welfare: Is There a Role for Social Work?" *Social Work* 37 (January 1992): 9.

[66] Wenocur and Reisch, *From Charity to Enterprise*, 268.

[67] Mark Courtney, "Psychiatric Social Workers and the Early Days of Private Practice," *Social Service Review* 66 (June 1992): 211.

[68] Florence Styz, "Desegregation: One View from the Deep South," *Social Work* 2 (July 1957): 4, 7.

[69] As defined by Frederic Reamer, "The Free Will-Determinism Debate and Social Work," *Social Service Review* 57 (December 1983): 631.

[70] Meinert, Pardeck, and Kreuger, *Social Work*, 6.

[71] James Hackshaw, "Race and Welfare," *Encyclopedia of Social Welfare*, Vol. II (Washington, DC: National Association of Social Workers, 1971): 1066.

[72] For additional discussion of social work and its environment, see Jansson, *Social Policy—From Theory to Practice*, 13–19.

[73] Hackshaw, "Race and Welfare," 1065.

[74] An example of writings in this area can be found in Roy Bailey and Mike Brake, *Radical Social Work* (New York, 1975); and a contemporary discussion on radical social work can be found in DiNitto and McNeece, *Social Work*, 91–92.

[75] DiNitto and McNeece, *Social Work*, 12.

[76] See Jimenez, *Social Policy and Social Change*, 46–76, for a discussion of American values.

[77] The comparison between Richmond and Addams is drawn from Donna Franklin, "Mary Richmond and Jane Addams: From Moral Certainty to rational Inquiry in Social Work Practice, *Social Service Review* 60 (June 1986): 504–525.

[78] Mary Richmond, *Social Diagnosis* (New York: Russell Sage Foundation, 1917).

[79] Popple and Leighninger, *The Policy-based Profession*, 7.

[80] Donald Van Meter and Carl Van Horn, "The Policy Implementation Process: A Conceptual Framework," *Administration and Society* 6 (February 1975): 446.

[81] This discussion is drawn from Neil Betten and Raymond Mohl, "From Discrimination to Repatriation: Mexican Life in Gary, Indiana, During the Great Depression," *The Pacific Historical Review* 42 (August 1973): 370–388; Leobardo Estrado, F. Chris Garcia, Reynaldo Macías, and Lionel Maldonado, "Chicanos in the United States: A History of Exploitation and Resistance," *Daedalus* 110 (Spring 1981): 103–131; Abraham Hoffman, *Unwanted Mexicans in the Great Depression—Repatriation Pressures 1929–1939* (Tucson: The University of Arizona Press, 1979); Norman Humphrey, "Mexican Repatriation from Michigan Public Assistance in Historical Perspective," *The Social Service Review* 15 (September 1941): 497–513; Eric Meeks, "Protecting the 'White Citizen': Race, Labor, and Citizenship in the South-Central Arizona, 1929–1945," 91–113; Francisco Rosales and Daniel Simon, "Mexican Immigrant Experience in the Urban Midwest: East Chicago, Indiana, 1919–1945," *Indiana Magazine of History* 77 (Number 4, 1981): 333–357; and Zaragosa Vargas, "Life and Community in the 'Wonderful City of the Magic Motor': Mexican Immigrants in 1920s Detroit," *Michigan Historical Review* 15 (Number 1, 1989): 45–68.

[82] As quoted in Humphrey, "Mexican Repatriation from Michigan Public Assistance in Historical Perspective," 498.

[83] Estrada, García, Macías, and Maldonado, "Chicanos in the United States," 117.

[84] Adena Rich, "Case Work in the Repatriation of Immigrants," *The Social Service Review* 10 (December 1936): 569–605.

[85] Yoosun Park, "Facilitating Injustice: Tracing the role of Social Workers in the World War II Internment of Japanese Americans," *Social Service Review* 82 (September 2008): 447–483.

[86] F. Ellen Netting, Peter Kettner, and Steven McMurtry, *Social Work Macro Practice*, 4th ed. (New York: Pearson, 2008), 3.

[87] Netting, Kettner, and McMurtry, *Social Work Macro Practice*, 160.

[88] DiNitto and McNeece, *Social Work*, 74.

[89] Ray Johns and David DeMarche, *Community Organization and Agency Responsibility* (New York: Association Press, 1951), 38–40; Leighninger, *Social Work Search for Identity*, 11; Beverly Stadum, "A Critique of Family Case Workers 1900–1930: Women Working with Women," *Journal of Sociology and Social* Welfare 16 (September 1990), 75.

CHAPTER
8

Ethnicity,
Voluntary Associations,
and Community Services

The history of ethnic minorities is characterized by adversity, hard work, community initiative, heartache, triumphs, indomitable spirits and hope for the future. People of color in the United States have often been depicted as helpless victims of discriminatory practices with little appreciation of their strengths and their struggle with adversity.[1]

While social work was evolving into a profession, ethnic and racial minority communities were working diligently to respond to their community needs. Just about every group mobilized whatever resources it could to provide support, both tangible and intangible, to those who needed it. Community responses were part of American history before the emergence of social work, continued in existence during the evolution of social work, and persisted after the professionalization process. In essence, the country had two streams of social services—one of mainstream services and the other of community-based services, many of which were associated with ethnic and minority communities. These streams continue to parallel each other today.

The community-based social services—those formal and informal services provided by ethnic members to their own particular group—were not limited to ethnic and racial minorities. Religious groups also established services and missions for their members and for service to other nonmembers. Often, however, many religious services represented the intersection of ethnicity and religion. The services may have become part of the community infrastructure to support community life and respond to community needs. From a systems theory perspective, ethnic minority communities fought for their survival, and the provision of basic support may have buffered community members from abject poverty and destitution. In some cases, the support extended by the community filled a void because other, developing mainstream services were not available to marginalized groups.

This chapter focuses on the need for ethnic services and the types of community-based services, informal and formal, that were available in particular ethnic and racial communities. Voluntary associations and ethnic agencies are both examples of the community self-help and community mutual aid that operated in ethnic communities. Although these associations and agencies emerged at different points in time, their commonality of goals did not change. The chapter then identifies the common themes found across these services and the implications they pose for mainstream services. The chapter concludes with interpretations and analyses of ethnic group services in America.

ETHNIC COMMUNITIES AND VOLUNTARY ASSOCIATIONS

As previously indicated, ethnic and racial groups created community-based mechanisms for addressing community concerns and problems. Some of the mechanisms were informal voluntary associations that loosely organized to address specific community goals. Members were volunteers who received no monetary compensation. Other mechanisms were formally organized voluntary associations with rules, officers, bylaws, and perhaps even a constitution, but members were still volunteers.[2] Still other later mechanisms came after the voluntary associations and included the formal ethnic agency that is outside the voluntary sphere.

These associations and agencies are unique in that ethnic or racial identity was the unifying element that brought members together. These "identity groups" had a commonality of history, group memory, culture, norms, values, customs, traditions, religion, and worldview.[3] This worldview defined the world around the community and its relationship with that world. The shared worldview gave members a vantage point from which to apply interpretations and explanations for the negative and positive events they experienced. Worldview was a significant factor in molding the group's ideology.

The voluntary association highlighted the commitment and motivation of its members because they devoted countless hours and their own resources to address community ailments and needs. The Progressive Era was a challenging period in American history when individuals and families faced a harsh, unforgiving environment. Despite this, individuals came together to plan and solve problems. The drive for community survival propelled them to carry out a vision they had for a better community. Their actions became an investment in the community's present and future.

Voluntary ethnic associations fall at one end of the ethnic services continuum while ethnic *agencies* fall at the other end. In some instances, an ethnic agency may have emerged from a voluntary association. In other instances, the ethnic agency began its life as an ethnic agency. The ethnic agency was often a formalized and institutionalized part of the community. As the social work profession evolved to develop social service agencies, ethnic communities were also, at the same time, working to establish ethnic service delivery structures.

Although the ethnic agency encompasses many of the same elements as the ethnic voluntary association, it is a formal organization whose members are paid for their time. The ethnic agency, like the emergent mainstream service delivery structures, was also nonprofit, but it differed significantly from these other service organizations. In the Progressive Era formal ethnic service delivery systems were started by members of a specific group, staffed by members of that group, served by members of that group, benefited from community support, and embraced the ideology of that group.

WHITE ETHNICS AND ETHNIC SERVICES

Ethnic group self-help appeared as far back as the colonial days of the early colonies. According to Tice and Perkins, the Scots Charitable Society of Boston was organized in 1657 by 27 Scotsmen.[4] By 1690, the society had grown to 180 members. This society managed to remain a viable resource for its members for decades. In 1767, the Charitable Irish Society of Boston began operating. The French Benevolent Society and the German Society of New York also blended nationalism with self-interest and compassion.

According to Gamm and Putnam, "Although many associations emerged in the first half of the nineteenth century, scholars generally argue that associations enjoyed their greatest flowering between 1870 and 1920."[5] These authors add that in the late nineteenth and early twentieth centuries, Italians, Jews, Poles and other immigrants from eastern and southern Europe started mutual aid societies as well as other clubs, churches, and synagogues. Berthoff noted,

> The immigrants, who had been accustomed to a more tightly knit communal life than almost any American could now recall, were quick to adopt the fraternal form of the American voluntary association in order to bind together their local ethnic communities against the unpredictable looseness of life in America.[6]

History is filled with examples of White ethnic services. The kinds of associations and their goals may have varied across groups, but children commanded a great deal of attention. For example, on August 31, 1879, church members from the Concordia German Evangelic Lutheran Church in Washington, D.C., agreed to start an orphanage.[7] On September 20 of the same year, the German Protestant Orphan Asylum Association of the District of Columbia was incorporated. The goal was "to provide, maintain, and support an Asylum for the destitute orphans and half-orphans of German parentage in the District of Columbia."[8] The men who established the Asylum were successful in a variety of occupations, and one founder left $100,000 to the Asylum upon his death—the largest gift it had ever received.

The Brooklyn Italian Settlement opened its doors in 1901 with the help of the Italian Settlement Society; and numerous other services emerged for specific immigrant groups, such as Catholic, Irish, and Slavonic immigrants.[9] Welfare activities for specific groups figured prominently in the lives of the immigrants and, in the absence of these groups, members of nationality groups looked to other agencies for assistance.[10]

Jewish associations appear to have been very active in numerous parts of the country. The Jewish Branch of the Roadside Settlement in Des Moines, Iowa, was organized in 1907 and supported by Jewish people; the Day Nursery and Neighborhood House was established in Newark, New Jersey, by the Jewish Sisterhood in 1905; the Harlem (New York) Federation for Jewish Communal Work was established in 1906 through the cooperation of all existing Jewish organizations in Harlem; In the South, the earliest Jewish women's societies filled "group-specific needs defined by gender, religion, and nationality."[11] According to Bauman:

> Rebecca Gratz of Philadelphia pioneered in the creation of these first Jewish benevolent associations in America. An officer in secular women's charities, she organized a foster home (1855), Sunday school association (1838), and Hebrew ladies benevolent society (1819). Gratz's example was quickly replicated in the South by her relatives and friends.[12]

Feldman chronicles social services in Los Angeles where the Jewish influence is significant.[13] The first social agency in Los Angeles was the Hebrew Benevolent Society that was established in 1854 by 15 of the 35 Jewish residents of Los Angeles for the purpose of purchasing land for Jewish burials and to provide assistance to worthy people. The first women's philanthropic society in that city was the Ladies Hebrew Benevolent Society established in 1870. The Hebrew Benevolent Society merged with the Ladies Hebrew Benevolent Society in 1918 to form the current Jewish Family Services of Los Angeles.

Chicago's National Council of Jewish Women, founded in 1893, developed in response to the needs of Jewish women and girls who arrived at Ellis Island.[14] Through its Department of Immigrant Aid, the Council attempted to assist immigrant women from the time of their entry into the United States to the time they reached their American destination. Assistance included an Americanization program to help the women with housing and health issues. Referrals were also made to other programs that could help them learn English. The Council undertook its program to help the newly arriving immigrants maintain a strong Jewish identity.

Voluntary associations served as buffers for immigrants and their communities as they assimilated into American life. These associations cared for parentless children, fostered the learning of the American way of life, and made sure their deceased were properly buried. Through the support of these associations, countless immigrants were able to adjust to life in a new country.

RACIAL/ETHNIC GROUPS AND ETHNIC SERVICES

African Americans, American Indians, Mexicans, Chinese, and Japanese had varying experiences with voluntary associations. These groups developed strategies for responding to the needs they defined. Because the assistance so readily available to the White ethnics was not forthcoming, these ethnic and racial communities had no recourse but to do for themselves. American Indians stand out as a distinct case because the intrusiveness of the government in their lives drastically limited their self-help capacity.

The fate of minority communities, however, was not under their control. They were not independent entities and could not determine for themselves the development of their communities and services. These communities were inexorably tied to the larger social systems in which they existed. What happened to these racial and ethnic subsystems internally was shaped by the external polity and external economy of the U.S. society surrounding them. This state of affairs continues to prevail today. The social, political, and economic institutions of society shape the minority community experience, and the community's reactions are often constrained by the larger system. According to Ringer and Lawless:

> The larger society's conception of the they-ness of the ethnic group has serious consequences for the ethnic group. For the larger society tends to accept the "validity" of its own definition and seeks to impose it in its relations with the ethnic group. Its conception of the they-ness of the group, for example, will govern its treatment of the ethnic group which in turn affects the life circumstances and opportunities of the ethnic group in the larger society.[15]

The development of a racial consciousness within an ethnic group is predicated on that group's relationship with the larger social system.[16] For example, African Americans and American Indians were valued because of their labor and their land, respectively; therefore, Cornell stated that African Americans were able to form a group identity earlier than were American Indians. African Americans' labor-based relationship with White America dissipated boundaries within the group and encouraged the formation of a group consciousness. Conversely, land-based relationships solidified boundaries within American Indian groups and impeded the emergence of a group consciousness.

Each minority group suffered discriminatory treatment, but the nature and type of discrimination varied from group to group. Although each group may have had a minority status, each brought a unique reaction from the society surrounding them. As a result of these differences, the particular needs of each group also varied. For this reason, all groups cannot be lumped together. The larger society had one response to African Americans, another to American Indians, and still another to Mexicans, Chinese, and Japanese. However, the agenda the African American community carved out for itself was different from the American Indian agenda, which was also different from the Chinese agenda, and so on.

The internal polity and internal economy of each group has also varied. The setting of a service agenda and the mobilization of resources to implement that agenda reflected the dominance of factions within the groups. Problem causality and problem resolutions were perceived in numerous ways, and the ideology of the dominant elite within each ethnic and racial minority group prevailed. As the power of factions rose and fell, the predominant ideology also shifted. The rise and fall of particular ideologies were also linked to the prevailing conditions in the larger social system.

The external polity and external economy exerted influences that encouraged as well as forced minority communities to develop their self-help capacity. The unavailability of outside help is a major factor in stimulating this self-help.[17] Although some groups received some outside assistance, it may not have been sufficient or appropriate for the problems facing these groups. Outsiders who adhered to the self-help doctrine may have been stingy in their support of minority communities. Marginalized status may have served to discourage generosity from the larger society.

As social work was planting its professional roots with the White ethnics (and, to a much less extent, African Americans), minority groups were beginning to create their own interventions. Mutual aid efforts of White ethnic communities preserved group culture and augmented the services of the charity organization societies and settlement houses. However, mutual aid efforts of minority communities served to fill the void left by lack of services or inadequate services. Miller captured the reality of these groups when he wrote: "To survive, these ethnic minority individuals and communities have had to make numerous adaptations to the institutions or create their own indigenous organizations, such as the ethnic churches and welfare institutions."[18]

Imposed segregation may serve to promote the growth of a community infrastructure so that dependency and reliance on "outsiders" for resources is reduced.[19] Again, the community infrastructure is often shaped by the external polity and the external economy. What occurred in the minority communities was indicative of what the larger social system *permitted* or *tolerated* to occur in those communities. The capacity for self-help was constrained by the environment. These environmental constraints, in turn, influenced what these communities perceived as feasible options available to them. Consequently, ethnic communities were not totally autonomous and free to develop whatever services they desired. Needless to say, segregation may have stimulated more self-help activity than would have resulted had discrimination not been practiced.

Segregation may have forced the emergence of community self-help and boosted the cohesiveness of ethnic minority communities. Group cohesiveness increases when members share a common external threat and feel that cooperation will reduce that threat, when members in low-status groups cannot elevate their status as individuals, and when stressful conditions exist.[20] For minority communities, membership in a minority group overrode the boundaries of education and social class. Because society's attack was based on the discrimination against and segregation of specific groups, ethnicity became a unifying point for those groups. Ethnicity continues to act as a unifying theme in forming and mobilizing particular organizations.[21]

The ethnic services that evolved in minority communities were predicated on the larger society's treatment of that group, the demographics of the community, the identification of problems by the group itself, the culture of the group, and the availability of resources to mount those needed services. A brief and general overview of the emergence of ethnic services in specific communities is presented to illuminate the distinct issues and responses of these groups. This overview is designed to be illustrative rather than exhaustive.

African Americans and Ethnic Services[22]

The history of benevolence and social welfare in the nineteenth century United States has been written overwhelmingly from the perspective of middle-class reformers who left in their wake an impressive trail of documentation that ensured their visibility in the historical record. . . . This scholarly emphasis mirrors the preoccupation of Victorian charitable institutions with the waves of European immigrants who statistically engulfed the relatively small numbers of African Americans among the destitute populations of America's greatest metropolises.[23]

Many factors have guided the development of African American voluntary associations and other service delivery structures. The literature on social services for African Americans is relatively extensive in comparison to that of other ethnic minority groups in the United States. For this reason, the discussion offered here is somewhat longer. This is not intended to diminish the significance of the history of other groups; rather, it reflects some of the numerous, varied, and complex issues that have been acknowledged in the relevant literature.

Persistence of Ideology.   In the face of exclusionary and separatist practices, the African American philosophy espoused historically has been one of African Americans helping African Americans.[24] According to Meier, White discrimination and exclusionary policies were the direct cause of the establishment of segregated institutions such as African American churches and fraternities.[25] The lack of economic advancement, compounded by growing poverty, spurred African Americans into action.[26] African American communities began to take on the task of addressing their own community needs because they felt abandoned by the world around them.

African Americans across the country seemed to accept the doctrine of ethnic group responsibility and believed that there were only a few others outside their community who would stand with them in the fight for equality. The self-help ethos was so strong that impoverished African Americans may have contributed a larger part of their income for charitable and religious causes than any group known in history.[27] Indeed, African Americans appeared to bear "almost the whole burden of their own internal social reform."[28] This self-help ethos encouraged African Americans to feel a responsibility to help those who were less fortunate. Successful community members were expected to "reach down" and "give something back" to their community so that others could be elevated. Regardless of social status, education level, and other signs of success, African Americans were expected or even obligated to use their success to help others in their community.

African Americans also lived in a world that continued to communicate the message that they should help themselves. The Social Gospel ideology and the home missions associated with it preached the gospel of self-help to African Americans. Now that they were unshackled from slavery, in the eyes of the larger society they were free to develop their potential (on their own). This message was pervasive, and they knew that they were the only ones who could help their communities. Unfortunately, the discriminatory practices and racist attitudes proved to be formidable obstacles.

Many of the writings on this racial self-help fail to note the class distinctions inherent in the ethnic responsibility doctrine. Those who were in a more comfortable position were expected to help those who had less or nothing at all. In fact, as can be expected, the middle-class African Americans led the drive for race improvement. With their status and the power of the church behind them, it was difficult for some of these leaders not to be patronizing in their attitudes toward the less fortunate. At the 1897 Second Atlanta University Conference, one of the African American speakers admonished her peers for not conducting friendly visits with the poor of the community and said, "How much better off we would be if we could cease to draw these lines of caste and each of us as we climb the ladder reach down and assist a struggling sister!"[29] This speaker thought these "low-spirited" struggling sisters could benefit from "just a word of cheer and hope, . . . just a word of sympathy."

White welfare relief concentrated on working with individuals. African Americans, on the other hand, saw their *race* as the focus of the uplift; racial improvement was the thrust. Service organizers had a vision of African Americans, as a people, taking their place in mainstream society with status, equality, and respect. For this reason, those services with the potential for elevating the future of the race were significant. The education and uplifting of children could reap benefits for generations to come and, if the tradition of ethnic group responsibility held, each generation would be better off than the one before it. African American service providers were also well aware of the oppressive social structures that perpetuated their marginalization. Dolgoff and Feldstein emphasize that unemployment and poverty are interwoven with the structure of the economy.[30] The social and political structures compound the disadvantaged status of African Americans.

African American social services were for the community of African Americans as defined by race, not by geographical location. A service for African Americans in one part of town would be utilized by African Americans from various parts of a city, because the service was rare and White doors were closed. For example, as the only African American settlement in Minneapolis, the Phyllis Wheatley House tried to serve all of the city's African Americans.[31] Because it had an African American clientele, this house was called on to perform duties not associated with other settlement houses. Serving the entire city was one of these additional functions.

Another dimension of African American services warrants comment. Social reform and changes in public attitudes were not the goals for many of the services developed. Racial betterment, alleviating the harsh effects of poverty, and sustaining the community were primary goals of many early interventions.[32] Perhaps, during this era, African Americans were acutely aware of their powerlessness in the U.S. political and social system. In addition, political activism may have been the domain of political associations rather than social service ones. The times were neither favorable to nor supportive of movements for integrating African Americans, many of whom had not yet found their political and social muscle. Also, the effects of outside funding on the course of self-help development may be a relevant factor here in guiding African Americans away from political activities. Thus, although African American services were analogous to services of mainstream America, in the African American communities individual-level change was replaced with group-level change for an entire race of people.

The Significance of the Church.   The African American church, in all its forms and configurations, has figured prominently in the history of African American community self-help, and that history has been richly documented.[33] From this history, several themes emerge: belief in the unity of the race, belief in self-help as the primary means of addressing problems and social conditions, and a commitment to improving the race.[34] African Americans fervently believed that their survival was intricately linked to self-reliance because the social, economic, and political forces surrounding them appeared to undermine that survival.

For African Americans, the church emerged as one of the first organizations to pursue the betterment of the African American community. According to DuBois, it was natural "that charitable and rescue work among Negroes should first be found in the churches and reach there its greatest development."[35] The church was second only to the African American extended family as a care-giving institution in these communities.[36] As the scope and extent of social needs exceeded the church's ability to respond and as the number of other voluntary organizations such as clubs and fraternities increased, the church lost its dominance as a service center.[37]

The Role of Women.   Women have played vital roles in African American voluntary associations. In fact, the origins of voluntary associations in African American communities can be traced through the work of African American women. African Americans who lived in free communities were able to establish these voluntary associations, and Scott has provided details of their history with African American women. [38] Indeed, the history of African American women's voluntary associations is as long as that of White women's. The Female Benevolent Society of St. Thomas was established in Philadelphia in 1793, and the Colored Female Religious and Moral Society were established in 1818 in Salem, Massachusetts. In 1830, a mutual aid society in Philadelphia pooled the savings of its members to aid each other in times of sickness, unemployment, or family troubles. Even though they made significant contributions to communities, Scott asserts that the voluntary associations of African American women are virtually invisible in American history.

Service endeavors offered African American women a voice in the community, and they often led fund-raising and organizational development campaigns. As mentioned earlier, participation for White women was a way of escaping the confines of traditional roles. This was not necessarily the case for African American women, many of whom were heads of households and had to work outside the home to support their families. African American women were identified as industrious while some of the men were becoming stereotyped as vagrant and drunk.[39] Many African American women service leaders were not using this work to promote civic housekeeping or social mothering. The belief in racial unity brought African American men *and* women together in the struggle for racial improvement.

Victoria Earle Matthews' White Rose Mission in New York serves as an example of several of the factors previously mentioned.[40] She was one of the leaders of the African American women's movement and participated in a number of causes of that era. She became involved in Ida B. Wells' anti-lynching campaign. Matthews took up the cause of the exploitation of African American women from the South by unscrupulous men and envisioned a plan for helping these women and girls. In 1898, she opened a mission to house and feed them until they could obtain employment. Several years later, the mission became a settlement house and offered such services as a mother's club, adult classes, travelers' aid, relief assistance, and a library. White Rose was the city's second settlement to serve an exclusively African American clientele. White Rose was funded by patrons in the local community and had the support of Booker T. Washington, the founder of Tuskegee Institute, and noted poet Paul Lawrence Dunbar. In the ten years that Matthews led the settlement, about 50,000 females utilized the services there. Matthews died of tuberculosis at the age of 45. The White Rose Home ceased operation in the 1960s.

The Value of Education and Morality.   Improving the race meant that education was emphasized as a way out of poverty. African Americans established countless educational programs around the country and designated education as a type of self-improvement that could not be stripped away from its possessor. As education was frequently denied to African Americans, it was no wonder that these communities struggled to attain it. Education became synonymous with liberation and enlightenment, and it was also one means of assuring the betterment of the next generation. Consequently, numerous schools were established, usually through the efforts of church organizations, and they also provided a multiplicity of social welfare and child welfare functions.[41]

Improving the race was also interpreted to mean uplifting the morality of the race. "Immorality" was reflected in the high incidence of fatherless families in ghetto communities in the cities of the Progressive Era. This so-called immorality was defined as "sexual laxity" and "indifference to family ties," and it was associated with "vagrancy and drunkenness" among African American men.[42] During and since that time, numerous debates have ensued about the validity of statistics on African American families and the effects of slavery on African American family forms. During this period, however, these middle-class helpers were not only patronizing but were moralizing as well.

Issues of morality may also have been influenced by the presence of the church as a service delivery agent. The church was a central figure in African American communities and was the largest and most visible African American organization. Issues of immorality, drunkenness, and vice in general received immeasurable attention from the church. The inescapable presence of vice and the absence of law enforcement in African American communities (as noted in Chapter 3) exacerbated issues of vice and immorality in these communities.

Identifying the Deserving.   Pollard's study, as well as others, of African American welfare developments of the Progressive Era reveals several trends that may still characterize ethnic services today.[43] First, as with the White welfare efforts, African American services targeted populations that were perceived as the "most deserving." For African Americans, "most deserving" generally included the "most worthy" members of the community in need of assistance, such as children, young girls, widows, and the elderly.

Relief efforts for the general poor were not a priority for most U.S. communities. Although provisions could be made for some form of emergency relief, stable, ongoing relief-assistance measures were not forthcoming. Groups and organizations rallied around those who were poor through no fault of their own. Those individuals deemed responsible for their own poverty were extended little sympathy.

Orphanages, reformatories, homes for young girls, and homes for the aged were established for the vulnerable groups. [44] Segregated or nonexistent services had resulted in large numbers of jailed young African American women, children as young as age seven "serving time" with adult criminals, and the elderly spending their twilight years in almshouses. Child welfare reform, as well as other service reforms, bypassed African American communities, and these populations appeared to be especially needy within these communities.

The concern of African American communities about their pernicious treatment at the hands of law-enforcement officials and in jails and prisons spurred organizations to include juvenile justice and law-enforcement issues. In a 1908 visit to a Georgia court, a visitor observed that 578 boys and girls, mostly African American and under the age of 12, had been arrested and brought to court.[45] Offending African American youths were confined either to jails, penitentiaries, stockades, or chain gangs. In Pollard's words, "No one worried about the soul of the black child but black people."[46]

White Philanthropy as Social Control.   Another trend in African American services involved the tension between self-sufficiency and the acceptance of contributions from government and/or White philanthropists. For some African American service providers, the ethos of self-help extended to self-help for the provision of services themselves. For other service providers, however, acceptance of donations from "outside" the community was necessary for the establishment and maintenance of services. The availability of outside funds indicated that Whites of the larger society supported and encouraged self-help in the African American community—as long as those self-help activities were consistent with White expectations. For example, White philanthropists provided significant funding for African American education, but many were only willing to support industrial programs. White support for academic, professional, and artistic pursuits was almost nonexistent. Outside funding could serve to steer the community in the direction defined by the donors and thus act as a means of social control. The history of African American self-help appears to be inextricably interwoven with the history of White philanthropy among African Americans.[47] An example can be found in Peeps' analysis of the relationship between northern philanthropy and the rise of African American higher education.[48] The author concludes that support from the North was needed because of the pressure in the South to repress African American progress.

African American Services and Social Work.   Social work, as an activity and as a profession, was accepted and integrated into the ethnic services of the African American community. In a 1928 article, Jones recounted the history of social work among African Americans and indicated that social work activities as generally understood had been going on among African Americans throughout their lives in America.[49] He traced early "social work" activities back to 1793 when a New York City African American woman organized the first Sunday school in the United States and also "reared and placed in suitable private homes forty-eight children," some of whom were White. She was no doubt among the first African Americans to work in what would now be called child placement or foster care. For Jones, as well as others, effective social work was a means of raising the social and economic level of the African American community and developing the self-sufficiency of the group.

Several points on social work by African Americans are worthy of emphasis. First, in the history of social work in this ethnic community, specialized training appears to have been less of a prerequisite for providing services than in the White communities. As the profession was carving out its specialized knowledge base and building special training programs, African Americans were continuing to do "social work" without the benefit of that training. As noted in Chapter 6, only about a third of African American social workers in 1928 were thought to have had special training. Lack of access to White programs and the limited number of African American programs contributed to this situation. For African Americans, the qualifications for doing social work and being a social worker appear to have involved factors other than professional credentials.

African American social workers also had distinct expectations placed on them by White social workers, as Dexter observed in 1921.[50] They were expected to know their people's background; have intellectual training, a progressive outlook, and a pleasant personality; be in touch with the movements for improvement among African Americans; possess faith in the destiny of the African American race; and deal with effects of race prejudice on the African American, something that White people were not believed to understand or realize.

As the profession of social work continued to develop and expand, that expansion spilled over into the arena of African American self-help activities. White social work leaders wanted to cast their net over the care of dependent African American children in Chicago.[51] Segregation, discrimination, and benign neglect had previously excluded African American children from the mainstream child welfare programs. African Americans responded by trying to operate their own programs in their communities, and the social work profession was seeking to absorb these programs into the profession. The social workers justified their actions by citing what they saw as problems with the African American community-based services: (a) African American institutions were outdated and substandard, (b) African Americans had a difficulty managing programs, and (c) African Americans had difficulty managing money. Some have concluded that wresting these services and others from the African American community had the effect of silencing the community's self-help tendencies. In addition, questions may be raised about the quality of care that dependent African American children received under professional (White) supervision. Perhaps those same questions could be raised about the care they received within their community.

There were other tensions between the profession and the African American community. Because the budding profession needed to distance itself from its Social Gospel and mission roots, many of the social work-type services provided through church affiliation or under church supervision were dismissed and deemed to be outside of the profession. Church-affiliated missions that were similar to the settlement houses were not counted in the settlement-house census.[52] The hundreds of social work-related services in the African American community were relegated to the margins or overlooked completely. Thus, the history of the profession has discounted the contributions of countless African Americans.

As mainstream America developed mechanisms for responding to the social needs of its people, African American communities were also developing their responses to the needs of their own people. Parallel service delivery systems were in the making, each with its own ideologies, missions, and practices.

American Indians and Ethnic Services

American Indians represent a unique group in American history. Policies of the U.S. government inhibited some of the self-help capacity of American Indians and, for this reason, American Indians stand out as a distinct case. Despite this, the voices of American Indians were raised in protest about their treatment.[53] Some American Indian leaders made advocacy their life's mission. Many of their beliefs were consonant with those of the progressive reformers, but they were not powerful enough to place racial equality on the progressives' agenda. These advocates used their writing as a tool of advocacy. While they may have been victimized, they did not perceive themselves as victims.

The lives of American Indians who migrated to the cities differed dramatically from those on the reservations. Shoemaker describes the urban lives of American Indians in Minneapolis from 1920 to 1950.[54] They adjusted to their new urban life and created social organizations to support their ethnic identity. A national survey conducted in 1928 found that the American Indians who had resided in the city for longer periods of time were middle-class while the new Native American residents lived in poorer sections of town.

For this group, as with the other racial and ethnic groups, there is no homogenous life or lifestyle that defines the entire group. American Indians lived on reservations, in towns, and in cities. Maintaining ethnic identity was necessary for some and perhaps less so for others. They were united, however, in the history they shared and in their desire for equality.

Several sources have documented the history of the American Indian and the effects of oppressive policies.[55] Confinement to reservations prevented these groups from continuing their cherished way of life. Forced acculturation was the country's mandate for them. Life on the reservation was dictated and controlled by the polity and economy of the larger society. In addition, the reservation's own internal polity and economy were not powerful enough to combat these external forces. U.S. goals for American Indians ranged from extermination and genocide, to expulsion, to exclusion, to forced Americanization, to ethnic responsibility.[56]

The U.S. government had defined what it perceives to be the problems of American Indian peoples and the solutions to those problems, including their social welfare needs. What these people wanted for themselves was in opposition to what America wanted for them, and they were powerless to halt the imposition of U.S. policies. In essence, the country demanded that American Indians renounce their lifestyles, their cultures, their languages, and their ways of survival. American Indians represent the most extreme example of Americanization. Even though they were denied the right to self-determination and the freedom to help themselves in the ways they thought necessary, several conclusions can be drawn from their history.

As detailed in Chapter 3, at the turn of the century American Indians were enduring the Americanization efforts of missionaries and, in the eyes of the missionaries, were proving to be recalcitrant to those efforts. For this and perhaps other reasons, the adult American Indian was dismissed as lost or hopeless; thus, efforts focused on saving the American Indian child. Hence, the boarding school movement was launched. The removal of children as young as six years old from their families and the placement of these children in institutional, off-reservation boarding schools is just one of the extreme ways in which assimilation policy operated.

Although the off-reservation boarding schools were discontinued during the Depression years, mainstream child welfare continued the practice of removing American Indian children from their families and placing them in non-Indian settings. The perpetuation of rescuing children from "harmful" American Indian influences was reflected in the child placement rate of American Indian children. In 1976, for example, the out-of-home placement rate for American Indian children was 12 to 18 times higher than that for non-Indian children, and 85 percent of the American Indian children were placed in non-Indian homes.[57]

Because of the country's desire to save American Indian children from the alleged harmful effects of the reservations, American Indians struggled to protect their children and to continue the transmission of cultural values to the next generation. Tensions, and even hostility, have developed over time between American Indians and child welfare systems with their non-Indian service providers. The Indian Child Welfare Act of 1978 gives the jurisdiction of American Indian child-custody cases to the tribes. However, because many tribes needed time to develop their own programs, mainstream child welfare agencies, the Bureau of Indian Affairs, and other nontribal entities were often used. In the aftermath of the passage of the Indian Child Welfare Act, numerous tribes struggled to hire staff, formulate program guidelines, and create program structures.

The Indian Child Welfare Act illuminates one of the paradoxes of the self-determination policies that have emerged since the 1960s and are exemplified in the Indian Self-Determination and Education Assistance Act of 1975. This act extended to tribes on reservations the right of self-government and the freedom to establish independent services. Many tribes did not have the resources to respond to these newly given rights. To a certain extent, government resources and leadership were still needed to make that transition. Deloria was critical of these governmental efforts to foster American Indian control of their reservations and asserted, "In the misguided hope that withdrawal of support services to the reservations would create a new wave of individualism among Indians, Congress terminated federal responsibility for them."[58]

In the years since the passage of the Indian Child Welfare Act, questions have been raised about the efficacy of the policy in reducing out-of-tribe placements. For example, Limb and Brown found that more measurable outcomes and monitoring procedures are needed to actually assess states' compliance with the law.[59] Cross observes that courts have been applying an Indian Family Exception Doctrine that uses a narrow definition of "Indian child" and, as a result, some Indian children continue to be placed in non-Indian homes.[60] Consequently, the passage of legislation has not guaranteed the desired outcomes.

With the Indian Self-Determination Act of 1975 (ISDA), American Indians could "control their relationships both among themselves and with non-Indian governments, organizations and persons" and acknowledge that "the prolonged federal domination of Indian service programs has served to retard rather than enhance the progress of Indian people and their communities."[61] Herein lies another paradox: Policies developed and imposed by the government have resulted in a plethora of pernicious conditions on the reservations. The government then places the control of the communities in the hands of the residents to deal with these conditions. Government control was so extensive that American Indians' self-determination was legislated—they did not have the right to decide for themselves when and how they could become self-determining. No doubt they would have preferred tribal empowerment years earlier.

In the years following the passage of the ISDA, legal issues arose regarding the funding of contracts under the legislation. The Department of the Interior and the Department of Health and Human Services transferred certain programs to the tribes and then entered into contractual agreements with the tribes so that the programs could be funded.[62] Since this funding did not include administrative costs, many tribes fell financially short. Legal battles resulted that eventually led to a Supreme Court decision. The Court ruled in favor of the tribes. This litigation amplifies the type of disconnect that can occur between policy as it is written and policy as it is implemented.

As American Indians develop self-help activities, efforts aimed at rebuilding or re-creating family support systems are priorities.[63] In addition, many of the sovereign nations are developing their own programs that integrate tribal customs and values.[64] This focus is a direct response to policies that reduced the role of the extended family, clan systems, and natural child welfare systems within American Indian communities.[65] The ethnic services now forming seem to be realistic program reactions to the damage inflicted by mainstream child welfare practices and other practices of the welfare state.

Mexican Americans and Ethnic Services

Latino communities in the US have a long history of launching, contributing to and participating in "sociedades mutualistas" (mutual aid organizations). Although the form and structure of previous mutual aid societies have changed, Latino community based organizations (formal) and informal community associations now fill the vacuum left by the demise of "mutualistas" serving Latino families in the US.[66]

Mexican American community-based self-help has a long and sustained history in the United States.[67] The early efforts of Mexicans in the Southwest to provide for the needs of their communities revolved around the family unit. Mexican American communities organized *mutualistas* that provided insurance, funeral, and limited welfare benefits. These organizations served a social as well as an instrumental function, had constitutions, and conducted meetings. Since many of the members thought of themselves as Mexicans (rather than Mexican Americans) and anticipated returning to Mexico, politics of the United States did not occupy their time. Some of these mutualistas existed prior to the Treaty of Guadalupe Hidalgo. These were organizations of Mexicans helping and supporting Mexicans and maintaining loyalty to Mexico. They observed Mexican holidays and traditions, and they spoke Spanish.

A secret Roman Catholic lay organization called La Fraternidad Piadosa de Nuestro Padre Jesus Nazareno, known as the Penitentes, was active in responding to community needs in the Progressive Era.[68] The Penitentes were known for their self-flagellation during religious holidays as part of their desire to live like Christ. They also functioned as a charitable association, performing acts of charity for members of the community. These acts included helping with burials by making caskets, preparing the body for burial, and overseeing funerals. The female auxiliary, the Auxiliadoras de la Morada, comforted those who were grieving and nursed the sick. The Penitentes maintained a fund and a storehouse so they could distribute relief as needed. For rural, isolated communities, the voluntary association filled a void.

For numerous Mexicans, a return to Mexico was not realized and they continued to reside in the United States and raise families. With this second generation, "Mexican American" was more an identity than it had been with their parents. These Mexican Americans turned their eyes toward the United States and wanted to be part of its society. They wanted to promote their integration and change negative perceptions about them. The organizations they developed attempted to achieve these goals.

As a group, Mexican Americans have been subjected to deportation in the past, regardless of whether they were citizens, legal residents, or undocumented workers. Indeed, in some situations, one's only infraction was simply "looking Mexican." Associations were often established to fight deportation in crisis times, such as economic slumps and depressions. These were times the United States wanted to rid itself of expendable Mexican workers.

Some organizations were concerned with promoting the rights of Mexicans who were native born or who had achieved citizenship through naturalization. The citizen status reflected a permanency and commitment to the United States, and the goal of these organizations was to assist Mexican Americans in obtaining their constitutional rights. One example of such an organization was *La Orden de Hijos de America* (The Order of Sons of America), founded in 1921 in San Antonio. It was the forerunner of the League of

United Latin American Citizens (LULAC) established in Texas in 1928. During this period, it was more acceptable to be "Spanish" or "Latin" rather than "Mexican."[69] The anti-Mexican sentiment (discussed in Chapter 4) was a factor in the emergence of this organization.

LULAC had an integrationist perspective (as reflected in its taking an English rather than a Spanish name) with middle-class members. The organization had a commitment to children, and teaching them English was a priority as implemented in the LULAC-established preschools. LULAC was a vehicle for Mexican American Americanization. As this organization grew, it expanded its scope to serve political as well as social functions.

Self-help community efforts among Mexican Americans were also directed toward uplifting the group. The group's status as "outsider" and "Mexican" led to harsh discriminatory treatment, and the muting of their "Mexican-ness" was envisioned as leading to social acceptance and social justice. As mentioned in Chapter 4, mainstream America often made no distinction between the Mexican and the Mexican American.

The Mexican American presence in social work has not been well documented in the social work literature. Aranda reviews the development of the Latino social work profession in Los Angeles.[70] Her review reveals that this development began in the 1960s with the creation of a training center for Latino social workers, the first center of this type in California. The contributions of this group to the profession commands recognition as the American population grows in diversity.

Chinese Americans and Ethnic Services

The early Chinese communities were closed social systems in which boundaries were crossed for economic purposes but other group needs were met within the subsystem of the communities.[71] There were several types of associations: clans that united males of a common ancestry, *hui kuan* that united those who spoke the same dialect or came from the same geographical area of China, and tongs that were secret mutual-aid associations not based on ancestry or language. In some communities, clan, *hui kuan,* and tong associations would come together to form one large organization.

One of the most powerful influences in the lives of the Chinese immigrant was the Chinese Consolidated Benevolent Association (CCBA), or the "Chinese Six Companies," established in the mid-1850s. Its membership included members of six *hui kuan.* According to the CCBA-authorized historian, the CCBA "was empowered to speak and act for all the California Chinese in problems and affairs which affect the majority of the population."[72] The association collected various fees that were used to defray costs for services and community welfare.

The Chinese Six Companies also engaged in smuggling Chinese laborers into the United States after the immigration exclusion laws went into effect.[73] This is yet another example of the informal association working on behalf of its members. As with voluntary associations, the group members determine the needs and the strategies for meeting those needs. The association devised ways of circumventing the law so that Chinese workers could seek employment. These actions further reveal the marginalized status of the Chinese community in America. This community perceived laws as obstacles that could be overcome, albeit illegally.

In general, merchants, landlords, and factory owners led the voluntary organizations and served as gatekeepers and spokespersons between the community and the rest of society. In these positions, leaders often worked to maintain the separateness of the Chinese communities to protect their own power within these communities. This meant that the merchant class controlled the voluntary organizations and, to some extent, exploited the immigrant laborers. On the other hand, workers who needed assistance because of sickness or loss of job had the organization's help. Wong and colleagues stated,

> The benevolence of the traditional organizations in protecting their members from the vicissitudes of economic and other misfortunes must be weighed against their malevolence in maintaining as well as shielding the exploitative relationship between employers and workers in the enclave economy from external scrutiny.[74]

Thus, the focus of much of the voluntary organizations' efforts seems to have been heavily economic, since the protective associations acted as a type of "trades-union" that launched boycotts and strikes for better wages.[75]

The aims of the voluntary organizations were derived from the demographic makeup of the Chinese communities and the response of the larger society to the Chinese immigrants. Because of segregation, discrimination, and mob violence, the Chinese were clustered in ethnic enclaves, isolated from White Californians. All social life and activities took place within the ethnic enclave. As noted in Chapter 4, these communities were primarily male, so issues of family and children did not need attention. Because the immigrants came to the United States to work, their economic needs were of greater significance.

The isolation of the Chinese community from the "outside" world resulted in the Chinese community being perceived [by outsiders] as self-contained and able to take care of itself. An 1895 study of women in almshouses in San Francisco found that the Chinese "are practically unknown in the almshouse, probably owing to the fact that they *always care for their own poor*" [emphasis added].[76]

As mentioned earlier, Chinatown was under siege whenever there was an outbreak of some kind because mainstream American associated "foreignness" with disease. Although the city and county of San Francisco did not open a health clinic or hospital in Chinatown until 1970, the Chinese Six Companies led the way in organizing a healthcare system for Chinatown.[77] In 1900 the Tung Wah Dispensary opened and employed Western-trained doctors and Chinese herbalists. The community worked to fill a major void in its Chinatown. The Dispensary treated patients who had been rejected by the city and county hospitals.

Although the doctrine of ethnic group responsibility was operative for this group, the group's internal polity and internal economy was driven by economic definitions of presenting problems. In addition, the barriers erected around this community, by those outside and inside the community, may have persisted over time.

Japanese Americans and Ethnic Services

Fukuin Ka, established in 1877, was the first Japanese American organization in this country.[78] The Fukuin Ka provided English classes, ran a boarding house, and had meeting rooms. The Japanese Christian churches sprang from this association. The first language school opened in 1902, and by the 1930s just about every Japanese community was overseeing its own Japanese-language school. The Japanese American Citizens was created in the 1930s but ceased operating during World War II with the internment of Japanese communities.

Japanese Americans first arrived in Chicago in the 1890s and began operating small businesses.[79] By the 1920s their population had increased to 300. They had their own Japanese Mutual Aid Society, and the YWCA mission favored Japanese students but it closed in the 1930s. In New York, the Japanese Mutual Aid Society formed in 1907 and purchased land in 1912 for Japanese burials.[80] In 1914, Japanese community leaders replaced the Japanese Mutual Aid Society with the Japanese American Association of New York (New York Nihonjinkai). It continues to exist as a nonprofit that serves the Japanese American community. Through the use of volunteers, the JAA supported its community with social welfare services.

The Japanese followed a pattern in social services similar to that of the Chinese. As with the Chinese, the Japanese immigrants were primarily males who came to the United States for economic reasons. They formed voluntary associations that promoted economic survival and success.[81] Some of these associations provided burial and financial assistance. Members of the same *ken,* or Japanese state, frequently pooled resources for starting businesses or other economic ventures. The *tanomoshi* (to rely on or depend on) was another type of organization that assisted business ventures. The *tanomoshi* was akin to a small bank in which money was pooled and then extended, with credit, for business start-up costs.

Cohesion within the Japanese community was a key factor in its development. In comparing the voluntary organizations of the early Chinese and Japanese communities, according to Wong, Applewhite, and Daley, those in the Japanese community might have contributed more to fostering ethnic group solidarity and less to promoting class cleavage.[82] The ethnic group solidarity, as manifested in the activities of the voluntary organizations, contributed to the economic success of the ethnic group at the turn of the century.

As with the Chinese community, economic issues dominated the focus of the Japanese associations. Again, this is related to the group's purpose for immigrating to the United States, the composition of the group that immigrated, and the economic constraints confronting this group. At this point in the history of Japanese American voluntary organizations, political issues were generally outside the purview of the community. The Issei (first generation) concentrated on economic and sociocultural interests.

Observations on Early Ethnic Services

Trends and patterns begin to surface when reading the self-help histories of each group. When the patterns and the history are analyzed, some observations about early ethnic services can be advanced:

1. Social work, as a practice and as a budding profession, was interwoven with the self-help activities of African American communities. African Americans wanted and even demanded that these services be extended to them, and they wanted social work training so they could become social workers and work for the betterment of their race. Social work was a part of their world and it was growing around them, over them, beyond them, but not *through* them. As White programs and services proliferated, African Americans longed to bring these same services to the poor and vulnerable in their communities.

African Americans were members of U.S. society without being integrated into that society. They possessed American values and considered themselves "native Americans"—more native than the old-stock immigrants. They emulated, as much as they could, the mainstream social-service developments around them. If services, programs, friendly visitors, settlement houses, and the vast array of other services were going to help the immigrant become a better American, then African Americans wanted these same things to help their community members be better Americans. African Americans still clung to the hope that with education, employment, and related services they could become fully integrated into the world around them.

African Americans defined their needs in "social work" terms, and their books, articles, and newspapers documented their unique problems and their self-help work. Volumes of literature exist about the "Colored" problem, the "Negro" problem, the "Black" problem, and most recently the "African American" problem. History is replete with African Americans analyzing, describing, and studying their community's problems and what should be done about them by African Americans themselves as well as the larger society.

2. Although all racial minority groups were involved in the provision of "hard" services (tangible, concrete services), African Americans appear to be the only group that also identified a need for "soft" services (the "talking services"). Individuals from the African American community became friendly visitors to lift the spirits of the less fortunate. Social work's relationship with the African American community may have influenced this development, and whatever services were being provided to the White ethnic immigrants may have then been adopted by African Americans. On the other hand, the community may have independently recognized this service as necessary for its members.

3. White social workers knew more about the issues, needs, and conditions of African Americans than they did about any other ethnic/minority group. Through the COS and settlement houses, the plight of African American communities was discussed, dissected, and debated. The size of the African American population and the migration of African Americans in large numbers to centers of social work growth were factors fueling this interest. It may have led to social work historically viewing African Americans as the primary or

major racial minority group in the country and to the profession displaying a greater interest in this group than in the other racial groups.

4. Other ethnic minority groups did not share the African American enthusiasm for the public discussion of its internal issues or for social work. It is doubtful that these other groups were even aware of the budding profession or of its practices. Of course, as these groups ventured into other parts of the United States, they were exposed to settlement houses and "social service," but a comparable integration of social work into their communities and cultures did not take place.

5. Society influenced the direction of self-help efforts in the African American communities. These communities became a "cause" for philanthropists, settlement organizers, religious groups, and others as they funded, guided, and encouraged the self-help response among African Americans. Because African Americans were perceived by many as being in a primitive stage of race development, the external polities, including social workers, were only too happy to provide the gentle nudge needed to stimulate ethnic responsibility.

6. Although American Indians are currently creating, defining, and implementing their own solutions to their issues, they fought long and hard for this right. While other groups have historically had opportunities to do this, American Indians had to have this right legislated because of the heavy-handedness of prior policies. Because many American Indians have never viewed social work in a favorable light, the role of the profession in guiding and supporting these self-help developments is unclear. The distrust of the "system," particularly the child welfare system, held by numerous American Indians cannot be easily dismissed.

7. Mexican Americans were removed by geography, culture, and language from the development of social work so that their self-help efforts were, in fact, derived from the needs as perceived by members of this group. Because early self-help activities were geared to integration through English acquisition, language emerged as an area of great concern. They were also focused on reducing the threat of deportation (see item #10), as the line between "legals" and "illegals" was firmly etched in their communities. Unfortunately, the public often refused to make this distinction and simply lumped all persons of Mexican origin in the same category; thus, the threat of deportation was very real, as shown by the repatriation of Mexicans as well as many Mexican Americans.

8. Because the history of self-help organizations in the Chinese and Japanese communities centered on economic self-help, they have often been perceived in terms of their economic success. In addition, they have maintained the image of the early communities: "closed," close-knit, and able to take care of themselves. Because of the perpetuation of this image, these communities may be perceived as problem free or not in need of "outside" help. The history of these two groups as related to exclusionary policies and practices suggests that outside help might be received with distrust.

9. Issues related to children were priorities for African Americans, Native Americans, and Mexican Americans, whose communities included families, whereas the early Chinese and Japanese communities did not. Child-related

issues for these groups did not become important until the demographics of these groups shifted. For those groups that included a significant percentage of families and children, hopes for the betterment of the group were anchored to the next generation and to each successive generation. For these reasons, the communities sought to protect this investment in their future.

10. Law enforcement figured prominently in the self-help responses of African American and Mexican communities. African American children were subjected to the harshness of the criminal justice system and had few advocates. African Americans wanted reformatories and other services for juveniles. In the criminal justice system, race was the pivotal factor, not age, as African Americans—young and old, male and female—were jailed.

For Mexican Americans, the threat of deportation was driven by the enforcement of laws by police, border patrols, and anyone operating under the authority of a badge. A Mexican American could easily be deprived of his or her freedom, even if only temporarily. It is no wonder that early organizations tried to combat mass deportations because, during those times, law-enforcement agents may have indiscriminately deported countless U.S.-born Mexicans. Law enforcement does not appear to have been a friend of the Mexican American, particularly in Texas and the Southwest.

For populations of color, law enforcement officials refused to protect them from vigilantism and violence. Lynching, beatings, and property destruction continued as law enforcement stood by and watched.

11. Self-help activities of the African Americans, Mexican Americans, and Chinese Americans illuminate the intragroup issues of each culture. The African Americans were distinguished by class, as the "haves" reached back/down to help the "have-nots." Some of the former could be patronizing and moralizing in their work with the poor and unfortunate. Skin color, mentioned in Chapter 2, was likely a factor in defining status within this group.

For Mexican Americans, social class and status as a native-born or naturalized citizen were important for some of the groups that formed. Middle-class, native-born "Spanish" or "Latin" individuals seemed to have had a higher status in the development of early organizations. This suggests that a gulf separated this group from the poor Mexican American and the immigrant Mexican. "Looking Mexican" may have also served to decrease one's social worth within this group.

In the Chinese communities, certain classes dominated community governance. These merchants, business owners, and others were able to offer employment in the ethnic enclave to immigrants, and this was the basis of their power.

Each group had an internal polity and an internal economy that helped to define the dominant elite of that group. An ethnic minority group may have been united by race or ethnicity, but it did not constitute a homogeneous group. Within each group, there were specific dimensions along which status and hierarchy may be plotted. The larger society may not have been aware of or interested in these intragroup differences, but the dynamics between members of the same ethnic/racial group were affected by these differences.

12. The history of ethnic minorities in the United States, the history of social work's development, and the history of ethnic self-help are relevant for forging contemporary links between social work and these diverse communities.

Endnotes

[1] "The History of Japanese Immigration," *The Brown Quarterly* 3, no. 4 (2000). http://brownvboard.org/brwnqurt/03-4/03-4a.htm (accessed December 3, 2009).

[2] For the definition of the formal voluntary association, please see Don Doyle, "The Social Functions of the Voluntary Associations in a Nineteenth-Century American Town," *Social Science History* 1 (Spring 1977): 333.

[3] Ayelet Shachar, *Multicultural Jurisdictions: Cultural Differences and Women's Rights* (Cambridge, MA: Cambridge University Press, 2001), 2f.

[4] Carolyn Tice and Kathleen Perkins, *The Faces of Social Policy* (Pacific Grove, CA: Brooks/Cole, 2002), 43.

[5] Gerald Gamm and Robert Putnam, "The Growth of Voluntary Associations in America, 1840–1940," *Journal of Interdisciplinary History* 29 (Spring 1999): 520.

[6] As quoted in Gamm and Putnam, "The Growth of Voluntary Associations in America, 1840–1940," 531.

[7] Anna Watkins, "To Help a Child: The History of the German Orphan Home," *Washington History* 18(1/2) (2006): 121.

[8] As quoted in Anna Watkins, "To Help a Child," 121.

[9] Edith Bremer, "Development of Private Social Work with the Foreign Born," *Annals of the American Academy of Political and Social Science* 262 (March 1949): 139; Robert Woods and Albert Kennedy, *Handbook of Settlements* (New York: Russell Sage Foundation, 1911), 85, 163, 183, 237.

[10] Yaroslav Chyz and Read Lewis, "Agencies Organized by Nationality Groups in the United States," *Annals of the American Academy of Political and Social Science* 262 (March 1949): 155.

[11] Mark Bauman, "Southern Jewish Women and Their Social Service Organizations," *Journal of American Ethnic History* 22 (Spring 2003): 35.

[12] Ibid., 36.

[13] Frances Feldman, *Human Services in the City of Angels* (Los Angeles: Historical Society of Southern California, 2004), 14.

[14] Seth Korelitz, "'A Magnificent Piece of Work': The Americanization Work of the National Council of Jewish Women," *American Jewish History* 83(2) (1995): 177–203.

[15] Benjamin Ringer and Elinor Lawless, *Race-Ethnicity and Society* (New York: Routledge, 1989), 20.

[16] Stephen Cornell, "Land, Labour and Group Formation: Blacks and Indians in the United States," *Ethnic and Racial Studies* 13 (July 1990): 367–388.

[17] George Weber, "Self-Help and Beliefs," in *Beliefs and Self-Help,* ed. George Weber and Lucy Cohen (New York: Human Sciences Press, 1982), 21.

[18] Samuel Miller, "Themes and Models in Primary Prevention with Minority Populations," in *Primary Prevention Approaches to the Development of Mental Health Services for Ethnic Minorities,* ed. Samuel Miller, Gwenelle O'Neal, and Carl Scott (New York: Council on Social Work Education, 1982), 122–123.

[19] Carl Milofsky, "Neighborhood-Based Organizations: A Market Analogy," in *The Nonprofit Sector— A Research Handbook,* ed. Walter Powell (New Haven, CT: Yale University Press, 1987), 280.

[20] Marcia Guttentag, "Group Cohesiveness, Ethnic Organization, and Poverty," *Journal of Social Issues* 26(2) (1970): 111.

[21] Charles Stevens, "Organizing the Poor," *Journal of Sociology and Social Welfare* 5 (September 1978): 744–762.

[22] The sources cited in this section offer rich detail about African American benevolent and voluntary associations:

[23] Gunja San Gupta, "Black and 'Dangerous'? African American Working Poor Perspectives on Juvenile Reform and Welfare in Victorian New York: 1840–1890." *The Journal of Negro History* 86 (Spring 2001): 100.

[24] See, for example, Marybeth Gasman and Katherine Sedgwick, eds., *Uplifting a People—African American Philanthropy and Education* (New York: Peter Lang, 2005).

[25] August Meier, *Negro Thought in America: 1880–1915*, 4th ed. (Ann Arbor: University of Michigan Press, 1966).

[26] Iris Carlton-LaNey, "Old Folks' Homes for Blacks during the Progressive Era," *Journal of Sociology and Social Welfare* 16 (September 1989): 44.

[27] Joanne Martin and Elmer Martin, *The Helping Tradition in the Black Family and Community* (Silver Spring, MD: National Association of Social Workers, 1984), 53.

[28] W. E. B. DuBois, "Social Effects of Emancipation," *The Survey* 29 (February 1913): 572.

[29] As quoted in Pollard, *A Study of Black Self Help*, 63.

[30] Ralph Dolgoff and Donald Feldstein, *Understanding Social Welfare*, 7th ed. (Boston, Pearson, 2007): 3.

[31] Judith Trolander, *Settlement Houses and the Great Depression* (Detroit, MI: Wayne State University Press, 1975): 141.

[32] This point is supported by the literature on the history of African American self-help, especially William Pollard, *A Study of Black Self Help* (San Francisco: R and E Associates, 1978)

[33] See, for example, Andrew Billingsley and Jeanne Giovannoni, *Children of the Storm* (New York: Harcourt Brace Jovanovich, 1972), 47–59; Lilian Brandt, "The Negroes of St. Louis," *Publications of the American Statistical Association* 8 (March 1903): 206, 234, 241, 257–262; Carlton-LaNey, "Old Folks' Homes for Blacks," 43–60; Steven Diner, "Chicago Social Workers and Blacks in the Progressive Era," *Social Service Review* 44 (December 1970): 394, 405; John Dittmer, *Black Georgia in the Progressive Era, 1900–1920* (Urbana: University of Illinois Press, 1977), 50, 62–65; W. E. B. DuBois, *Efforts for Social Betterment Among Negro Americans* (Atlanta, GA: The Atlanta University Press, 1909); Maude Griffen, "The Negro Church and Its Social Work—St. Mark's," *Charities and the Commons* 15 (October 7 1905): 75–76; Florette Henri, *Black Migration* (Garden City, NY: Anchor Press/Doubleday, 1975), 98–99; 126–131, 159, 186; Martin and Martin, *The Helping Tradition*; Meier, *Negro Thought in America 1880–1915*, 121–138; Tom Moore, "The African American Church: A Source of Empowerment, Mutual Help, and Social Change," *Prevention in Human Services* 10(1) (1991): 147–167; Pollard, *A Study of Black Self Help*; Edyth Ross, ed., *Black Heritage in Social Welfare 1860–1930* (Metuchen, NJ: The Scarecrow Press, 1978); Lennox Yearwood, "National Afro-American Organizations in Urban Communities," *Journal of Black Studies* 8 (June 1978): 423–438.

[34] As identified by Meier, *Negro Thought in America*, 121–138.

[35] DuBois, *Efforts for Social Betterment*, 6.

[36] Martin and Martin, *The Helping Tradition*, 38.

[37] Yearwood, "National Afro-American Organizations," 423–438.

[38] Anne Firor Scott, "Most Invisible of All: Black Women's Voluntary Associations," *The Journal of Southern History* 56 (February 1990): 3–22.

[39] Henri, *Black Migration*, 99.

[40] This discussion is drawn from Ralph Luker, *The Social Gospel in Black and White* (Chapel Hill: The University of North Carolina Press, 1991), 178–179; Steve Kramer, "Uplifting Our 'Downtrodden Sisterhood': Victoria Earle Matthews and New York City's White Rose Mission, 1897–1907," *The Journal of African American History* 3 (Summer 2006): 243–266; and Cheryl Waites, "Victoria Earle Matthews: Residence and Reform," in *African American Leadership—An Empowerment Tradition in Social Welfare History*, ed. Iris Carlton-LaNey (Washington, DC: NASW Press, 2001), 1–16.

[41] Billingsley and Giovannoni, *Children of the Storm*, 47–49.

[42] Henri, *Black Migration*, 98, 99.

[44] Pollard, *A Study of Black Self Help*.

[44] See, for example, Iris Carlton-Laney and Vanessa Hodges, "African American Reformers' Mission: Caring for Our Girls and Women," *Affilia* 19 (Fall 2004): 257–272; and San Gupta, "Black and 'Dangerous'," 99–131.

[45] As detailed in Pollard, *A Study of Black Self Help*, 93.

[46] Ibid., 96.

[47] Ruth Crocker, *Social Work and Social Order* (Urbana: University of Illinois Press, 1992), 7.

[48] J. M. Stephen Peeps, "Northern Philanthropy and the Emergence of Black Higher Education—Do-Gooders, Compromisers, or Co-Conspirers?" *The Journal of Negro Education* 50 (Summer 1991): 251–269.

[49] Eugene Jones, "Social Work among Negroes," *The Annals of the American Academy of Political and Social Science* 140 (November 1928): 287–293.

[50] Robert Dexter, "The Negro in Social Work," *The Survey* 46 (June 25 1921): 439–440.

[51] Sandra O'Donnell, "The Care of Dependent African American Children in Chicago: The Struggle between Black Self-Help and Professionalism," *Journal of Social History* 27 (Summer 1994): 763–776.

[52] Elizabeth Lasch-Quinn, *Black Neighbors—Race and the Limits of Reform in the American Settlement House Movement, 1890–1945* (Chapel Hill: The University of North Carolina Press, 1993), 52.

[53] This discussion is based on Frederick Hoxie, "Introduction: American Indian Activism in the Progressive Era," in *Talking Back to Civilization—Indian Voices from the Progressive Era*, ed. Frederick Hoxie (Boston: Bedford/St. Martin's, 2001), 11–15.

[54] Nancy Shoemaker, "Urban Indians and Ethnic Choices: American Indian Organizations in Minneapolis, 1920–1950," *The Western Historical Quarterly* 19 (November 1988): 431–447.

[55] See, for example, Terry Cross, "Drawing on Cultural Tradition in Indian Child Welfare Practice," *Social Casework* 67 (May 1986): 283–289; Diana DiNitto and Thomas Dye, *Social Welfare—Politics and Public Policy*, 2nd ed. (Englewood Cliffs, NJ: Prentice-Hall, 1987), 256; Michael Dorris, "The Grass Still Grows, the River Still Flows: Contemporary Native Americans," *Daedalus* 110 (Spring 1981): 43–69; E. Dan Edwards and Margie Egbert-Edwards, "Native American Community Development," in *Community Organizing in a Diverse Society*, ed. Felix Rivera and John Erlich (Boston: Allyn & Bacon, 1992), 30–33; Grafton Hull, Jr., "Child Welfare Services to Native Americans," *Social Casework* 63 (June 1982): 340–347; Teresa LaFromboise, "American Mental Health Policy," *American Psychologist* 43 (May 1988): 388–397.

[56] Edwards and Egbert-Edwards, "Native American Community Development," 31–33.

[57] Cross, "Drawing on Cultural Tradition," 287.

[58] Vine Deloria, Jr., "Identity and Culture," *Daedalus* 110 (Spring 1981): 16.

[59] Gordon Limb and Eddie Brown, "An Examination of the Indian Child Welfare Act Section of State Title IV-B Child and Family Services Plans," *Child and Adolescence Social Work Journal* 25 (April 2008): 99–110.

[60] Suzanne Cross, "Indian Family Exception Doctrine: Still Losing Children Despite the Indian Child Welfare Act," *Child Welfare* 85 (July/August 2006): 672.

[61] Dorris, "The Grass Still Grows," 55.

[62] This discussion is drawn from, "Indian Self-determination and Education Assistance Act Contracts and Cherokee Nation of Oklahoma v. Leavitt: Agency Discretion to Fund Contract Support Costs" (Washington, DC: Congressional Research Service, The Library of Congress, updated 2005). https://www.policyarchives.org (accessed November 10, 2009).

[63] Hull, "Child Welfare Services to Native Americans," 345.

[64] Ceilia Belone, Edwin Gonzalez-Santin, Nora Gustavsson, Ann E. MacEachron, and Timothy Perry, "Social Services: The Navajo Way," *Child Welfare* 81 (September/October 2002): 773–790.

[65] Cross, "Drawing on Cultural Tradition," 286.

[66] Barbara Robles, "Latino Families: Formal and Informal Help Networks," Prepared for the Annie E. Casey Foundation (August 2003): 1. http://olp.asu.edu (accessed November 14, 2000).

[67] This discussion is drawn from Rodolfo Acuña, *Occupied America: A History of Chicanos*, 7th ed. (Englewood Cliffs, NJ: Prentice-Hall, 2010); José Hernandez, *Mutual Aid for Survival* (Malabat, FL: Kreiger Publishing, 1983); and Robles, "Latino Families: Formal and Informal Help Networks," 1–3.

[68] This discussion is drawn from Thomas Krainz, "Culture and Poverty: Progressive Era Relief in the Rural West," *The Pacific Historical Review* 74 (February 2005): 97–101.

[69] Maria Aranda, "The Development of the Latino Social Work Profession in Los Angeles," *Research on Social Work Practice* 11 (March 2001): 256–257; Carlos Arce, "A Reconsideration of Chicano Culture and Identity," *Daedalus* 110 (Spring 1981): 184.

[70] Aranda, "The Development of the Latino Social Work Profession in Los Angeles," 254–265.

[71] A detailed account of the voluntary organizations in early Chinese communities, from which this discussion is drawn, can be found in Paul Wong, Steven Applewhite, and J. Michael Daley, "From Despotism to Pluralism: The Evolution of Voluntary Organizations in Chinese American Communities," *Ethnic Groups* 8, no. 4 (1990): 215–233.

[72] As quoted in Wong et al., "From Despotism to Pluralism," 217–218.

[73] Lawrence Hansen, "The Chinese Six Companies of San Francisco and the Smuggling of Chinese Immigrants across the U.S.–Mexico Border, 1882–1930, *Journal of the Southwest* 48 (Spring 2006): 37–61.

[74] Wong et al., "From Despotism to Pluralism," 221.

[75] Philip Foner, *History of the Labor Movement in the United States*, vol. III (New York: International Publishers, 1964), 274.

[76] Mary Smith, "Almshouse Women," *Publications of the American Statistical Association* 4 (September 1895): 228.

[77] Joan Trauner, "The Chinese as Medical Scapegoats in San Francisco, 1870–1905," *California History* 57 (Spring 1978): 70–87.

[78] This discussion is based on "The History of Japanese Immigration," *The Brown Quarterly* 3 (Spring 2000): 1. http://brownvboard.org/brwnqurt/03-4/03-41.htm (accessed November 23, 2009).

[79] This discussion is drawn from "Japanese," *Encyclopedia of Chicago*. http://www.encyclopedia.chicagohistory.org (accessed November 23, 2009).

[80] The Japanese American Association of New York, "A Historical Overview of the Japanese American Association of New York, Inc." http://www.jaany.org/historyen.htm (accessed November 23, 2009).

[81] This discussion is drawn from Harry Kitano, *Japanese Americans* (Englewood Cliffs, NJ: Prentice-Hall, 1976), 18–20; and Kenji Murase, "Organizing in the Japanese American Community," in *Community Organizing in a Diverse Society* (Boston: Allyn & Bacon, 1992), 162–163.

[82] Wong et al., "From Despotism to Pluralism," 221.

Social Services and the Ethnic Community
The Ethnic Agency

The voluntary associations, mutual aid societies, and community services of the late nineteenth and early twentieth centuries were precursors to the modern ethnic agency. The volunteers have been transformed into paid staff. The mutual aid and community self-help traditions are still apparent in ethnic minority communities and can be found in the ethnic agencies that exist around the country. "Old" ethnic minority groups and "new" groups continue the tradition of developing, providing, and maintaining services to members of their groups.

The ethnic agency encompasses many of the same elements as the ethnic voluntary association with the exception that the ethnic agency is a formal organization that pays its members for their time. The ethnic social service agency, like mainstream service delivery structures, also tends to be nonprofit, but the ethnic agency differs significantly from these other service organizations. The formal ethnic service delivery systems are started by members of a specific group, are staffed by members of that group, benefit from community support, and embrace the ideology of that group. The ethnic minority agency, however, still stands apart in other ways from other kinds of agencies. There is the perception that ethnic minority status creates a unique dilemma for communities that requires special attention.

As the profession responds to the challenge of providing ethnic-sensitive services, the ethnic agency should be carefully analyzed so that what they do, why they do it, and how they do it can be better understood by those outside the ethnic agency system. These agencies may be an overlooked bridge between mainstream services and ethnic minority communities.

This chapter examines the ethnic agency and its ideologies, practice, and structure, as well as the ethnic agency's links to group history.

SEMINAL RESEARCH

To date, the most definitive work on the ethnic agency is the research completed by Shirley Jenkins and reported in 1981 in her book, *The Ethnic Dilemma in Social Services.*[1] The findings from her work are still relevant today. She studied 54 agencies that served five ethnic/racial groups (Asian Americans, African Americans, Puerto Ricans, Chicanos, and Cherokees). These agencies were located in six states and included day-care centers, foster care and adoption agencies, residential centers, youth services, multipurpose service centers, and other programs providing services to children.

From this research, Jenkins concluded that an ethnic agency has the following characteristics:

- it serves primarily ethnic clients,
- it is staffed by a majority of individuals who are of the same ethnicity as the client group,
- it has an ethnic majority on its board,
- it has ethnic community and/or ethnic power structure support,
- it integrates ethnic content into its program,
- it views strengthening the family as a primary goal, and
- it maintains an ideology that promotes ethnic identity and ethnic participation in the decision-making processes.

In a sample of 574 workers from the agencies studied, Jenkins also found that 43 percent of the workers had less than a B.A. degree, 18 percent had a B.A., 13 percent had some master's work, 17 percent had an MSW, and the remainder (9 percent) had done doctoral work. These figures reflect a tendency for these ethnic agencies to rely on paraprofessional staff.

Jenkins wanted to know more about the ethnic attitudes of social workers and asked whether workers are more likely to be helpful if they have a social work degree, or if they belong to the same ethnic group as the client. In comparing the responses of ethnic agency workers to those of a national sample of trained social workers in mainstream child welfare agencies, she found that 79 percent of the child welfare sample answered "degree" and 21 percent answered "ethnicity." For the ethnic agency workers, 62 percent replied "degree" and 38 percent replied "ethnicity." These differences were statistically significant (21 percent versus 38 percent) and further underscore the ethnic ideology of ethnic agency staff.

Additional survey questions delineated the attitudes of ethnic agency staff. Two-thirds of the ethnic agency workers believed that those minority groups who wanted to operate programs for their own group should be allowed to do so and be given public funds. About half of the national sample of workers felt this way. More than half the ethnic agency workers thought that Spanish should be compulsory in schools of social work, yet less than a quarter of the national sample concurred. Since the Mexican American and Puerto Rican ethnic agency workers comprised 22 percent of the sample, their presence alone cannot account for the percentage of ethnic agency response on the Spanish question. Workers in ethnic agencies seem more likely to support those ideas and practices that promote ethnic/racial identity and consciousness in comparison to social workers in general.

Jenkins also found that African American social workers in the ethnic agencies placed more value on credentials in comparison to the other ethnic groups studied and that more of them actually had credentials. The place of social work in the history of African American communities attests to the faith that many of this group have in the value and recognition of the social work degree. This may also suggest that, among those entering the ethnic agency workforce, the African American ethnic agencies will have a larger pool of degreed workers from which to choose.

For the ethnic agency workers the social work degree was important, but so was ethnicity; the ethnic factor was also acknowledged in responding to the needs of clients. The ethnic agency, in its own way, promotes the contemporary uplift of the group by providing services in addition to attempts to assist the basic primary unit of the ethnic group—the family. This pioneering work by Jenkins amplifies the ethnic factor in service delivery that is receiving more attention in mainstream services.

The ethnic agency has been viewed as the most efficient way to deliver services that promote ethnic cohesiveness and identity.[2] The ethnic agency appears to offer its clients psychological well-being, cultural affinity, a nurturing environment, emotional support, the incorporation of their unique sociohistorical experiences in the treatment process, and interventions often based on the concept of empowerment.[3]

WHY ETHNIC AGENCIES?

In colonial America and the subsequent Progressive Era, American society needed the ethnic group associations to care for its vulnerable members. In the absence of any formal services or service delivery systems, group members had no recourse but to devise their own solutions. As can be seen from the previous chapter, just about every ethnic or racial group had its own means of garnering resources for community care. With the rise of the welfare state and the evolution of a profession to implement its programs, the need for these agencies should have lessened. Still, ethnic agencies have remained enduring fixtures on the social-services landscape. Thus, the reasons for their continued use warrant consideration.

The Immigration Factor

Tens of thousands of immigrants and refugees come to the United States each year seeking a better life for themselves and their families. Most are leaving their countries for economic and political reasons and hope to prosper in this new environment. Many are totally unprepared for the stresses and extreme hardships they will encounter in a new country, where opportunities for employment and success are limited because of language and cultural differences, in addition to discrimination and preju-

> dice. The hope for better life may actually prove to be a life of back-break-
> ing work and disappointment.[4]

Even though this quotation was written in 2004, it could have been penned a
hundred years ago, for it captures the world of immigrants as it was in a
younger America. While America, as a nation, has grown and matured, the
experiences of immigrants seem to remain frozen in time. The immigrants of
contemporary America include Filipinos, Koreans, Asian Indians, Salvadorans,
and Hmongs.[5] Apparently, America has not really changed its attitudes
toward immigrants who are "foreign" in appearance and culture.

Although Asian Americans represent one the fastest-growing ethnic
minority groups and have been part of America since the nineteenth century,
"professional social services for Chinese and their communities did not exist
before the 1970s."[6] This lack of professional services may be tied to perceptions of Chinatowns as closed communities that care for their own (as discussed in Chapter 4). The Progressive Era witnessed the marginalization of
Asian immigrants, particularly the Chinese and Japanese. As the profession of
social work was forming, these groups were outside its sphere of service.
Chapters 5 and 6 indicated that, while the tools and techniques for work with
other ethnic groups were crafted, none was crafted for the marginalized
groups. The results of this history are revealed in the schism that exists today
between mainstream social work and the Chinese community. In the twenty-
first century, the ethnic agency is responding to its needs. As the profession
seeks to embrace ethnic-sensitive service delivery, its response to marginalized groups is gaining greater significance.

Building Communities and Community Capacity

The ethnic agency may help promote community capacity and contribute
to community building. Through community capacity, the community can
work toward problem solving and change. By using the strengths of the community and its members, the community can build its capacity to solve problems. The focus here is on community strengths and not on deficits. According
to Netting, Kettner, and McMurtry, capacity building involves both participation and empowerment.[7] Members must be empowered to overcome obstacles to their participation in advocacy and change-seeking activities. At the
community level, empowerment is the process through which residents attain
power and control over forces affecting community life.[8] The presence of the
ethnic agency in a community may serve to reaffirm the importance of the
community and inspire residents to advocate for other resources. The ethnic
agency itself may be the result of members' mobilization efforts. In response
to a need, the community and/or specific members worked to address that
need. With the opening of the ethnic agency, the community's capacity had
dramatically increased.

In describing the multiservice centers in three different Chinese communities, Chow notes that, to fill the social service void, "professionally trained
Chinese American social workers, many of whom were immigrants themselves, began to seek public support to develop social programs to meet the

needs of the Chinese immigrant communities.[9] These grassroots programs began as storefronts and gradually expanded into the multimillion-dollar-complex service agencies that exist today. The ethnic agency, in this case, offers a striking example of community capacity building. The community now has the capacity to respond to the varied needs of the community in a myriad of ways.

Community building can target the internal dynamics of the community system. The building of a sense of community involves forging ties and relationships between the people and other social units that define a community. Holley asserts that recent immigrants of color can benefit from community building as a means of addressing the isolation and lack of support they face in this country.[10] The author adds that ethnic minority communities may face social and economic conditions that render them invisible to the larger society and result in feelings of isolation and hopelessness. In addition, some members may greet outsiders with apprehension and distrust and also dismiss them as not understanding the community.

The ethnic agency becomes a tool for community building.[11] It provides an arena for reinforcing group identity, strengths, worldview, and resiliency. It symbolizes the self-help capacity of the community, with members of the group assuming leadership positions in directing the services and administration of the agency. The community-building process also adds to the members' feelings of empowerment. The ethnic agency becomes a critical component of both processes.

Inadequacy of Mainstream Service Delivery Systems

Another reason for the existence of the ethnic agency may be the manner in which traditional service systems have responded (or not responded) to ethnic minority populations. Western intervention strategies may differ dramatically from the indigenous strategies of the ethnic group.[12] The meaning and use of community and its supports to ethnic minority groups may vary from that of mainstream America. The application of Western values and interventions may alienate some ethnic minority clients and communities. This difference poses a major challenge for service delivery.

Traditional systems may not be able to accommodate the language and/or culture of particular clients. The lack of bilingual and bicultural staff may be interpreted by clients as being dismissive of the group in question. Programs may be located outside of the community, thereby creating transportation problems for some individuals. Issues in access and a perceived nonresponsiveness may foster a sense of alienation or distrust on the part of ethnic minority clients.

Organizational climate is a set of characteristics that distinguish the organization from other organizations, are relatively enduring over time, and influence the behavior of people in the organization.[13] The climate of the bureaucratized agency can become a barrier to service delivery. Bureaucratization can refer to the increase in size and structural complexity of organizations, including social service agencies.[14] As social service agencies expand, that expansion may be accompanied by increased specialization, increased formalization with the requisite paperwork, and decreased worker autonomy. Potential clients may encounter workers who are facing the pressures of maintaining accurate and complete case files. The demands of the job may inadvertently communicate that the worker is too busy to give the client full attention or give the impression that the worker is not interested in the client. Ethnic minority group members under duress from their presenting problem may not be willing to disclose, and the worker–client interaction is reduced to a level of superficiality.

A related concept, *organizational culture*, may also distinguish the ethnic agency from other agencies. This concept can be defined as "the way things are done around here" and includes those shared norms, beliefs, and behavioral expectations that influence workers and help them to understand who or what is important to the agency.[15] Some mainstream agencies may have cultures that are subtly uninviting to ethnic minority clients. These clients may have to wait a little longer for service and may receive the minimal amount of service and information. Although they are being served by the agency, that service represents the floor of service, not the ceiling. Workers at such agencies are doing their job, but clearly without the enthusiasm that may be extended to White clients. Furthermore, workers may be unaware of this differential treatment. When the client responds in a closed, unfriendly manner, the worker may simply conclude that the group is that way in general. There may be no interest in pursuing alternative explanations for the lack of rapport between the two. Rather than being one interaction in time between two individuals, the interaction is the outcome of decades of stereotyping, distrust, and mistrust. If the agency does not value the ethnic minority client, there may be no attempt to alter or reshape these kinds of interactions. The agency culture becomes a microcosm of society and its treatment and perception of ethnic minorities.

Minority clients may also feel that they have no input into the systems that provide them services. They may face what is defined by Gilbert, Specht, and Terrell as nondistributive participation (no real input) or normal participation (tokenism) without really being able to change or influence these systems.[16] Such feelings of powerlessness reinforce the marginalized position these groups may occupy in society.

Myths and gross generalizations may also decrease the efficacy of mainstream services to ethnic minorities. For example, the "myth of the model minority" has followed many Asian Americans because of their apparent educational and economic successes.[17] This illusion of assimilation suggests that they do not warrant special attention. As can be seen in chapters 2, 3, and 4, stereotypes were fairly rampant in the history of ethnic and racial groups. Although some ethnic groups have succeeded in banishing their stereotypes with the passage of time, for other groups time may have served to further reinforce the stereotypes in American society. This means that, for some groups, the stereotypes are still "contagious," being "caught" by some service planners and service providers.

The lumping of ethnic groups into global categories also decreases system responsiveness to these groups. *Asian American* is used typically to define Chinese, Japanese, and Korean Americans, but the term is also being expanded to include Filipino, Vietnamese, Cambodian, Samoan, and Guamanian Americans.[18] As an example Tezcatlipoca argued, "The terms *Hispanic* and *Latino* are insulting to Chicanos and Mexicanos because these words deny us [Chicanos] our great Native Mexican heritage."[19] Clearly, with the passage of time group names may change, and that change may actually come from outside the group. Labels such as *Hispanic* or *Spanish-speaking* mask the differences that exist between Cuban, Puerto Rican, and Mexican Americans. These global labels also ignore the fact that, for some groups, Latino ethnic identification can be situational and political.[20] American Indians did not consider themselves as a collective group; rather, they were separate and distinct sovereign nations with cultural and language variations. The society around them categorized them as a group, thereby ignoring the self-identification of the nations. The imposition of artificial labels communicates a false homogeneity between ethnic groups. Services designed to meet the needs of both Asian Americans and Hispanic Americans, for example, ignore between-group differences and tensions and may only superficially attend to the needs of the clients.

Challenges confronting the larger social system have not been the only factor associated with the formation of ethnic agencies. Another set of explanatory factors lies in the ethnic community subsystems themselves.

Cultural Challenges to Mainstream Services

As mentioned previously, distrust and apprehension of the larger social systems may figure prominently in attitudes toward mainstream services. In a review of the literature on service utilization among Asian American elderly, Salcido, Nakano, and Jue found that distrust and skepticism played a role in the underutilization of services by Chinese Americans, Korean Americans, and Filipino Americans.[21] For the Japanese Americans, differences were found in the attitudes between the generations. For individuals isolated from and distrustful of "outside" service systems, the ethnic agency functions as a point of contact as well as a provider of services. In this study, the ethnic agency provided needed services to individuals who otherwise would have been isolated, alone, and neglected.

Some ethnic agencies are a manifestation of a group cohesiveness that supports organizational development and organizational participation.[22] For example, in a study of American Indians' preference for counselors, Johnson and Lashley found that participants with strong commitment to the American-Indian culture preferred a same-race counselor.[23] For ethnic group members with strong ethnic identity, the ethnic agency becomes a tool for further solidifying group cohesiveness. Because participation in traditional ethnic organizations was related to success and life satisfaction among first-generation Japanese Americans, the ethnic agency can also potentially serve as a crucial source of support.[24]

A history of self-help may foster a belief that self-help social services have better outcomes than mainstream programs. For example, in an article entitled, "Why African American Adoption Agencies Succeed: A New Perspective on Self-Help," the authors are inadvertently implying that these agencies can be superior to other agencies.[25] As discussed in the previous chapter, African Americans have a long-standing history of formal and informal self-help activities that dates back to the early nineteenth century. This history has led to years of developing community-based mechanisms to address community needs. Readers, African American and others, who see the article on African American adoptions, may conclude that this group can certainly do it better. The reality is that *some* mainstream agencies and *some* ethnic agencies provide effective services.

THE ETHNIC AGENCY: SOCIAL SYSTEM PARAMETERS

The ethnic agency, thus, represents a bridge to ethnic communities—a bridge that may be useful to mainstream agencies as they strengthen their service delivery capacity for working with ethnic minority communities. Ethnic agencies are already reaching and serving those populations in need of ethnic-sensitive practice from mainstream agencies. The ethnic agency does not represent a monolithic entity; rather, it covers a range of agencies that provide a variety of services to a spectrum of ethnic groups. The ethnic agency is affected by cultural traditions that become manifested in both structure and operations. Thus, as ethnic groups differ in history, cultural traditions, belief systems, and norms, these differences become reflected in the structure and operations of an ethnic agency serving a particular group.[26] There is no single model that defines the ethnic agency.

Some ethnic agencies mirror traditional system services. This form of duplication is referred to as *separatism*.[27] New agencies that are established outside the mainstream service delivery system may not try to penetrate that mainstream system. These agencies serve disenfranchised groups that are also outside of the mainstream. Separatism may act as a political and social strategy for advocating for needs and obtaining resources.

Since the ethnic agency emerges from within the ethnic community, an understanding of the community itself is important in order to understand the necessity of the ethnic agency. Several factors seem to determine whether ethnic agencies develop in ethnic communities. These factors include the city or part of the country where the group is located, the length of time the group has been in the United States, the degree of diversity or homogeneity of the group, intragroup class system,[28] and the group's relationship with the larger social system.[29]

Location is important because values, norms, and social systems vary by region. For example, the Japanese Americans of St. Louis have had a different interaction with their larger social system and external polity as compared with the Japanese of California.[30] In St. Louis, the Japanese Americans were upwardly mobile and the city provided better pathways to employment and entrepreneurship. The polarization between Whites and African Americans in that city did not impede the progress of the Japanese Americans. This may have been related to the smaller size of the St. Louis community as compared to the one in California, so that the Japanese community was not perceived as a threat. The race conflict in St. Louis was a Black–White problem, not a Japanese American one. The rapid integration of the Japanese into the larger social system may have reduced some of the need for this group to establish its own social service agencies.

Immigration patterns, as they relate to specific regions of the country, affect the nature and extent of ethnic community organization and ethnic agency development in numerous other cities and states. For example, in Miami the polarization between African Americans and Whites is still apparent, while the Cuban American community, in general, has attained greater economic and political success in comparison to African Americans. As other "Black" groups (Afro-Caribbean immigrants, for example) immigrate to the southeastern states, their experiences have also differed somewhat from those of American-born Blacks.[31] In addition, some Black immigrants have tried to distance themselves from African Americans because of the negative stereotypes surrounding African Americans. This is reminiscent of the experiences of White ethnics (discussed in Chapter 2) who did not want to be seen as African American.

For those groups that are recent arrivals, the newness of the culture, the establishing of economic security, and the transition from the old home to the new may not immediately encourage the development of ethnic agencies. For example, for Guatemalans immigrating to the United States (from Central America), divisions by political ideology and district of origin may stifle group cohesiveness and reduce the likelihood of Guatemalan ethnic agencies. As these former identifications give rise to a consensus in identity as Guatemalans, ethnic agencies that serve Guatemalans regardless of political ideology and district of origin may be forthcoming. Thus, the longer this group is in the United States, the more likely group members are to create their own ethnic agencies. Recency and diversity are the operative factors here.

An ethnic group, as a subsystem, interfaces with other subsystems as well as with the larger system of which it is a member. Discriminatory practices may foster group cohesiveness and encourage ethnic agencies to develop, both to meet group needs and to provide intragroup support. Thus, the initial motivation to form an ethnic agency may arise from external conditions such as inadequate facilities, inappropriate facilities, or no facilities.[32] In a prevailing environment of anti-immigration sentiment directed toward Hispanics, immigrants from Central America may find the climate less than hospitable and services less than forthcoming. They may be forced to provide for the needs of their own community, and the creation of ethnic agencies may be one option. For the Central Americans, the development of ethnic agencies may be accelerated by a hostile environment.

The presence of a sizable lower class within an ethnic group may also promote the establishment of ethnic agencies. When added to minority status, poverty may create a truly disadvantaged, disenfranchised class that warrants assistance from ethnic-specific agencies. Within ethnic communities, class becomes another force that propels ethnic agency development. Indeed, Jenkins found that the ethnic agencies she studied served primarily low-income groups.[33]

Class may also be an indication of some degree of integration into the larger society. For example, in a study of Korean Americans in Cleveland, Han found that middle-class Korean Americans had knowledge of mental health professionals and accepted the purpose they served.[34] Although this group seemed receptive to these service providers, it was not ascertained whether this belief was actually supported through action. Class could be interpreted as a measure of one's awareness of and integration into the larger social system. For middle-class ethnic group members, the ethnic agency may be less of a necessity than for the impoverished lower class.

The ethnic community is a dynamic, fluid entity that adapts and responds to its environment. Ethnic agencies rise and fall in tune with the system in which they are situated. Integration into and acceptance by the larger social system may decrease the need for ethnic agencies, while polarization and differential treatment compel minorities to seek stations of solace. Because of the significance of these agencies to their communities, what these agencies do and how they do it command consideration.

Defining the Ethnic Agency: Ethnicity and Ideology

A number of factors serve to define the ethnic agency, and some of them were identified in the previous chapter on early ethnic services. A discussion of these factors will help to underscore the manner in which the ethnic agency is similar to and different from mainstream services.

The foremost distinction of the ethnic agency is its ideology of the value of ethnicity and its integration into the service delivery process. Ideologies reflect those beliefs that are held with fervor and help explain cause-and-effect relationships.[35] Ideologies shape the agency's receptivity to the clients and their presenting problems. Typically, these ideologies are manifested in the worker–client interaction, agency technology, agency structure, distribution of power, and the extent to which clients are held responsible for causing their situation.

Generally, the worker–client relationship is analyzed in terms of the degree of discretion the workers have in their interactions with their clients; the removal of the worker–client interaction from the scrutiny of the organization; the compatibility of value between worker and client goals; and the centrality of trust and rapport in effective helping relationships.[36] Another aspect of the worker–client relationship commands attention. According to Iglehart, the worker represents the interface between the agency and the client and, in this role, embodies the agency to the client.[37] The client "sees" the agency through a worker who interprets the agency to the client. Through the worker, the client enters the organization's system. What occurs between the worker and client is frequently generalized by the client as being representative of the rest of the agency. If the organization has a commitment to its clients, workers will be expected to develop trust and rapport in working with these clients. Ethnicity may be a crucial factor in the commitment of the agency and the worker to the client.

Racial sameness between worker and client is assumed to foster close, sensitive interactions that are generalized to the agency. According to Etzioni, a close relationship between worker and client leads to sensitivity to the client, which in turn leads to client-responsive services.[38] In the ethnic agency, ethnicity becomes a factor that advances rather than impedes the service delivery process. For the agencies Jenkins studied, this ethnic content was located in food, music, art, history, and holidays. It seems, however, that these are just symbolic of a much deeper meaning of ethnicity.

Dexter's 1921 observation about the qualification for social work among one's own people can be generalized to other groups besides African Americans. That qualification was faith in the destiny of the race.[39] The worker who symbolizes the agency joins with the client in those steps necessary to improve and uplift the ethnic/racial group. In this regard, the worker and client become part of the same system, rather than being members of the helping system versus the client system. As a member of that ethnic group, the worker does not have to be convinced of, lectured about, or advised about the destiny of the race since he or she already has inside knowledge about this destiny.

Ethnicity may facilitate service delivery by exposing clients to role models with whom they can identify. Freudenberger[40] emphasized this point by noting that, in a youth drug-treatment program, it is easier for the Latino client to identify with a successful member of his own group than with someone from another group:

> As staff members of minority programs it is incumbent on us to keep in mind that if there are Latino residents, then we need Latino staff; the same applies for Asian Americans, Native Americans, and Mexican Americans. This does not mean that there needs to be exclusivity, but the majority of the treatment staff in a dominant minority group neighborhood ought to be from the same ethnic background.[41]

Petr has urged workers to position themselves *within* the client system to allow for reciprocity and mutuality in the relationship.[42] If this occurs, Petr stated, "then the role of worker must be noninterventionist, or somehow beyond intervention. Attention to the subjective world of values, meaning, and process would displace objective understanding of problems and their resolution."[43] Although this type of mutuality is not promoted by the professional and bureaucratic imperatives of mainstream agencies, the ethnic agency at least seems more sympathetic to this point of view.

In the ethnic agency, the worker and client are already more likely to attend to the world of values, meaning, and process. In a study of 13 ethnic agencies, Holley found that all the agencies supported an ideology of ethnic awareness.[44] For example, an American Indian client does not have to hide his or her use of native healers or other culturally sanctioned healers from the ethnic agency worker. For some groups, these healers may be a crucial source of help.[45] The worker would already have knowledge of the practice and may even inquire about it. The ethnic agency and the ethnic worker are less likely to frown on these practices and are more likely to support and validate the client's values. For example, the Papago Psychological Service (run and staffed by members of the Papago Indian tribe) used, when necessary, the combination and cooperation of the medicine man and the mental health technician for client intervention.[46]

Cross described a ceremony used at the Anishnaabe Child and Family Services in Manitoba, Canada, that welcomes children returning home from placement away from the reservation.[47] This ceremony greeted the children and gave the community an opportunity to begin reestablishing bonds with them. This type of community practice can probably be conducted only under the auspices of an ethnic-focused agency. Mainstream agencies may not have the capacity for this type of culturally based innovation. Besides, most child welfare agencies have diverse client populations and the special needs of one particular group may be overshadowed by the needs of other groups.

As members of the same system, the worker and clients may share the commonality of history, background, experiences, and worldview. For the Korean individual new to this country, the ethnic agency means that he or she can assume that the Korean American worker has some knowledge of Korean cultural heritage, including some awareness of the significance of *haan*—a belief system about emotions associated with suffering.[48] If the worker is working in an ethnic agency, there is a strong probability that he or she is grounded in the culture of that group.

The significance of ethnicity in the worker–client interaction may be so subtle as to be rendered invisible. Communication patterns and processes may be culturally based and so endemic to the organization, to the staff, and to the clients that these patterns and processes are a "given." Language patterns may connote a unity and familiarity to clients that enable them to feel comfortable and open to staff feedback. For example, the African American language patterns of verbal inventiveness and call/response may be understood and used freely in some African American agencies and thus promote ethnic cohesiveness.[49]

Trust, rapport, and mutuality may be more likely to occur in the ethnic agency because the worker and client share similar ethnic-based goals. For many ethnic groups, the family is the cornerstone of the group. Jenkins found that the majority of the ethnic agencies she studied sought to strengthen the family.[50] These ethnic agencies saw individuals as members of a family *system* and worked to improve the functioning of that unit.

Because the worker and client share the commonality of history, there does not seem to be a need to interpret that history to each other. As a Mexican American, the client does not need to explain to the Mexican American worker what it is like to be a Mexican American in the United States. Although each person is different and has different experiences, there is still a common thread that brings people together—the thread of ethnic group experience.

The ethnic factor suggests that barriers that often exist in mainstream agencies are minimized or are nonexistent. A layer of potential static in the communication process has been removed. For example, minority clients often have a dual consciousness that results from negotiating life in a White world and in their ethnic world.[51] Because these cultures are not compatible, communication between Whites and minorities is frequently delivered and received at two levels—one based on the reality of being a minority and the other based on the history of minority–majority interactions. In these cross-race exchanges, the *perception* of what is being said may override what is *actually* being said. In same-race exchanges, some confusion in interpretations and meaning (the noise or state of the interaction) has been reduced.

The ethnic factor in service delivery moves beyond the worker–client interaction. It also prevails in other aspects of organizational practice.

Empowerment as Technology

Client empowerment is a major feature of the agency's ideology that is mirrored in agency technology. Organizational empowerment is located in the efforts, methods, and strategies used in organizations to reduce disempowering conditions.[52] The ethnic agency attempts to foster client empowerment in the agency. The organizational level of empowerment connotes the *organization's* ability to empower individuals and communities.[53] Hasenfeld stated that "empowerment is a process through which clients obtain resources—personal, organizational, and community—that enable them to gain greater control over their environment and to attain their aspirations."[54] Through its ideology of empowerment, the ethnic agency rejects the "victim" label that is all too freely attached to poor minorities, especially African Americans. The "clinicalism" of the effects of differential treatment that frequently guides mainstream casework interventions is replaced by a more powerful, uplifting ethos. Victimization breeds victimization, and as long as individuals continue to see themselves as victims, they will continue to be victimized.[55] Empowerment is a foundation for practice that replaces the victimization label.

Empowerment may be a by-product of the agency's development. Ethnic workers and organizers successful enough to create and maintain a service agency for their community in a turbulent environment may feel empowered by the results of their work and may extend this air of confidence and empowerment to their clients. The feeling of accomplishment and contribution to the community may find its expression in practices that encourage clients to find their voice. A stronger sense of satisfaction may emanate from helping members of one's group. Thus, the helper benefits from organizing and contributing to the agency.

Ethnic agencies attempt to empower clients in a number of ways, such as providing them with the information they need to make decisions, providing them with information about community resources and services, involving clients in the agency decision-making process, hiring former clients as workers and/or using clients as volunteers, and creating opportunities for clients to learn the skills they desire.

Information, participation, and *skills* are three primary areas that distinguish the ethnic agency from other agencies. The client often has to negotiate numerous systems in order to resolve problems and/or seek assistance. The ethnic agency can be one of those systems. The agency often begins by providing clients with the information they need about the agency. In the ethnic agency, information seems readily available and, generally, freely given. In addition, information is also provided about those other agencies and services that may be of use to the clients. The worker is acting as resource consultant and teacher/trainer for the clients, and this is a role that can facilitate ethnic-sensitive practice. Knowledge is an example of concrete power,[56] and when clients are provided information, they can become empowered.

In the ethnic agency, client participation appears to be redistributive participation in which clients are able to exert influence in the agency decision-making process.[57] Over half of the ethnic workers studied by Jenkins felt that parents should have input in the decisions made in day care, whereas this was true for about 43 percent of the national social work sample.[58]

Ethnic agencies also empower clients by using them as volunteers and/or by hiring former clients. Because the worker and client are members of the same "system," the transition from client to worker is fairly smooth. The use of clients in these capacities further attests to the way in which the client becomes a partner in the helping process. The client volunteer or employee can function as another role model for other clients, and the empowerment process continues. The satisfaction and sense of accomplishment felt by the worker is then shared with clients who become agency volunteers or with former clients who join the agency staff. The benefits of helping are passed along to the client. Thus, the helping role in and of itself has significant value to the helper as well as to the service recipient.

Ethnic agencies seem to have a "group" focus in that they seek to empower the ethnic group as well as the individual client. Providing services that strengthen the family unit is indicative of this focus. In the Jenkins study, strengthening the family was the primary goal for over 90 percent of the agencies.[59] These agencies also wanted to provide growth and leadership for minority children.

As noted by Jenkins, changing majority attitudes is not the agency goal.[60] The goal of these agencies, as was true with the early minority self-help efforts, is to improve the conditions of the group.

Nonprofessionalism and the Ethnic Agency.   According to Powell, "The issue of professionalization is partly a question of who determines the nature of the merit good to be received by the organization's client."[61] Workers who identify with the community and its residents may define the "merit good" (services) as empowerment and the helping process as interactive. In contrast, the professionally trained worker may be guided by a commitment to the profession and the tenets of professional practice. Ethnic agencies have a pattern of relying on nonprofessional staff to carry out agency practices. This practice is generally taken to mean that these organizations reject professionalism and the professional. Professionalization is seen as a wedge that distances the worker from the client. For those advocating client empowerment, this distance becomes a significant disadvantage to understanding and engaging the client. According to Musick and Hooyman, the client is the one who has to live with the problems, not the professional.[62] This "living with the problem" minimizes the expertise that an "outsider" brings to the intervention. Professionalism may also be associated with individual-level explanations about the cause of the client's problem and may view the client as being responsible for solving it.

The controversy centers on who is the most qualified: the nondegreed paraprofessional with personal experience (group membership) or the degreed professional with specialized knowledge.[63] For ethnic agencies, ethnic group membership has primacy over professionalism. This general perception of ethnicity over professionalism may be an oversimplification of a more complex issue. Ethnic agencies may be extremely interested in and supportive of professionalism. In fact, these agencies may be *rejecting the nonminority professional rather than professionalism itself.* With the issues confronting ethnic minority clients, agencies may have made the decision to subject them to the untrained, same-group worker rather than to the expertly trained, distanced worker.

The staffing patterns selected by an ethnic agency are based on the effort to maintain an internal polity that supports a particular agency ideology. The agency seeks control of the practice, and if professionals are involved, the agency seeks control of the professional practice as well. Professionalism in the context of ethnic agency practice is the predominant goal. The ethnic agency seems to have more confidence that the untrained ethnic worker is more likely than the professional to value and maintain the "merit good" (services) to be received by clients. In the absence of identification with the clients and the community, the professionally trained nonminority individual may be more likely to define the "merit good" in other ways.

Unlike the distanced professional, the untrained worker may effectively function in the role of a supportive peer with a sympathetic ear. Mutuality and rapport, a basis for the helping relationship, are presumed to be established almost immediately through the bonds of ethnic identification, group cohesiveness, and sociohistorical commonality. Thus, the interaction becomes part of the intervention process in both direct and indirect practice.

As previously mentioned, among the ethnic agency workers in the Jenkins study, the highest number of workers with Masters degrees (MSW) was found among the African Americans. African Americans may be ahead of the other ethnic groups in their involvement in professional social work education. It may be the *absence* of the professional ethnic worker that leads agencies to utilize the paraprofessional. Jenkins also found that the highest overall level of ethnic commitment came from the MSW ethnic agency workers in comparison to other ethnic agency workers and the national sample of social workers.[64] Professionalism, as reflected in the MSW, is strongly supportive of ethnic commitment.

Debureaucratization and the Ethnic Agency. The climate or atmosphere of the ethnic agency may differ from that of most mainstream agencies. In reviewing studies of organizational climate, Bunker and Wijnberg found that *structure* (perceptions of formality versus informality) and *social inclusion* (friendly sociability versus disagreement and criticism) were among the dimensions of this climate.[65] These two seem to have significant relevance for understanding the climate of ethnic agencies.

Within the ethnic agency a relaxed and friendly climate seems to prevail, and this type of atmosphere is desired and maintained by the agencies. This is accomplished, in part, by the reduction in the bureaucratic red tape that is commonly associated with formal organizations. The less formal and less rigid nature of the agency climate also applies to the staff. The interactions between staff members may also be less formal in an organization structure that has a flattened hierarchy.

The debureaucratized agency with its diffusion of power may serve as a source of empowerment for the workers. Workers can empower clients only if they themselves feel empowered. Worker participation in decision making and agency governance promotes the efficacy of the worker. Empowered workers may be more committed to the agency, and the degree of worker commitment affects the quality of the worker–client interaction.[66] Worker empowerment may be correlated with job satisfaction and high worker morale, factors that may also contribute to the agency's climate.

Organizational Development

As they grow and develop, organizations move through several stages, including (1) innovation and niche creation, (2) cohesion and commitment, (3) rule formation and structure stabilization, (4) structure elaboration, and (5) adaptation.[67]

According to Kramer, most voluntary organizations become more bureaucratic and professionalized over time in their quest for domain and identity.[68] Kramer further added that, over time, local voluntary organizations grow, prosper, and build professional staffs that obtain federal support. The transformation of an agency is related to its search for and dependency on external funding. Hardina, for example, found that the acceptance of government funding limits the organization's flexibility in responding to client needs.[69] Fabricant recommended that public funding should not exceed 25 percent of an agency's budget if that agency wants to maintain its objectives.[70] Grants bring with them commitment to particular goals and the demands for greater formalization of operating procedures.[71] This means that agency administrators are likely to become more responsive to the wishes of the funding sources rather than the wishes of the staff and clients.[72]

Fisher and Fabricant provide an example of the transformation of an agency in their analysis of the changing funding base of the Henry Street Settlement House in New York.[73] As a settlement house that relied on private support from donors and community support, Henry Street could devote its resources to services and community building. As funding from these sources decreased, the settlement was forced to pursue other channels of funding. As it began receiving public contract dollars for categorical programs, the settlement began to look more like mainstream service agencies. Rather than the maturation of an organization, the authors attribute this transformation to a political economy that experiences shifts over time. The authors further theorize that in social change eras like the Progressive Era and the 1960s, settlement ideas receive more support. In conservative periods, funding declines for progressive programs and shifts to recreational, categorical, and individualized programs.

In addition to the influence of funding requirements, age contributes to agency size, complexity, and diversity independent of funding source.[74] As agencies survive, they also tend to expand and add additional programs that require more staff. Increasing complexity and specialization are also factors that promote the agency's bureaucratic development.

What does this mean for the ethnic agency? The ethnic agency appears to be a special case that may be outside the traditional organizational development pattern. For example, over 94 percent of the ethnic agencies Jenkins studied were receiving public funds.[75] The Chicano Training Center, a vehicle for training Latino social workers, was started in 1969 with a grant from the National Institute of Mental Health. The training center developed into a multi-purpose social service agency that continues to serve the Latino community in Los Angeles. Numerous ethnic agencies have originated with federal, state, and local public dollars.

Several explanations may be offered for why, comparatively speaking, ethnic agencies seem able to retard their rate of bureaucratic growth: (1) agencies protect their core technologies, (2) agencies protect their clients, and (3) government funding is not as intrusive to these agencies as it is to mainstream agencies. According to Meyer:

> The effort to maintain a structure that meets the criteria of externally defined rationality may make it necessary or wise to leave that structure inconsistent with the work that needs to get done. *Decoupling results, buffering the formal structure from ongoing activity* [emphasis added].[76]

Where decoupling is not feasible, agencies may operate as loosely coupled systems with subsystems maintaining autonomy and identity with marginal interactions.[77] In other words, ethnic agencies are able to decouple their ideology and practices from the bureaucratic imperatives that accompany funding, or function as loosely coupled systems that can also protect technologies and ideologies. Conformity with the externally imposed requirements of bureaucracy and formalization occurs, yet the ideology and practices are minimally affected. As new programs emerge in the agency, the bureaucratic mandate is met while the prevailing ideology and technology are incorporated into the program. Each individual program can be aligned with the community, but all programs together may comprise a complex, bureaucratic system.

The ethnic agency may also seek to protect its clients from the effects of bureaucratization. The agency administrators may feel that the clients should not have to experience the inconvenience and problems associated with bureaucracy, and efforts are undertaken to shield the clients as much as possible from its intrusiveness. Ideally, clients would not have to be bombarded with volumes of forms and mounds of rules. The staff would also try to keep the service delivery process as uncomplicated as possible for the clients. The agency can serve to buffer the client, thereby allowing the client to continue to feel that a certain informality has prevailed in the agency.

It is also possible that the ethnic agency augments and complements mainstream services so that its practices and ideologies are assumed to meet the needs of a nontraditional population. Nontraditional populations may require nontraditional interventions so that the day-to-day operations of the ethnic agency may not be scrutinized. If the ethnic agency is regarded as an expert in service delivery to the ethnic population, funding sources may be less likely to want to modify the agency's practices.

The ethnic agency, as a voluntary agency, may reflect the democratization and decentralization of the welfare state discussed by Ostrander, since many of them do rely on public funding.[78] This public support brings client-responsive services to communities that are more likely to be outside of mainstream service delivery. Community participation on the boards of these agencies may indirectly link these constituencies with the welfare state. For these reasons, the organizational development of the ethnic agency may differ from that of mainstream organizations.

Tseng raises concern about ethnic agencies relying on public dollars for survival.[79] In a study of two Chinese and two Vietnamese community-based organizations (CBOs) in the San Francisco Bay area, the researcher found that in times of economic crisis, ethnic and immigrant CBOs appear to be the most vulnerable to budgetary cuts. These CBOs represent groups that are powerless and voiceless in the political process. Public funding can be indicative of a government–ethnic community partnership, but this partnership may be valueless if the constituency cannot affect the political process.

THE EXTERNAL POLITY OF THE ETHNIC AGENCY

The community served by the ethnic agency appears to be a powerful force in the life of the agency. The agency and its community share a symbiotic relationship. The community provides the legitimacy and the clients needed by the agency, and the agency provides the services that the community needs. Agency reputation influences client trust; the better the reputation, the higher the level of client trust.[80] The *ethnic community* rather than an individual is the service recipient/consumer, and this community bestows legitimacy and credibility. Consequently, this community consumer has a powerful voice in the agency.

Mainstream social services may be funded by sources who are not the recipients of services. The agency is, however, accountable to its sponsors and not to the service recipients. This situation is radically different in the ethnic agency, which is a response to community need. In some instances, the community may have been the original service sponsors.

The ethnic agency belongs to the community and is accountable to its community constituency. For this reason, community participation on boards, in programs, and at meetings is necessary. Citizen involvement, especially through board membership, is vital to the agency/community relationship,[81] and the ethnic agency relies heavily on citizen involvement. The community advocates for the agency and can buffer the agency from public attack. The community can also "interpret" the agency to others in the larger social system. Funding cutbacks and other processes that threaten to harm the agency may be offset by community advocacy that literally protects the agency.

The agency's commitment to its community is found in the approaches it takes to client needs. For example, the agencies studied by Jenkins seemed to address as many client needs as possible.[82] This was referred to as the "more integrated approach" because many service areas were addressed. This occurred even if the agency had only one or two "official" specific service areas. The agency's role was to ease as many problems as possible, perhaps due to the perception that if the agency did not help, no one else would. This attests to the strength of the agency/community link.

The agency/community link is often reflected in the agency director's relationship with the community. The distance between the director and a community resident is minimal in comparison to the distance between mainstream administrators and the community. Community residents and the ethnic agency director continue the pattern of meaningful personal interactions. The director belongs to the community and may be called on to participate in community activities. Rich made this observation about African American administrators and the African American community years ago, but it appears to be especially true for the ethnic agency administrator and the ethnic community.[83]

Consequently, the boundaries between the ethnic agency and the community it serves are fluid, as energy is exchanged between the two. In addition to responsiveness to its clients, the ethnic agency also must be responsive to the community if it is to survive.

THE ETHNIC AGENCY AND SOCIAL CHANGE/SOCIAL REFORM

The ethnic agency's position on social reform bears additional comment. As previously mentioned, this agency seems to be committed to improving the condition of the community it serves. For example, in the Jenkins study agencies seemed committed to helping clients "make it" in American society.[84] Efforts included bilingual-bicultural programs, career development programs, and support for families. These agencies want their clients to be a part of the American dream. However, the business of facing the problems of daily living may be overwhelming for both staff and clients, and there is often no time or energy left for planning or implementing other activities.

The question arises: To what extent is social change the *real* goal of ethnic agencies? These are *service* agencies and, within their communities, service provision is a major task. Furthermore, it appears that ethnic agencies and ethnic groups may be more concerned with obtaining their piece of the pie rather than changing the pie. The ideologies of the meritocracy, individualism, and Protestant work ethic encourage citizens to toil hard and expect the rewards that accrue. The ethnic agency may pursue strategies that urge group members to work hard to achieve success. There may not be a perception that, regardless of how hard one works, some avenues to success may continue to be blocked. Ethnic minorities may be accepting the intractability of institutions and structures in U.S. society. Perhaps they have no issue with them. The issue may be one of access, opportunity, and right—access to the riches and rewards of mainstream life, opportunity to participate in U.S. society, and the right to equality.

The ethnic agency serves a vital purpose in American society. Its organization, ideology, and climate invite community members to make use of its services. As it continues to play a vital role in the nation's service delivery process, there are still many disadvantages that must be acknowledged.

Unique Challenges

No agency, practice, or ideology is perfect. The ethnic agency is no exception. Several pitfalls surround the ethnic agency and its approach to practice:

1. Because the ethnic agency may serve an underserved population, it may try to do too much with too little. A shotgun approach to service delivery may erode the agency's effectiveness and undermine the community's confidence.

2. The most talented workers of a particular ethnic group may not view the ethnic agency as a wise career move or as a rung on the ladder to success.

3. The "we-ness" between clients and staff may result in role ambiguity as boundaries become blurred.

4. The "we-ness" of the atmosphere may inhibit client self-disclosure because of fear that confidentiality will be breached.

5. The "we-ness" may cloud worker objectivity.

6. Because workers and clients share cultural norms and values, workers may not wish to intrude in areas that may be deemed culturally inappropriate, even if this intrusion promotes effective service delivery.

7. Group cohesiveness may lead to stereotyping of the out-group.[85] In the ethnic agency, negative perceptions of White America may be perpetuated and reinforced as individuals trade "discrimination" stories, and the need for racial tolerance may not be addressed.

8. Homogeneity among ethnic agency members may stifle innovation and creativity. New ideas may be frowned on because of the agency's organizational culture ("That is not how things have been done.").

9. Group cohesiveness may force individuals to conform to group norms.[86] Individuality may not be valued, as it may be a sign of deviancy.

10. Because of the staff members' investment in and identification with the agency, conflict becomes personal. Conflict within the agency may be personalized—that is, issues that are nonpersonal may be seen as personal, and the reaction may be a personal one.

11. The intragroup patterns of sexism, classism, and status differentials may persist in the ethnic agency.

12. Because "we're all in this together," clients may expect to have fewer demands placed on them.

13. The intensity and amount of work coupled with the degree of emotional investment may lead to worker burnout.

14. Community participation in an agency may mean participation by only a dominant few while some segments of the community may be excluded.[87]

15. Some ethnic agencies may become "sacred cows" that defy change or innovation. These agencies may be "institutionalized" in the community and have the community's support regardless of the effectiveness of their services.

16. While the ethnic agency seeks to promote the integration of the client into the larger society, it practices a type of separatism. This separatism may be needed to ensure that community needs receive attention, but it may inadvertently work against integration. White America may react with skepticism and even hostility to special services for special groups. Racial polarization may be perpetuated by the presence of the ethnic agency.

However, these limitations may be overshadowed by the strengths and advantages that are associated with the ethnic agency.

Social Work and the Ethnic Agency

The very existence of the ethnic agency may be antithetical to the tenets of the social work profession. Because ethnic group members are providing services to other members of their ethnic group, ethnicity serves as a type of credential needed for this practice. Thus, the ethnic agency appears to support the "insider" doctrine: You have to be one in order to understand one.[88] This doctrine suggests that, by virtue of group membership, individuals have a monopoly on or special access to the knowledge needed for practice with that particular group.

With the insider doctrine, the role of the profession's knowledge base in extending services is discounted. The existence of this knowledge base implies that social work training prepares individuals to practice with the various groups of society. Knowledge and skills are expected to be transferred from one setting to another, and applications to specific ethnic groups are held to be extrapolated from this knowledge base. Because the ethnic agency emphasizes ethnicity over professional expertise, a gulf may exist between the ethnic agency and the mainstream social work agency.

The ethnic agency poses another significant challenge to the social work profession in its perceptions of and interfaces with the client. Rather than endorsing the worker–client power differential as part of agency practice, the ethnic agency equalizes the power between the service provider and the service recipient, accepts the client's definition of the problem, actively involves the client in the change process, teaches skills to the client, and advocates for the client.[89] Ethnicity is the common denominator that builds on a "one-ness" or a "we-ness" as the worker identifies with the client. Such views may define *subjective* practice as opposed to *objective* practice, and this subjective practice may be outside the boundaries of professional social work. Although ethnic agencies and mainstream social work share a commitment to service delivery, fundamental differences exist in their ideologies and methods of service delivery.

From this discussion, some propositions can be outlined to summarize the ethnic agency and its practices:

Proposition 1: The ethnic agency is controlled by, staffed by, and provides services to a specific ethnic group.

Proposition 2: The ethnic agency seems to be a special type of voluntary, self-help, alternative, community-based service agency.

Proposition 3: The ethnic agency may fill a void left by deficiencies in mainstream service delivery systems and/or be a response to cultural barriers that impede a group's utilization of traditional services.

Proposition 4: The ethnic agency is shaped by the larger social system in which it is located.

Proposition 5: Ethnicity is an integral part of the ideology and technology of the ethnic agency.

Proposition 6: The ethnic agency operationalizes the concept of empowerment.

Proposition 7: There is a tension between ethnicity and professionalism in the ethnic agency.

Proposition 8: The ethnic agency seeks to simplify the organization for the client.

Proposition 9: The ethnic agency tries to protect its ideology and technology from bureaucratic intrusion.

Proposition 10: The ethnic agency and its community share a symbiotic relationship.

Proposition 11: The ethnic agency may not be social-reform oriented.

Proposition 12: The ethnic agency may augment, rather than compete with, mainstream services.

Proposition 13: There may be limitations surrounding ethnic agency practice that are not associated with mainstream agencies.

Proposition 14: A tension seems to exist between the ethnic agency and mainstream social work practice.

Historically, with mainstream social work, ethnic/racial minorities have frequently been underserved or unserved, an adherence to ethnic group responsibility has prevailed, and service providers have defined problems and their solutions. Although it too seems to support the ethos of ethnic group responsibility, the ethnic agency, in contrast, focuses primarily on an ethnic/

racial minority group and engages in an interactive problem-defining/problem-resolving process with that group.

According to Kwong, organizations reflect the institutionalized patterns of interactions among their members and capture the group's self-definition.[90] She further added that an understanding of an ethnic group's perspective can be achieved by studying the dynamics of the ethnic group through its ethnic organizations. Service delivery to ethnic minorities may be more effective if (1) the manner in which their agencies provide services is respected and, where feasible, adopted by other service delivery systems; and (2) more of these ethnic agencies were more fully incorporated into larger service delivery networks. The next chapter will explore avenues for achieving these goals.

Endnotes

[1] Shirley Jenkins, *The Ethnic Dilemma in Social Services* (New York: The Free Press, 1981).

[2] Elaine Pinderhughes, *Understanding Race, Ethnicity, and Power* (New York: The Free Press, 1989), 203.

[3] Melvin Delgado and John Scott, "Strategic Intervention—A Mental Health Program for the Hispanic Community," in *Human Services for Cultural Minorities*, ed. Richard Dana (Baltimore: University Park Press, 1981), 251–264; Lorraine Gutierrez, "Empowering Ethnic Minorities in the Twenty-First Century," in *Human Services as Complex Organizations*, ed. Yeheskel Hasenfeld (Newbury Park, CA: Sage Publications, 1992), 320–338; Jenkins, *The Ethnic Dilemma in Social Services*; Marvin Kahn, Cecil Williams, Eugene Galvez, Linda Lejero, Rex Conrad, and George Goldstein," The Papago Psychology Service," in *Human Services for Cultural Minorities*, ed. Richard Dana (Baltimore: University Park Press, 1981), 79–94; Pinderhughes, *Understanding Race, Ethnicity, and Power*, 202–205; Barbara Solomon, *Black Empowerment* (New York: Columbia University Press, 1976).

[4] Nancy Webb, "Series Editor's Note," in *Culturally Competent Practice with Immigrant and Refugee Children and Families*, ed. Rowena Fong (New York: The Guilford Press, 2004), xi.

[5] For a discussion of these and other immigrant groups see Rowena Fong, ed., *Culturally Competent Practice with Immigrant and Refugee Children and Families* (New York: The Guilford Press, 2004).

[6] Julian Chow, "Multiservice Centers in Chinese American Immigrant Communities: Practice Principles and Challenges," *Social Work* 44 (January 1999): 71.

[7] F. Ellen Netting, Peter Kettner, and Steven McMurtry, *Social Work Macro Practice*, 4th ed. (Boston: Pearson 2008), 351.

[8] Stephen Fawcett, Adrienne Paine-Andrews, Vincent Francisco, Jerry Schultz et al., "Using empowerment Theory in Collaborative Partnerships for Community and Health and Development, *American Journal of Community Psychology* 23 (October 1995): 677–697.

[9] Chow, "Multiservice Centers in Chinese American Immigrant Communities: Practice Principles and Challenges," 72.

[10] Lynn Holley, "Emerging Ethnic Agencies: Building Capacity to Build Community," *Journal of Community Practice* 11(4) (2003): 41.

[11] Holley, "Emerging Ethnic," 40–41.

[12] Carmen Tolentino, "Filipino Children and Families," *Culturally Competent Practice with Immigrant and Refugee Children and Families*, ed. Rowena Fong (New York: The Guilford Press, 2004), 70–72.

[13] Forehand and Gilmer, as quoted by Lawrence James and Allan Jones, "Organizational Climate: A Review of Theory and Research," *Psychological Bulletin* 81(12) (1974): 1097.

[14] Netting, Kettner, and McMurtry, *Social Work Macro Practice*, 54.

[15] Anthony Hemmelgarn, Charles Glisson, and Lawrence James, "Organizational Culture and Climate," in *Human Services as Complex Organizations*, 2nd ed., ed. Yeheskel Hasenfeld (Thousand Oaks, CA: Sage Publications, 2010), 231.

[16] Neil Gilbert, Harry Specht, and Paul Terrell, *Dimensions of Social Welfare Policy*, 3rd ed. (Englewood Cliffs, NJ: Prentice-Hall, 1993), 140–141.

[17] David Crystal, "Asian Americans and the Myth of the Model Minority," *Social Casework* 70 (September 1989): 405–413.

[18] Crystal, "Asian Americans," 405.

[19] Leo Tezcatlipoca, "We're Chicanos—Not Latinos or Hispanics," editorial, *Los Angeles Times*, 22 November 1993, section B.

[20] Felix Padilla, "On the Nature of Latino Ethnicity," *Social Science Quarterly* 65(2) (1984): 651–664.

[21] Ramon Salcido, Carol Nakano, and Sally Jue, "The Use of Formal and Informal Health and Welfare Services of the Asian American Elderly: An Exploratory Study," *Californian Sociologist* 3 (Summer 1990): 213–229.

[22] Thomas Guterbock and Bruce London, "Race, Political Orientation, and Participation: An Empirical Test of Four Competing Theories," *American Sociological Review* 48(4) (1983): 439–453.

[23] Mark Johnson and Karen Lashley, "Influence of Native Americans' Cultural Commitment on Preference for Counselor Ethnicity and Expectations About Counseling," *Journal of Multicultural Counseling and Development* 17 (July 1989): 115–122.

[24] Eric Woodrum and Nelson Reid, "Migration, Ethnic Community Organization, and Prosperity among Japanese Americans," *Arete* 12 (Summer 1987): 31–46.

[25] Geraldine Jackson-White, Cheryl Dozier, J. Toni Oliver, and Lydia Garner, "Why African American Adoption Agencies Succeed: A New Perspective on Self-Help," *Child Welfare* 76 (January–February 1997): 239–254.

[26] Richard Hall and Weiman Xu, "Research Note: Run Silent, Run Deep—Cultural Influences on Organizations in the Far East," *Organizational Structures* 11(4) (1990): 569–576; James Lincoln, Mitsuyo Hanada, and Kerry McBride, "Organizational Structures in Japanese and U.S. Manufacturing," *Administrative Science Quarterly* 31 (September 1986): 338–364.

[27] Gilbert, Specht, and Terrell, *Dimensions of Social Welfare Policy*, 140–141.

[28] These issues were raised by Jenkins, *The Ethnic Dilemma in Social Services*, 196.

[29] Discussed by Gunter Baureiss, "Towards a Theory of Ethnic Organizations," *Canadian Ethnic Studies* 14(2) (1982): 21–42.

[30] Miyako Inoue, "Japanese Americans in St. Louis: From Internees to Professionals," *City and Society* 3 (December 1989): 14–152.

[31] Kay Deaux, Nida Bikmen, Alwyn Gilkes, Ana Ventuneac, Yvanne Joseph, Yasser Payne, and Claude Steele, "Becoming American: Stereotype Effects in Afro-Caribbean Immigrant Groups," *Social Psychology Quarterly* 70 (December 2007): 384–404.

[32] Felice Perlmutter, "A Theoretical Model of Social Agency Development," *Social Casework* 50 (October 1969): 468.

[33] Jenkins, *The Ethnic Dilemma in Social Services*, 45.

[34] In Young Han, "A Study of Help-Seeking Patterns among Korean Americans," Ph.D. dissertation, Case Western Reserve University, 1989.

[35] This concept is defined in Chapter 1.

[36] See, for example, Burton Gummer, "On Helping and Helplessness: The Structure of Discretion in the American Welfare System," *Social Service Review* 53 (June 1979): 214–228; Hasenfeld, *Human Service Organizations*, 197–200.

[37] Alfreda Iglehart, "Adolescents in Foster Care: Factors Affecting the Worker Youth Relationship," *Children and Youth Services Review* 14(3/4) (1992): 308.

[38] Amitai Etzioni, *Modern Organizations* (Englewood Cliffs, NJ: Prentice Hall, 1964), 100.

[39] Robert Dexter, "The Negro in Social Work," *The Survey* 46 (June 25, 1921): 439–440.

[40] Herbert Freudenberger, "The Dynamics and Treatment of the Young Drug Abuser in an Hispanic Therapeutic Community," in *Human Services for Cultural Minorities*, ed. Richard Dana (Baltimore: University Park Press, 1981), 226.

[41] Freudenberger, "The Dynamics and Treatment of the Young Drug Abuser," 226.

[42] Christopher Petr, "The Worker–Client Relationship: A General Systems Perspective," *Social Casework* 69 (December 1988): 625.

[43] Ibid.

[44] Lynne Holley, "The Influence of Ethnic Awareness on Ethnic Agencies," *Administration in Social Work* 27(3) (2003): 47–63.

[45] Damian McShane, "Mental Health and North American Indian/Native Communities: Cultural Transactions, Education, and Regulation," *American Journal of Community Psychology* 15(1) (1987): 101–102; Scott Nelson, George McCoy, Maria Stetter, and W. Craig Vanderwagen, "An

Overview of Mental Health Services for American Indians and Alaska Natives in the 1990s," *Hospital and Community Psychiatry* 43 (March 1992): 258.

[46] Kahn et al. "The Papago Psychology Service," 85.

[47] Terry Cross, "Drawing of Cultural Tradition in Indian Child Welfare Practice," *Social Work* 67 (May 1968): 289.

[48] *Haan* is discussed Sung Sil Lee Sohng and Kui-Hee Song, "Korean Children and Families," in *Culturally Competent Practice with Immigrant and Refugee Children and Families,* ed. Rowena Fong (New York: The Guilford Press, 2004), 90–95.

[49] For a discussion of these patterns, see Anita Foeman and Gary Pressley, "Ethnic Culture and Corporate Culture: Using Black Styles in Organizations," *Communication Quarterly* 35 (Fall 1987): 293–307.

[50] Jenkins, *The Ethnic Dilemma in Social Services*, 49.

[51] Creigs Beverly, "Treatment Issues for Black, Alcoholic Clients," *Social Casework* 70 (June 1989): 373–374.

[52] Linda Turner and Wes Shera, "Empowerment of Human Service Workers: Beyond Intra-organizational Strategies," *Administration in Social Work* 29(3) (2005): 79–94.

[53] Gutierrez, "Empowering Ethnic Minorities," 330.

[54] Yeheskel Hasenfeld, "Power in Social Work Practice," *Social Service Review* 61 (September 1987): 478–479.

[55] Robert Elias, *The Politics of Victimization* (New York: Oxford University Press, 1986).

[56] P. Johnson, "Women and Power," *Journal of Social Issues* 32(3) (1976): 99–110.

[57] Gilbert, Specht, and Terrell, *Dimensions of Social Welfare Policy*, 134.

[58] Jenkins, *The Ethnic Dilemma*, 88.

[59] Ibid., 49.

[60] Ibid.

[61] David Powell, "Managing Organizational Problems in Alternative Service Organizations," *Administration in Social Work* 10 (Fall 1986): 65.

[62] John Musick and Nancy Hooyman, "Toward a Working Model for Community Organizing in the 1970's," *Journal of Sociology and Social Welfare* 4 (September 1976): 14–18.

[63] E. W. Studt, "Professionalization of Substance Abuse Counseling," *Journal of Applied Rehabilitation Counseling* 21 (Fall 1990): 11–15.

[64] Jenkins, *The Ethnic Dilemma in Social Services*, 102.

[65] Douglas Bunker and Marion Wijnberg, "The Supervisor as a Mediator of Organizational Climate in Public Social Service Organizations," *Administration in Social Work* 9 (Summer 1985): 61.

[66] Hasenfeld, *Human Service Organizations*, 198.

[67] David Bargal, "The Early Stage in the Creation of Two Self-Help Organizations: An Exploratory Study," *Administration in Social Work* 16(3/4) (1992): 84.

[68] Ralph Kramer, "Voluntary Agencies and the Personal Services," in *The Nonprofit Sector—A Research Handbook*, ed. William Powell (New Haven, CT: Yale University Press, 1987), 243.

[69] Donna Hardina, "The Effect of Funding Sources on Client Access to Services," *Administration in Social Work* 14(3) (1990): 44.

[70] Michael Fabricant, "Creating Survival Services," *Administration in Social Work* 19 (Fall 1986): 80.

[71] Carl Milofsky, "Structure and Process in Community Self-Help Organizations," *Community Organization Studies in Resource Mobilization and Exchange*, ed. Carl Milofsky (New York: Oxford University Press, 1988), 211.

[72] Patricia Martin, "Multiple Constituencies, Dominant Societal Values, and the Human Service Administrator: Implications for Service Delivery," *Administration in Social Work* 4 (Summer 1980): 19.

[73] Robert Fisher and Michael Fabricant, "From Henry Street to Contracted Services: Financing the Settlement House." *Journal of Sociology and Social Welfare* 29 (September 2002): 3–25.

[74] Carl Milofsky and Frank Romo, "The Structure of Funding Arenas for Neighborhood Based Organizations," *Community Organization Studies in Resource Mobilization and Exchange*, ed. Carl Milofsky (New York: Oxford University Press, 1988), 238.

[75] Jenkins, *The Ethnic Dilemma*, 45.

[76] John Meyer, "Organizations as Ideological Systems," in *Leadership and Organizational Culture*, ed. Thomas Sergiovanni and John Corbally (Chicago: University of Illinois Press, 1984), 188.

[77] Hasenfeld, *Human Service Organizations*, 150.

[78] Susan Ostrander, "Voluntary Social Service Agencies in the United States," *Social Service Review* 59 (September 1985): 435.

[79] Winston Tseng, "Government Dependence of Chinese and Vietnamese Community Organizations and Fiscal Politics of Immigrant Services," *Journal of Health and Social Policy* 20(4) (2005): 51–74.

[80] Hasenfeld, *Human Service Organizations,* 198.

[81] Ann Ward Tourigny and Joe Miller, "Community-Based Human Service Organizations: Theory and Practice," *Administration in Social Work* 5 (Spring 1981): 81.

[82] Jenkins, *The Ethnic Dilemma,* 48–49.

[83] Wilbur Rich, "Special Role and Role Expectation of Black Administrators of Neighborhood Mental Health Programs," *Community Mental Health Journal* 11 (Winter 1975): 399.

[84] Jenkins, *The Ethnic Dilemma,* 60–66.

[85] Guttentag, "Group Cohesiveness, Ethnic Organization, and Poverty" *Journal of Social Issues* 26(2) (1970): 123–124.

[86] Marie Killilea, "Mutual Help Organizations: Interpretations in the Literature," *Support Systems and Mutual Help: Multidisciplinary Explorations,* ed. Gerald Kaplan and Marie Killilea (New York: Grune and Stratton, 1976), 70.

[87] Gilbert, Specht, and Terrell, *Dimensions of Social Welfare Policy,* 135.

[88] Robert Merton, "Insiders and Outsiders: A Chapter in the Sociology of Knowledge," *American Journal of Sociology* 78 (July 1972): 15.

[89] Gutierrez, "Empowering Ethnic Minorities," 331.

[90] Julie Kwong, "Ethnic Organizations and Community Transformations: The Chinese in Winnipeg," *Ethnic and Racial Studies* 7 (July 1984): 374–386.

Strengthening the Links
to the Ethnic Community

The history of racial and ethnic minorities in American society clearly shows that these groups seek *validation*, *visibility*, and *voice*. They want their history of discrimination to be recognized and validated as a factual occurrence that should not be dismissed or overlooked. They want increased visibility so that they can move from the margins to the core of society. They want a voice in the processes that shape their lives and control their future. Social work can work with them in advancing all three of these goals in the profession and in the larger society.

The contemporary place of social work in American society is the result of years of accumulated history that formed the identity and interventions of the profession. Social work is a product of the era in which it was born—an era that incorporated the ideologies of Social Gospel and Social Darwinism. This was the era that defined some groups as White and others as not White. As society shifted and changed, so did the profession. Social work can be considered as the outgrowth of a country that was suffering from growing pains. From this seemingly chaotic world, charity organization societies and settlement houses emerged to assist White ethnics with the process of assimilation. These workers were inspired by the hope that foreign immigrants would one day melt into the pot of Americanism. Through the modeling examples of the COS visitors and the teachings of the settlers, immigrants were aided in their transformation. The foundations of casework and social reform were cemented in the Progressive Era—an era known for its advances in social welfare legislation.

The history of the marginalized ethnic and racial minorities who were struggling during the Progressive Era does not receive as much attention and interest as it should. Caste-like racial attitudes of White America hampered African Americans' dreams of assimilation. Isolation and marginalization made poverty a persistent way of life for American Indians. Mexican Americans have been hounded by questions about their citizenship. Mexican, Chinese, and Japanese immigrants labored in a country that refused to protect them from the legal and physical assaults of others.

As products of their environment, the profession's founders acquiesced to what was happening to the country's minority populations. These leaders had been socialized by American values and beliefs about these groups. They were not immune to all the negative and pervasive messages about the place of minority groups in society. As the profession matured, its members continued to be socialized in the norms of the larger society. Socialization is, after all, one of the major functions of society.

As social work continues in its challenging mission to infuse ethnic-sensitive practice into its interventions, the reality of the past must be considered. This reality forms the context of practice with populations of color. The formulation of techniques cannot occur in a vacuum with the current environment as the starting point. The effects of decades of neglect and differential treatment cannot be overcome in a few years with new models and techniques of practice.

As an example of the significance of history, Langer discusses the effects of history on the American Indian ethnic identity.[1] She recounts many of the events mentioned in Chapter 2 as well as other significant occurrences that befell this group. She further discusses the implications of this past for policy and practice. She noted that the effects of the past might be cultural dislocation and that models for working with American Indians could possibly include fostering reconnections or enhancing the connections that may already exist. The separation of the tribes from their land and the resulting tribal dispersion are factors that almost certainly have eroded cultural identification. Without knowledge of this history, workers may reach erroneous conclusions to explain a seeming lack of American Indian identity among some members of this group.

Because the historical context is such a vital element of service delivery to ethnic minority populations, it is necessary to discuss those issues that may affect the profession's willingness and ability to incorporate a historical perspective in the service delivery process. This chapter discusses ethnic-sensitive practice, at the worker, organization, community, and societal levels.

WHAT IS ETHNIC-SENSITIVE PRACTICE?

Ethnic-sensitive practice, diversity practice, and multicultural practice are all terms that have been used to designate practice with ethnic and racial minorities as well as other groups that have experienced some type of discrimination. Lum asserts that cultural competency involves cultural awareness, development of a knowledge base that supports practice, development of relevant skills for intervention, and a commitment to continuing professional development.[2] Devore[3] adds that when knowledge, values, and skills merge, layers of understanding emerge that include:

- awareness of and positive response to social work values,
- basic understanding of human behavior,
- knowledge and skills of social welfare policy and services,
- insight into one's own ethnicity and how it may affect one's practice,
- understanding of the effect of ethnic reality on daily life,

- knowledge of the various ways that may lead minority group members to the social worker, and
- the adaptation of skills for ethnic-sensitive practice.

Davis and Organista provide literature reviews on this topic that are helpful in revealing slight variations in definitions.[4] Davis concludes that, in general, the models focus primarily on ethnic-sensitive practice at the micro level.

The interest in and literature on this topic may be a response, in part, to the Council on Social Work Education's education policy standards on nondiscrimination mentioned in Chapter 1. The goal of ethnic-sensitive practice is to promote practice that does not discriminate against any group that may encounter or have encountered discrimination and to provide the training that supports this practice. For this reason, ethnic-sensitive practice can be subsumed under the larger heading of multicultural practice.

Ethnic agencies seem to have a different approach to ethnic-sensitive practice than do mainstream agencies. According to the previous chapter, it seems that in ethnic-sensitive practice the agency:

- adopts an ideology of mutuality with the client through same-ethnic/race workers,
- implements a technology of empowerment that focuses on building strengths,
- buffers clients from agency bureaucracy,
- promotes and utilizes input from clients and the ethnic community it serves, and
- maintains accountability to its ethnic community.

Ethnic-sensitive practice in the ethnic agency appears to focus more on macro elements of practice, possibly as a result of historical factors that have shaped the group's worldview and ideology.

There seems to be a disconnect between the ethnic agency's approach to ethnic-sensitive practice and mainstream agencies' approach. As the levels of intervention are discussed below, the factors that can account for this divergence are explored. The goal is not to provide answers; rather, it is to identity issues for consideration and discussion.

THE WORKER–CLIENT LINK

A major approach in the quest for ethnic-sensitive practice is the use of worker training. Because the worker–client interaction is a core feature of service delivery process,[5] there is a tendency to locate ethnic-sensitive practice under this umbrella. Consequently, much of the attention has been on what occurs between worker and client. The focus on the worker implies that he or she needs additional learning in order to enhance the quality of service delivery to ethnic and racial minority groups. Clearly, the worker is at the center of the service delivery process. In a profession that has micro interventions as the core technology, this emphasis on worker training seems reasonable. In summarizing the literature on worker discretion, Sosin asserts:

Even though human service organizations can be heavily controlled by outsiders, their staffs may have considerable autonomy in dealing with clients. For example, the "line" (direct service) workers of some organizations may have leeway to convince eligible clients to refrain from applying for welfare benefits, to deny available services to some clients and to expand services to others, or less pejoratively, to interpret and use professional standards to determine whether clients require treatment or services. As one expert suggests, workers so frequently exercise autonomy as to regularly create policy in practice.[6]

Worker sensitivity to ethnic and racial differences could potentially minimize any bias or negativity a worker may feel about a client who is a member of a particular minority group. The worker would have to be aware of the bias and committed to retarding its use in practice. This perspective suggests that the worker is in command of his or her attitudes and can alter them at will. While this may be true for some beliefs and attitudes, it may be less so for others.

The worker–client relationship reinforces problem definitions at the individual level. Recurring echoes from the past persist in defining the individual as the cause and solution to whatever problem or need she or he presents. As was discussed in previous chapters, minority group members define problems in more macro terms. Micro interventions may often invalidate a group's history of racism and discrimination and erect barriers between worker and client. To use the language of Seccombe, workers persist in wanting to help clients "beat the odds" against them rather than engage in interventions that would help "change the odds."[7]

While focus on the worker has merit, this focus alone is not sufficient for advancing ethnic-sensitive practice. In addition, there are several factors that reduce the efficacy of this approach.

Beliefs about race and ethnicity are formed over years of socialization and may not be altered through several training sessions. Williams and Land argue that some Whites systematically internalize racist attitudes, stereotypes, jokes, folklore, assumptions, fears, resentments, discourses, and images.[8] They may not be aware of this socialization because these beliefs are virtually "in the air." These authors also raise the possibility that such images and ideologies may be part of the national identity. Because of the seemingly intractable nature of race and race ideology in this country, this possibility cannot be easily dismissed.

In a study of White social workers' attitudes about people of color, researchers found that most respondents expressed positive and supportive attitudes.[9] These attitudes were more positive than those found among the general public. The White workers were, however, "reluctant to express a desire for more closeness and interaction with people of color. This reticence about intimacy and social distance from people of color was clearly reflected by responses to individual [survey] items. . . ."[10] Historically, social distance and marginalization have often characterized the relationship between White America and its people of color. It is not surprising, then, that as members of society, social workers would have some ambivalence about minority groups. The provision of support and validation may be very challenging to workers who harbor attitudes that appear somewhat contradictory. Again, the efficacy of training to minimize or eradicate these attitudes seems doubtful.

While workers may be aware of the history of discrimination in this country, many may feel that the civil rights era effectively eliminated this problem and adopt a color-blind view of race and ethnicity.[11] In their eyes, America is now the land of meritocracy, in which people are free to rise and fail according to the level and intensity of their effort and ambition. They see legislation as powerful enough to overcome a century or more of discrimination. To these workers, oppression is obsolete and does not exist in today's modern society. If these workers were aware of Cox and Ephross's definition of oppression as the "enactment of racism through policies and behaviors,"[12] they might be more receptive to training for ethnic-sensitive practice. As mentioned in Chapter 3, Massachusetts' desegregation act of 1855 was not as effective as anticipated in changing White attitudes and behaviors. Without monitored implementation and sanctions for noncompliance, the legislation had limited success. This color-blindness may also encourage workers to believe that if race is ignored, then racism is no longer an issue.[13] Some workers may, therefore, resist the new knowledge that training offers.

As noted previously, self-awareness seems to be a vital component of effective ethnic-sensitive practice. This entails an awareness of one's position as a White person and an awareness of the privileges that accompany whiteness.[14] Although the concept of White privilege may emphasize history as a social context for discussing race in America, there might be resistance from some White workers who question the validity of this concept. It may imply that Whites have used their privileged position to "lord over" other groups or that somehow Whites are benefiting from a social status that discriminates against ethnic and racial minority groups. Although the concept of White privilege places "whiteness" in a social context, learner resistance may be hard to overcome.

In teaching about race and racism,[15] the concept of White privilege and concern about the discomfort of some Whites regarding this concept seem to imply that Whites are the ones who need training in ethnic-sensitive practice. This may be the case, since Whites in American society represent the dominant elite. It may be difficult, however, for some Whites to see themselves as being dominant over anyone, so they may have hostile reactions to the suggestion that they would benefit from participating in ethnic-sensitive training.

A focus on the individual worker is also consonant with the prevailing ideology of social work. The individual, in this case the social worker, has to be transformed through training to become an ethnic-sensitive practitioner. The issue and its solution rest with the individual worker. The thread that has been woven throughout the profession since its infancy is micro ideology. As discussed in Chapter 7, the micro perspective was the underpinning of the Social Darwinism of the Progressive Era and the American value of individualism. Its application to worker training as method to foster ethnic-sensitive practice is not surprising.

For those workers who have experienced the benefits of training, there may be some frustration in trying to apply the newly acquired learning in an organizational setting that has not changed. In actuality, the training may educate the worker about cultural differences and lead to *worker* empowerment rather than to *client* empowerment. However, worker empowerment in a disempowering agency may be a disservice to both the worker and the client. Without opportunities to effectively act on new learning, the training is virtually useless in making any tangible difference in the agency.

In the agency setting, it is all too easy for committed workers to feel powerless to bring about change in service delivery to ethnic minority populations. The forces that inhibit change activities for workers are powerful, and the social costs may be high. Workers may react with silence—withholding valuable suggestions or comments on issues of diversity because they fear negative reactions.[16] Organizational silence is a threat to organizational change and undermines the development of an ethnic-sensitive agency[17] Worker silence, unfortunately, may actually be a rational reaction to this difficult situation.

Consequently, emphasis on the worker–client interaction ignores the way agency parameters shape that interaction. Glitterman and Miller asserted,

> The organization influences and shapes services, problem definition, assessment and intervention, and "careers" of clients. These in turn influence our professional behavior and view of ourselves. . . . Organizational structures . . . can become the mechanisms which create numerous tensions and obstacles for professionals and clients.[18]

For these reasons, it is necessary to focus on the agency's role in promoting ethnic-sensitive practice.

THE AGENCY LINK

Worker training ignores the power of the agency in the worker–client interaction. The worker, through practice, implements the ideology and the technology of the agency. After training, the worker may continue to implement the same ideology and technology, only this time with heightened cultural awareness. The worker can provide only those services sanctioned by the agency, whether or not these services support ethnic-sensitive practice. Workers cannot visit clients in their neighborhoods if home visits are not part of the agency's technology. A worker cannot enter into a "sameness" or "oneness" with the client if the agency's service ideology calls for professional distance and the authority of expertise. The worker alone cannot and should not bear the entire responsibility for providing ethnic-sensitive service.

The organization—with its structure, goals, and technology—remains unchanged, while its workers are taught how to be culturally sensitive and relate to members of other groups. Holloway and Brager stated,

> There is, we believe, a too ready disposition to define organizational problems in terms of the abilities or attitudes of incumbents and thus to overemphasize people change. . . . It is implicitly critical of the organization's personnel rather than the organization's program and structure or its ideology and is therefore less controversial.[19]

Worker training is not necessarily accompanied by agency change or innovation.

After an extensive review of the literature, Chow and Austin propose a definition of a culturally responsive agency that has five components: (1) services that are responsive to group needs, (2) processes that are responsive, (3) agency policies and operating procedures that are responsive, (4) ongoing renewal, and (5) effective relationships with the community.[20] Numerous barriers, however, inhibit change in organizations, and ethnic-sensitive practice is susceptible to these roadblocks. These obstacles are often imbedded in the agency itself and may not be indicators of staff attitudes toward minority groups. The barriers can be categorized as ideological, technological, and structural. The ideology of the agency is controlled by the internal polity (dominant elite) of the agency or those who are in charge. While all in the agency may not agree with the prevailing ideology, it remains functional in the agency because of the agency's history and because of power of the dominant elite. The technological barriers are tied to the implementation of practice (what the agency *does* with clients), and the structural barriers refer to power, complexity, and formalization of the agency.

The Power of Ideologies

Many agencies have established service ideologies that have been formalized and supported by the agency structure and climate. These ideologies are the beliefs held about why people need assistance and the form that assistance should take. For example, Antler and Antler traced the evolution of the child-protective movement in the United States and commented that *protecting* the family came to be interpreted as *controlling* the family.[21] As public responsibility for safeguarding the health and welfare of children grew, social work methods were integrated into the movement. Identification and investigation, indications of the significance of child-abuse reporting, suggest that society still remains concerned with finding instances of abuse, determining the guilt or innocence of suspected abusers, and trying to prevent the abuse from happening again. The *prevention of the recurrence* of abuse differs markedly from the *prevention of cruelty and neglect.*[22]

Thus, a prevailing ideology around child abuse focuses on correcting family situations that have already resulted in the abuse and/or neglect of children. A body of literature exists about the correlates of child abuse and a "profile" of the abuser based on the compilation of the correlates. Abuse has been associated with such factors as poverty, substance abuse, stress, family isolation, poor self-control, and the gender of the abused child.[23] With this ideology, interventions are identified that correspond to the definition of the problem. In child-abuse cases, parents may be referred for counseling, parenting classes, substance-abuse treatment, and numerous other services geared to eradicate the abusive behavior. The abuse has been located in the traits and characteristics of the abusing parent, and interventions aim to correct these inadequacies. This, then, defines the child-abuse ideology. There are programs, such as family preservation, that attempt to reframe this ideology into one that is supportive of early intervention *before* there is a need to remove the child from the home. The prevailing ideology of preventing *recurrence*, however, is still dominant.

Such service ideologies may be further refined or completely altered when they are applied to ethnic minority groups. Because of the history of discrimination and disenfranchisement, minority groups may be perceived in much harsher terms than Whites. For example, African American families may be perceived by child welfare service providers as multi-problem, hard to work with, resistant, and hostile, while African American children become "hard to place."[24] The overrepresentation of minority children in the foster care system may be the manifestation of an ideology that says that these children are in greater need of protection from the effects of those harmful, dysfunctional families and their environments. It is conceivable that the foster care placement rates for ethnic minorities are more reflective of the ideologies of these service delivery systems than of the behavior of these families themselves.

Furthermore, these ideologies have confirming, reaffirming, and self-confirming qualities—a kind of self-fulfilling prophecy. Minority families may react with anger, hostility, and resistance to the treatment they receive from mainstream agencies. These reactions serve to reaffirm the beliefs of those in the agency. The dynamics perpetuate the historically held beliefs of both parties. Families with cultural lifestyles and patterns that deviate from the expected may be perceived as "dysfunctional." Families who react with anger to the punitiveness of the child-welfare system are "hostile." Parents who are unfairly singled out for scrutiny are "uncooperative." Children who do not meet the adoption profile are "hard to place" and, since minimal efforts may be expended to place them, they *do* become hard to place. These ideologies are perpetuated because they have been found to be "true."

Although these service ideologies interact with notions of ethnicity and the ways in which it affects service delivery, they may not be inherently racist or reflective of malicious intent of the people who believe them. They are grounded in a century of stereotypes and differential treatment of people of color. Agencies have incorporated these ideologies as *truths* and have operated in specific ways for so long that their members may not be able to imagine any other way of seeing things or even the necessity for seeing things differently. These ideologies are held with conviction and great tenacity, and they are grounded in years of practice wisdom and professional judgments. The organization of the workplace and the technology of the agency are the outgrowth of ideologies about problems and solutions. These ideologies are grounded in history and are not just limited to the way people perceive problems and client groups, also becoming a blueprint for the agency.

Agencies may operate on the premise that equality in treatment and services is the same as responsiveness of services. Sue, Allen, and Conaway observed that it may be possible for all minorities to receive equal but unresponsive services.[25] Because all clients in an agency are treated the same without regard to ethnicity, staff and administrators may be lulled into believing that minority access and the absence of differential treatment are all that are needed for ethnic-sensitive services.

This is not to be confused with color blindness. The agency is very aware of ethnicity and race and may extend special efforts to recruit minority clients. The sensitivity is in working to promote access. If there is a disregard for ethnicity, it happens in other places in the agency. For some agencies, special attention to outreach efforts is seen as ethnic-sensitive practice rather than as a step in a continuing process.

Each minority group's unique history in this country dictates that it has its own worldview, goals, and aspirations. What (and how) it defines as problems and needs will vary from group to group. A validation of the past cannot occur if every group is seen as the same and in need of the same intervention.

Technological Challenges

Workers' attempts to import the new technology of ethnic-sensitive practice may be neutralized by the agency as a way of protecting its equilibrium. In reality, it is not easy for agencies to change practices that have been established over a period of time. As systems, these organizations have developed their own homeostasis or steady state. According to Anderson and Carter,

> A steady state occurs when the system is "in balance"; maintaining a viable relationship with its environment and its components, and its functions are being performed in such a fashion as to ensure its continued existence.[26]

The work is predictable. The clients are predictable. The administrators are predictable. Processes have been routinized, informally and formally. Change—any change—is a threat to that equilibrium. The threat lies in the uncertainty of the change and its consequences. Workers and administrators strive to continue with "business as usual." "But this is how we've always done it" is one of the enemies of ethnic-sensitive practice.

The agency resists change in a battle to keep to the old ways. Indeed, Katz and Kahn observed that any internal or external factor that threatens to disrupt the system is countered by forces that *restore the system as closely as possible to its previous state.*[27] Efforts to bring about change may be co-opted by the existing system. Innovative approaches may be altered or handled in such a way to accommodate existing practices.

Threats to the equilibrium may be absorbed by the agency so that they are no longer disruptive to the agency. Iglehart stressed this point in discussing organizational responses to turnover:

> Turnover is commonly held to be disruptive to the agency . . . [but] in the face of turnover, even high rates of turnover, an agency will be likely to create mechanisms that will minimize the disruptive effects of this turnover on the organization. . . . Organizations, in fact, are dynamic systems capable of adapting to and gaining control over disruptive forces in order to return to their previous stability or to redefine a new stability.[28]

The agency that supports ethnic-sensitive training but continues to implement the same old practices may be protecting its service delivery and its ideologies. In these situations, an *appearance* of change may occur without change itself. Change and innovation may be met with such organizational resistance that ethnic-sensitive practice remains a goal rather than a reality.

Agencies may resist new technologies for other reasons. For some private, nonprofit agencies with a tradition of family service to majority groups, the move into multicultural practice may be undesirable because it could jeopardize the agency's status. Agencies often take on the status of the clients they serve, and all clients are not equal. In order to protect its status, the agency may wish to dissociate itself from "minority" issues. As the country continues to move toward greater diversity, there will probably always be some agency somewhere that will remain untouched by the mark of multiculturalism.

This means that some agencies will try to protect themselves from becoming too African American, too Mexican American, or too Asian American in terms of clients served and staff hired. Controls may be informally instituted to limit the access of special ethnic populations. With this controlled access, there may be little need to think or plan ethnic-sensitive practice since, in these settings, it is not of value.

Absence of Formalized Structures. There may not be a structure in place to reward staff and administrators for excellence in ethnic-sensitive service delivery. Those activities of worth to the agency generally have some sanction attached to them so that worker discretion in whether to implement these activities is minimized. When left to the whim of individuals in the agency, culturally sensitive practice may be lost in the shuffle. Interventions aimed at promoting culturally aware workers may be only marginally effective if the worth of those interventions is not validated by the agency. As long as the value of those interventions lies outside of the incentive structure, then a permanent, routinized change is not going to take place.

Typical evaluations of administrator and staff performance do not include performance measures on ability to create and maintain an ethnic-sensitive agency and ethnic-sensitive practice. Some may argue that these measures would be difficult to articulate, but if they were of worth to the agency, efforts would be underway to tackle the task.

A formal structure for obtaining client input and feedback about the agency and its service may also be lacking. This renders the clients voiceless in the service delivery process. According to Hasenfeld,

> There is generally an asymmetry of power between the agency and the client. . . . First, most agencies are not directly dependent on their clients for procurement of resources. . . . Second, the demands for services often outstrip their supply. . . . Third, many agencies have a quasi-monopoly over their services.[29]

Those who would benefit from ethnic-sensitive services may be the least powerful in bringing this practice to fruition. The funding structure of services works against clients and highlights their disadvantaged status. Since the consumers of service may not be the sponsors of service, agencies may not be motivated to hear what these consumers have to say. This situation may be exacerbated by the powerlessness of ethnic minorities. Clients, particularly ethnic minority clients, are not the dominant elite in most agencies. Etzioni elevated the issue to the level of society:

> Here separation between consumption and control is supported by a strong ideology . . . namely, that those who administer the service are in

a better position to judge what is good for the consumer than he is for himself; hence separation of control from consumption is the best way to maximize the happiness of the greatest number.[30]

This powerlessness of clients may be part of an underlying ideology about the service delivery process. If this is true, then fee-paying clients of private agencies may have only limited control over the services they receive. Although paying for services increases the status of the clients, the distance between helper and client may reduce the power typically associated with that status.

The voicelessness of clients is typified by the lack of effort to obtain client evaluations of services. Many agencies do not routinely collect information on client opinions. Exit interviews may not be part of agency procedures. The absence of procedures for collecting evaluation data serves to retard the development of ethnic-sensitive practice. For minority clients, this voicelessness is reflective of their status in the larger society and further distances them from the agency.

Sunk Costs.   Agencies also resist change because of the sunk-cost factor. According to Patti:

Sunk costs refer to the investments that have been made by an organization (or its members) to develop and sustain any institutional arrangement or pattern of behavior that is currently in force. Investments are . . . inputs of money, time, energy, or personal commitment.[31]

The internal economy of the agency indicates the distribution of resources, and those investments may not be recovered if there is a change in the practices of the agency. For example, the agency that has spent a great deal of time and money developing foster-home recruitment and maintenance strategies may not be willing to put those strategies aside, even temporarily, to develop culturally sensitive ones for ethnic groups.

The shift in service populations, technologies, and staff is a costly one for many agencies. The training or retraining of staff or the hiring of bilingual, bicultural workers may not be cost efficient in the eyes of the agency. The cost involved in servicing new client groups may be seen as prohibitive. Change may receive even less support in times of fiscal austerity, when the agency may attempt to protect resources rather than expend them.

Agencies have significant amounts of resources committed to maintaining their steady state. The technology of "how things usually get done" requires a particular configuration of services as well as a particular organizational structure, and relations among staff and between staff and administrators may be derivatives of the technology. Conversions, transformations, or eliminations of the existing technology may not be feasible for the agency.

Minority Staff as Technology.   Some agencies assume that the ethnic presence on the staff is a sufficient indicator of ethnic-sensitive service. Ethnic-sensitive practice is expected to occur between the minority professional and the minority client, with the minority professional then becoming the

embodiment of ethnic-sensitive practice. In addition, the minority professional is expected to impart knowledge to his or her colleagues. Wright,
Saleeby, Watts, and Lecca made this assumption when they commented,
"Organizations committed to hiring minority personnel can expect, in some
instances, that those individuals will not be only workers and administrators
but *teachers* as well" [emphasis added].[32]

This assumption subscribes to the "myth of homogeneity," because
within-group differences are ignored and ethnic sensitivity is presumed to
reside in the individual because of his or her ethnicity. However, some minority professionals who have "made it" may have little sympathy for those who
are "keeping the race down." Montiel and Wong stated,

> For these professionals, "problems" may be seen as being surmountable
> within the boundaries of a functional society that has provided satisfaction
> to its participants. This view points to the need to examine critically the
> disparity between minority professionals and the minority community.[33]

Minority professionals are also presumed to increase minority service utilization through their presence on the staff.[34] The assumption of the minority
worker as the embodiment of ethnic-sensitive practice places a tremendous
burden on the worker. In addition to performing daily responsibilities, he or
she is expected to be the resident expert on ethnic issues, teach colleagues
the nuances of ethnic-sensitive practice, and act as a magnet to attract minority clients. In this approach, the agency remains unchanged and the success
or failure of ethnic-sensitive practice becomes the responsibility of the minority worker(s). Thus, the problem would continue to be seen as a *minority*
problem and not an *agency* problem.

The "minority as expert" assumption disregards the kinds of issues that
may hamper staff collegial interactions. Staff and administrators may assume
that minority members are only expert in minority issues and with minority
clients. The African American may be expected to interface with the African
American community, the Hispanic with the Hispanic community, the Asian
with the Asian community, and so on. These assumptions may create tensions
between staff members, as professional expertise is second to ethnic group
membership. Although many of these agency practices may be informal, they
are nevertheless well known and extremely visible in the agency. Ambivalence about the role of ethnicity at the organizational level may not be the
cultivating ground for ethnic-sensitive practice.

Other Agency Considerations.   Several other agency features warrant
attention. One such feature involves the agency's staffing patterns. The specific positions occupied by minority staff in an agency communicate a great
deal of information to the clients and to the larger society. Ely and Thomas
reviewed the literature on diversity and work-group processes.[35] This literature revealed that the distribution of power between culturally identified
groups inside the agency is important because it affects the way people feel,
think, and act at work. In addition, the status value ascribed by the larger
society also affects how people think about group membership inside the

agency. These authors also cite literature that argues, "In organizations, status differentials are reinforced when higher-status identity groups are disproportionately represented in positions of organizational authority and are challenged when they are not."[36]

If minority clients see an agency in which the decision makers are predominantly White, the conclusions they draw may not be limited to that agency at that moment in time. They may see this as indicative of their historic marginalization and lack of power. This also further reinforces voicelessness within the agency. Clients may conclude that their group is not of value to the agency because its members are not represented in the agency's power structure.

Another feature that should be considered is the agency climate. In a study of climate, researchers found that organizational factors influenced the relationship between the staff of a community mental health center and their African American clients.[37] Involvement with clients, clear goals, the provision of physical comfort, and an ideology of positive outcomes for clients were interrelated and affected the treatment relationship. This type of climate indicates that the agency works to minimize the social distance between the worker and the client. Social distance apparently can be reduced without jeopardizing the professional relationship. The creation of such a climate represents agency innovation that enjoys agency support.

In general, agency change and innovation are complex subjects that involve ideologies, technologies, structures, people, and history. Hasenfeld summed up the issues on agency change and innovation in this manner:

> While many individual human service practitioners may be change oriented and ready to intervene on behalf of clients, their organizations are often likely to resist change and innovation. On balance the forces that promote stability outweigh those that push for innovation and change. Human service organizations seem to change only when under duress—that is, when external conditions have reached a point at which they cannot be ignored.[38]

THE AGENCY–COMMUNITY LINK

Minority populations desire to have a voice in planning and implementing services for their communities. Historically, this right has been denied, and others have determined the destiny of these groups. Ethnic-sensitive practice should foster the relationship between agencies and minority communities by creating opportunities for their voices to be heard. Factors that affect this relationship should be addressed. The agency's willingness and capacity to interface with ethnic communities may be significantly influenced by the *history* of that agency with particular ethnic groups. For example, the history of American Indians in the United States would suggest that tension may exist between some group members and the mainstream child welfare agencies. Because of the historical issues that surround reporting and deportation, segments of the Hispanic community may be skeptical about accessing services. Ethnic service delivery cannot disregard the history of ethnic groups in America and how agencies have responded or contributed to that history.

The Young Women's Christian Association (YWCA) has had a history of locating branches in ethnic communities. This presence of and responsiveness to ethnic communities seems rooted in the history of the YWCA. For example, in 1906, the association was working in African American schools in the South and, in 1915, at its Louisville Conference, the association affirmed:

1. That we believe the time has come for the appointing of a committee composed of white and colored women from or of the South.

2. That we recognize that the best method of cooperation in city associations is through branch relationships.[39]

This history has been instrumental in elevating the image and reputation of this agency in minority neighborhoods. It has supported an agency–community relationship that values the minority group's presence and its voice. In the absence of this history, there are other strategies that support the inclusion of voice in the agency.

The Minority Community's Visibility and Voice

Communities are composed of residents, informal associations, voluntary agencies, religious organizations, businesses, and numerous other cliques and factions. Mainstream agencies can use many resources in the planning of services for communities. Because many ethnic minority communities may be disproportionately located in low-income areas, use of their community structures is often excluded from planning bodies. It may be customary for services to be planned according to some perception of their community's *best interest* rather than according to its *expressed wish*. Agencies may use their power of professional authority in deciding what services to offer, how to offer them, and where to locate them. Actions like this continue to perpetuate the historic invisibility and voicelessness of minority communities.

Ethnic-sensitive practice at the community level suggests that the minority community should become more visible. Private, nonprofit agencies tend to rely on the board as their preferred structure of governance. Through board participation, the minority community can have both a presence and a voice in the agency's operations. However, ethnic minorities may be underrepresented on the boards of many of the mainstream social work agencies and, hence, are not able to influence the agency. Because many of these agencies rely on public funding,[40] they may be even less likely to "hear" minority voices. In casting a net for board members, these agencies may not target minority communities, particularly if they are not a powerful external agency constituency. Minority community input, then, is not structured into the agency's organization.

Maximum feasible participation was a popular phase of community groups in the 1960s. As noted in Chapter 7, many groups were forcing the "establishment" to listen to them. Regrettably, that movement has passed, and the cry for citizen participation may have passed with it. As public attitudes shift, the demands placed on agencies also shifts. Grassroots organizing seems dated as society becomes more advanced and technologically sophisticated. Citizen involvement in agencies may now be predicated on who can help the agency the most. Individuals with specialized skills rather than the representatives of minority communities may be more likely to take a seat at the agency's board table. Thus, there may not be a great deal of political pressure on agencies to seek participation from a broad spectrum of the community.

While the agency maintains a structure for securing community input (typically the board), other methods may be used to encourage input from the ethnic community. Agencies can establish community councils, ad hoc task forces of community members, and advisory groups to meet with staff and administrators to discuss common interests, issues, and special agency needs. These are useful only if the agency responds to the issues raised by these groups. These groups are typically formed when the agency needs some type of assistance from the community in reaching special populations. For example, in the past, local community councils were formed in African American neighborhoods as a means of locating foster homes for African American children.[41]

As the previous chapters indicate, religious institutions are an integral part of ethnic communities. This is also true for immigrant and refugee populations that have recently arrived to the United States.[42] Mainstream agencies can recruit religious leaders for membership on boards and other planning bodies. The religious institutions act as a gathering place for community members and promote community building. In addition, because many of them offer some types of social-related services (for example, child care, language classes, and food banks) they also contribute to community capacity building. Many may be funded to provide employment training, parent education classes, and other social services. They constitute a valuable resource in the agency–community link.

Some agencies cannot be accountable to an ethnic community because of the structure of their service delivery. These agencies will continue to be accountable to the publics that sponsor them. Relationships with communities can, however, be established to create a symbiotic tie between the agency and the community in specific areas in which the tie benefits both parties. To further establish this tie, mainstream social work may have to utilize the services of ethnic agencies to reach specific communities. The ethnic agency is already involved in service delivery in the community, has legitimacy in that community, and is committed to serving that group. The ethnic agency can be a vital, viable bridge between mainstream agencies and the ethnic community.

The Role of the Ethnic Agency

As society becomes more diverse, service demands from ethnic minority communities will increase. Mainstream social services, public and private nonprofit, will have to respond to the needs of a diverse population. It is doubtful that mainstream social services will evolve into ethnic agencies in the near future. It is also doubtful that ethnic agencies will proliferate and expand to respond to all the needs of all ethnic communities. Ethnic agencies do, however, appear to practice a type of service delivery that reaches and engages numerous communities that may be unserved or underserved, for a myriad of reasons, by mainstream services. The goals and ideology of these agencies support approaches to service delivery that appear to be responsive to ethnic communities.

Mainstream, public-supported health, welfare, and other social services, on the other hand, have a mandate to address the needs of the public. The mandate of the modern welfare state includes the provision of services to its populace. The service net is cast wide enough to reach as many as possible who meet service requirements. Services and programs of the welfare state may operate under the myth of homogeneity to develop standardized, uniform programs that may not vary, even though the communities do. Some service nets may have gaping holes through which segments of the population fall, thereby being excluded from services. In other cases, the holes are not as great and a much smaller number is excluded.

It bears repeating that for mainstream service providers, the ethnic agency can be a bridge to ethnic communities. Ethnic agencies have access to the community, visibility in the community, and intimate knowledge of the community's structure and processes. The ethnic agency is a subsystem of the ethnic community system. As such, it may have a significant presence in its community.

Relationships between mainstream agencies and ethnic agencies connect social service systems that generally exist as parallel systems. The purpose of this section is not to determine what could, should, or ought to occur between mainstream agencies and ethnic agencies. Rather, these relationships are examined to determine those factors that affect their development, dynamics, and outcomes. The purpose is also to place these relationships in the model of ethnic-sensitive practice.

In identifying those factors that influence mainstream agency and ethnic agency linkages, it is important to develop a framework for the analysis. The resource-dependence approach indicates that organizations will become powerful if they can control the resources needed by other organizations and if they can reduce their own external dependency. A second approach looks at organization sets or organization networks—organizations that interact and exchange resources on a frequent and continuing basis—and the activities within them.[43] The third approach, the political-economy perspective, looks at the external linkages an organization has to the larger social system. Two basic types of resources are at the core of the political economy of interorganizational networks: money and authority.[44]

All these approaches incorporate the focal organization's environment and the exchange of energy (resource inputs) between that organization and others in the environment. These approaches are consistent with the theoretical perspectives presented in Chapter 1. The ethnic agency is a subsystem interacting within a larger system (one organization in an organizational set) as well as a system unto itself (seeking to maintain its functional independence and organizational identity).[45]

Power is a key factor in the relationships between organizations and can be defined in this manner: A has power over B to the extent that A can get B to do something B would not otherwise do.[46] Interorganizational power is frequently expressed in the negotiations that take place between organizations and according to Benson,

> The powerful organization can force others to accept its terms in negotiations. . . . Power permits one organization to reach across agency boundaries and determine the policies or practices in weaker organizations. Failure or refusal of the weaker organization to accede to the demands of the stronger can have serious repercussions for the resource procurement of the weaker organization.[47]

The ethnic agency's ability to obtain resources and to survive becomes critical in analyzing their relations with mainstream agencies. In addition, the exchanges between systems are relevant. The points at which the ethnic agency's service delivery system interfaces with mainstream service delivery systems are important for understanding when and how race and ethnicity shape these interfaces.

From what is already known about the nature of interorganizational relationships and what has been presented here on ethnic agencies, some propositions can be advanced to describe those factors that influence the ethnic agency's relationship with organizations external to the ethnic community. Some of the factors focus on power, status, and dependency issues that have their base in the historical context of majority–minority interactions.

Over 90 percent of the agencies Jenkins studied received public dollars.[48] This suggests that ethnic agencies are likely to receive public funds. For that reason, attention is directed to the relationships that are established between *public* agencies and ethnic agencies. Less attention is given to the relationships that develop between ethnic agencies and other kinds of agencies.

Proposition 1. Ethnic agencies are not in competition with mainstream social services for clients.

Previous discussions indicated that ethnic agencies can receive public funds to provide services to groups that would not ordinarily receive them or access them. Deficits in mainstream service systems and/or cultural barriers appear to create a need for ethnic agencies. Thus, as a service delivery system, the ethnic agency is not robbing mainstream services of clients.

Proposition 2. In an interorganizational relationship, the ethnic agency is of importance because of its access to a particular ethnic population.

In the social service marketplace, ethnicity becomes a potential commodity that gives importance to the ethnic agency. According to Hasenfeld and English, because of political, social, and demographic changes in the social environment of agencies, new interorganizational relations may be developed to respond to these changes.[49] These authors further indicated that pressures to serve indigent populations may lead a family service agency, for example, to interact with another agency that has access to that population. Thus, the ethnic community represents a specialized service market to which the ethnic agency has access. The identification of neglected groups "at the boundaries of governmental welfare programs" has generally come from indigenous, less bureaucratized, less professionalized organizations.[50]

The ethnic agency does not receive interest because of its innovations, technologies, or ideologies, but rather because of its presence in the ethnic community and its access to clients. Although accessibility is related to its technology and ideology, the external polity and the external economy are attracted to the ethnic agency because of its relationship with specific targeted populations.

Proposition 3. *Redefining approaches to service delivery may promote interorganizational relations that include ethnic agencies.*

As programs develop to test new configurations of service delivery, the ethnic agency may be called on to contribute to a network or constellation of services. Service delivery as a system or organizational process continues to be a dynamic process that is altered by technological, ideological, political, and economic factors. The mode of service delivery has varied from specialization to integrated, comprehensive services. As service fragmentation, duplication, and cost rise and fall as issues, the ethnic agency may be called on to participate in alternative approaches to service delivery.

Proposition 4. *As privatization increases, the ethnic agency may be called upon to extend services to its special population.*[51]

Through the purchase of service contracts, mandated services can be tailored to reach specific ethnic communities. New policies are emerging in response to government retrenchment and other environmental changes. Privatization of human services is becoming more widely embraced. According to Bendick, *privatization* is defined as shifting into nongovernmental hands some or all roles in providing a good or service that was once publicly provided.[52] Bendick also listed contracting out, franchises, grants, subsidies, and vouchers as examples of the types of privatized arrangements that can exist between government and nongovernment entities. For many years, purchase-of-service contracting has been the major mode of human service delivery nationally.[53] Government agencies frequently call on voluntary agencies to obtain specialized programs "to serve a clientele for whom there is a public responsibility" and by utilizing the "access of neighborhood-based, ethnic-sponsored organizations," government "can more effectively serve needy clients."[54]

Proposition 5. *Interorganizational relationships are more likely to develop between public agencies and the ethnic agency rather than between mainstream agencies in general and the ethnic agency.*

Public agencies are mandated to meet the needs of their populations. These mandates are in the form of social policies and regulations that specify client groups, service eligibility requirements, and services to be provided. In addition, policies bring with them fiscal support for implementing them. Thus, the public agency may be a rich source of funding for ethnic agencies when particular ethnic groups are targeted for service delivery.

Proposition 5a. In the contractual relationship with a public agency to deliver service to a special population, the ethnic agency becomes a substitute for government provision of those services.[55]

This further suggests that the ethnic agency becomes part of the welfare state indirectly through the contracting process. The ethnic agency is assisting the government in the provision of mandated services and becomes the entity through which those services flow.

Proposition 5b. The relationship between the ethnic agency and the public funding agency is usually asymmetrical.

Saidel defined an *asymmetrical relationship* as one in which two or more organizations are not equally dependent on each other for the resources each has access to or controls.[56] According to Cook, dependence is lessened to the extent that alternatives are available to an organization in the exchange network.[57] Public agencies typically have more options for reaching ethnic populations than ethnic agencies have for funding sources. The ethnic agency depends more on the public agency than that agency depends on it. To reach special populations public agencies can create special programs, hire special staff, and/or launch aggressive outreach efforts. Although some of these options may be costly to the public agency, they nonetheless exist and may, on occasion, be utilized.

The ethnic agency, on the other hand, is far more limited in its funding options. Funding available for agencies varies from government grants/contracts to foundations to membership in an umbrella fund-raising organization to private donations. Agencies often find themselves commitment rich and cash poor. In many instances, contracts and grants from public agencies provide a rich source of support that cannot be matched in the private sector.

Proposition 5c. Because of the asymmetrical nature of the relationship, public agencies tend to have power over ethnic agencies.

Because ethnic agencies may be dependent on public agencies for resources, public agencies can influence and alter the services and service delivery processes of ethnic agencies. Diversification of funding sources as a means of managing environmental dependency is less of an option for the ethnic agency. Funding options are limited and the search for other, additional funding sources requires technical expertise, agency supports, and time. Many small ethnic agencies are not equipped to mount diversification efforts. Thus, these agencies may be more responsive to public agencies than public agencies are to them.

Proposition 5d. The greater the ethnic agency's access to the ethnic community, the more power the agency has in its funding relationships with public agencies.

Access to the ethnic community gives the ethnic agency visibility and status in relating to public agencies, which may be able to gain a degree of legitimacy in the ethnic community from its relationship with ethnic agencies.[58] External agencies attempting to reach ethnic communities may use an ethnic agency with access to the community as a means of community penetration. Organizational dominance may emerge from the significant linkage the ethnic agency has to a particular racial or ethnic group, which is the reason the ethnic agency is important to other organizations.[59] The strength of this community penetration may boost the power of the ethnic agency.

> **Proposition 5e.** *The greater the bond between the ethnic agency and the dominant elite of the ethnic community, the more power the agency has in its funding relationships with external agencies.*

The dominant elite members of an ethnic community have access to the residents of the community and may serve as an interface between the community and the larger social system. The dominant elite can advocate for the community and emerge as visible members of that community. An ethnic agency that has the support and even participation of its community's elite further solidifies its community penetration.

> **Proposition 5f.** *The greater the ethnic agency's monopoly of services in that community, the more likely the agency is to be involved in its funding relationships with external agencies.*

Those ethnic agencies with a dominant presence in the community as seen in range and number of services offered may act as a magnet to attract the interest of those agencies that seek to reach that ethnic community. A prevailing public sentiment may be that if any services are to be provided in that particular community, it must go through a certain agency in order for that service to be sanctioned by the community.

The proposition may reflect "the more, the more" principle in that the more services, resources, and community penetration an agency has, the more likely it is to acquire more of these. Expansion and diversification may be indicative of the extent and degree of an agency's monopoly over the community.

> **Proposition 5g.** *The more physically established the ethnic agency, the more likely the agency is to be involved in a funding relationship with external agencies.*

Physically established here means that the ethnic agency actually has an office, space, equipment, and other support facilities. Thus, in entering into a fiscal arrangement with an external agency, the funds received by the ethnic agency are not used to literally create the physical presence of the agency.

> **Proposition 5h.** *The ethnic agency may not be a skilled player in the "contract game."*

Bernstein discussed at length the nuances of the contract game and the informal, formal, and subtle communication that takes place.[60] This is a process that one apparently learns from repeated contract experiences. The rules, requirements, compliance, unofficial operations, and conflict that arise in the contracted relationship seem to call for a special expertise. Many ethnic agencies may not have a strong enough history in this area to adequately prepare them for the process.

Proposition 5i. *A competitive funding process may work to the detriment of the ethnic agency.*[61]

According to Milofsky, an agency's ability to attract funders and funding is related to the agency's history of grant/proposal writing, the agency's history with funding agencies, and the number of people the agency has available to write proposals.[62] Many smaller ethnic agencies may not have the history and staff to develop competitive proposals.

Competition may also work against the relationships between ethnic agencies within the same community. Schmid defines competition as rivalry between agencies for scarce resources.[63] Smith further notes that an increasingly competitive fiscal environment may complicate collaboration between agencies.[64] Groups can become so focused on their needs and meeting those needs that they fail to recognize the benefits of forging ties with other agencies. Perceived differences between groups can inhibit the recognition of common goals and the undertaking of collaborative ventures.

Proposition 5j. *Formal evaluation processes that accompany contracts and grants may not acknowledge those activities that reflect the strength of the ethnic agency's work.*

Sewell argued that an emphasis on end products may not adequately reflect the effectiveness of an ethnic agency.[65] Thomas and Morgan suggested that formative evaluation rather than summative evaluation should be the primary evaluation effort.[66] Formative evaluation creates a feedback loop that feeds information back into the program *during* its development, whereas summative evaluation is done *after* the program has been completed.[67] In other words, one focuses on process and the other focuses on outcome.

Some ethnic agencies expend a great deal of time and resources in developing programs. Special approaches may have to be developed to tailor programs to their specific populations. The success of the program, however, is generally not measured in terms of creating the technology of service delivery but rather in the *outcome* of that service delivery.

Proposition 6. *Changing federal funding requirements have the potential for developing partnerships between mainstream agencies and ethnic agencies.*

Major funding sources stipulate that the grantee must address the needs of women and minorities when developing program and service proposals. For example, the 57 municipalities studied by Terrell and Kramer were likely to use "compatibility with ethnic and foreign groups" as one of the factors on which funding proposals were rated.[68] Many mainstream agencies may not have the history, staff, or compatibility for service delivery to an ethnic community. For these agencies, the ethnic agency then becomes the vehicle for complying with this stipulation.

Proposition 7. *The ethnic agency's interface with mainstream agencies is predicated on the availability of funding to support that interface.*

Because the degree of cooperation occurring between organizations in the same network is contingent on the amount of resources available to that network, a decrease in funds will affect the cooperation and/or conflict between organizations.[69] The interorganizational linkages likely to occur between mainstream agencies and ethnic agencies derive from a funding environment that supports and encourages these linkages. Increased attention to the development of partnerships in service delivery, efforts to reduce service duplication, and efforts to reach special populations have promoted interorganizational relations, and the funding mandates reflect this. A change in policy direction and/or funding direction could easily remove the ethnic presence from service delivery areas. What occurs between ethnic agencies and mainstream agencies appears to be environmentally induced.

Proposition 8. *In the ebb and flow of the fiscal environment, ethnic agencies are particularly vulnerable.*

Because many ethnic agencies do not have a diversified funding base, they may grow dependent on contracts and grants with publicly sponsored agencies. In a study of Chinese and Vietnamese community organizations, Yseng found that, in times of shortage of public dollars, ethnic community-based organizations and immigrant service organizations are extremely vulnerable to budget cuts.[70] This was attributed to the lack of political voice of these groups. Smith noted that, in times of financial austerity, funds for contracts are likely to be cut first if this can be accomplished legally and politically.[71] Ethnic agencies may have to continuously scramble for funds as contracts are terminated and priority areas change.

Proposition 9. *Ideological conflicts can occur between ethnic agencies and mainstream agencies.*

While resource dependence, power, and organizational exchanges are being determined, ethnicity is an additional variable affecting the interorganizational relationship. Rose suggested that the empowerment orientation of ethnic agencies may clash with the individual–defect framework associated with mainstream agencies.[72] Thus, ethnic agencies may attempt to use their technology of information, education, and participation in planning and implementing programs while program sponsors may have a different approach in mind.

Proposition 10. *The problems of race relations that exist in the larger society permeate the dynamics of the relationship between ethnic agencies and mainstream agencies.*

In the relations between ethnic agencies and mainstream agencies, the expertise of staff and administrators who are predominantly White may be interpreted by ethnic agency staff as yet another indicator of race superiority.

Power, in this case, is derived from individual perceptions that are located in historical experiences and not in the interaction that is taking place. The authority of expertise, as determined by specialized skills and knowledge, may appear to be evidence of race superiority in the eyes of ethnic agency members. Whites may be perceived as viewing the ethnic agency staff in need of teaching and leadership. Interactions are then filtered by the "color" lens, and tensions develop because different individuals are responding differently to the same stimulus.

The propositions listed above define the basis of power for the ethnic agency and for the other agencies in its organizational network. Exchanges often provide the source of power for an organization, particularly if it has resources in demand by other organizations. The reciprocity of the exchange is important for determining who has the most bargaining chips. The ethnic agency increases its ability to bargain by having access to special populations and access to the dominant elite of the ethnic community. In exchange for this access, the ethnic agency receives revenues and whatever legitimacy the funding may bring.

Schmidt and Kochan concluded that interorganizational relationships should be conceptualized as "mixed motive" because each organization is motivated by self-interest as well as other interests.[73] The ethnic agency seeks services for its clients while at the same time it is trying to create a secure funding niche. This is true for other agencies as well. With the ethnic agency, ethnicity becomes a fundamental part of the exchange process.

These propositions are presented as a way of framing the relationship that can develop between mainstream agencies and ethnic agencies. The interorganizational relationships serve as another vehicle for promoting the validation, visibility, and voice of ethnic communities.

THE AGENCY–SOCIETY LINK

Social service agencies implement social policy and, in doing so, are implementing the public will (as noted in Chapter 7). Social policy is an expression of public values, priorities, and beliefs about the kinds of social services that should be available. The legislation that gives rise to social programs typically defines the services to be offered, to whom they should be offered, and how they should be offered. The legislative arena dictates, to a great extent, the nature of social services in this country. Constituencies that influence the legislative process have validation, visibility, and voice. For many ethnic minority communities, these three may be lacking. For this reason, ethnic-sensitive practice must also include practice in the policy arena.

The history of ethnic and racial groups in America that was described in the earlier chapters revealed that legislation determined their treatment, opportunities, and survival. Discrimination often found form in legislation that propagated racism and mandated unequal treatment. Prevailing social climates dictated this legislation. As the political and social atmosphere changed over time, legislation became more sympathetic to minority groups.

Social work's role in the policy process is activated at the back end of the process. By the time the services are being delivered, the policies have already defined the client population and the services it is to receive. Although social work is active in implementing, or enforcing, the legislative mandates, it is more passive at the front end of the policy process that entails policy formulation. This passivity may inadvertently communicate to minority communities that social work is not that interested in their welfare but rather in protecting its status and domain. Some in the profession may also view political advocacy as outside the sphere of the profession.

Historically, ethnic minorities have defined their issues in structural terms and not in individual terms. This places the profession at odds with many minority groups, who feel that they could benefit from interventions that help to change the odds instead of interventions that seek to help them beat the odds. For these groups, a return to social reform would elevate the profession in their eyes.

As indicated in Chapter 7, Jane Addams did not propose technologies for social change or social reform. Hudson asserts that the theory needed for social change has "languished" in the profession.[74] Social change and social reform, in American society, have often occurred through legislation, so policy practice seems central to any reform process. The macro discussions in social work, however, often omit the mention of policy advocacy or policy practice.[75] While there is literature on the theory and techniques of policy practice in social work,[76] these works are not prolific in the profession, which continues to be reactive rather than proactive in the political process. Agencies adjust to legislated budget cuts that reduce their capacity to serve their clients, and they continue to do more with less. As Jimenez states:

> From the point of view of our history, the question social workers themselves might ask is whether the drive for professionalism contributes to our becoming agents of social control, rather than social justice. The potential for social workers to be agents of social change is high, since with more professional autonomy, social workers have more room to work for social reform and potentially do more good for clients.[77]

As an instrument of the public will, social workers may not have any opposition to the policy they are implementing. If there is some ambivalence, it may be muted by a desire not to rock the boat. Indeed, social work has not been in the forefront of modern social movements.

There may be numerous factors that quell the social reform impulse in the profession. With the waning of the settlement house movement and the social reform arm of the profession, a clear career trajectory for reformers did not surface. In addition, social work educational programs did not define a clear course of study for social reformers. Social casework became the definitive domain of the profession. There may be some social workers who think that the path to macro practice must first pass through the micro door. Consequently, within the profession, there may be mechanisms that continue to silence policy reform.

As more literature is produced in the profession about social justice, a revival in social reform may result.[78] Perhaps today's social work student will have a different perspective of the profession. Perhaps the era of ethnic-sensitive practice is but a bump in the road of business as usual. It is clear that the *validation, visibility*, and *voice* desired by America's minority communities are not being fully achieved through mainstream social service agencies. For this reason, the ethnic organization will remain a vital part of the minority community as it has been for over a hundred years.

Endnotes

[1] Carol Langer, "The Effect of Selected macro Forces on the Contemporary Social Construction of American Ethnic Identity," *Journal of Health and Social Policy* 20(2005): 15–32.

[2] Doman Lum, *Culturally Competent Practice—A Framework for Understanding Diverse Groups and Justice Issues,* 3rd ed. (Pacific Grove, CA: Brooks/Cole, 2007).

[3] Wynetta Devore, "Ethnic Sensitivity: A theoretical Framework," in *Beyond Racial Divides—Ethnicities in Social Work Practice,* ed. Lena Dominelli, Walter Lorenz, and Haluk Soydan (Burlington, VT: Ashgate, 2001), 34.

[4] Tamara Davis, "Diversity Practice in Social work: Examining Theory in Practice," *Journal of Ethnic and Cultural Diversity in Social Work* 18 (January–June 2009), 40–68; Kurt Organista, "New Practice Model for Latinos in Need of social Work Services," *Social Work* 54 (October 2009): 297–305.

[5] Yeheskel Hasenfeld, "Worker-Client Relations," in *Human Services as Complex Organizations,* 2nd ed., ed. Yeheskel Hasenfeld (Thousand Oaks, CA: Sage Publications, 2010):405–425.

[6] Michael Sosin, "Discretion in Human Service Organizations," in *Human Services as Complex Organizations,* ed. Yeheskel Hasenfeld (Thousand Oaks, CA: Sage Publications, 2010), 380.

[7] Karen Seccombe, "'Beating the Odds' versus 'Changing the Odds': Poverty, Resilience, and Family Policy," *Journal of Marriage and Family* 64 (May 2002):384–394.

[8] Dawn Williams and Roderic Land, "The Legitimation of Black Subordination: The Impact of Color-Blind Ideology on African American Education," *Journal of Negro Education* 75 (Fall 2006): 580.

[9] Robert Green, Mary Kiernan-Stern, and Frank Baskind, "White Social Workers' Attitudes about People of Color," *Journal of Ethnic and Cultural Diversity in Social Work* 14 (2005): 47–68.

[10] Green, Kiernan-Stern, and Baskind, "White Social Workers' Attitudes about People of Color," 62.

[11] Williams and Land, "The Legitimation of Black Subordination: The Impact of Color-Blind Ideology on African American Education," 580.

[12] Carole Cox and Paul Ephross, *Ethnicity and Social Work Practice* (New York: Oxford University Press, 1998), 14.

[13] Michalle Mor Barak and Dnika Travis, "Diversity and Organizational Performance," in Human Services as Complex Organizations," ed. Yeheskel Hasenfeld (Thousand Oaks, CA: Sage Publications, 2010), 346.

[14] See, for example, Laura Abrams and Priscilla Gibson, "Reframing Multicultural Education: Teaching White Privilege in the Social Work Curriculum," *Journal of Social Work Education* 43 (Winter 2007): 147–160.

[15] See, for example Joshua Miller, Cheryl Hyde, and Betty Ruth, "Teaching about Race and Racism in Social Work: Challenges for White Educators," *Smith College Studies in Social Work* 74 (March 2004): 409–426.

[16] Mor Barak and Travis, "Diversity and Organizational Performance," 346–347.

[17] Elizabeth Morrison and Frances Milliken, "Organizational silence: A Barrier to Change and Development in a Pluralistic World," *The Academy of management Review* 25 (October 2000): 707.

[18] Alex Glitterman and Irving Miller, "The Influence of the Organization on Clinical Practice," *Clinical Social Work Journal* 17 (Summer 1989): 151, 154.

[19] Stephen Holloway and George Brager, "Some Considerations in Planning Organizational Change," *Administration in Social Work* 1 (Winter 1977): 351.

[20] Julian Chow and Michael Austin, "The Culturally Responsive Social Service Agency: The Application of an Evolving Definition to a Case Study," *Administration in Social Work* 32 (2008): 46.

[21] Joyce Antler and Stephen Antler, "From Child Rescue to Family Protection," *Children and Youth Services Review* 1 (Summer 1979): 177–204.

[22] Antler and Antler, "From Child Rescue," 202.

[23] Peter Pecora, James Whittaker, Anthony Maluccio, with Richard Barth and Robert Plotnick, *The Child Welfare Challenge* (New York: Aldine de Gruyter, 1992).

[24] For a discussion of the history of child-welfare services and the African American family, see Andrew Billingsley and Jeanne Giovannoni, *Children of the Storm* (New York: Harcourt Brace Jovanovich, 1972).

[25] Stanley Sue, David Allen, and Linda Conaway, "The Responsiveness and Equality of Mental Health Care to Chicanos and Native Americans," *American Journal of Community Psychology* 6(2) (1978): 145.

[26] Ralph Anderson, Irl Carter, with Gary Lowe, *Human Behavior in the Social Environment,* 5th ed. (New York: Aldine de Gruyter, 1999), 24.

[27] Daniel Katz and Robert Kahn, *The Social Psychology of Organizations* (New York: Wiley, 1978), 27.

[28] Alfreda Iglehart, "Turnover in the Social Services: Turning over to the Benefits," *Social Service Review* 64 (December 1990): 649, 652–653.

[29] Yeheskel Hasenfeld, "Power in Social Work Practice," *Social Service Review* 61 (September 1987): 475.

[30] Amitai Etzioni, *Modern Organizations* (Englewood Cliffs, NJ: Prentice-Hall, 1964), 97.

[31] Rino Patti, "Organizational Resistance and Change: The View from Below," in *Social Administration,* ed. Simon Slavin (New York: Haworth Press and Council on Social Work Education, 1978), 551.

[32] Roosevelt Wright, Dennis Saleeby, Thomas Watts, and Pedro Lecca, *Transcultural Perspectives in the Human Services* (Springfield, IL: Charles C. Thomas, 1983), 153.

[33] Miguel Montiel and Paul Wong, "A Theoretical Critique of the Minority Perspective," *Social Casework* (February 1983): 116–117.

[34] I-Hsin Wu and Charles Windle, "Ethnic Specificity in the Relative Minority Use and Staffing of Community Mental Health Centers," *Community Mental Health Journal* 16 (Summer 1980): 156–168.

[35] Robin Ely and David Thomas, "Cultural Diversity at Work: The Effects of Diversity Perspectives on Work Group Processes and Outcomes," *Administrative Science Quarterly* 46 (June 2001), 231.

[36] Ely and Thomas, "Cultural Diversity at Work: The Effects of Diversity Perspectives on Work Group Processes and Outcomes," 231.

[37] Christopher Larrison, Susan Schoppelrey, Eric Hadley-Ives, and Barry Ackerson, "Organizational Climate and Treatment Outcomes for African American Clients Receiving Services at Community Mental Health Agencies," *Administration in Social Work* 32 (2008), 111–138.

[38] Hasenfeld, *Human Service Organizations,* 245–246.

[39] C. H. Tobias, "The Work of the Young Men's and Young Women's Christian Associations with Negro Youth," *The Annals of the American Academy of Political and Social Science* 240 (November 1928): 286.

[40] Susan Ostrander, "Voluntary Social Service Agencies in the United States," *Social Service Review* 59 (September 1985): 434.

[41] See, for example, Valora Washington, "Community Involvement in Recruiting Adoptive Homes for Black Children," *Child Welfare* 66 (January /February 1987): 57–68.

[42] See, for example, Fong (ed.), *Culturally Competent Practice with Immigrant and Refugee Children and Families* (New York: The Guilford Press, 2004).

[44] Hasenfeld, "Worker-Client Relations," 414–415.

[44] J. Kenneth Benson, "The Interorganizational Network as a Political Economy," *Administrative Science Quarterly* 20 (June 1975): 232.

[45] Alvin Gouldner, "Reciprocity and Autonomy in Functional Theory," in *Symposium on Sociological Theory,* ed. Llwellyn Gross (New York: Harper and Row, 1959), 241–270.

[46] Mary Zey-Ferrell, *Dimensions of Organizations* (Santa Monica, CA: Goodyear Publishing, 1979), 142.

[47] Benson, "The Interorganizational Network as Political Economy," 234.

[48] Shirley Jenkins, *The Ethnic Dilemma in Social Services* (New York: The Free Press, 1981), 45.

[49] Yeheskel Hasenfeld and Richard English, "Interorganizational Relations," in *Human Service Organizations,* ed. Yeheskel Hasenfeld and Richard English (Ann Arbor: University of Michigan Press, 1978), 543.

[50] Ralph Kramer, "Voluntary Agencies and the Personal Social Services," in *The Nonprofit Sector— A Research Handbook,* ed. Walter Powell (New Haven, CT: Yale University Press, 1987), 249.

51 For a discussion of the effects of contracts on agency services, see Steven Smith, "The Political Economy of Contracting and Competition," in *Human Services as complex Organizations,* 2nd ed., ed. Yeheskel Hasenfeld (Thousand Oaks, CA: Sage Publications, 2010), 154–156.

52 Marc Bendick, Jr., "Privatizing the Delivery of Social Welfare Services: An Idea to be Taken Seriously," in *Privatization and the Welfare State,* ed. Sheila Kamerman and Alfred Kahn (Princeton, NJ: Princeton University Press, 1989), 98.

53 Peter Kettner and Lawrence Martin, "Purchase of Service Contracting: Two Models," *Administration in Social Work* 14(1) (1985): 15.

54 Paul Terrell and Ralph Kramer, "Contracting with Nonprofits," *Public Welfare* 42 (Winter 1984): 36.

55 For a definition of substitute services, see Kramer, "Voluntary Agencies and the Personal Social Services," 249.

56 Judith Saidel, "Resource Interdependence: The Relationship between State Agencies and Nonprofit Organizations," *Public Administration Review* 51 (November/December 1991): 550.

57 Karen Cook, "Exchange and Power in Networks of Interorganizational Relations," *The Sociological Quarterly* 18 (Winter 1977): 66.

58 Winston Tseng, "Government Dependence of Chinese and Vietnamese Community Organizations and Fiscal Politics of Immigrant Services," *Journal of Health and Social Policy* 20 (2005), 51–74.

59 For a discussion of organizational dominance, see Benson, "The Inter-organizational Network as a Political Economy," 233–234.

60 Susan Bernstein, *Managing Contracted Services in the Nonprofit Agency* (Philadelphia: Temple University Press, 1991).

61 Smith, "The Political Economy of Contracting and Competition," 139–160.

62 Carl Milofsky, "Neighborhood-Based Organizations: A Market Analogy," in *The Nonprofit Sector— A Research Handbook,* ed. Walter Powell (New Haven, CT: Yale University Press, 1987), 277–295.

63 Hillel Schmid, "Agency-Environment Relations," *The Handbook of Human Services Management,* 2nd. ed., ed. Rino Patti (Thousand Oaks, CA: Sage Publications, 2009), 424.

64 Smith, "The Political Economy of Contracting and Competition," 157.

65 Carl Sewell, "Impact of External Public Funding Policies on the Development of Black Community Organizations," *Black Scholar* 9 (December 1977): 42.

66 Stephen Thomas and Cynthia Morgan, "Evaluation of Community-Based AIDS Education and Risk Reduction Projects in Ethnic and Racial Minority Communities: A Survey of Projects Funded by the U.S. Public Health Service," *Evaluation and Program Planning* 14(4) (1991): 247–255.

67 Carol Weiss, *Evaluation Research* (Englewood Cliffs, NJ: Prentice-Hall, 1972), 42.

68 Terrell and Kramer, "Contracting with Nonprofits," 34.

69 Patrick Wardell, "The Implications of Changing Interorganizational Relationships and Resource Constraints for Human Services Survival: A Case Study," *Administration in Social Work* 12(1) (1988): 89–105.

70 Tseng, "Government Dependence of Chinese and Vietnamese Community Organizations and Fiscal Politics of Immigrant Services," 51–74.

71 Bruce Smith, "Changing Public-Private Sector Relations: A Look at the United States," *Annals of the American Academy of Political and Social Science* 466 (March 1983): 158.

72 Stephen Rose, "Community Organization: A Survival Strategy for Community-Based, Empowerment-Oriented Programs," *Journal of Sociology and Social Welfare* 13 (September 1986): 491–506.

73 Stuart Schmidt and Thomas Kochan, "Interorganizational Relationship: Patterns and Motivations," *Administrative Science Quarterly* 22 (June 1977): 220–234.

74 Christopher Hudson, "From Social Darwinism to Self-Organization: Implications for Social Change Theory," *The Social Service Review* 74 (December 2000): 533.

75 See, for example, F. Ellen Netting, Peter Kettner, and Steven McMurtry, *Social Work Macro Practice,* 4th ed. (Boston: Pearson, 2008).

76 See, for example, Karen Haynes and James Mickelson, *Affecting Change—Social Workers in the Political Arena,* 7th ed. (Boston: Pearson, 2010) and Bruce Jansson, *Becoming an Effective Policy Advocate—From Policy Practice to Social Justice,* 5th ed. (Belmont, CA: Thomson Higher Education, 2008).

77 Jillian Jimenez, *Social Policy and Social Change* (Thousand Oaks, CA: Sage Publications, 2010), 252–253.

78 See, for example, Jimenez, *Social Policy and Social Change* (Thousand Oaks, CA: Sage Publications, 2010); and Josefina Figueira-McDonough, *The Welfare State and Social Work—Pursuing Social Justice* (Thousand Oaks, CA: Sage Publications, 2007).

CHAPTER 11

Social Services and the Ethnic Community
Unresolved Issues and Themes

> Historically, the social work profession has been committed to working with different ethnic and racial communities and has defined its purpose as working with the oppressed . . . As a result, social work has directed considerable attention toward issues of social reform and civil rights.[1]

This quotation was written in 2009 and, no doubt, captures the sentiments of many social workers as they reflect on the profession's history. This is the view that is often projected and accepted about the profession. The previous chapters of this book raise serious questions about this view. Is it a fact or is it a myth? Readers are asked to reach their own conclusions as they ponder the meaning of the contents of this book. What is factual is the current thrust to provide ethnic-sensitive practice to vulnerable populations of color. In order to develop effective practice, this historical context of the profession and of minority populations has to be understood and acknowledged.

A number of issues have been raised in this analysis of the history of social services and the ethnic community. There is no intention here to try to resolve these issues. Such an effort would be fruitless, since many of them are embedded in the history of this country and in the profession itself. These issues are presented with the goal of stimulating dialogue.

HISTORICAL CONTEXT

This book began with a review of the historical context in which social work, personal services, and social practice—or the "helping professions"—found roots. The nation was in the midst of transition as industrialization, urbanization, immigration, and migration cast a dark cloud over the burgeoning cities. A new poverty was invading the lives of millions of people with destitution, disease, and despair. Americans had been poor in the past and doing without at that time meant learning to sacrifice. This new poverty, however, was one of unparalleled abjection and wretchedness.

247

Even then, the suffering was not distributed equally throughout the tenements or throughout the country. Some people seemed to suffer poverty in its most pernicious forms, and the records of the time bear witness to this fact. The "new" and unpopular White ethnic immigrants were really only a temporary disruption to U.S. society. It was expected that, after a few generations, they would be indistinguishable from the native-born Americans. They could melt into the American pot and rise from the poverty and the slums to join the ranks of middle America. African Americans, however, had no such prognosis. Economic success was not sufficient enough to hurdle the segregation that walled African Americans from mainstream society.

While cities swallowed the "new" White ethnics and African American migrants, the American Indian population suffered on the reservations. Inadequate resources resulted in an abhorrent aberration of former reservation life. The forced transition from the old ways to the new ways was an ordeal that has been referred to as *acculturation under duress*.

The American Indian had something in common with the Mexican American: Their land was important, but they were not. While the White ethnics and African Americans lived under the most extreme of conditions and while American Indians remained on the reservations, thousands of Mexican Americans were stripped of their land and the rights that should accompany citizenship. As immigration from Mexico increased, these immigrants were always "foreigners" who were not expected to make the United States their home. They did have *brazos fuertes* (strong arms), so they were expendable and dispensable and needed at the same time. The labor was valued but not the laborer.

Meanwhile, the contributions that the Chinese were making in building the United States were little appreciated and soon were almost forgotten. What is left is the memory of the Chinese Exclusion Acts that banned an entire group of people from these shores. Documents of the period tell of racial hatred, violence, and fear. In the eyes of Californians and the rest of the country, the new land needed protection from the invasion of foreign countries and foreign people.

The Japanese were welcomed as another source of labor but they, too, were "foreign" and were destined to be seen that way for years to come. In their reach for the American dream their success was their downfall. Fear that they would take over and fear that they were taking land and business from "real" Americans revealed the ambivalence that the United States had about those who looked and acted "foreign."

In this time period, the sorrow of the slums could not be addressed by the old ways of problem solving. The fragmentation of efforts and the uncoordinated giving needed to be replaced with more organized approaches to poverty. The provision of alms was not enough, and the alms supply was dwindling. Throwing money at the problems could not contain the problems. The English model of poverty work was imported to the United States and the charity organization societies were established with paid agents, friendly visitors, investigations, and coordination of efforts. In the Progressive Era, the beginnings of social casework or direct practice are evident.

The White ethnics needed more than friendly visiting and case investigations; they needed political advocacy, community organization, and community planning. This need could be met through the settlement houses, another import from England. Although the reform nature of the settlement house movement is continuously emphasized, closer scrutiny of history reveals that most settlement houses were trying to Americanize the White ethnics to make them better and "real" Americans.

The charity organization societies and the settlement houses gave a passing nod to African Americans and did not bother to nod at all to the American Indians, Mexicans, Chinese, and Japanese. These groups were not their target "clients"; they were not good candidates for Americanization. Although each group was different, they all had something in common—they did not conform to the commonly accepted image of Americans. Moreover, no amount of Americanization could transform them into this image. Services extended to them were spotty, inconsistent, an afterthought, a footnote to primary services, or nonexistent.

The helping professions of today emerged from the responses of established White Americans to the needs of "new" White ethnic Americans. Although the "new" immigrants were from unpopular parts of Europe and had religions, customs, and values that differed from those of America, these immigrants were considered "redeemable" and major efforts were undertaken toward that end to protect America from erosion. Thus, the help extended had dual purposes: to assist the immigrants with adaptation to a new world and to protect White middle-class America.

Three themes dominated early helping organizations: ethnic minorities were ignored, the doctrine of ethnic group responsibility prevailed, and those extending the help were the ones defining the problems and the solutions. Ethnic minorities were assumed and expected to care for their own group members.

From the need to rescue the "unfortunates" from the squalor of the slums, a new occupation eventually arose. Members who practiced its craft wanted specialized knowledge, specialized skills, and legitimacy as a profession. As these were developed, the new helping profession tended to focus on those immigrants of European stock. Casework overpowered social reform in the profession and less attention was given to the needs of the ethnic minority groups, who were more concentrated in the West while the profession grew in the East.

There were those in the profession who challenged its direction and preoccupation with professionalization, but the rank-and-file movement of the 1930s and the human services movement of the 1960s were just momentary distractions—little blips on the radar that tracked the trajectory of the profession. These movements have been absorbed into the profession, and they have expanded the profession to include new workers and new service areas. The profession, however, has had more effects on them than they have had on the profession. They were absorbed by the profession—they did not absorb it. The influence and its direction seem clear. Further, many people in these movements eventually aspired to be professional social workers.

While the profession was crystallizing, the ethnic minority groups were organizing their own community responses to their ills. African Americans were concerned about children, widows, the elderly and young girls. Crime in the communities was also receiving attention. Second-generation Mexican Americans desired integration and used the acquisition of English as a tool. They were also concerned about issues of deportation because like new Mexican immigrants they, too, were faced with the threat just because they "looked Mexican." The Chinese and Japanese wanted to succeed in the new country, and their community associations reflected this desire.

The ethnic agency rose from these early community self-help efforts. These ethnic communities responded to the needs of their residents, as defined by their residents, and provided services to individuals who could not receive services elsewhere. In this manner, these agencies filled service gaps and substituted for government services as public agencies "hired" them to provide mandated services. The social work profession and other helping professions have not fully recognized or appreciated the accomplishments and importance of the ethnic agency.

THE CHALLENGES OF TODAY

Ethnic-sensitive practice does not start today with the here and now. Rather, it is lodged in the historical continuum that includes the unique cultural, social, political, and economic context of each group in the United States. The development and implementation of responsive service delivery systems are predicated on the awareness and acknowledgment of a group's history as *perceived by that group.*

The Importance of In-Depth Historical Analyses

The historical experiences of African Americans, Mexican Americans, American Indians, Chinese Americans, Japanese Americans, and other ethnic minority Americans have shaped their interface with mainstream agencies. This history suggests that ethnic minority groups may be justified in perceiving mainstream services with suspicion and cynicism. The crumbling of many racial walls has not led these groups to warmly embrace those institutions and structures that previously limited their opportunities for full participation in society. Services that were supposedly designed to foster upward mobility and enhance the quality of life were often guilty of reinforcing racial stereotypes, practicing racial segregation, and excluding ethnic minorities.

Some people may believe that the past is dead and should therefore be buried. Since the past cannot be changed, some may question its relevance to contemporary issues, especially if this history includes issues of racism and discrimination. However, the legacy of that past is often reflected in the present and transformed into more subtle and insidious modes of operation. Knowledge of that past becomes crucial for protecting organizational change and innovation from the perpetuation of inequality.

What are the effects of this history today? Some groups may see their own ethnic agencies as the primary conduit for service delivery and may shun mainstream agencies. Other groups may view any mainstream change as purely superficial and resist outreach efforts made to their communities. Others may wonder whether traces of past discrimination still persist today. The past thus becomes useful for identifying pitfalls to be avoided and patterns to be changed. Community responses may also be understood and predicted in the context of group history.

A significant message from the past is that the ethnic community attempted to define and solve its own problems. History indicates that each ethnic group defined what it saw as major social concerns and also developed its own interventions to address those concerns. Each group had some capacity for self-help and self-determination. Thus, because priorities and needs may vary from group to group, interventions should be developed in partnership with each community. It is of paramount importance that their voices be heard.

An examination of history will further indicate that, based on past experiences, groups and professions develop a collective identity and a collective memory.[2] The meaning of the past is passed from generation to generation in the stories, writings, language, dialogue, and other symbols that frame each group's history. This collective memory serves to shape a collective identity for the group. Polleta and Jasper offer the following definition of the collective identity:

> To avoid overextension of the concept, we have defined collective identity as an individual's cognitive, moral, and emotional connection with a broader community, category, practice, or institution. It is a perception of a shared status or relation, which may be imagined rather than experienced directly, and it is distinct from personal identities, although it may form a part of a personal identity. . . . Collective identities are expressed in cultural materials—names, narratives, symbols, verbal styles, rituals, clothing, and so on—but not all cultural materials express collective identities.[3]

The interactions between social workers and ethnic minority communities are lodged, to a certain extent, in the collective memories and identities of each. Ethnic-sensitive practice builds on these memories and histories to foster linkages that support rapport and mutual respect.

While history is important as a context for understanding the relationship between society and the minority community, ways of encouraging in-depth historical reviews and analyses must be identified. For too many social workers, Jane Addams and Mary Richmond are all they know about social work's past—a past that has been glorified and romanticized. More needs to be done to foster an appreciation of social work history as it is, not as people want it to be. This appreciation will result in a recognition and acceptance of the profession's progress from the Progressive Era to present-day America. Following are some important issues to consider in this process.

Ethnic Group Responsibility

The doctrine of ethnic group responsibility continues to receive support in the larger society as well as within ethnic communities. This belief in the responsibility of an ethnic group to provide for its own relief may account, in part, to the reluctance of the country to respond to the needs of various ethnic groups. Ethnic responsibility in and of itself is neither desirable nor undesirable. The emphasis may need to be redirected from the group itself to the external constraints placed upon a group as it attempts to help itself. The doctrine of ethnic group responsibility often disregards the effects of the external polity and the external economy in constraining self-help efforts within communities.

While social and human services are developing practice methods that may be more responsive to the needs of ethnic minorities, the minorities continue to stress the responsibility of each group to help itself. This position seems to imply the deficit model of social service delivery rather than a partnership model: Mainstream efforts are deficient in their responses to the group, so the group must do for itself. The "Lifting As We Climb" motto of the National Association of Colored Women during the early 1900s is analogous to the "what we ourselves can and must do" message of the more contemporary National Urban Coalition.[4] Although client participation is laudable here, it must be recognized as having arisen from problems inherent in the mainstream service delivery systems.

The current century certainly differs from that of the nineteenth and twentieth centuries, but similar questions emerge: When is ethnic group self-help needed, and when is assistance from other groups needed?[5] In the past, African Americans were urged by numerous African American leaders to develop habits that advanced their race because their suffering could be attributed to poor circumstances—circumstances that could be overcome by diligence and determination. Other leaders advocated self-help efforts because they believed that White America cast a blind eye and responded with benign (and sometimes overt) neglect to the conditions of African American communities. Regardless of the reasons, the message was firmly etched in African American literature and ideologies.

Existing service delivery systems and the doctrine of ethnic group responsibility do not appear to work in partnership to bring more effective services to ethnic minorities. There is a tension between the two, with ethnic group responsibility being evoked, at times, as a means of overcoming service delivery problems. The professional should continue to seek ways of reducing this tension.

Defining Community Needs

Who defines the needs of a community? For ethnic minority groups, the external polity seems to have the loudest and strongest voice in determining how problems are defined and which solutions are utilized. Public policy responses are not always sympathetic to minority perspectives of problems.

The external polity (the larger society) continues to define problems and solutions, acting "on" its minority communities rather than acting "in partnership with" those communities. The helping professions, as part of this external polity, may also be acting on ethnic communities by embracing ideologies and implementing policies that are counter to the expressed wishes of these groups.

Social service and social work may be continuing with the "middle course" by walking a fine line between the needs and desires of the larger social system and the needs and desires of ethnic subsystems. While this middle-ground position may offer some conflict resolution for the practitioners, it does nothing to encourage ethnic communities to take advantage of services offered by social work and other helping professions.

Some efforts are currently underway to build partnerships with communities by creating opportunities for resident input. For example, Mathie and Cunningham report on the use of asset-based community development (ABCD) strategies that respond to community-identified strengths and resources.[6] ABCD solicits and utilizes community input and participation in the problem-solving process. ABCD may be one type of intervention that has potential for forging partnerships between mainstream agencies and ethnic minority communities. The goal of partnership-building strategies is the inclusion of the community's voice in problem identification and the service delivery process. This voice renders the ethnic community as a visible and viable resource that should not be discounted.

Cultural Pluralism versus the Melting Pot

The demand for ethnic-sensitive social services is growing as the ethnic diversity of U.S. society grows. As the prevailing social environment moves toward the acknowledgment, acceptance, and appreciation of cultural differences, social institutions and systems are expected also to keep pace with the changing times. The days of the melting-pot metaphor are melting away as cultural pluralism takes hold. Ethnic groups are no longer thrown into the great American pot and melted into a unique individual—the American. Rather, today's metaphors describe America as a patchwork quilt and as a "mosaic" society in which the uniquely individual and diversely colored pieces join together to form a cohesive and vibrant whole. According to Kiser,

> The newer concept of cultural pluralism, on the other hand, recognizes the ethnic diversity of our population. . . . As a philosophy, cultural pluralism denies the assumption that there is one American culture fixed once and for all by our colonial ancestors. It assumes that our culture is variegated and dynamic, and that all immigrant groups have contributed toward its enrichment.[7]

Kiser made this observation in 1949, and U.S. society is still in a tug-of-war between the melting pot and cultural pluralism metaphors.

On one hand, the prevailing and dominant ethos has been against the formation and maintenance of subgroup identities in favor of an overall *American* one.[8] But, as Kiser noted, the concept of cultural pluralism differed markedly from policies and practices related to the "colored" groups. Or, as Solomon said, "The proponents of the melting pot theory could be terribly cruel to ethnics who would not melt."[9] On the other hand, ethnic and racial differences seemed too often diagnosed rather than defined, and treated rather than tolerated. Despite generations of life in the United States, some groups still bear the stigma of being "foreign."

Thus, American society, as well as its professions and ethnic minorities, continues to struggle with issues of race and ethnicity. Can differences be noted without penalizing those who are different? When are differences to be ignored? Can this be done without jeopardizing practice effectiveness? In efforts to minimize or discount ethnic differences, ethnicity became glaring in its attempts to become "invisible." Now it has become glaring in its visibility.

The period of ethnic/cultural awareness has appeared on the horizon while traces of the melting-pot ideology still persist. Social workers and other helpers are faced with the ambivalence that pervades society about the significance (or insignificance) of race and ethnicity. This ambivalence leads to questions and confusion about the meaning of ethnic-sensitive practice. This is one of the dilemmas confronting mainstream social-service delivery.

A related dilemma is the seemingly unique status of African Americans as an ethnic minority group. Cox and Ephross note, "In the United States, racism tends to be associated with African Americans, but at various times other racial groups—Chinese, Japanese, and Hispanics—have been targets of racism."[10] In addition, while numerous ethnic groups were able to assimilate into American society, the assimilation of African Americans has not been swift or easy. Sears and Savalei suggest that the African American experience can represent "Black exceptionalism" to typical patterns of assimilation.[11] These authors state:

> To be sure, America has in the past subordinated and sometimes perse-
> cuted Latinos and Asians. But the differences between their histories and
> that of African Americans are crucial, with the result that Latinos and
> Asians have not been the target of the same rigid color line and highly
> crystallized prejudices as have African Americans. . . . Latinos and Asians
> are behaviorally already considerably more assimilated than are African
> Americans in the domains most governed by individual choice, such as
> intermarriage and residential segregation.[12]

Is there some type of hierarchy among ethnic minority groups that need to be addressed in social work practice? Does this apparent distinction between African Americans and other ethnic minority groups pose a challenge for intergroup collaboration? These questions require the attention of educators and practitioners as they continue to focus on ethnic-sensitive practice.

Ethnicity as a Credential

Ethnic-sensitive practice may not become the new ideology of helping professions and social work until the contradictions surrounding the meaning of ethnicity in service delivery are resolved. On one hand, White practitioners are urged to become culturally sensitive, culturally aware, and culturally responsive. On the other hand, trained ethnic-group members are needed to work with members of their own group. Historically, ethnic-group members have been identified with service delivery to their own communities. Hispanic American workers, Asian American workers, and American Indian workers are needed.

Ambivalence is reflected in discussions of who is the best person to work with whom. It is implied that the *preferred* worker is the trained worker of the same ethnic group as the client. In the absence of such an individual, White workers who are culturally sensitive are viewed as preferred substitutes. In reality however, the credibility of the White worker may be in doubt because he or she is not a member of that group and therefore cannot fully understand the ethnic issues and concerns at hand. Although individuals may say that ethnicity is not a credential, it still seems to be treated as if it were. This issue is compounded by literature that supports ethnic matching of client and service worker. For example, in a study of home–based support programs, the authors found that African American clients who had African American workers remained in the program longer than those who had other workers.[13] Furthermore, the same study revealed that ethnic matching seemed to have promoted more involvement of non–English-speaking clients. The authors suggest that programs with African American and first-generation Latino clients consider hiring workers ethnically similar to these clients.

With ethnicity being revered as a credential in many situations, issues may be raised about the role of Whites working with minorities and the role of minorities working with Whites. The expertise of each group in working with the other is often overlooked and minimized. For ethnic-sensitive practice to take place, credentials reside with *all* workers who are culturally aware—regardless of their ethnicity. Culture then becomes something that everyone has and everyone learns. In probing beneath the surface of this issue, the focal point may not be ethnic matching in itself but rather which clients or client groups seem to benefit from same race service providers.

Separatism versus Integration

The existence of the ethnic agency mirrors another contradiction that was noted by Jones in 1928:

> The Negro attitude seems paradoxical. The whole idea of racial segregation is obnoxious to him, yet he demands that the Negro social worker specialize in the Negro's peculiar social problems, treat the problems of the Negro as special group problems.[14]

The existence of special ethnic agencies that work with particular ethnic groups seems antithetical to the norms of racial integration.

Questions are then raised about the need for these agencies and about their possible promotion of racial separatism. This is another dilemma that must be addressed in order for ethnic-sensitive practice to find a place in mainstream social work.

Ethnic-Sensitive Practice: Whose Domain?

The ethnic agency appears to play a continuing part in the development of ethnic communities. Is ethnic practice the exclusive domain of ethnic agencies? Should ethnic practice be the exclusive practice of ethnic agencies?

A continuum of services seem to unfold in which the ethnic agency may serve as the first line of defense for filling service gaps, responding to the needs of marginalized groups, and helping when no other agency does. It may also substitute for public agencies in delivering uniquely packaged and specially tailored services. In the quest for ethnic-sensitive practice it seems to be a resource that has been underutilized.

Mainstream social services and agencies will continue to vary in the degree to which they adopt ethnic-sensitive practice. This variation is due to agency history, ideologies, structure, and technologies. Mainstream agencies have a history of responding to the needs of a mainstream America, and shifts in paradigms do take years to accomplish.

The first stage of the journey to ethnic sensitive practice is already underway as service providers begin to acknowledge the need to do something different with diverse populations. That acknowledgment should now move beyond changing workers to changing systems.

Diversity of Ethnic-Sensitive Practice?

Use of the category of "diversity" has increased. This term includes ethnic minorities and groups such as women; the disabled; the elderly; lesbian, gay, bisexual, and transgendered individuals; and others that are at risk for discriminatory treatment. A diversity focus may, however, shift attention from the needs of ethnic minority groups. Race and ethnic minority group status seem to occupy a unique position on the discrimination scale. By placing ethnic minority groups in such a global category, the significance of their experiences may be overshadowed and minimized. In addition, agencies may succeed with their diversity goals without hiring minorities or serving minority clients.

More needs to done to ensure that ethnic and racial minorities remain a crucial aspect of any diversity-driven or multicultural practice. This is one way to strengthen the profession's link with minority communities.

Religion, Spirituality, and Social Work

The profession worked hard to distance itself from its Social Gospel roots and its home missions roots. In the twenty-first century, minority communities and others continue to embrace religious institutions as central to their lives. In addition, many social workers themselves have significant religious identification. Perhaps it is necessary for the profession to further explore the place of religiosity and spirituality in the provision of social services. Some workers may already use religion in their work with clients. Forging stronger links with minority communities may require a way of validating the power of their faith. This may be a more difficult challenge in that the general public may continue to equate social work with a religious-like calling for those who are committed to helping the poor. Discussions of a tie with religion may further reinforce this perception. At the same time, the importance of religion in the lives of many minority group members cannot be ignored.

There appears to be a growing interest since the literature on religion, spirituality, and social work has increased significantly in the last decade.[15] According to Sherr, Singletary, and Rogers, three main categories of this literature can be identified: religion, spirituality, and direct practice; religious organizations and service delivery; and educational preparation of social work students.[16] In addition, in reviewing the literature on how social workers used spiritually based interventions Sheridan found that social workers were, indeed, using a variety of spiritually-influenced interventions.[17]

As noted in Chapter 6, the settlements differed from the religious-based home missions in their lack of effort to indoctrinate service users about a particular religion or point of view. This distinction may be of importance today as the profession begins to address the need for ethical standards, an educational curriculum, and service accountability since more attention is now focused on religion, spirituality, and social work. Recognition of the centrality of religion in the lives of many people of color (as well as many White individuals) may serve to increase the relevance of the profession to these groups.

Race and Racism

Race continues to a sensitive and difficult topic for many workers to discuss. Separating *difference* from *inequality* can be a daunting task in today's society. It may be assumed that minorities are better than Whites at teaching and dealing with racial issues. Many White practitioners may experience some degree of discomfort when the topic is raised. The profession must find ways to discuss race and ethnicity that generate light, not heat.

The profession mirrors the attitudes and beliefs of the larger society. Everyone is a prisoner of his or her times. The prevailing public perceptions may be that this is a new day and racism is a part of the past. The election of America's first African American president may lead some to conclude that race is no longer a problem in America so there is no need to discuss it. People may not realize that contagious racist attitudes are still "in the air" and are being "caught" and spread every day. This means that new ways of talking about race and racism, inside and outside the profession, must be generated. Open, frank, and honest dialogue is the first step toward understanding the problem.

Determining the Place of Reform in the Profession

The debate about the place of social reform in contemporary social work continues. Periodically, a book or an article surfaces to challenge the profession to resurrect its social reform roots. This is truly a dilemma for the profession. While there may be individuals involved in social reform activities who happen to be social workers, the profession itself does not seem to have been identified with any recent social reform movements. Explanations for this state of affairs abound, from the effects of professionalization to dependency on public dollars. Whatever the explanation, the outcome remains the same—social reform in the profession remains stifled. If the profession is committed to social reform and social justice, then educational programs must begin teaching future social workers the tools and techniques for achieving reform and social justice. Models must be developed, and educational programs must be motivated to incorporate them into the curriculum. Unfortunately, the forces working against this practice may be more powerful than those that support them.

The Progressive Era: Progressive for Whom?

This historical analysis suggests that the written history of America does not accurately reflect the history of minority groups in this country. The Progressive Era was progressive only for the White ethnic immigrants and the people who tended to their needs. This era was successful for them because they became Americanized and were able to blend into the American mainstream without an ethnic designation of Irish American, Italian American, or any other White ethnic label. The founders of the profession invested their time and energy in the White ethnic groups, an endeavor that was successful.

In contrast, African Americans, American Indians, Mexican Americans, Chinese Americans, and Japanese Americans did not experience a Progressive Era. For African Americans and Mexican Americans in particular, this was a bloody period filled with vigilantism, lynching, and other forms of brutality. The Chinese were assaulted and, in some cases, run out of town. The Japanese began their history in this country with questions being raised about their loyalty—a situation that worsened during World War II and resulted in their imprisonment in camps. These groups were denied the progressiveness of the Progressive Era. The designation of this period by that name further communicates the invisibility of these groups during those "progressive" years.

Social work was part of that world. While the past cannot be changed, it can be acknowledged as a step toward strengthening the link between social work and minorities. Minority communities desire *validation, visibility,* and *voice.* Social work can join with them in realizing these goals.

Endnotes

[1] Flavio Marsiglia and Stephen Kulis, *Diversity, Oppression, and Change* (Chicago: Lyceum, 2009), 13.

[2] See, for example, Ron Eyerman, "The Past in the Present: Culture and the Transmission of memory," *Acta Sociologica* 47 (June 2004): 159–169; and Francesca Polleta and James Jasper, "Collective Identity and Social Movements," *Annual Review of Sociology* 27 (2001): 283–305.

[3] Polleta and Jasper, "Collective Identity and Social Movements," 285.

[4] August Meier, *Negro Thought in American 1880–1915* (Ann Arbor: University of Michigan Press, 1966), 120; Wynetta Devore, "The African-American Community in 1990: The Search for Practice Method," in *Community Organizing in a Diverse Society,* ed. Felix Rivera and John Erlich (Boston: Allyn & Bacon, 1992), 79.

[5] See Gayle McKeen, "Whose Rights? Whose Responsibility? Self-Help in African-American Thought," *Polity* 34 (Summer 2002): 409–432.

[6] Alison Mathie and Gordon Cunningham, "From Clients to Citizens: Asset-Based Community Development as a Strategy for Community-Driven Development," *Development in Practice* 13 (November 2003): 474–486.

[7] Clyde Kiser, "Cultural Pluralism." *The Annals of the American Academy of Political and Social Science* 262 (March 1949): 129.

[8] Marcia Guttentag, "Group Cohesiveness, Ethnic Organization, and Poverty," *Journal of Social Issues* 26(2) (1970): 125.

[9] Barbara Solomon, "Social Work in Multiethnic Society," in *Cross-Cultural Perspectives in Social Work Practice and Education,* ed. M. Sotomayor (New York: Council on Social Work Education, 1976): 2.

[10] Carole Cox and Paul Ephross, *Ethnicity and Social Work Practice* (New York: Oxford University Press, 1998), 14.

[11] David Sears and Victoria Savalei, "The Political Color Line in America: Many 'Peoples of Color' or Black Exceptionalism? *Political Psychology* 27 (December 2006): 895–924.

[12] Ibid., 898–899.

[13] Karen McCurdy, Robin Gannon, and Deborah Daro, "Participation Patterns in Home-Based Family Support Programs: Ethnic Variations," *Family Relations* 52 (January 2003): 3–11.

[14] E. K. Jones, "Social Work among Negroes," 288.

[15] Michael Sherr, Jon Singletary, and Robin Rogers, "Innovative Service or Proselytizing: Exploring When Services Delivery Becomes a Platform for Unwanted Religious Persuasion," *Social Work* 26 (April 2009): 157.

[16] Ibid.

[17] Michael Sheridan, "Ethical Issues in the Use of Spiritually Based Interventions in Social Work Practice: What Are We Doing and Why?" *Journal of Religion and Spirituality in Social Work* 28 (January 2009): 99–126.

Index